Essentials of Athletic Training

Essentials of ATHLETIC TRAINING

DANIEL D. ARNHEIM, D.P.E., A.T., C.
Fellow, American College of Sports Medicine;
Professor of Physical Education,
California State University, Long Beach

Illustrated by
HELENE ARNHEIM, M.A.

FIRST EDITION

With 314 illustrations and
122 photographs

TIMES MIRROR/MOSBY COLLEGE PUBLISHING

ST. LOUIS   TORONTO   SANTA CLARA   1987

Executive editor   Nancy K. Roberson
Developmental editor   Michelle A. Turenne
Project editor   Suzanne Seeley
Art director   Kay Kramer
Editing and production   Publication Services
Cover design   Susan E. Lane

Cover art by Bart Forbes. Reprinted with permission from the copyright owner, Bristol-Meyers Company © 1983, makers of VITALIS.

This text was based on the most up-to-date research and suggestions made by individuals knowledgeable in the field of athletic training. The author and publisher disclaim any responsibility for any adverse effects or consequences from the misapplication or injudicious use of information contained within this text. It is also accepted as judicious that the coach and/or athletic trainer performing his or her duties is, at all times, working under the guidance of a licensed physician.

Credits for all materials used by permission appear after the glossary.

Library of Congress Cataloging-in-Publication Data

Arnheim, Daniel D.
   Essentials of athletic training.

   Includes bibliographies and index.
      1. Sports — Accidents and injuries.   2. Sports —
Accidents and injuries — Prevention.   3. Physical
fitness.
I. Title.   [DNLM: 1. Athletic Injuries.
2. Physical Education and Training.   3. Sports
Medicine.   QT 260 A748e]
RD97.A76   1987   617'.1027   86–14533
ISBN   0–8016–0335–8

PS/VH/VH   9 8 7 5 4 3 2   03/A/377

PREFACE

Purpose of Text

The first edition of *Essentials of Athletic Training* is to provide the reader with the most current information possible on the subject of prevention and basic care of sports injuries.

Who is it Written For?

Essentials of Athletic Training is designed as a primary text for the student going into the field of coaching and/or physical education. Its major thrust is toward injury prevention and the immediate care of the most common sports injuries. Basic foundations are also provided for the student interested in more substantive areas of rehabilitation.

Organization and Coverage

Essentials of Athletic Training was created from the foundations established by the sixth edition of *Modern Principles of Athletic Training*. Where *Modern Principles of Athletic Training* serves as a major text for athletic trainers and those individuals interested in sports medicine, *Essentials of Athletic Training* is written for the coach and physical educator.

The general approach to the text is that adverse physical problems arising from sports participation should be prevented whenever possible. Secondly, when adverse problems do arise, quick and proper care can reduce their seriousness.

Essentials of Athletic Training is divided into three parts: Foundations; Sports Injury Causation, Response, and Management; and Sports Conditions. Overall, this text is designed to take the beginning student from general to more specific concepts. As the student progresses from the first to the last chapter, understanding of the prevention and care of athletic injuries will occur.

Part One, Foundations, consists of five chapters. It explores the origin of athletic training, the current status of sports injuries, and athletic training and sports medicine. It also presents the relationship of proper physical conditioning and protective equipment to the prevention of injury as well as application of good taping, bandaging, and emergency care to injury.

Part Two, Sports Injury Causation, Response, and Management, includes three chapters. These chapters provide an understanding of how the body is susceptible to traumatic musculoskeletal injuries and how these injuries are classified, recognized, and evaluated. Chapter 8 discusses the body's response to musculoskeletal injuries and provides a foundation for basic management.

Part Three, Sports Conditions, includes eight chapters covering major sports injuries that occur to the different body regions. Each of these chapters present related anatomy, methods of prevention, and immediate and follow-up care. Where appropriate, chapters contain taping techniques that may be used as a means of achieving injury prevention or protective support following an injury. Chapter 17, the last chapter, covers a number of health-related conditions that may adversely affect the athlete.

Pedagogical Features

A number of teaching devices have been included in this text:

1. *Chapter objectives* Objectives are presented at the beginning of each chapter to reinforce important learning goals.
2. *Color throughout the text* A second color appears throughout the text to enhance the overall appearance and accentuate illustrations.
3. *Boxed material within chapters* Important information such as special taping techniques have been boxed to make key information easier to find and to enhance the text's usefulness.
4. *Illustrations* The text includes 122 photographs and 314 line drawings. All illustrations are presented to increase the student's comprehension of injury prevention and athletic training.
5. *Margin information* For greater emphasis, key concepts, selected definitions, helpful training tips, salient points, and some illustrations have been placed in the margin throughout the text. These increase ease of reading and improve upon the teaching/learning process.
6. *Review questions and class activities* A list of questions and suggested class activities follow each chapter to review and apply the concepts learned.
7. *References* All chapters have a bibliography of pertinent references that includes the most complete and up-to-date resources available.
8. *Annotated bibliography* As an additional aid to learning, relevant and timely articles, books, and topics from the current literature have been annotated to provide additional resources.
9. *Glossary* An extensive list of key terms and their definitions are presented to assist students in applying the content learned.
10. *Appendix* The appendix provides the student with a conversion table for units of measure.

Ancillaries for the Instructor

Instructor's Manual An Instructor's Manual is provided that keys the content and organization of *Essentials of Athletic Training* with *Modern Principles of Athletic Training*. Practical features include:

- Brief chapter overviews
- Learning objectives
- Key terminology
- Discussion questions
- Class activities
- Appendixes include answer keys, additional resources, and transparency masters
- Perforated format, ready for immediate use

In addition, approximately 2000 examination questions are included. Each chapter contains true-false, multiple choice, and completion test questions. Worksheets including matching, short answer, listing, and essay questions can be used as self-testing tools for students or as additional sources for examination questions. The appendix includes part tests that can be used in evaluating student knowledge for each of the three parts of the text.

A special note of appreciation must be given to Marcia Anderson, M.S., A.T., C., Director of the Athletic Training program, Bridgewater State College, Bridgewater, Massachusetts, for her enthusiastic contribution in preparing the Instructor's Manual.

Transparencies Twenty-four acetate transparencies are available to maximize the teaching and learning process. These can be used with either *Essentials of Athletic Training* or *Modern Principles of Athletic Training*.

Acknowledgments

It is with great pleasure that I acknowledge those individuals who helped to make this project possible. With deep appreciation to my wife, Helene, whose help in all aspects of this project, as in the past, has been immeasurable. A special thanks is extended to the manuscript reviewers whose critical suggestions have been very helpful and are present in every chapter:

Doris E. Flores,   California State University at Sacramento
Ron Pfeiffer,   Boise State University
James G. Nespor,   Iowa State University
Teresa E. McHugh,   Monmouth College (N. J.)
Bobby Patton,   Southwest Texas State University
Suzanne Shoemaker,   Pennsylvania State University
Lowell C. Bailey, Jr.,   Phoenix College

Finally, gratitude must be expressed to Nancy K. Roberson, Editor, who initiated *Essentials of Athletic Training* and has provided a constant basis of support throughout its development. Special thanks is also extended to Michelle Turenne, my Developmental Editor at Times Mirror/Mosby College Publishing. Once again she has guided me through turbulent waters.

Daniel D. Arnheim

CONTENTS

Part Three
SPORTS CONDITIONS

Essentials of Athletic Training

Part One | # FOUNDATIONS

Part One explores the origins of athletic training, the current status of sports injuries, and athletic training and sports medicine. The relationship of proper conditioning and protective equipment to injury prevention is discussed. The application of good taping, bandaging, and emergency care is also stressed.

INTRODUCTION TO ATHLETIC TRAINING

When you finish this chapter, you will be able to:

Describe the historical foundations of athletic training

Define collision, contact, and noncontact sports and the types of injuries they commonly sustain

Describe the role of a coach, athletic trainer, and team physician and their functions within an athletic training program

Define epidemiological data gathering of sports injuries

Chapter 1 is concerned with introducing the field of sports medicine/athletic training to the reader.

Sports medicine, of which athletic training is a major part, can be traced back in history to the earliest period of human existence. These early humans spent their daily lives in the pursuit of basic survival. A healthy, able body was absolutely necessary to effectively forage for food.

Sports medicine and athletic training in early civilizations are best reflected in the civilizations of ancient Greece and the early Roman empire. With the rise of the Greek civilization and their desire to achieve physical perfection through athletics came the professional specialities of coaching and the development of specialists.[12] Professional coaches and trainers also played an important role in the life of the gladiators of the early Roman period.[12] Galen, the greatest name in Roman medicine, served as a physician at gladiatorial contests, in addition to other pursuits. Herodicus, a Roman physician for the ancient Olympic Games, was considered by many to be the first sports medicine physician.[16]

MODERN SPORTS MEDICINE AND ATHLETIC TRAINING

Modern athletic training and the athletic trainer, although having roots in ancient Greece and the Roman empire, are for the most part unique to North America.[12] The growth of the training profession in general has followed the growth of American football. Currently athletic training is one of the fastest growing paramedical fields under the umbrella of sports medicine. Sports medicine, as described by the American College of Sports Medicine (ACSM), is concerned with:

the study of the physiological, **biomechanical**, psychological, and pathological phenomena associated with exercise and athletics and the clinical application of the knowledge gained from this study to the improvement and maintenance of functional capacities for physical labor, exercise and athletics and to the prevention and treatment of disease and injuries related to exercise and athletics.[8]

Athletic training is a subspecialization of sports medicine providing a major link between a sports program and the medical community for the implementation of injury prevention, emergency care, and rehabilitation procedures.[7] It had evolved as a major paramedical profession when the National Athletic Trainers' Association (NATA) was formed in 1950.[12]

THE ATHLETE'S HEALTH AND SAFETY

Athletes, while participating in an organized sport, have every right to expect that their health and safety is of the highest priority at all times. A major rule to be considered by sports professionals is that the prevention of a health problem is much preferred over caring for the problem once it has occurred.

The three persons having the closest relationship to the athlete are the coach, the athletic trainer, and the team physician. Ideally, they should work together as an injury prevention team.[2]

The Coach

The coach is directly responsible for preventing injuries by seeing to it that the athlete has undergone a preventive injury conditioning program. He or she must ensure that sports equipment, especially protective equipment, is of the highest quality and is properly fitted. The coach must also make sure that protective equipment is properly maintained.[9] A coach must be keenly aware of what produces injuries in his or her particular sport and what measures must

biomechanical
Branch of study that applies the laws of mechanics to living organisms and biological tissues

Figure 1-1

The coach is directly responsible for preventing injuries in his or her sport.

be taken to avoid them. A coach should be able, when called upon, to apply proper first aid. This is especially true in cases of serious head and spinal injuries (Fig. 1-1).

It is essential that a coach have a good understanding of skill techniques as well as environmental factors that may adversely affect the athlete. Poor biomechanics in such skill areas as throwing and running can lead to overuse injuries of the arms and legs, while overexposure to heat and humidity may cause death. Just because a coach is experienced in coaching does not mean that he or she knows proper skill techniques. It is essential that coaches engage in a continual process of education to further their knowledge in a particular sport.

The Athletic Trainer

Athletic training, more specifically the athletic trainer, is a major link between the athletic program and the medical community for the implementation of preventive measures, emergency care, and injury management.[2] Ideally, every organized sports program should have a professional athletic trainer on its staff. Too often, however, a coach or student trainer assumes these responsibilities.

As mentioned earlier, the athletic trainer has evolved into a highly educated and well-trained professional. The titles *athletic trainer* and *athletic training* remain because of tradition. In reality, *trainer* is synonymous with *coach*, and *training* with *coaching* or *teaching*. A better title to describe the role of an athletic trainer is *sports therapist* or, perhaps, *sports medicine therapist* (Fig. 1-2).

Qualifications of the Professional Athletic Trainer

The professional athletic trainer is expected to be a college graduate with extensive background in biological and health sciences, having taken specific courses in athletic training. He or she should be certified by the NATA and should hold a cardiopulmonary resuscitation (CPR) certification.

NATA Certification

Currently there are two ways to become NATA certified[*]: (1) graduate from a NATA-approved curriculum and pass the national examination, or (2) hold an internship and pass the national examination. A person can become certified after successfully completing a NATA-approved athletic training program from a college or university sponsoring a NATA-approved graduate or undergraduate program.

Certification by the NATA may be attained under this category for schools that do not offer an approved curriculum; however, the candidate for certification must have spent a minimum of 1800 hours over a minimum of 4 years and not more than 5 years under the direction of a NATA-certified athletic trainer. It is also recommended that athletic trainers obtain an emergency medical technician (EMT) certificate.

---

[*]All requirements are subject to change. Students may contact the NATA Board of Certification, 1001 E. 4th St., P.O. Drawer 1865, Greenville, N.C. 27835-1865 for updated information.

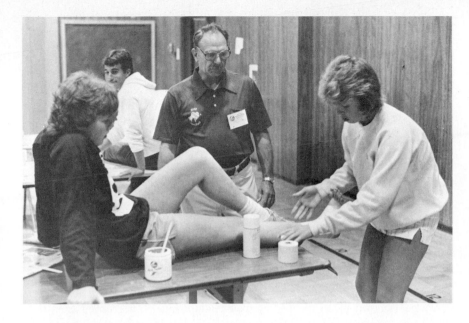

Figure 1-2

The athletic trainer is a major
link between the athletic
program and the medical
community.

The Trainer's Functions

Today's professional athletic trainer performs numerous and diverse functions. In general, he or she is concerned with six major task areas: injury prevention, injury recognition and evaluation, injury management/treatment and disposition, injury rehabilitation, program organization and administration, and program education and athletic counseling.[5]

The prevention of injury is a
major goal of athletic training.

Athletic trainers are employed by individual high schools, school districts, colleges and universities, professional teams, and more recently by sports medicine clinics. Athletic trainers must work closely with coaches, the team physician, and other medical personnel.

The athletic trainer is
considered a paramedical
specialist in sports medicine.

Many states now license athletic trainers and officially establish their relationship with the physician, their scope of function of athletic training, and the use of therapeutic methods.

The Team Physician

The team physician must have a full understanding of sports injuries. It is ideal that the team physician has a background in sports medicine. Currently physicians with varied specializations act as team physicians. These may be family physicians, pediatricians (specialists with children), internal medicine specialists, or orthopedic surgeons (specialists in the **musculoskeletal** system). These physicians may be medical doctors (M.D.) or doctors of osteopathy (D.O.). Their primary duties entail:

musculoskeletal
Pertaining to muscles and the
skeleton

1. Seeing that a complete medical history of each athlete is compiled and is readily available
2. Determining through a physical examination the athletes' health status

3. Diagnosing and treating injuries and other illnesses
4. Directing and advising the athletic trainer on health matters
5. Acting, when necessary, as an instructor to the trainer, assistant trainer, and student trainers on special therapeutic methods, therapeutic problems, and related procedures
6. Attending all games, athletic contests, scrimmages, and practices; if this is not feasible, arranging for attendance by other qualified medical personnel; when personal attendance is not possible, being available for emergency call
7. Deciding when, on medical grounds, athletes should be disqualified from participation and when they may be permitted to reenter competition
8. Serving as an advisor to the trainer and the coach and, when necessary, as a counselor to the athlete
9. Working closely with the school administrator, school dentist, trainer, coach, and health services personnel to promote and maintain consistently high standards for the care of the athlete

The Health Screening Examination

All athletes must have a thorough health screening examination before participating in a competitive sport.

A health screening examination is an essential part of the athletic health program and is often given by the team physician. Health screening examinations must be given not only at the entry level but must be conducted each season that an athlete participates. It must serve as a screening device that allows only physically and psychologically fit individuals to enter highly vigorous sports competition. The examination must take into consideration cardiovascular, neurological, orthopedic, or respiratory irregularities that could be further aggravated by certain sports participation. Such findings should be grounds for disqualification.[6] Individuals with a loss of one organ or with an impaired organ(s), such as an eye or a kidney, must be considered candidates for disqualification, especially for collision sports. Other conditions, such as being seriously overweight or underweight, might be correctible through an individual program of diet and conditioning. Postural and orthopedic conditions that may prove to be a handicap or predispose the participant to injury should also be noted during the examination.

The physician should rule out disease states that contraindicate participation in certain activities. Such states might include: metabolic, cardiovascular, and renal disease; neurological problems; and pulmonary, musculoskeletal, and abdominal aberrations. Athletes having past injuries must be carefully examined for any residual weaknesses or problems. Medicinally controlled disorders such as asthma, diabetes, and convulsive disorders must be individually considered.

The first step in the health screening examination is to obtain a complete medical history. Second, a thorough physical examination is given. This includes the cardiovascular, respiratory, musculoskeletal, and central nervous systems. A major part of this examination should also be determining urine and blood chemistry (Figs. 1-3 and 1-4).

Other Specialists Concerned with Athletic Health

In addition to those personnel concerned with prevention (coach, athletic trainer, and team physician), there are many other specialists concerned with

ATHLETIC MEDICAL EXAMINATION FOR _____
                                          (Sport)

Name _____ Age ____ Birthdate _____ S.S.# _____

Address _____ Phone no. _____
         (Street)   (City)   (Zip)

Instructions:
    All questions must be answered. Failure to disclose pertinent medical informa-
    tion may invalidate your insurance coverage and, under NCAA rules, may cancel
    your eligibility to participate in interscholastic athletics. Any further
    health problems must be discussed with the physician at the time of this
    examination.

Medical history:
    Have you ever had any of the following: If "yes" give details to the
    examining doctor.

	NO	YES	DETAILS (IF YES)
1. Head injury or concussion			
2. Bone or joint disorders, fractures (broken bones), dislocations, trick joints, arthritis, back pain			
3. Eye or ear problems (disease or surgery)			
4. Dizzy spells, fainting or convulsions			
5. Tuberculosis, asthma, bronchitis			
6. Heart trouble or rheumatic fever			
7. High or low blood pressure			
8. Anemia, leukemia or bleeding disorder			
9. Diabetes, hepatitis or jaundice			
10. Ulcers, other stomach trouble or colitis			
11. Kidney or bladder problems			
12. Hernia (rupture)			
13. Mental illness or nervous breakdown			
14. Addiction to drugs or alcohol			
15. Surgery or advised to have surgery			
16. Taking medication regularly			
17. Allergies or skin problems			
18. Other illness, injury not named above			
19. Menstrual problems; LMP			

Signature _____

Date _____

Figure 1-3

Suggested medical history form
for athletes.

II
ATHLETIC MEDICAL EXAMINATION

Name _____ S.S.# _____

Physical examination   Sport _____

Height_____ Weight_____ Pulse_____ B.P. _____/_____

    Vision: Right_____/_____ with/without glasses   Dip/Tet

             Left _____/_____ with/without glasses

    Hearing: Right_____ Left_____   (Date)

Laboratory_____ Blood: HCT_____ RPR_____ Sickledex_____
      (Date)   Urine: Sugar_____ Alb_____

Chest x-ray_____   Yes_____ no_____
        (Date)

System examination	Comments	Initials
Group 1 Eyes		
Ears		
Nose		
Throat		
Neck		
Group 2 Skin		
Heart		
Lungs _____ Breasts		
Group 3 Abdomen, groin, genitals, rectum		
Group 4 Spine, extremities		

Cleared, unrestricted_____ Not cleared_____

Cleared, restricted_____ Further evaluation_____

                Appointment to be made_____
                                (date)

Comments:_____
         _____
         _____

                        Team Physician   Date

Figure 1-4

Suggested medical examination form for athletes.

the health and safety of the athlete. They include the dentist, podiatrist, equipment personnel, and referees.

The Team Dentist

The role of team dentists is somewhat analogous to that of team physicians. They serve as dental consultant for the team and should be available for first aid and emergency care. Good communication between the dentist and the coach or trainer should ensure a good dental program.

The Team Podiatrist

Podiatry, the specialized field dealing with the study and care of the foot, has become an integral part of sports health care. Many podiatrists are trained in surgical procedures, foot biomechanics, and the fitting and construction of orthotic devices for the shoe. Like the team dentist, a podiatrist should be available on a consultative basis for major problems.

Equipment Personnel

Increasingly, sports equipment personnel are becoming specialists in the purchasing and proper fitting of protective equipment. They work closely with the coach and athletic trainer.

Referees

Referees must be highly knowledgeable regarding rules and regulations, especially those that relate to the health and welfare of the athlete. They must be able to check the playing facility for dangerous situations and equipment that may predispose the athlete to injury.[2]

THE TRAINING PROGRAM

Most high schools and colleges have some type of athletic training program. They may range from very basic offerings to those that are highly complex. The degree to which the athletic training program provides services to the athlete depends on the philosophy of the administration, the availability of a professional trainer, available facilities, and the budget. Athletic training and sports medicine form a health care unit that requires careful organization and administration.[4]

The Training Facility

The only use for the training facility is the prevention and care of sports injuries and related health functions. The training room is a special facility often with many rooms designed to meet the many requirements of a sports training program. Larger, more complex facilities found in some universities and professional teams have areas for first aid, physical examinations, pregame and prepractice bandaging and taping, and an area where a variety of therapeutic techniques can be carried out (Fig. 1-5). In these complexes there also may be separate offices for trainers and physicians.[15] In contrast, some high schools may have only one small room to carry out a multitude of health and safety functions. Above all, a training facility should never become a club room for athletes, a meeting room for coaches and athletes, nor a storage room for athletic equipment. Unless strict rules on the function of the training are made and kept, the training room soon loses its major purpose. A major goal is that the training room be kept in a hygienic and sanitary condition at all times. The following are some general rules to which athletes should adhere:

1. No cleated shoes are allowed.
2. Game equipment is kept outside.
3. Shoes are kept off of treatment tables.
4. Athletes must shower following activity and before receiving treatment except in an emergency situation.
5. Roughhousing and profanity are never allowed.

Example of Service Areas

Modern training rooms are usually organized into service areas. Some examples of special service areas are:

The only use for the training room is the prevention and care of sports injuries and related health functions.

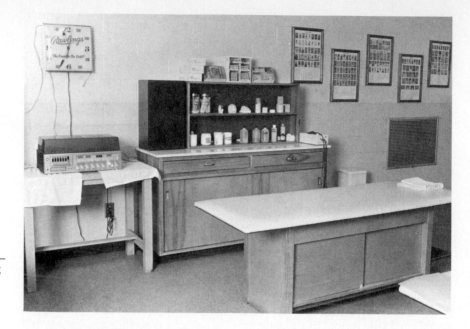

Figure 1-5

The primary use of the training facility is the prevention and care of sports injuries and health-related functions.

1. Taping, bandaging, and orthotics section
2. Superficial thermal and mechanical therapy section—this area might have infrared heat lamps and massage tables
3. Electrotherapy section—this area commonly has ultrasound and electrostimulation machines
4. Hydrotherapy section—this area has whirlpool baths, sinks, and in some cases a steam room (Fig. 1-6)
5. Exercise rehabilitation section—this area specializes in resistance apparatus and bicycle exercises

In addition to these service sections, there must be a trainer's office and plentiful storage facilities.

SUSTAINING SPORTS INJURIES

Understanding sports injuries requires knowledge of the types of sports involved and how injuries are sustained.

An **accident** is defined as an unplanned event capable of resulting in loss of time, property damage, injury, disablement, or even death.[3] On the other hand, an **injury** may be defined as damage to the body that restricts activity or causes disability to such an extent that the athlete is confined to his or her bed.[3]

An athlete runs a 50% chance of sustaining some injury. Of the 50 million estimated sports injuries sustained each year, approximately 50% require only minor care with no activity restriction.[3] Ninety percent of sports injuries are considered minor, while 10% are of the more serious type. It should be noted, however, that repeated **acute** minor injuries can eventually lead to more serious **chronic** conditions in later life.

accident
Occurring by chance or without intention

injury
An act that damages or hurts

acute injury
An injury with sudden onset and short duration

chronic injury
An injury with long onset and long duration

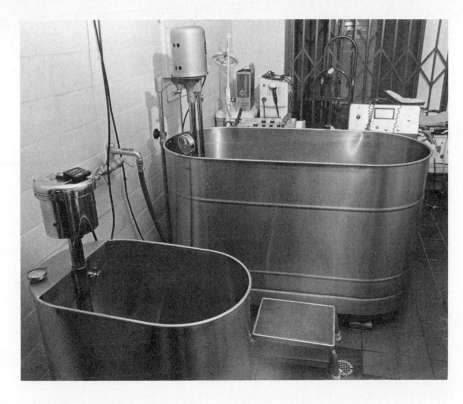

Figure 1-6

A whirlpool bath is a common therapeutic modality in the athletic training facility.

Sports Classification

Sports injuries cannot be studied without an examination of the different types of sports classifications. Sports can be classified in many different ways. The classifications that best describe the extent to which a sport produces situations for accidents and subsequent injuries are collision, contact, and noncontact sports. In **collision** sports, athletes use their bodies to deter or punish opponents (Fig. 1-7). American football, ice hockey, boxing, and rugby are common American collision sports. In **contact** sports athletes make physical contact, but not with the intent to produce bodily injury (Fig. 1-8). Examples of contact sports are soccer, basketball, baseball, and touch and flag football. As the name implies, **noncontact** sports have no physical contact (Fig. 1-9). Archery, crew rowing, and cross country running are examples of noncontact sports.

collision sport
Athletes use their bodies to deter or punish opponents

contact sport
Athletes make physical contact, but not with the intent to produce bodily injury

Sports Injury Information

By their very nature many sports activities invite injury. The "all-out" exertion required, the numerous situations requiring body contact, and play that involves the striking and throwing of missiles, create hazards that are either directly or indirectly responsible for the many different injuries suffered by athletes.

In general, accurate assessment of why sports injuries occur is very difficult. As many factors as possible must be known about why the injury oc-

noncontact sport
Athletes are not involved in any physical contact

epidemiological approach
The study of sports injuries involving the relationship of as many injury factors as possible

curred. Such information as the skill level of the athlete, how much exposure to an injury was sustained by the athlete, and environmental conditions are but a few of the bits of information needed before a complete understanding can be accomplished.

There are vast numbers of people involved with organized and recreational sports who become injured. However, the collection of accurate data that stem from these injuries is weak for the most part. Most data collection systems report that an injury occurred, but they do not collect details of the occurrence. A good data collection system is one that takes an **epidemiological approach**, such as the NATA's High School Athletic Injury Registry conducted by John Powell, Ph.D, of San Diego State University.[14] This system not only documents an injury's occurrence, but it also collects as many factors related to the injury as possible.[1]

Collision sports, primarily American football, are associated directly with causing catastrophic injuries and even death. However, fatalities in organized football have dropped significantly since rules were adopted that prevent the head from being used as a primary and initial contact area.[10] From 1976 to 1984 there have been a total of 72 deaths from head injury, most of which occurred in high school football.[17,18] Mueller and Schindler indicate that out of the 1,575,000 participants in American football in 1984, there were 6 direct fatalities and 3 indirect fatalities from heat stroke.[11] From 1977 there has been a gradual decline in injuries due to stricter adherence to the rules of play, better conditioning, medical supervision, and continued research in the improvement of protective equipment (e.g., the helmet).

The highest incidence of indirect sports death stems from heat stroke. Other less common indirect causes include cardiovascular and respiratory problems or congenital conditions not previously known. There has been a

Figure 1-7

In collision sports, athletes use their bodies to deter or punish opponents.

Figure 1-8

In contact sports some physical contact is made but not with the intent to punish the opponent.

catastrophic injury
A permanent injury to the spinal cord that leaves the athlete quadriplegic or paraplegic

steady decline in permanent spinal injuries leading to quadriplegia from 1976 to 1984. In 1976 there were 34 such injuries, and in 1984 there were 5 — a decline of about 85%. The expression **catastrophic injury** refers to permanent spinal injuries.

It should be noted that although millions of individuals participate in organized and recreational sports, there is a relatively low incidence of serious injuries. Ninety-eight percent of individuals with injuries requiring hospital emergency room medical attention are treated and released immediately.[13] Deaths from sports have been attributed to chest or trunk impact by thrown objects, other players, or nonyielding objects. Deaths have occurred when players were struck in the head by sports implements (bats, golf clubs, hockey sticks) or by missiles (baseballs, soccer balls, golf balls, hockey pucks). Deaths have also resulted when an individual received a direct blow to the head from another player or the ground. On record are a number of recreational sports deaths in which a playing structure, such as a goalpost or backstop, fell on a participant.

In general, in most popular organized and recreational sports activities, the legs and arms are most at risk, with the head and face next. Muscle strains, joint sprains, contusions, and skin abrasions are the most frequent injuries sustained by the active sports participant.

SUMMARY

Modern sports medicine and athletic training have their roots in ancient Greece and early Rome. Today athletic training is a subspecialization of sports medicine. A major concern of the coach and athletic trainer is the prevention of sports injuries.

The coach is directly responsible for preventing injuries to the athlete by avoiding hazardous situations, providing well-made and properly fitted protective equipment, and making sure the athlete is in top physical condition to withstand the rigors of the sport.

The athletic trainer is an essential member of any athletic department. The athletic trainer provides a major link between the athletic program and the medical community. It is important that the athletic trainer is well educated in the prevention and care of sports injuries and is nationally certified.

A team physician who has a thorough understanding of sports medicine is a necessary part of any athletic program. The team physician is an integral part of the athletic department's health and safety program. In addition to conducting the health screening program, he or she advises the coach and trainer, attends sports contests, and makes decisions on when an athlete is disqualified from participation.

A training facility varies in size from a small room to a complex of many rooms. The training program has as its major concern the health and safety of the athlete. It provides services such as first aid, physical examinations, preventive taping, and the carrying out of therapeutic procedures.

REVIEW QUESTIONS AND CLASS ACTIVITIES

1. How do modern sports medicine and athletic training compare to ancient Greek and Roman approaches to the care of the athlete?
2. Compare the coach, athletic trainer, and team physician health care and safety responsibilities to the athlete.

Figure 1-9

Noncontact sports do not
involve physical contact with
an opposing player.

3. How should sports injury data gathering be improved to provide more information?
4. American football is the nation's most injurious sport. How may it be made safer?
5. What is the scope of an athletic trainer's job?
6. Have the athletic director from your school talk about his or her concern for health and safety.
7. Visit with your athletic training program to understand the services it provides the total athletic program.
8. Talk with a team physician and find out his or her major problems and frustrations.

REFERENCES

1. Caldwell, F.: Epidemiology in sports medicine overview: epidemiologists take their place on the sports medicine team, Phys. Sportsmed. **13**:135, March 1985.
2. Cutting, V.J.: Development of "A student handbook for prevention of athletic injuries," an unpublished master's thesis, San Diego, 1985, San Diego State University.
3. Dean, C.H., and Hoerner, E.F.: Injury rates in team sports and individual recreation. In Vinger, P.F., and Hoerner, E.F. (editors): Sports injuries: the unthwarted epidemic, Boston, 1981, John Wright, PSG, Inc.
4. Gaunya, S.T.: The role of the trainer. In Vinger, P.F. and Hoerner, E.T. (editors): Sports injuries: the unthwarted epidemic, Boston, 1981, John Wright, PSG, Inc.
5. Grace, P., and Ledderman, L.: Role delineation study for the certification examination for entry-level athletic trainers, Ath. Train. **17**:264, 1982.
6. International Congress on Sports and Health, Sept. 22–23, 1983, Int. J. Sports Med. (supplement) **5**:1, Nov. 1984.
7. Kegerreis, S.: Sports medicine: a functional definition, J. Phys .Educ. Rec. Dance **52**(5):22, 1981.
8. Lamb, D.R.: "Sports medicine" - what is it?, ACSM President's report, Sports Medicine Bulletin, 16:2, 1981.
9. Lester, R.A.: The coach as codefendant: football in the 1980's. In Appenzeller, H. (editor): Sports and law: contemporary issues, Charlottesville, Va., 1985, The Michie Co.
10. Mueller, F.O., and Blyth, C.S.: Fatalities and catastrophic injuries in football, Phys. Sportsmed. **10**:135, 1982.
11. Mueller, F.O., and Schindler, R.D.: Annual survey of football injury research – 1931–1983, Ath. Train. **20**(3): 213, 1985.
12. O'Shea, M.E.: A history of the National Athletic Trainers' Association, Greenville, N.C., 1980, National Athletic Trainers' Association.
13. Overview of sports-related injuries in persons 5–14 years of age, Washington D.C., Dec. 1981, U.S. Consumer Product Safety Commission.
14. Powell, J: Coordinator, NATA high school athletic injury registry, San Diego State University, San Diego, California, Jan. 1986.
15. Secor, M.R.: Designing athletic training facilities, or "where do you want the outlets?" Ath. Train. **19**:19, Spring 1984.
16. Southmayd, W., and Hoffman, M.: Sports health, New York, 1981, A Perigee Book, The Putnam Publishing Group.
17. Torg, J.S.: Epidemiology, pathomechanics, and prevention of athletic injuries to the cervical spine, Med. Sci. Sports Exer. **17**:295, June 1985.
18. Torg, J.S., et al.: The national football head and neck injury registry, J.A.M.A., **254**:3439, 1985.

ANNOTATED BIBLIOGRAPHY

Bilik, S.E.: The trainers bible, ed. 9, New York, 1956, T.J. Reed & Co. Publishers.
    A classic book by a major pioneer in athletic training and sports medicine. It was first published in 1917.

Kulund, D.N.: The injured athlete, Philadelphia, 1982, J.B. Lippincott Co.
  Chapter 1 discusses the many ramifications of the athletes' physician. In Chapter 8 Joe H. Gieck discusses in detail the athletic trainer and rehabilitation.
Myers, G.C., and Garrick, J.G.: The preseason examination of school and college athletes. In Strauss, R.H. (editor): Sports medicine, Philadelphia, 1984, W.B. Saunders Co.
  An excellent discussion on what a preseason physical examination should contain. The American Medical Association's "disqualifying conditions for sports participation" are also included.
O'Shea, M.E.: A history of the National Athletic Trainers' Association, Greenville, N.C., 1980, National Athletic Trainers' Association.
  An interesting text on the history of the NATA. Any student interested in athletic training as a career should know something about the pioneers in this field.
Rawlinson, K.: Modern athletic training, ed. 2, North Palm Beach, Fla, 1980, The Athletic Institute.
  Introductory material provides interesting information on the National Athletic Trainers' Association.

Injury Prevention: Physical Conditioning, Nutrition, and Psychological Considerations

When you finish reading this chapter you will be able to:

Describe the major aspects of developing strength, flexibility, and endurance for performance and injury prevention

Identify the major conditioning seasons

Explain the major procedures in warm-up and cool down

Describe how nutrition enhances performance and also aids in the prevention of sports injuries

Explain how psychological factors can increase or decrease the possibilities of athletic injuries

Describe the implications of hard physical training and competition during childhood

Chapter 2 is concerned with two major areas of sports injury prevention: physical conditioning and psychological considerations.

CONDITIONING AND TRAINING

Physical conditioning for sports participation, besides preparing athletes for high-level performance, also prevents injuries. Coaches and trainers alike now recognize that improper conditioning is one of the major causes of sports injuries. Muscular imbalance, improper timing due to faulty neuromuscular coordination, inadequate ligamentous or tendinous strength, inadequate muscle or cardiovascular endurance, inadequate muscle bulk, problems of flexibility, and problems related to body composition are some of the primary causes of sport injury directly attributable to insufficient or improper physical conditioning and training.

Training is usually defined as a systematic process of repetitive, progressive exercise or work, involving the learning process and acclimatization. The great sports medicine pioneer Dr. S.E. Bilik[3] correctly stated that the primary objective of intense sports conditioning and training must be as follows: "To put the body with extreme and exceptional care under the influence of all agents which promote its health and strength in order to enable it to meet extreme and exceptional demands upon it."

Conditioning Seasons

No longer do serious athletes engage only in preseason conditioning and in-season competition. Sports conditioning is now a year-round endeavor, often encompassing four training seasons: postseason, off-season, preseason, and in-season. This is especially true for collision-type sports, such as football. For American tackle football, the postseason generally is from mid-December through January; off-season from February to July; preseason from July to September; and in-season from September to January.

Sports conditioning often falls into four seasons:
  Postseason
  Off-season
  Preseason
  In-season

Postseason

The postseason period is immediately after a sport season. It is often dedicated to physical restoration, especially when athletes have been injured during the season. This is a time for postsurgical rehabilitation and detailed medical evaluation.

Off-season

It is not essential that athletes continue an intensive conditioning program during the off-season. It is, however, a good idea for the athlete to engage in another sport during this period. Such sports engagement should be physiologically demanding so that strength, endurance, and flexibility are maintained.

Preseason

If the athlete has maintained a reasonably high level of physical fitness during the off-season, the preseason work will not be especially difficult. During this period the athlete should achieve the highest possible level of conditioning and training specific to the position played.

In-season

It should be noted that the intensive preseason conditioning training program that brought the athlete to the competitive season may not be maintained by the sport itself. Unless there is conditioning throughout the season, a problem of deconditioning may occur. In other words, athletes who do not undergo a maintenance conditioning program may lose the ideal entry level of physiological fitness.

The Ten Cardinal Conditioning Principles

The following ten cardinal principles can be applied to sports conditioning:
1. *Warming up*. See that proper and adequate warm-up procedures precede all activities.
2. *Gradualness*. Add small daily increments of work. **REMEMBER**: It takes 6 to 8 weeks to get into top-level condition.
3. *Timing*. Prevent overdoing. Relate all work to the athlete's general condition at the time. Practice periods should extend for 1 hour to 1 hour and 45 minutes, depending on the sport. **REMEMBER**: The tired athlete is prone to injury.
4. *Intensity*. Stress the intensity of the work rather than the quantity. Usually coaches and athletic trainers fail to work their athletes *hard* enough in terms of intensity. They make the mistake of prolonging

the workout rather than increasing the tempo or the work load. As the degree of training increases, the intensity of training must also increase.

5. *Capacity level.* Expect from the athlete performance that is as close to his or her physiological limits as health and safety factors will allow. Only in working to capacity will the desired results be achieved.

6. *Strength.* Develop strength as a means of producing greater endurance and speed.

7. *Motivation.* Motivation is a prime factor in sports conditioning. Use circuit training and isometric exercises as means of further motivating the athlete.

8. *Specialization.* Exercise programs should include exercises for strength, relaxation, and flexibility. In addition, exercises geared to the demands made on the body in specific activities should be used to develop specialization.

9. *Relaxation.* Specific relaxation exercises, which aid in recovery from fatigue and tension, should be taught.

10. *Routine.* A routine of exercise, 3 to 4 times per week "year-round," should be established.

Foundations of Conditioning

The SAID principle indicates that conditioning and training should be directed toward the specific demands of a sport.

Logan and Wallis[14] identified the *SAID principle*, which expressly relates to sports conditioning and training. SAID is an acronym for *s*pecific *a*daptation to *i*mposed *d*emands. The SAID principle indicates that conditioning and training are directed toward the specific demands of a given sport.

Gradually increasing the strenuousness of an exercise is an application of the *overload principle*, which holds that an activity must always be upgraded to a consistently higher level through maximum or near-maximum stimulation.

Fat and the Lean Body

The human body is generally composed of fat and a lean body mass. *Essential fat* is the survival fat that is stored around vital organs, in the bone marrow, and nervous system. This usually constitutes about 2% to 4% of the total body fat in adult males and 6% to 8% in adult females. Fat, other than essential fat, is primarily found subcutaneously. A normal total body fat of 13% to 15% has been shown for young adult males and 22% to 25% for young women.[7]

In terms of sports injuries prevention, excess body fat should be avoided. Excess body fat is weight that is considered "dead" and not viable. This extra weight places an added stress on the body, especially the joints, and therefore increases susceptibility to overuse problems.

Body Density

Over time, regular exercise produces density changes within the musculoskeletal system. Depending on the sport, muscles display girth changes. There is a reduction of adipose tissue and an increase of connective tissue within muscle bundles, which increases the resistance to strains and stresses the muscle may undergo. Ligaments and bones also become denser through a gradual overload exercise program.

Warming Up and Cooling Down

Both the processes of properly warming up and cooling down are believed by many authorities to have major implications in the prevention of sports injuries.[21]

Warming up   Although warm-up is still a subject of study and results are somewhat conflicting, most evidence favors its use. The use of warm-up procedures has been traditional in sports and is still advocated as the means of preparing the body physiologically and psychologically for physical performance, in the belief that it will not only improve performance but will lessen the possibilities of injury. The term *warming up* in this discussion refers to the use of preliminary exercise procedures rather than the use of hot showers, massage, counterirritants, diathermy, or other forms of passive warm-up.

Warm-up is used as a preventive measure, although limited data exist to substantiate this. It is believed that a proper warm-up will prevent and/or reduce strains and the tearing of muscle fibers from their tendinous attachments. Most frequently the antagonist muscles are torn. Their inability to relax rapidly, plus the great contractile force of the agonist muscles added to the momentum of the moving part, subject the antagonists to a sudden severe strain that can result in a subsequent tearing of the fibers themselves, as well as their tendinous attachments. Proper warm-up can help to reduce or prevent muscle soreness.

Physiological purposes of warming up   The main purposes of warming up are to raise both the general body and the deep muscle temperatures and to stretch connective tissues to permit greater flexibility. This reduces the possibility of muscle tears and ligamentous sprains and helps to prevent muscle soreness. As cellular temperature increases, it is accompanied by a corresponding increase in the speed of the metabolic processes within the cells, since such processes are temperature dependent.[23] For each degree of internal temperature rise there is a corresponding rise in the rate of metabolism of about 13%. At higher temperatures there is a faster and more complete dissociation of oxygen from the hemoglobin and myoglobins, which improves the oxygen supply during work.[19] The transmission of nerve impulses speeds up as well. Overloading the muscle groups before power activities results in improved performance. It is thought that there is an increased level of excitation of the motor units that are called into play to handle the increased load and that these motor units are then carried over into the actual performance. The result is an increase in the athlete's physical working capacity.

It takes at least 15 to 30 minutes of gradual warm-up to bring the body to a state of readiness with its attendant rise in body temperature and to adequately mobilize the body physiology in terms of making a greater number of muscle capillaries available for extreme effort and of readying blood sugar and adrenaline. The time needed for satisfactory warm-up varies with the individual and tends to increase with age.

Warm-up differs in relation to the type of competition. It is advisable for athletes to warm up in activities similar to the event in which they will compete. Accordingly, a sprinter might start by jogging a bit, practice a few starts, and use some stretching techniques and general body exercises. A baseball player might first use general body exercises, swing a bat through a number of

> Warming up involves general body warming plus specific warming to the demands of the sport.

practice swings, and do preliminary throwing, alternating these activities with stretching exercises. Both overload and the use of mimetic activities appear to be important for those events in which neuromuscular coordination is paramount.

On cool days warm-up should be increased somewhat in duration and should be performed in sweat clothing. Only when athletes are fully warmed up and ready to move directly into competition should they remove their sweat clothing. In some events, for example, field events, sweat clothing should be replaced immediately after the competitive effort. If rather long periods of time elapse between trials or events, the performer should use light warm-up procedures during the intervals.

The process of warming up   Generally, warm-up is considered as falling into two categories: (1) the *general*, or *unrelated*, warm-up, which consists of activities that bring about a general warming of the body without having any relationship to the skills to be performed; and (2) *specific*, or *related*, warm-up, which is mimetic, that is, similar to or the same as skills to be performed in competition (running, throwing, swinging, etc.).

General warm-up   General warm-up procedures should consist of jogging or easy running, gradual stretching, and general exercises. These procedures should mobilize the body for action and make it supple and free. They must be of sufficient duration and intensity to raise deep tissue temperatures without developing marked fatigue. When athletes attain a state of sweating, they have raised their internal temperature to a desirable level. The nature of the warm-up varies to some degree in relation to the activity. Some procedures lend themselves well to athletic activities of all types and should be performed along with others that are specifically designed for the sport in which the athlete is to participate.

The exercises described in this discussion provide balance and depth in procedures, so that total body warm-up may be achieved. The athlete's daily workout, either for practice or for competition, should begin with running and the static stretches and then proceed to the calisthenic exercises.

Specific event warm-up   After completing the general exercises in the warm-up, the athletes should progress to those that are specific for their events or activities. They should start at a moderate pace and then increase the tempo as they feel body temperature and cardiovascular increases taking place. The effects of warm-up may persist as long as 45 minutes. However, the closer the warm-up period is to the actual performance, the more beneficial it will be in terms of its effect on the performance. For the athlete to benefit optimally from warm-up, no more than 15 minutes should elapse between the completion of the warm-up and the performance of the activity itself.

Cooling properly decreases blood and muscle lactic acid levels more rapidly.

Cooling down   Cooling down applies to exercise of gradually diminishing intensity that follows strenuous work and permits the return of both the circulation and various body functions to preexercise levels. From 30 seconds to 1 minute of jogging, followed by 3 to 5 minutes of walking, permits the body to effect the necessary re-adjustments.

Physiologically, an important reason for cooling down is that blood and muscle lactic acid levels decrease more rapidly during active recovery than during passive recovery. Also, active recovery keeps the muscle pumps active, which prevents blood from pooling in the extremities.

Muscle Conditioning

Muscles are complex types of tissue composed of contractile cells of fibers that affect movement of an organ or body part.

Muscle strength   *Strength* can be defined as the capacity to exert force or as the ability to perform work against resistance. The most noticeable change that takes place in the muscle as a result of placing an overload on the muscle over time is an increase in girth. The overload principle follows the concept that strength and endurance of a muscle will increase only when the work loads are above those normally encountered. It should be noted, however, that size alone is not an index of strength of a muscle, since muscles vary in size due to their various amounts of fatty tissue.[18]

Size alone is not an index of muscle strength.

Muscle contraction and exercise   Exercise for the development of strength is related to the type of muscle contraction (Fig. 2-1).

Isometric muscle contraction   An isometric muscle contraction is one in which there is no change in the length of the muscle or in the angle of the joint at which the contraction takes place. **Isometric exercise** has been shown to be most effective when a maximal contraction is held for at least 6 seconds. After resting between each bout, the athlete repeats the exercise five to ten times. Strength gained through an isometric exercise is specific to the joint angle at which the contraction takes place.

isometric exercise
Contracts the muscle statically without changing its length

Isotonic muscle contraction   Shortening or lengthening the muscle causing a skeletal part to be moved through a full range of motion involves an isotonic contraction. **Isotonic exercise** involves moving a resistive force, either a body part or some object, and may also be referred to as *dynamic* contraction. An isotonic exercise does not involve the same muscle fibers throughout a particular movement because the load remains constant regardless of the angle of contraction or the degree of fatigue. Thus the greatest strength gain is in those fibers used in the initial part of the movement when

isotonic exercise
Shortens and lengthens the muscle through a complete range of motion

Figure 2-1

An example of an isotonic exercise.

inertia is overcome. The least strength gain is at the midpoint of the contraction.

The major values of performing exercises involving isotonic contraction are that they promote joint range of motion and increase circulation and endurance. When performing an isotonic movement against resistance, the muscle should first be placed in a stretched position to ensure maximal innervation to the muscle fibers. After full stretch, the body part is *concentrically* moved as far as possible and then *eccentrically* moved to the beginning stretch position. Concentric contraction refers to the muscle becoming shortened, while eccentric contraction refers to muscle lengthening. Slow, eccentric muscle contraction against resistance is known as **negative resistance**, which enervates more muscle fibers than positive, or concentric, contraction. In contrast to concentric contraction, eccentric contraction tends to cause more muscle soreness.

Recovery from muscular fatigue is more rapid in isotonic than in isometric exercise. Isotonic exercises that involve increasingly greater resistance are known as progressive resistance exercises (PRE) and were introduced by DeLorme and Watkins.[8] Although there are many variations to the DeLorme method, it originally made use of a series of three exercise sets having ten repetitions in each set. The first set is performed against a resistance equal to one-half of one's maximum effort, the second at three-fourths maximum effort, and the final set against a full maximum effort. When the athlete is able to easily perform the third set, the weight increment is increased between 2 1/2 and 5 pounds. Workouts commonly take place every other day, or three to four times weekly. Although ten repetitions will increase strength, four to eight repetitions will produce the greatest strength.

Isokinetic muscle contraction Isokinetic muscle contraction occurs through an *accommodating and variable resistance exercise* (ARE). This method more nearly uses total involvement of the muscle fibers, since the resistance varies according to the angle of pull and the degree of fatigue developed throughout the exercise. The resistance is also variable in that it changes throughout the exercise range of motion. The inertia of the resistance, a definite factor in the isotonic exercise, is not a factor in isokinetics, since the resistance automatically adjusts to the degree of force exerted against it, thus maintaining a constant and consistent force. Exercises can be performed throughout the entire range of the performer's speed. A decided advantage of this type of exercise is that muscle soreness does not usually result. It is postulated that the muscle has a brief period of relaxation between repetitions, thus allowing the blood to circulate freely throughout the fibers and cleanse away the accumulated lactic acid and metabolites from the muscle cells. Isotonic exercises do not permit such relaxation, hence there is a buildup of fatigue products. Neither isokinetic nor isotonic resistance is superior to the other. The goal of training must be satisfied according to the SAID principle. Over the last few years isokinetic resistance exercising has found a valuable place in rehabilitation, whereas free weights employing isotonic principles have become increasingly popular in sports conditioning.

Plyometric exercise Plyometric exercise produces an isometric-type overload, using the myotatic, or stretch, reflex. By means of an eccentric (lengthening) contraction, the muscle is fully stretched ("on stretch") im-

negative resistance
Slow eccentric muscle contraction against resistance

isokinetic exercise
Accommodating and variable resistance exercise (ARE)

mediately preceding the concentric (shortening) contraction. The greater the stretch put on the muscle from its resting length immediately before the concentric contraction, the greater the load the muscle can lift or overcome. A typical example of the plyometric concept occurs when a volleyball player trains to increase his or her vertical jump. The player jumps from a 30-inch (76.20 cm) height, lands on the floor, bends the knees 90 degrees, and immediately springs up as high as possible. The reader should note that although this technique maximizes the tendon stretch reflex, it also places a great deal of stress on the knee extensor mechanism causing injuries to some athletes.

Ways of achieving strength   Individuals can gain strength in numerous ways (see Table 2-1 for a comparison of strength exercises). This discussion briefly describes the more prevalent ways strength is developed; they are the nonequipment, equipment, and combined nonequipment and equipment approaches.

Nonequipment approaches   Three nonequipment approaches are presently employed in sports conditioning: calisthenics, or free exercise; partner, or reciprocal, resistance; and self-resistance.

Calisthenics, or free exercise, is one of the more easily available means of developing strength. Isotonic movement exercises can be graded according to intensity by using gravity as an aid, ruling gravity out, moving against gravity, or using the body or body part as a resistance against gravity. Most calisthenics require the athlete to support the body or move the total body against the force of gravity. Push-ups are a good example of a vigorous antigravity free exercise. When isotonic movements are made, ten or more repetitions are performed for each exercise and repeated in sets of two or three.

Some free exercises have a holding phase instead of employing a full range of motion. Examples of these are back extensions and sit-ups. When the exercise produces maximal muscle tension, it is held between 6 and 10 seconds and then repeated one to three times.

TABLE 2-1

Comparison of strength exercises

	Isometric	Isotonic	Isokinetic	Variable Resistance (Nautilus)
Resistance	Accommodating at one angle	Constant	Accommodating through range of motion	Fixed ration through range of motion
Velocity (speed)	Zero	Variable	Constant	Variable
Reciprocal contraction	None	None	Yes	None
Eccentric contraction	None	Yes	None	Yes
Safeness	Excellent	Poor	Excellent	Poor
Specificity to sport	Low	Medium	Very high	Medium
Motivation to exercise	Low	High	Medium	High

Figure 2-2

Modern athletic training programs provide many opportunities for their athletes to engage in a variety of resistive exercises.

Partner, or reciprocal, resistance exercise requires no equipment other than a partner who is about equal in size and strength. It is often highly motivating for both participants, and all types of exercise can be engaged using this method. When performing isokinetic resistance, the body part involved is taken into a stretched position by the partner. Resistance is accommodated through a complete range of motion. Three bouts of resistance usually are given for each exercise.

Figure 2-3

Dumbbells provide an excellent means for isotonic strength development.

Equipment approaches Modern athletic training programs include numerous devices designed to overload the musculature and develop strength (Fig. 2-2). These range from individual pieces to entire conditioning systems and generally are categorized as isotonic/isometric and isokinetic.

Isotonic/isometric equipment are almost too numerous to mention. Some of the more standard stationary apparatus, chinning bars, parallel bars, and stall bars, have numerous possibilities for increasing strength. Another standard piece of equipment is the wall pulley weight, which progressively exercises the major joints and muscles.

Free weights are very popular and are used for developing strength through both isotonic and isometric contraction. Sports programs commonly use a variety of free weights, including dumbbells (Fig. 2-3) and barbells (Fig. 2-4). Dumbbells range from 2 to 2 1/2 pounds to 50 to 75 pounds or more, and barbells range from 25 or 30 pounds to well over 200 pounds. Free weights

Figure 2-4

Barbell free weights assist the
athlete in developing isotonic
strength, balance, and muscle
coordination.

help in the development of balance and coordination and exercise the stabilizing and accessory muscles, which machine systems often do not provide.[16]

Machine exercise systems, such as the *Universal Gym*, allow a variety of exercise possibilities such as sit-ups, parallel bar dips, bench presses, pulldowns, rowing exercises, knee extensions, knee curls, and biceps curls, as well as arm pressing (Fig. 2-5). The Universal Gym employs graduated weights that are lifted by heavy cables as the athlete applies force against a bar. Newer Universal Gym machines provide variable resistance.

Isokinetic machines provide an accommodating and variable muscle resistance through a full range of motion. A maximal load is produced as the athlete dynamically performs work (Fig. 2-6). The amount of resistance depends on the extent of force applied by the athlete. Machines designed for isokinetic resistance develop flexibility and coordination, as well as strength.

The *Nautilus* training machines provide full range of movement and direct resistance to specific muscles or muscle groups. Both concentric and eccentric muscle contraction are provided by special cams and counterweights. In this system, negative, or eccentric, work is accentuated. Although Nautilus is not an isokinetic system, it does provide some variable resistance through a full range of motion. Each machine provides body stabilization to afford isolation of a specific muscle or muscle group (Fig. 2-7). This musculature isolation emphasizes negative, or eccentric, contraction. Because the amount of re-

Figure 2-5

Many machine exercise systems provide a variety of exercise possibilities for the athlete.

sistance varies during a full range of motion, resistance is indicated by the number of plates lifted rather than the number of pounds.

Other examples of exercise systems, such as the *Mini-Gym*, provide opportunities for specific strength development related to sports activities. Using variable resistance devices the athlete can concentrate on specific sports requirements (Fig. 2-8).

Fundamental principles of isotonic weight training   In a weight-training program certain fundamental principles must be followed by each athlete:

1. Precede all weight training with the general warm-up.
2. Begin all isotonic contractions from a position of "on stretch," immediately moving into the concentric contraction.

3. Perform isotonic movements slowly and deliberately, at approximately one-fifth maximal speed.
4. Apply the overload principle in all isotonic contractions. When you are able to complete the second or third series with some degree of ease, add more resistance.
5. Maintain good muscular balance by exercising both the agonist and antagonist muscles.
6. Confine heavy work to the off-season and the preseason period. A light to medium program can be maintained during the regular practice days of the competitive season, provided that it is confined to use of the weight schedule after the regular practice.
7. Work with weights every other day or no more than 4 days a week. This allows ample time for reduction of soreness and stiffness.
8. Initiate the training program first in terms of general body development and then progress to exercises tailored to the specific sport or event employing the SAID principle and geared to the type of muscle fiber involved in the activity.
9. After a general warm-up, begin a preliminary series of about ten repetitions using approximately half of the weight normally used. This is usually a sound procedure.
10. Observe proper breathing procedures during lifting to assist in fixing the stabilizing muscles of the trunk and therefore to give a firm base from which to work. Inhale deeply as the lift is being executed, and exhale forcefully and smoothly at the end of the lift.
11. Evaluate your progress at certain intervals of time by testing maximum lifts.
12. Develop a recording system using cards or a notebook. Common isotonic resistive exercises with free weights are illustrated on pp. 32-35.

Resistance Training for Specific Activities

After the general program of weight training, exercises specifically designed to develop the muscle groups that are most important for successful performance in a given activity should be assigned.[22] Sports demand rotational rather

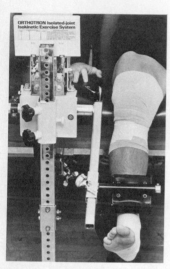

Figure 2-6

In isokinetic exercising the amount of resistance depends upon the extent of force applied by the athlete.

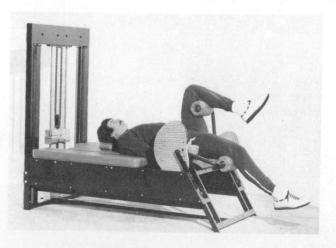

Figure 2-7

Nautilus training provides body stabilization and muscle group isolation.

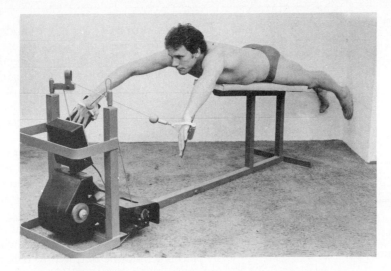

Figure 2-8

Exercise systems, such as that provided by the Mini-Gym, offer the athlete opportunities to concentrate on specific sports requirements.

than linear elements of the body. Exercises must be selected on the basis of their development construction, as well as mimetic activity, as specifically related to a given sport.

Flexibility Training

Most authorities in sports consider flexibility one of the most important objectives in conditioning athletes.[11] Good flexibility increases the athlete's ability to avoid injury. Since it permits a greater range of movement within the joint, the ligaments and other connective tissues are not so easily strained or torn. It also permits greater freedom of movement in all directions. There appears to be a definite relationship between injury and joint flexibility. The "tight" or inflexible athlete performs under a considerable handicap in terms of movement, besides being much more injury prone. Tight-jointed athletes seem to be more susceptible to muscle strains and tears. Repetitive stretching of the collagenous or fascial ligamentous tissue over a long period of time permits the athlete to obtain an increased range of motion.

Conversely, **hyperflexibility** — flexibility beyond a joint's normal range — must be avoided because loose-jointed players are more prone to joint injuries such as subluxations and dislocations.[24] Extremes of flexibility are indeed of little value and can result in weakness of the joint at certain angles. Flexibility, like strength, is specific to the joint and its surrounding tissues. It varies in its natural degree among individuals.

The athlete who possesses good flexibility can change the direction of a movement easily and is less likely to become injured if he or she should fall. The wise coach or athletic trainer will single out inflexible athletes and place them on a regimen of stretching exercises until they achieve a satisfactory degree of flexibility.

The athlete who gains improved flexibility and increased range of joint movement is able to use his or her body more effectively. In addition, when an injury situation is unavoidable, the joints involved very often can withstand a

Conditioning should be performed gradually, with work being added in small increments.

The "tight" or inflexible athlete performs under a considerable handicap in terms of movement.

hyperflexibility
Flexibility beyond a joint's normal range

Text continued on p. 37.

ISOTONIC EXERCISES

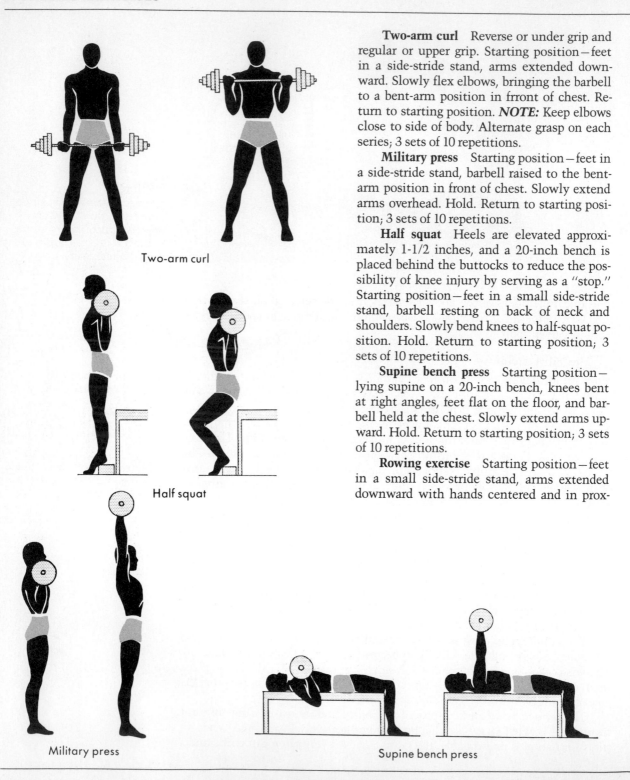

Two-arm curl   Reverse or under grip and regular or upper grip. Starting position—feet in a side-stride stand, arms extended downward. Slowly flex elbows, bringing the barbell to a bent-arm position in frront of chest. Return to starting position. *NOTE:* Keep elbows close to side of body. Alternate grasp on each series; 3 sets of 10 repetitions.

Military press   Starting position—feet in a side-stride stand, barbell raised to the bent-arm position in front of chest. Slowly extend arms overhead. Hold. Return to starting position; 3 sets of 10 repetitions.

Half squat   Heels are elevated approximately 1-1/2 inches, and a 20-inch bench is placed behind the buttocks to reduce the possibility of knee injury by serving as a "stop." Starting position—feet in a small side-stride stand, barbell resting on back of neck and shoulders. Slowly bend knees to half-squat position. Hold. Return to starting position; 3 sets of 10 repetitions.

Supine bench press   Starting position—lying supine on a 20-inch bench, knees bent at right angles, feet flat on the floor, and barbell held at the chest. Slowly extend arms upward. Hold. Return to starting position; 3 sets of 10 repetitions.

Rowing exercise   Starting position—feet in a small side-stride stand, arms extended downward with hands centered and in prox-

Two-arm curl

Half squat

Military press

Supine bench press

imity of the bar, head resting on a folded towel placed on a table. Slowly pull the bar up to a position in front of the chest. Hold. Return to starting position; 3 sets of 10 repetitions. *NOTE:* This may also be done with the lifter assuming and maintaining an angle stand — that is, trunk flexed forward at the hips at approximately a right angle.

Side-arm raises Starting position — prone or supine position on a bench, arms downward, hands grasping 10-pound dumbbells. Slowly raise arms sideward to a horizontal position. Hold. Return to starting position. *CAUTION:* Avoid locking the elbow joint in a complete extension, since this exerts severe strain on the joint. Do 3 sets of 10 repetitions, alternating the prone and supine positions daily.

Leg curl Starting position — face-lying position with boot weight fixed to one foot. The leg is curled upward as far as possible and then slowly returned to its original position; 3 sets of 10 repetitions and then repeat with other leg.

Heel raise Starting position — feet in a small side-stride stand, balls of the feet on a 2-inch riser, barbell resting on the back of the neck and shoulders. Slowly rise on toes. Hold. Return to starting position. Variations may be performed by having the feet either toes out or toes in; 3 sets of 10 repetitions.

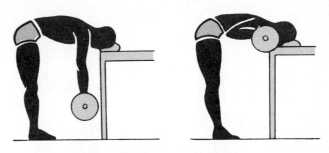

Rowing exercise

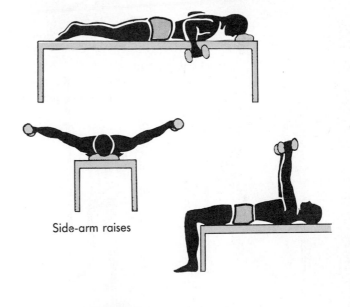

Side-arm raises

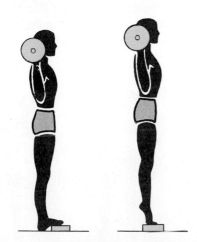

Heel raise

Leg curl

Continued.

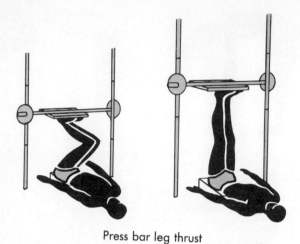

Press bar leg thrust

Press bar quadriceps
strengthener

Abdominal curl

Press bar leg thrust Starting position—angle-lying position under the press bar, balls of the feet in contact with the bar or bar platform, legs in a half-flexed position. Slowly extend the knees, keeping the buttocks in contact with the floor. Hold. Return to starting position; 3 sets of 10 repetitions. *NOTE:* To provide for better contact, fasten an 8-inch by 12-inch board to the bar. This prevents the feet from slipping off the bar.

Press bar quadriceps strengthener Starting position—a half-crouched position under the bar. Shoulders and neck in contact with the bar. (A folded towel may be used as a pad.) Slowly extend knees to an erect position. Hold. Return to starting position; 3 sets of 10 repetitions. *CAUTION:* Lift with the knee extensors, not the lower back muscles.

Abdominal curl Starting position—hook-lying, feet anchored, and dumbbell weighing 15 to 25 pounds held on the upper chest. Curl the upper trunk upward and as far forward as possible. Return slowly to the starting position. Maintain a moderate tempo and steady rhythm and avoid bouncing up from the floor; 3 sets of 10 repetitions. Number can be increased as capacity for more work increases.

Supination-pronation Start with feet in small side-stride stand, elbow bent at a right angle to upper arm, and hand grasping a 20-pound dumbbell. Rotate the dumbbell alternately left and right, using the muscles of the forearm and wrist only; 3 sets of 10 repetitions.

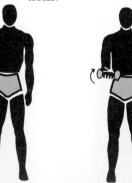

Supination-pronation

Wrist roll Begin with feet in a small side-stride stand. Slowly wind up a cord to which a 25-pound weight has been attached. Reverse the action, slowly unwinding the full length of the cord; 3 sets of 5 repetitions. *NOTE:* A wrist roller is easily constructed by securing one end of a 30-inch length of sash cord to the center of a 12-inch length of broomstick or dowel of a somewhat thicker diameter and the other end to a 25-pound weight.

Boot exercise Sit on plinth or table with lower legs hanging free over the edge and clear of the floor. A 20-pound boot is strapped to the foot. Do exercises involving knee flexion and extension and inversion, eversion, flexion, and extension of the ankle. The weight should be increased in terms of ability to handle it. Each exercise should be done for 3 sets of 10 repetitions.

Crossed-arm swings Starting position — small side-stride stand, a 20-pound dumbbell in each hand, arms raised directly sideward to shoulder height. Slowly swing the arms forward in a horizontal plane, continuing until each arm has progressed across the other and is carried as far as possible. Arms are extended, but elbow joints should not be locked. Return slowly toward the starting position, carrying the arms horizontally as far backward as possible; 3 sets of 10 repetitions.

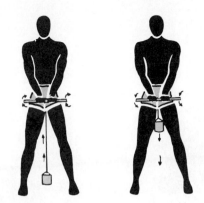

Wrist roll

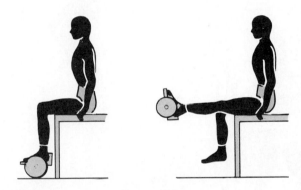

Boot exercise

Crossed-arm swing

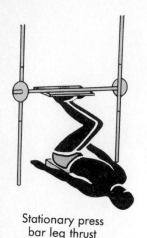

Stationary press
bar leg thrust

Stationary press
bar leg tensor

Wall press

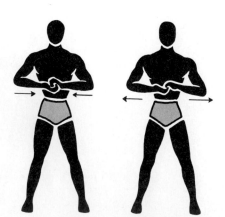

Shoulder-arm tensor

Stationary press bar leg thrust Starting position—angle-lying position under the press bar, balls of the feet in contact with the bar or bar platform, legs in a half-flexed position. Press bar is locked into place. Exert maximum force against the immovable bar, sustaining full pressure for 6 to 10 seconds. Following a short period of relaxation (5 to 10 seconds) repeat the procedure 2 or 3 times. *NOTE:* Hips may be elevated by a 2-inch pad.

Stationary press bar leg tensor Starting position—a half-crouched position under the bar, which is locked into place, shoulders and neck in contact with the bar. Exert maximum pressure against the bar by using the leg extensors and sustain full pressure for 6 to 10 seconds. Following a momentary relaxation, repeat the exercise 2 or 3 times.

Wall press Starting position—stand in a small side-stride stand in either the corner of a room or a doorway, placing the hands against the walls or the sides of the opening at about shoulder height. The elbows should be bent to about the halfway point in the normal range. Exert maximum force against the opposing surface, holding the position for at least 6 to 10 seconds. Relax pressure momentarily. Repeat 2 or 3 times.

Shoulder-arm tensor Starting position— feet in a small side-stride stand. Hook the fingers of the hands together, elbows bent so that hands are above waist height. Push the hands together forcefully, at the same time tensing the arm, shoulder, neck, and abdominal muscles. Hold for 6 to 10 seconds. Relax momentarily and then repeat the tensing action but reverse the hand action by pulling against the fingers with as much force as possible. Repeat 2 or 3 times.

stress or torque considerably in excess of that which can be resisted by a less flexible person. Increased flexibility further aids in reducing impact shock such as that encountered in the contact sports or in activities in which the body comes into forceful contact with a relatively unyielding surface (for example, the landing phase included in gymnastics, jumping, or vaulting).

Increasing flexibility The development of flexibility is a slow process. The myotatic (stretch) reflex, which is invoked during a stretching maneuver, is a muscle-protective mechanism. The muscle itself actively resists stretch as the result of a reflex inhibition in the antagonist muscle (the inverse myotatic reflex), which tends to reduce activation. The amount and rate of response of a stretch reflex are proportional to the amount and rate of stretching; hence the use of a repetitive vigorous ballistic (rebound) stretching maneuver would cause the muscle to contract with proportional vigor—not at all a desirable response for either warm-ups or the attainment of flexibility.[20]

In general, there are three methods of stretching in use today to increase flexibility: ballistic, static, and resistive stretching. As already discussed, ballistic (rebound) stretching should be avoided. The two methods that initiate the inverse myotatic reflex, which inhibits the stretching muscles and in turn facilitates further stretching, are the static and resistive stretching techniques.

Static stretching In static stretching the limb is moved to a point of maximal resistance, accompanied by active contraction of antagonist muscles. This position is held from 20 to 30 seconds, after which the muscle has relaxed and a new stretched position can be attained. For best results the exercise is performed several times daily, two or three repetitions each session. (Fig. 2-9).

Resistive stretching Another name for resistive stretching is *hold-relax stretching*. The athlete isometrically contracts the muscle to be stretched for 5 seconds followed by a complete relaxation of that muscle (about 3 to 5 seconds). Following muscle relaxation the limb is slowly moved to the point of resistance and held for about 10 seconds. This may be repeated two or three times (Fig. 2-10).

Figure 2-9

The back, shoulder, groin, and Achilles tendon regions can be effectively stretched by the static stretching method.

Gastrocnemius stretch

Shoulder stretch

Groin stretch

Back stretch

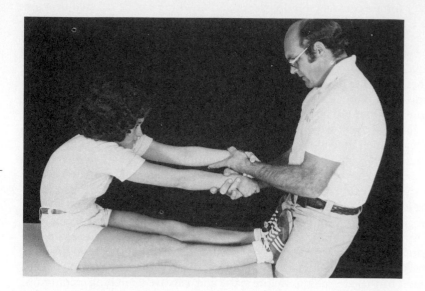

Figure 2-10

Releasing the muscles in the low back region can be accomplished by pulling back against an isometric resistance until fatigued, followed by 3 to 5 seconds of relaxation, and moving the trunk forward to a new position.

endurance
The ability of the body to undergo prolonged activity

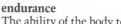

As a muscle tires, it loses some of its ability to relax.

Endurance and Stamina

The degree of ability to withstand fatigue is inherited, and the basis of the fatigue pattern is in each individual's constitution. Two factors modify an individual's capacity for improving endurance: (1) the ability to endure the pain and the discomforts of fatigue while endeavoring to improve the level of work tolerance and (2) the body's ability to effect the necessary adjustments, which can enable an athlete to increase energy production to as much as 20 times the resting level when such a demand is made.

Endurance is the ability of the body to undergo prolonged activity. Endurance involves a number of elements, each of which is partially responsible for success or failure in sustaining physical performance (Fig. 2-11). Endurance primarily depends on the various aspects of cardiac efficiency, which in turn exerts influence on the performance of the other portions of the human organism.

Training or conditioning builds a given economy—an efficiency in body adaptability—which is important as the body adjusts to the continued and prolonged stresses put on it in performing an activity that requires all-out or near-maximal performance over a considerable period of time.

Exercises for endurance improve muscle tonus. Endurance work improves circulation by calling into play more capillaries, thus providing the working muscles with more oxygen and fuel and facilitating removal of the metabolic by-products of the exercise.

As a muscle tires, it loses some of its ability to relax and thus increases the possibility of tearing. The character of a muscle is indicated not only by its ability to produce power over a period of time but also by its capacity to concurrently maintain its elasticity. As the muscle works, it restores its own oxygen and fuel supplies and disposes of metabolic products. As long as these

Figure 2-11

Endurance is the ability of the body to endure prolonged activity.

two processes continue to operate at basically the same rate, the muscle can continue to work with efficiency. In fatigue the reaction time slows down and is accompanied by stiffening or inability of the muscle to reach a condition of relaxation, which is a contributing factor to some sports injuries.[12]

Respiratory response to training   Training increases vital capacity (the maximal volume of air the lungs exchange in one respiratory cycle) and aids materially in establishing economy in the oxygen requirement. The conditioned athlete operates primarily on a "pay-as-you-go" basis as a result of his or her increased **stroke volume** and reduced heartbeat. An increase in the contractile power of the respiratory muscles, particularly the diaphragm, results in deeper respiration per breath. This enables the athlete to use a greater lung capacity and, consequently, to effect increased economy in the use of oxygen. The untrained individual attempts to compensate by increasing the rate of respiration and soon reaches a state of considerable respiratory indebtedness, which severely encumbers or even halts performance.

Endurance training not only significantly improves maximal oxygen consumption but is a key factor in injury prevention. The fatigued athlete not only has a diminished reaction capacity but, because of muscular fatigue, is less able to withstand extraneous forces, which means that such an athlete is more likely to sustain an injury under circumstances in which a better con-

stroke volume
The capacity of the heart to pump blood

ditioned performer will not. Aerobic endurance training uses slow interval training.

Neuromuscular Coordination

Neuromuscular coordination is a complex interaction between muscles and nerves to carry out a purposeful action. Major aspects of this coordination are the proprioceptors that are located in muscles, tendons, joints, and labyrinth of the inner ear. Proprioceptors give the athlete a knowledge of where the body is in space.

Athletes need to be able to recruit the appropriate muscles on demand. When recruitment of specific muscles is inappropriate, abnormal physical stresses can occur leading to acute or chronic injuries. This is also very true for proprioception. When the athlete is unable to adequately perceive the body in space, serious injuries can occur.

Special Conditioning Approaches

Circuit Training

The program should be planned so that the athlete can complete a circuit without becoming excessively fatigued.

Circuit training is a method of physical conditioning that employs both apparatus resistance training and calisthenic conditioning exercises. It provides a means of achieving optimal fitness in a systematized, controlled fashion. The intensity and vigor of circuit training are indeed challenging and enjoyable to the performer. This system produces positive changes in motor performance, general fitness, muscular power, endurance, and speed.

Circuit training is based on the premise that the athlete must do the same amount of work in a shorter period of time or must do considerably more work within the limits of an assigned training period. Numerous variations of this system are in use, but all employ certain common factors: (1) the use of PREs; (2) the use of calisthenics and apparatus exercises, the former being performed either with or without weights; (3) a circular arrangement of the activities that permits progression from one station to another until all stations have been visited, the total constituting a "circuit"; and (4) a limiting time factor within which the circuit must be concluded.

The circuit is usually set up around the perimeter of the exercise area. When a circuit is set up, the number and types of stations desired should be selected for their value in stressing development of the body parts most commonly called into play in a particular sports activity, as well as for their worth as activities promoting all-around body fitness. Six to twelve different stations can be set up, each with a specific exercise. The program should be planned so that the athlete can complete a circuit without becoming excessively fatigued.

After a thorough orientation period, a time trial is given to ascertain the length of time required for completion of one to three laps, depending on the number of stations and the intensity and design of the various exercises. Progress is from one station to the next immediately on completion of the assignment at the first station. A "target" time, which is one-third lower than the initial trial time, is then assigned. The weight exercises are usually performed at 50% to 70% of the athlete's maximal number of repetitions, and the resistance is usually arbitrarily determined by the trainer, in accordance with the athlete's capability. A sample circuit program is shown in Fig. 2-12.

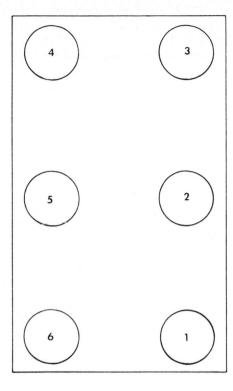

Figure 2-12

Station **1**, squat thrusts, 75% maximum number of repetitions performed in 1 minute; **2**, general flexion exercise, performed for 2 minutes; **3**, abdominal curls with weights, 75% maximum number of repetitions; **4**, two-arm curls, 75% maximum number of repetitions; **5**, vertical jump (Sargent), 75% maximum number of repetitions performed in 1 minute; **6**, half squat, heels raised, exercise with weight, 75 % maximum number of repetitions.

Cardiorespiratory Improvement

A number of training methods are designed to specifically enhance cardiorespiratory performance according to the requirements of a particular sport. Those discussed here are continuous training and interval training.

Continuous training   The continuous training approach is designed for long-endurance activities such as marathon running. Long, uninterrupted work is engaged in at a constant intensity. The steady pace in a situation of constant overload draws on the athlete's energy reserves over a long period of time. This method develops the athlete's aerobic capacity, functional stability, and energy reserves.

Interval training   All sports call for endurance. Some sports, such as soccer, football, lacrosse, hockey, and cross-country skiing, make tremendous aerobic demands on the body. Improvements in training methods have enabled athletes to significantly reduce their times in running events. Resistance to the various effects of fatigue can be accomplished only through intensive, rigorous training that loads the circulorespiratory system to a level above an established threshold. In this way improvement in training, notably endurance, can occur. Below the training threshold no training effect is visible. This is the application of the overload principle to the cardiorespiratory system. The working pulse rate should be 60% of the heart rate reserve; therefore, the target heart rate equals the resting heart rate plus 60% of the heart rate reserve. Others have suggested 160 beats/min as a rule-of-thumb threshold. (A 10-second value of 27 beats/min may be used.)

Four factors are significant in interval training: (1) a specified distance that is repeated a given number of times; (2) a recovery period during which the athlete jogs slowly and relaxes; (3) a predetermined pace, carefully timed, at which the athlete covers the set distance; and (4) a predetermined number of repetitions in running the distance. Alternating 30-second intervals of work with rest intervals, which terminate when the pulse rate reaches 120 beats/min, appears to be the best pattern.

It is best to start the program 6 to 8 months before the opening of the competitive season. A relatively slow pace is used in the beginning and is sufficiently increased every 4 weeks to bring the runner to the desired time peak at the start of competition.

This type of conditioning program is quite flexible and permits adaptation. However, it is best not to tamper with the pace factor, since this is the key to a successful, planned performance. The number of repetitions should be increased if one wishes to intensify the workout, but the pace, recovery period, and distance should remain unchanged.

NUTRITION

A very important component of injury prevention is the athlete's diet. If the physical stresses that are imposed by hard training and competition are not adequately replenished by good nutrition, proper physical restoration cannot be achieved.[4] In many cases an athlete follows the nutritional patterns of elite performers, whether they are sound or not, in hopes of emulating his or her achievements. The coach and athletic trainer must consider nutrition education as a means toward optimal performance and injury prevention or, when injuries do occur, toward optimal healing.

Basic Nutritional Guidelines

Exercise often makes severe metabolic demands on the body. Keeping the body's tissues strong, repairing damaged tissues, recuperating fatigued muscles, and regenerating lost energy necessitates a proper diet.

The Athlete's Training Diet

In general, the athlete's daily diet should consist of 55% to 60% carbohydrates, 30% fat, and 10% to 15% protein. Adhering to the suggestions in Table 2-2 will provide these percentages for the most part.

Carbohydrates Carbohydrates are organic compounds composed of carbon, hydrogen, and oxygen. They make up the starches and sugars found in foods such as breadstuffs, pasta, potatoes, candy, and pastries. During digestion complex sugars are broken down into simple sugars to be absorbed into the blood and other tissues. Sugars are carried to the liver to be converted into glycogen. Glycogen can be stored in the liver, muscle cells, and other cells. Excess glycogen that is not used as energy and has not been converted into glucose is converted into fat. If the athlete's diet consists of less than 50% of the total energy requirement as carbohydrate, muscle glycogen may not be fully restored.[4] An athlete "in training" who wishes to reduce body fat should "cut down" on fat ingesta rather than carbohydrates.[4]

Fats Fats and carbohydrates are composed of the same elements: carbon, hydrogen, and oxygen, but in fat the hydrogen content is higher.[2] Fats

TABLE 2-2

Basic four food groups diet allowance

Food group	Servings
Milk	One cup of milk or equivalent Second cup of milk Third cup of milk or more
Fruits and vegetables	One serving of green or yellow vegetables One serving of citrus fruit, tomato, or cabbage Two or more servings of other fruits and vegetables, including potato
Breads and cereals	Three servings of whole-grain or enriched cereals or breads
Protein-rich foods	One serving of egg, meat, fish, poultry, cheese, dried beans, or peas One or more additional servings of egg, meat, fish, poultry, or cheese

represent a concentrated source of reserve energy. Fats are used when carbohydrate stores are depleted. Examples of fats are butter, cream, mayonnaise, meat gravy, and lard. In terms of training, fats require more oxygen than carbohydrates for digestion. They are slower to digest and may cause gastric distress leading to diarrhea.

Protein　Proteins are nitrogenous organic compounds that are composed of amino acids. Amino acids are made of carbon, hydrogen, and oxygen atoms and are considered the ''building blocks'' of the body. Like fats, many athletes overingest proteins thinking proteins will automatically make them stronger. In fact, it is only when an individual engages in an extremely high level of muscle overload that the 10% to 15% of daily intake of protein may be slightly increased.[2] Overeating protein can displace carbohydrates from the diet and, in the case of animal protein, can introduce undesirable fats.[4] Digesting an excessive amount of protein can require extra water for urinary excretion and subsequently an increase in urination.[4]

Vitamins　Vitamins are chemical substances that act as metabolic catalysts. The body does not manufacture vitamins; they must be obtained from food. A varied diet that includes a balance of the basic four food groups will normally provide the athlete with all the vitamins needed.

Minerals and electrolytes　Essential to good health and life itself are inorganic salts known as minerals. They aid in metabolism, formation of tissue such as bone and teeth, and maintain the balance of the body's internal environment. In most cases a wide variety of fresh foods, especially fruits and vegetables, will provide the proper amount of minerals with the exception of iron, which will be discussed in dietary supplementation. The principal mineral elements are calcium, sodium, potassium, magnesium, phosphorus, chlorine, and sulfur. In addition, there are a number of trace elements such as iron, iodine, cobalt, copper, fluorine, manganese, molybdenum, selenium, vanadium, and zinc.

Electrolyte requirements　Electrolytes, such as sodium chloride and potassium, are electrically charged salts. They are primarily concerned with maintaining the balance of water outside the cell. There may be a need for electrolyte replenishment when a person is poorly fit or is suffering from extreme water loss. In most cases of heavy sweating, however, there must be water replacement instead of electrolyte supplementation. Electrolytes can be sufficiently replaced with exercise and a balanced diet.

Water　Water is necessary for the various metabolic chemical reactions to occur within the body. It forms about 75% of all living matter; it dilutes the toxic by-products of metabolism; and it helps to regulate body temperature through dissipating excess heat and through perspiration. A water balance must be maintained at all times. When there is a large sweat loss during exercise, voluntary water intake usually is not adequate and may lead to a chronic dehydration. In other words, thirst is not an accurate indicator of the amount of water that is lost through perspiration. To prevent dehydration, at least 16 ounces (500 ml) of plain water should be ingested 10 to 15 minutes before engaging in activity.[4] It must also be noted that the sense of thirst satiation may not be an adequate indication of a full rehydration. Athletes must be advised to replace their sweat losses instead of simply satisfying their thirst.

Dietary Supplementation and Manipulation

Vitamins and minerals　If a variety of fresh foods are eaten daily, there is little reason for the athlete to supplement his or her diet with vitamins or minerals other than iron, especially for the menstruating female.[6] Taking vitamins in excess quantities (megavitamin dosage) can have adverse effects and lead to toxicity from the storage of fat soluble vitamins such as A, D, and E. Even for those athletes who sweat profusely, salt supplementation is unnecessary since salt is inherent in the usual Western diet.

Protein　Protein supplementation with the idea of stimulating muscle strength and size is a waste of the athlete's money. Only proper exercise can increase muscle mass.

Nutritional Readiness for Competition

It has often been said that the most important meal prior to competition is the one eaten the night before. This is especially true if the contest is to require 60 minutes or more of hard, sustained exercise.[4]

Carbohydrate loading　Events that call for sudden bursts of all-out energy are not particularly affected by pre-event nutrition modification. However, endurance activities may be positively affected by carbohydrate manipulation. In some cases, the amount of stored glycogen can be doubled through a loading process by increasing the ingestion of carbohydrates. Originally, athletes were instructed to deplete glycogen stores with hard training and a diet low in carbohydrates. It is now known that rest and a high carbohydrate diet 2 or 3 days before competition will store sufficient glycogen.

The pre-event meal　It is generally agreed that the pre-event meal should be consumed 3 to 4 hours before competition. The meal should be easily digestible; avoid fats, high cellulose foods such as lettuce, and heavily spiced foods.[5] Sugars should also be avoided because they retard stomach emptying. Extra salting of food should be avoided due to its dehydrating effects. Drinking at least two 8-ounce glasses of water before competition should be encouraged in endurance activities.

PSYCHOLOGICAL CONSIDERATIONS OF INJURY PREVENTION

When considering injury prevention in sports activities, the psychological conditioning, though less obvious, is as important as physical conditioning. The athlete who enters a contest while angry, frustrated, or discouraged or while undergoing some other disturbing emotional state is more prone to injury than is the individual who is better adjusted emotionally. The angry player, for example, wants to vent ire in some way and often loses perspective of desirable and approved conduct. In the grip of emotion, skill and coordination are sacrificed, and an injury that otherwise would have been avoided may be the result. Psychological conditioning is the responsibility of the coach. Often an individual's psychological condition has a direct bearing on neuromuscular or physical response.

Psychological conditioning is as important and as much the responsibility of the coach or trainer as physical conditioning or rehabilitation.

The Athlete's Level of Aspiration

A champion thinks like a champion. A positive attitude toward a competitive situation aids the performer. The mind is not hindered or cluttered with doubts and countless little nagging thoughts couched in terms of failure. Rather, the champion is determined to succeed and can concentrate all conscious efforts, physical and psychological, toward achieving the goal. Players will react emotionally to the importance of a contest (Fig. 2-13). If they are competing against a team that they believe will not give them much trouble, it is difficult for them to get "up" psychologically for the contest. An underrated team will often play far above its usual rated level of performance simply because it aspires to win. The players are determined. Conversely, their opponents, unquestionably the better team in terms of previous performances, cannot seem to get going.

Successful players and competitors have high levels of aspiration. They constantly raise these levels and maintain hopes of success even if at times they repeatedly experience failure. On the other hand, unsuccessful players tend to lower their level of aspiration. Individuals who have a low level of aspiration and then experience failure tend to escape by removing themselves from the failure situation through means such as rationalization or defeatism. If they are neither the favorite nor the underdog, they have a 50/50 chance of being successful.

The level of aspiration of either an individual or a team can be raised through pep talks, slogans, and various audiovisual materials in the training and locker rooms. Coaches can play an important role both in maintaining and raising the level of aspiration by using their position as a means of adding to the levels of motivation and encouragement so necessary in sports.[10]

Sports Participation as a Stressor

Sports participation serves as both a physical and an emotional stressor. Stress can be a positive or negative influence. All living organisms are endowed with the ability to cope effectively with stressful situations. Pelletier[17] stated: "Without stress, there would be very little constructive activity or positive change." Negative stress can contribute to poor health, whereas positive stress produces growth and development. A healthy life must have a balance of stress; too little can cause a "rusting out" and too much can cause "burn-out."[13]

Sports participation is both a physical and an emotional stressor.

Figure 2-13

Players often react emotionally
to the importance of a contest.

Athletes place their bodies in countless stress situations daily. Their
bodies undergo numerous "fight or flight" reactions to avoid injury or other
threatening situations. Inappropriate adjustment to fight or flight responses
can eventually lead to physical tensions and subsequently to physical injuries.[13]

TRAINING AND COMPETITION IN CHILDHOOD

Parents and professionals in the areas of education, psychology, and medicine
have long questioned whether vigorous physical training and competition are
advisable for the immature child. Increasingly, children are engaging in intense programs of training that require many hours of daily commitment and
may extend over many years. Swimmers may practice 2 hours, two times a
day, covering 6000 to 10,000 meters each season in the water; gymnasts may
practice 3 to 5 hours per day; and runners may cover as many as 70 miles each
week.[25]

The American Academy of Pediatrics has indicated that the nearly universal participation of young children of both genders in competitive sports requires realistic guidelines. It is recognized that sports have an important effect
on stamina and physiology and have lifelong value as recreational activities.[1]
The American Academy of Pediatrics also indicates that there is no physical
reason to separate preadolescent girls and boys by gender in sports activities
or recreational activities; however, separation of the genders should occur in
collision-type sports when boys have acquired greater muscle mass in proportion to body weight, making participation with girls hazardous. All partici-

pants should be properly grouped by physical maturation, weight, size, and skill (Figs. 2-14 and 2-15). Of major importance is for the child to always be given a proper physical examination before entering organized competitive sports. Also of importance is that coaches of children have some understanding of growth and development, injury causation, prevention of sports injuries, and the understanding and practice of correct coaching techniques.[15] Physical strength training as well as endurance training must be carefully coached and supervised to ensure proper execution and to avoid "overdoing."[9]

Of even more concern than the physical aspects of training in childhood are the psychological stresses that may be placed on children by overzealous parents and coaches. Enjoyment of the activity, rather than being winners at all cost, should be the focus of training and competition.

SUMMARY

Proper physical conditioning for sports participation should prepare the athlete for a high-level performance, while helping to prevent injuries that are inherent to that sport. Injury-preventive physical conditioning must include concern for strength, flexibility, endurance, and neuromuscular coordination. Physical conditioning is a year-round task.

Physical conditioning must be concerned with the SAID principle—an acronym for *specific adaptation to imposed demands*. It must work toward making the body as lean as possible, commensurate with the athlete's sport.

A proper warm-up should precede conditioning, and a proper cool-down should follow. It takes at least 15 to 30 minutes of gradual warm-up to bring the body to a state of readiness for vigorous sports training and participation. Warming up consists of general unrelated activity followed by specific related activity.

Strength is that capacity to exert a force or the ability to perform work against a resistance. There are numerous means to achieving strength development, including: isometric, isotonic, and isokinetic muscle contraction. Plyometric exercise maximizes the stretch reflex by first lengthening a muscle and immediately shortening the muscle against a resistance.

Optimum flexibility is a necessary attribute for success in most sports. However, too much flexibility can allow joint trauma to occur, while too little flexibility can result in muscle tears or strains. Ballistic stretching exercises should be avoided. The safest means of increasing flexibility are the static and resistive (hold-relax) methods.

Stamina, or endurance, is a necessary factor in most active sports, some more than others. It is the ability to undergo prolonged activity involving both the muscular and cardiorespiratory systems. Physical fatigue involves the loss of the ability to properly relax and coordinate muscles, making the athlete more prone to injury.

What an athlete eats is a major factor in attaining maximum performance. Diet is also a major factor in the general health of the athlete and is important to the relative strength and healing ability of both soft and bony tissue.

Injury prevention involves many psychological considerations as well as physical considerations. The athlete's emotions and aspirations (or lack of aspirations) can enhance or deter from physical performance. An athlete's psychological condition has a direct bearing on muscular coordination.

Injury Prevention
All children who participate in competitive activities should be properly grouped by physical maturation, weight, size, and skill.

Figure 2-14

It is particularly important to match children in sports according to physical maturity, weight, size, and skill.

Figure 2-15

Constant high-level competitive psychological pressure can lead to a child's becoming disinterested in sports and exercise.

REVIEW QUESTIONS AND CLASS ACTIVITIES

1. Why is year-round conditioning important for injury prevention?
2. Invite a coach and an athletic trainer to speak to the class on conditioning and training problems.
3. What is the value of a proper warm-up and cool-down?
4. Why is the SAID principle important to athletic physical conditioning?
5. Why can an abnormal amount of body fat be a potential injury-producing situation?
6. Compare the different strength development techniques in terms of specific sports requirements.
7. Relate neuromuscular coordination or lack of it to sports injuries.
8. Discuss the values of different equipment approaches to strength development.
9. Discuss the relative values of different flexibility training methods.
10. How can the acquisition of good endurance and stamina and strength and flexibility reduce the chance of injury?
11. Discuss psychological factors that may predispose an athlete to injury.
12. Describe the advantages and disadvantages of training and competition in childhood.

REFERENCES

1. American Academy of Pediatrics: Competitive sports for children of elementary school age, Committee on Pediatric Aspects of Physical Fitness, Recreation and Sports, Pediatrics, **67**:927, 1981.
2. Arnheim, D.: Modern principles of athletic training, ed. 6, St. Louis, 1985, Times Mirror/Mosby College Publishing.
3. Bilik, S.E.: The trainer's bible, ed. 9, New York, 1956, T.J. Reed & Co., Publishers.
4. Brotherhood, J.R.: Nutrition and sports performance, Sports Med. **1**:350, Oct. 1984.
5. Cheung, S.: The pregame meal for school-age children, Sports Med. Digest, **8**:6, March 1986.
6. Coleman, E.: Iron deficiency in athletes, Sports Med. Digest **8**:5, March 1986.
7. Cutting, V.J.: Development of "A student handbook for prevention of athletic injuries," an unpublished master's thesis, San Diego, 1985, San Diego State University.
8. DeLorme, T.L., and Watkins, A.L.: Progressive resistance exercise, New York, 1951, Appleton-Century-Crofts.
9. Duda, M.: Prepubescent strength training gains support, Phys. Sportsmed. **14**:157, Feb. 1986.
10. Finn, J.A.: Competitive excellence: it's a matter of mind and body, Phys. Sportsmed. **13**:61, Feb. 1985.
11. Hunter, S.T., et al.: Standards and norms of fitness and flexibility in high school athletes, Ath. Train. **20**(3):210, 1985.
12. Kirkendall, D.T.: Mobility: conditioning programs. In Gould, J.A., and Davies, G.J. (editors): Orthopaedic and sports physical therapy, vol. 2, St. Louis, 1985, The C. V. Mosby Co.
13. Landaw, S.: Burn-out and the athlete, Sports Med. Guide **4**:1, Feb. 1985.
14. Logan, G.A., and Wallis, E.L.: Recent findings in learning and performance, Paper presented at the Southern Section Meeting of the California Association for Health, Physical Education and Recreation, Pasadena, Calif., 1960.
15. Murphy, P.: Youth sports coaches: using hunches to fill a blank page, Phys. Sportsmed. **13**:136, April 1985.
16. Nosse, L.J., and Hunter, G.R.: Free weights: a review supporting their use in training and rehabilitation, Ath. Train. **20**:206, 1985.
17. Pelletier, K.R.: Mind as healer, mind as slayer, New York, 1977, Dell Publishing Co., Inc.
18. Sanders, M., and Sanders, B.: Mobility: active-resistive training. In

Gould, J.A., and Davies, G.J. (editors): Orthopaedic and sports physical therapy, vol. 2, St. Louis, 1985, The C.V. Mosby Co.

19. Shellock, F.G.: Physiologic benefits of warm-up, Phys. Sportsmed. **11**:134, Oct. 1983.

20. Surberg, P.R.: Flexibility exercise reexamined, Ath. Train. **18**:37, Spring 1983.

21. Tottössy, M.: Warming up. In Kulund, D.M. (editor): The injured athlete, Philadelphia, 1981, J.B. Lippincott Co.

22. Types of resistive exercises, Sports Med. Digest **6**:4, Oct. 1984.

23. Wiktörsson-Moller, M., et al.: Effects of warming up, massage, and stretching on range of motion and muscle strength in lower extremity, Am. J. Sports Med. **11**:249, July/Aug. 1983.

24. Wilmore, J.H.: Athletic training and physical fitness, Boston, 1977, Allyn & Bacon, Inc.

25. Zauner, C.W., and Benson, N.Y.: Physiological alterations in young swimmers during 3 years of intensive training, J. Sports Med. **21**:179, June 1981.

ANNOTATED BIBLIOGRAPHY

Exercise physiology — a primer, Sports Med. Digest **6**:1, Oct. 1984.
  An overview of the physiology of aerobic and anaerobic exercise with a thorough discussion of how to employ the level of excrcise of the metabolic equivalent (MET) proccss.
Garhammer, J.: Strength training (SI), New York, 1986, Harper and Row.
  Excellent book on the basics of strength training and conditioning.
Jobe, F. W., and Moynes, D.: The official Little League fitness book, New York, 1984, Simon & Schuster.
  A guide for coaches, parents and Little Leaguers on proper conditioning.
Katch, F.I., and Freedson, P.S. (editors): Training in Clinics in Sports Medicine, Vol. 5/No. 3, July 1986, W.B. Saunders Co., Philadelphia.
  An overview of physical training as related to sports perforrmance and injury prevention.
Leighton, J.R.: Weight training. Springfield, Ill., 1983, Charles C. Thomas, Publisher.
  Provides basic and advanced exercise programs using free weights plus off-season and preseason conditioning programs.
Neter, P.: High-tech fitness, New York, 1984, Workman Publishing.
  A catalog on "high-tech" exercise and fitness equipment.
Sharkey, B.J.: Physiology of fitness, Champaign, Ill., 1984, Human Kinetics Publishers.
  Written as a "why and how" of physical conditioning.

Chapter 3 | PROTECTIVE SPORTS DEVICES

When you finish this chapter, you will be able to:

Explain the major implications of sports equipment manufacturing standards

Identify selected protective equipment for various body parts in different sports

Differentiate between good and bad features of selected protective devices

Properly fit a football helmet, shoulder pad, and shoes

Demonstrate the use and construction of protective pads and orthoses

Protective equipment may be used to:
Disperse energy
Absorb energy
Slow down rate of energy
Deflect a blow
Transmit energy to other body areas
Protect body against sharp instruments
Limit excess movement

One function of the American Society for Testing and Materials (ASTM) is to test sports equipment.

Modifications and improvements in sports equipment are continually being made, especially for sports in which injury is common.[7]

The proper selection and fit of sports equipment are essential in the prevention of many sports injuries. This is of course particularly true in direct contact and collision sports such as football, hockey, and lacrosse, but it can also be true in indirect contact sports such as basketball and soccer. Whenever protective sports equipment is selected and purchased, a major decision in the safeguarding of the athletes' health and welfare is being made.

Currently there is serious concern about the standards for protective sports equipment, particularly material durability standards—including who should set these standards, mass production of equipment, equipment testing methods, and requirements for wearing protective equipment. Some people are concerned that a piece of equipment that is protective to one athlete might in turn be a weapon against another athlete.

Standards are also needed for protective equipment maintenance, both to keep it in good repair and to determine when to throw it away. Too often old, worn-out and ill-fitting equipment is passed down from the varsity players to the younger and often less experienced players, compounding their risk of injury. Coaches must learn to be less concerned with the color, look, and style of a piece of equipment and more concerned with its ability to prevent injury.

A major step toward the improvement of sports equipment has been through such groups as the American Society for Testing and Materials (ASTM).[1,12] Its Committee on Sports Equipment and Facilities, established in 1969, has been highly active in establishing "standardization of specifications, test methods, and recommended practices for sports equipment and facilities to minimize injury, and promotion of knowledge as it relates to protective equipment standards.[1,12] Engineering, chemistry, biomechanics, anatomy, physiology, physics, computer science, and other related disciplines are applied to solve problems inherent in safety standardization of sports equipment and facilities.

HEAD PROTECTION

Direct collision sports such as football and hockey require special protective equipment, especially for the head. Football provides more frequent opportunities for body contact than does hockey, but hockey players generally move faster and therefore create greater impact forces. Besides direct head contact, hockey has the added injury elements of swinging sticks and fast-moving pucks. Other sports using fast-moving projectiles are baseball, with its pitched ball and swinging bat, and track and field, with the javelin, discus, and heavy shot, which can also produce serious head injuries. In recent years most helmet research has been conducted in football and ice hockey; however, some research has been done on baseball headgear.[9]

Football helmets must withstand repeated blows that are of high mass and low velocity.

Football Helmets

A major influence of football helmet standardization in the United States has been the research of Hodgson and Thomas[10] and the National Operating Committee on Standards for Athletic Equipment (NOCSAE) for football helmet certification. To be NOCSAE approved, a helmet must be able to tolerate forces applied to it at three different sites. Football helmets typically must withstand repeated blows and high mass–low velocity impacts such as running into a goalpost or hitting the ground with the head.

Testing new football helmets to ensure their safety does not guarantee that they will remain safe. A random selection of helmets from a high school football team showed that 75% of those that were 3 years old failed the NOCSAE test.[11]

Schools must provide the athlete with quality equipment. This especially is true of the football helmet. All helmets must have an NOCSAE certification. Even though a helmet is certified, it does not mean that it is completely "failsafe." Athletes as well as their parents must be apprised of the dangers that are inherent in any sport, particularly football.[4] To make this especially clear, the NOCSAE has adopted the following recommended warning to be placed on all football helmets:

> Do not use this helmet to butt, ram or spear an opposing player. This is in violation of football rules, and can result in severe head, brain, neck injury, paralysis or death to you and possible injury to your opponent. There is a risk these injuries may also occur as a result of accidental contact without intent to butt, ram or spear. No helmet can prevent all such injuries.[14]

There are many types of helmets in use today. They currently fall into two categories: (1) padded and (2) air and fluid (Fig. 3-1). There are also helmets that are combinations of the two. In general, the helmet should adhere to the following fit standards:

1. It should cover the base of the skull.
2. It should not come down over the eyes.

Figure 3-1

Football helmets basically fall into two categories, air and fluid filled.

3. It should not shift when manual pressure is applied.
4. It should not recoil on impact.
5. The ear and ear cut-out should match.
6. The front edge of helmet shell should sit 3/4-inch (1.91 cm) above the player's eyebrows.
7. The chin strap should be an equal distance from the center of the helmet.
8. The cheek pads should fit snugly against the sides of the face.

Whichever football helmet is used, it must be routinely checked for proper fit, especially in the first few days that it is worn. A check for snugness should be made by inserting a tongue depressor between the head and liner. Proper fit is determined when the tongue depressor resists firmly when moved back and forth.

Chin straps are also important to maintaining the proper head and helmet relationship. There are two basic types of chin straps in use today, a 2-snap and a 4-snap strap. Many coaches prefer the 4-snap chin strap because it tends to keep the helmet from tilting forward and backward. The chin strap should always be locked so it cannot be released by a hard external force to the helmet (Fig. 3-2).

Jaw pads are also essential to keep the helmet from rocking laterally. They should fit snugly against the player's cheek bones. Even if a helmet is certified as to its ability to withstand the forces of the game, it is of no avail if not properly fitted or maintained.

Even high-quality helmets are of no avail if not properly fitted or maintained.

Figure 3-2

A, Pull down on face mask; helmet must not move. **B**, Turn helmet to position on the athlete's head. **C**, Push down on helmet; there must be no movement. **D**, Try to rock helmet back and forth; there must be no movement. **E**, Check for a snug jaw pad fit. **F**, Proper adjustment of the chin strap is necessary to ensure proper helmet fit.

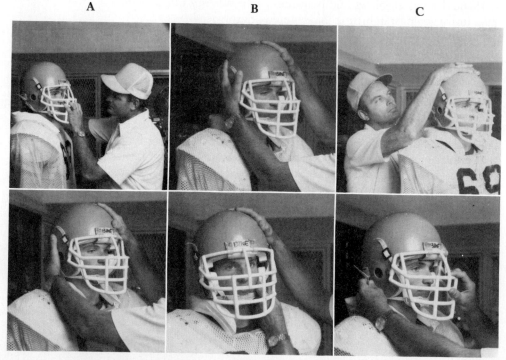

A   B   C

D   E   F

Ice Hockey Helmets

As with football helmets, there has been a concerted effort to upgrade and standardize ice hockey helmets.[2] In contrast to football, blows to the head in ice hockey are usually singular rather than multiple. An ice hockey helmet must withstand both high-velocity impacts, such as being hit with a stick or a puck (which produces low mass and high velocity), as well as the high mass–low velocity forces produced by running into the sideboard or falling on the ice. In each instance, the hockey helmet, like the football helmet, must be able to spread the impact over a large surface area through a firm exterior shell and at the same time be able to decelerate forces that act on the head through a proper energy-absorbing liner.[2]

Ice hockey helmets must withstand the high-velocity impact of a stick or puck and the low-velocity forces of falling or hitting a sideboard.

Baseball Batting Helmets

Like ice hockey helmets, the baseball batting helmet must withstand high-velocity impacts. Unlike football and ice hockey, baseball has not produced a great deal of data on batting helmets.[9] It has been suggested, however, that baseball helmets do little to adequately dissipate the energy of the ball at impact (Fig. 3-3). An answer might be to add external padding or improve the helmet's suspension.[9]

Figure 3-3

There is some question as to how well baseball batting helmets protect against high-velocity impacts.

FACE PROTECTION

Devices that provide face protection fall into four categories: full face guards, mouth guards, ear guards, and eye protection devices.

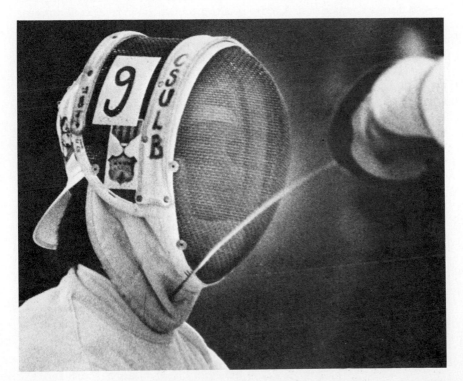

Figure 3-4

Sports such as fencing require complete face protection.

Face Guards

Face guards are used in a variety of sports to protect against collision of flying or carried objects with another player (Fig. 3-4). Since the adoption of face guards and mouth guards in football, mouth injuries have been reduced over 50% (Fig. 3-5). The catcher in baseball, the goalie in hockey, and the lacrosse player all should be adequately protected against facial injuries, particularly lacerations and fractures (Fig. 3-6).

The face in sport may be protected by:
  Face guards
  Mouth guards
  Ear guards
  Eye protection devices

There is a great variety of face masks and bars available to the player, depending on the position played and the protection needed. In football no face protection should have less than two bars. Proper mounting of the face mask and bars is imperative for maximum safety. All mountings should be made in such a way that the bar attachments are flush with the helmet. A 3-inch (7.62 cm) space should exist between the top of the face guard and the lower edge of the helmet. No helmet should be drilled more than one time on each side. There should be a space of 1 to 1 1/2 inches (3.81 cm) between the player's nose and the face guard. As with the helmet shell, pads, and chin strap, the face guard must be checked daily for defects.

Mouth Guards

The majority of dental traumas can be prevented if the athlete wears a correctly fitted intraoral mouth guard, as compared to an extraoral type (Fig. 3-7). In addition to protecting the teeth, it absorbs the shock of chin blows and obviates a possible cerebral concussion. The mouth protector should afford the athlete a proper and tight fit, comfort, unrestricted breathing, and unimpeded speech during competition. A loose mouthpiece will soon be ejected onto the ground or left unused in the locker room. The athlete's air passages should not be obstructed in any way by the mouthpiece. It is best when it is retained on the upper jaw and projects backward only as far as the last molar, thus permitting speech. Maximum protection is afforded when the mouth guard is composed of a flexible, resilient material and is formfitted to the teeth and the upper jaw.[6]

Several commercial protectors are available that can either be self-molded or fitted by a dentist. Many high schools and colleges are now requiring that mouth guards be worn under certain circumstances. Such a protector should be considered as much a part of standard protective equipment as is a helmet or a pad.

Figure 3-5

A variety of face guards are used in football.

Figure 3-6
Baseball catcher's mask.

Figure 3-7
Customized mouth protector.

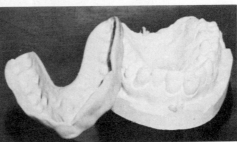

Ear Guards

With the exception of boxing and wrestling, most contact sports do not make a special practice of protecting the ears. Both boxing and wrestling can cause irritation of the ears to the point that permanent deformity may result. To avoid this problem special ear guards should be routinely worn. Recently a very effective ear protection has been developed for the water polo player (Fig. 3-8).

Eye Protection Devices

The athlete who wears glasses must be protected during sports activities. Of course, glasses broken during the heat of competitive battle may pose considerable danger. The eyes of the athlete can be protected by glass guards, case-hardened lenses, plastic lenses, or contact lenses.

Eye protection must be worn by all athletes who play sports with fast-moving projectiles.

Spectacles

For the athlete who must wear corrective lenses, spectacles can be both a blessing and a nuisance. They may slip on sweat, get bent when hit, fog up from perspiration, detract from peripheral vision, or be difficult to wear with protective headgear. Even with all these disadvantages, properly fitted and designed spectacles can provide adequate protection and withstand the rigors of the sport. If the athlete has glass lenses, they must be case-hardened to prevent them from splintering on impact. When a case-hardened lens breaks it crumbles, eliminating the sharp edges that may penetrate the eye. The cost of this process is relatively low. The only disadvantages involved are that the weight of the glasses is heavier than average, and they may be scratched more easily than regular glasses.

Another sports advantage to glass-lensed spectacles is a process by which they can become color-tinted on exposure to ultraviolet rays from the sun and then return to a clear state when removed from the sun's rays. These are known as *photochromic lenses*.

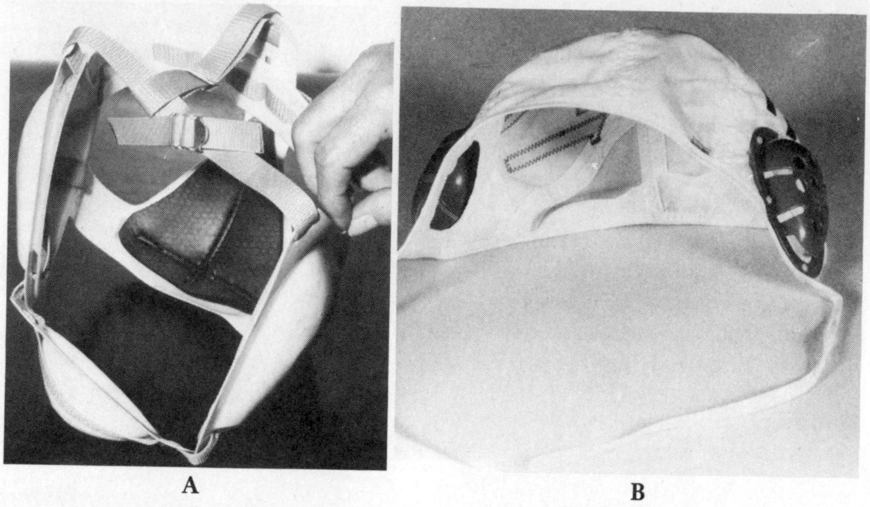

Figure 3-8

Ear protection. **A,** The wrestler's ear guard. **B,** The water polo player's ear protection.

A   B

Plastic lenses for spectacles are becoming increasingly popular with athletes. They are much lighter in weight than glass lenses; however, they are much more prone to scratching.

Contact Lenses

In many ways the athlete who is able to wear contact lenses without discomfort can avoid many of the inconveniences of spectacles. Their greatest advantage is probably the fact that they "become a part of the eye" and move with it.

Contact lenses come mainly in two types: the corneal type, which covers just the iris of the eye, and the scleral type, which covers the entire front of the eye, including the white or scleral portion. Peripheral vision, as well as astigmatism and corneal waviness, is improved through the use of contact lenses. Unlike regular glasses, contact lenses do not normally cloud up during temperature changes. They also can be tinted to reduce glare. For example, yellow lenses can be used against ice glare and blue ones against glare from snow. One of the main difficulties with contact lenses is their high cost compared to regular glasses. Some other serious disadvantages of wearing contact lenses are the possibility of corneal irritation caused by dust getting under the lens and the possibility of a lens becoming dislodged during body contact. Besides these disadvantages, only certain individuals are able to wear contacts with comfort, and some individuals are unable to ever wear them because of certain eye idiosyncrasies. There is currently a trend toward athletes preferring the soft, hydrophilic lenses to the hard type. Adjustment time for the soft lenses is shorter than for the hard, they can be more easily replaced, and they are more adaptable to the sports environment.

Eye and Glass Guards

It is essential that athletes take special precautions to protect their eyes, especially in those sports that employ fast-moving projectiles and implements (Fig. 3-9). Besides the more obvious sports of ice hockey, lacrosse, and baseball,

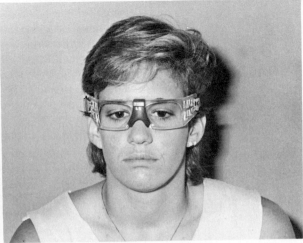

Figure 3-9

Athletes playing sports that
involve small, fast projectiles
should wear the closed type of
eye guards.

the racquet sports may also cause serious eye injury. Those athletes not wearing spectacles should wear closed eye guards to protect the orbital cavity.[3] Athletes who normally wear spectacles with plastic or case-hardened lenses are to some degree already protected against eye injury from an implement or projectile; however, greater safety is afforded by the metal-rimmed frame that surrounds and fits over the athlete's glasses. The protection the guard affords is excellent, but it does hinder vision in some planes.

BODY PROTECTION

Body protection is essential in contact sports. Those areas that are most exposed to impact forces must be properly covered with some resilient material that offers protection against tissue compression injuries. Of particular concern are the hard, bony protuberances of the body that have insufficient soft tissue for protection, such as the shoulders, chest, ribs, elbows, knees, and shins (Figs. 3-10 and 3-11). The protection of soft tissue body areas is also a concern (Fig. 3-12).

The problem that arises in the wearing of protective head, face, and body equipment is that while it is armor against injury to the athlete wearing it, it can also serve as a weapon against all opponents. Standards must become more stringent in determining what equipment is absolutely necessary for body protection and at the same time is not itself a source of trauma.

Recently many lightweight pads have been developed to protect the athlete against external forces. A jacket developed by Byron Donzis for the protection of a rib injury incorporates a pad composed of air-inflated, interconnected cylinders that protect against severe external forces.[5] This same principle has been used in the development of other protective pads.

Shoulder Protection

Manufacturers of shoulder pads have made great strides toward protecting the football player against direct force to the shoulder muscle complex. There are

Figure 3-10

The ice hockey goalie's equipment represents the ultimate in body protection.

two general types of pads—flat and cantilevered. The player who uses the shoulder a great deal in blocking and tackling requires the bulkier cantilevered type as compared to the quarterback or ball receiver. Over the years the shoulder pad's front and rear panels have been extended along with the cantilever. The following are rules for fitting the shoulder pad:

1. The tip of the inside shoulder pad should come in a direct line with the lateral aspect of the shoulder and flap covering the deltoid muscle.
2. The neck opening must allow the athlete to extend the arm overhead without placing pressure on the neck but not allow sliding back and forth.
3. Straps underneath the arm must hold the pads firmly but not so they constrict soft tissue.

Breast Protection

Until recently the primary concern for female breast protection had been against external forces that may cause bruising. With the vast increase in physically active women, concern has been redirected to protecting the breasts against movement that stems from running and jumping. This is a particular problem for women with very heavy breasts. Many girls and women in the past may have avoided vigorous physical activity because of discomfort felt from uncontrolled movement of their breasts. Manufacturers are making a concerted effort to develop specialized bras for women who participate in all types of physical activity.

A brassiere should hold the breasts to the chest and prevent stretching of Cooper's ligament, which causes premature sagging[8] (Fig. 3-13).

Figure 3-11

Standard football protective pads. This system uses open cell foam and air management to disperse a direct impact over the entire surface area of the pad, minimizing the blow to the athlete.

KNEE, FOOT, AND ANKLE PROTECTION

Footwear can mean the difference between success, failure, or injury in competition. It is essential that the coach, athletic trainer, and equipment personnel make every effort to fit their athletes with proper shoes and socks.

Socks

Poorly fitted socks can cause abnormal stresses on the foot. For example, socks that are too short crowd the toes, especially the fourth and fifth. Socks that are too long can also cause skin irritation because of their wrinkles. All athletic socks also should be clean, dry, and without holes to avoid irritations. Manufacturers are now providing a double-knit tubular sock without heels that considerably decreases friction within the shoe (Fig. 3-14). The tubular sock is especially good for the basketball player. The material composition of the sock also should be noted. Cotton socks can be too bulky, while a combination of materials, such as cotton and polyester, allow for less bulk and faster drying.

Shoes

Even more damaging than improperly fitted socks are improperly fitted shoes. Chronic abnormal pressures to the foot often lead to permanent structural deformities as well as to potentially dangerous calluses and blisters. Besides these local problems occurring to the feet, improper shoeing results in mechanical disturbances affecting the body's total postural balance, which may eventually lead to pathological conditions of the muscle and joint.

Figure 3-12

The body areas that are prone to bruising often require protective padding.

A

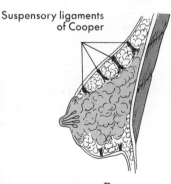

Suspensory ligaments of Cooper

B

Figure 3-13

A, A sports bra must hold the breasts to the chest to avoid excessive motion. **B**, Cooper's ligament.

Figure 3-14

The tubular double-knit sock can prevent friction in the shoe.

Shoe Composition

The bare human foot is designed to function on uneven surfaces. Shoes were created to protect against harmful surfaces but should never interfere with natural functioning. Sports shoes, like all shoes, are constructed of different parts, each of which is designed to provide function, protection, and durability. Each sport places unique stresses and performance demands on the foot. In general, all sport shoes, like street shoes, are made of similar parts. For example, shoes are composed of a sole, uppers, heel counter, and toe box. The sole or bottom of a shoe is divided into an outer, middle, and inner section, each of which must be sturdy, flexible, and provide a degree of cushioning, depending on the specific sport requirements. A heel counter should support and cushion the heel, while the toe box protects and provides an area so that the toes do not become crowded. The uppers must give the foot support and freedom to withstand a high degree of stress (Fig. 3-15).

Shoe Fitting

Fitting sports footgear is always difficult, mainly because the individual's left foot varies in size and shape from the right foot. Therefore, measuring both feet is imperative. To properly fit the sports shoe, the athlete should approximate the conditions under which he or she will perform, such as wearing athletic socks, jumping up and down, or running. It is also desirable to fit the athlete's shoes at the end of the day to accommodate the gradual increase in size that occurs from the time of awakening. The athlete must carefully con-

Figure 3-15

Properly fitted and constructed shoes can prevent foot injuries.

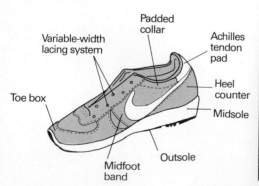

Figure 3-16

Variations in cleated shoes—the longer the cleat, the higher the incidence of injury.

sider this shoe choice because he or she will be spending countless hours in those shoes.

Under performance conditions the new shoe should feel snug but not too tight.[15] The length of the sports shoe should allow enough space that all toes can be fully extended without being cramped. Its width should permit full movement of the toes, flexion, extension, and some spreading. A good point to remember is that the wide part of the shoe should match the wide part of the foot. This allows the shoe to crease evenly when the athlete goes on the balls of the feet. The shoe should bend (or "break") at its widest part; when the break of the shoe and the ball joint coincide, the fit may be considered to be correct. However, if the break of the shoe is in back or in front of the normal bend of the foot (metatarsophalangeal joint), the shoe and foot will be opposing one another, causing abnormal skin and structural stresses to occur. Two measurements must be considered when fitting shoes: (1) the distance from the heel to the metatarsophalangeal joint and (2) the distance from the heel to the end of the longest toe. An individual's feet may be equal in length from the heels to the balls of the feet but different between heels and toes. Shoes, therefore, should be selected for the longer of the two measurements. Other factors to consider when buying the sports shoe are the stiffness of the sole and the width of the shank or narrowest part of the sole. A shoe with a too rigid, nonyielding sole places a great deal of extra strain on the foot tendons. The shoe with too narrow a shank also places extra strain because it fails to adequately support the athlete's inner longitudinal arches. Two other shoe features to consider are inner soles to reduce friction and built-in arch supports.

The cleated or specially soled sports shoe presents some additional problems in fitting. For example, American football uses the multi-short-cleated polyurethane sole and the five-in-front-and-two-in-back cleat arrangement with the soccer-type sole, both of which have cleats no longer than 0.5 inches (1.27 cm) (Fig. 3-16). Special soled shoes are also worn when playing on a synthetic surface. If cleated shoes are used, no matter which sport, the cleats must be properly positioned under the two major weight-bearing joints and not felt through the soles of the shoes.

Figure 3-17

The hand, which is an often-neglected area of the body in sports, can be protected by the use of gloves.

HAND PROTECTION

One of the finest physical instruments, the human hand, is perhaps one of the most neglected in terms of injury, especially in sports. Special attention must be paid to protecting the integrity of all aspects of the hand when encountering high-speed missiles or receiving external forces that contuse or shear. Constant stress to the hand, as characterized by the force received by the hand of the baseball catcher, can lead to irreversible pathological damage in later life (Fig. 3-17).

SPECIALIZED PROTECTIVE DEVICES

In recent years many lightweight and very strong synthetic materials have been developed. As a result, a number of very useful and specialized protective pieces of equipment are now available to the athlete. They can be made by hand or are available commercially.

One must have a very optimistic feeling about the progress that has been made in protective sports equipment. Researchers, coaches, trainers, physicians, and manufacturers are working together to provide the athlete with the safest possible equipment. Although there is a continuous need for safer protective equipment, the future is bright in this important area.

Ankle Supports

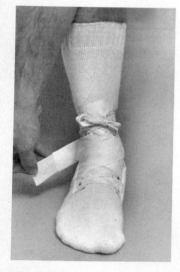

Figure 3-18

The spat-type commercial ankle support may be able to give mild support to an uninjured ankle.

Most commercial ankle supports are of either elastic or spat type (Fig. 3-18). The elastic type is a flexible, fibered sheath that slides over the foot and ankle, purportedly giving mild support to a weak ankle. It has little use either as a strong support or as a protection to the postacute or chronically weakened ankle in sports. The spat type is usually less resilient than the elastic and has an open front that permits it to be fitted directly over the ankle and then snugly tied like a shoe. Some spats have vertical ribs to effect added inversion or eversion. Though providing some assistance, no commercial ankle support affords as much protection as does adhesive tape properly applied directly to the skin surface. A fabricated orthoplast strip brace cut 3 or 4 inches (7.62 or 10.16 cm) wide has been found to be an effective semirigid support for sprained ankles.

Knee Supports and Protective Devices

Knees are next in order to ankles and feet in terms of incidence of injury in sports. As a result of the variety and rather high frequency of knee afflictions, many protective and supportive devices have been devised. The devices most frequently used in sports today are braces, elastic supports, and elastic pads.

Protective knee braces are extremely varied. Currently popular are the singular hinge-type braces that are designed to protect against a lateral force and to distribute the load away from the joint (Fig. 3-19). It should be noted, however, that although these devises are designed to withstand lateral forces, they may increase rotary forces to the knee joint. Other types of protective knee braces are the ribbed brace, consisting of a series of vertical ridged strips contained within an elastic sleeve, and the elastic sleeve, containing a rigid hinge on either side of the knee joint. Another support that is commonly used is the neoprene sleeve, which provides a great deal of pressure around the knee. Careful engineering and testing must be conducted to produce the knee brace that will protect adequately.

Elastic knee pads or guards are extremely valuable in sports in which the athlete falls or receives a direct blow to the anterior aspect of the knee. An elastic sleeve containing a resilient pad helps to dissipate anterior striking force but fails to protect the knee against lateral, medial, or twisting forces.

Abdominal and Low Back Supports

Because low back strain is a national problem, there are many gimmicks on the market that claim to give relief. Such devices may be classified as *abdominal and low back supports*. Where freedom of activity is desired, as in sports, a rigid and nonyielding material may be handicapping. A material that per-

Figure 3-19

A preventive knee brace designed to protect against a lateral force and distribute load away from joint. Losse knee defender.

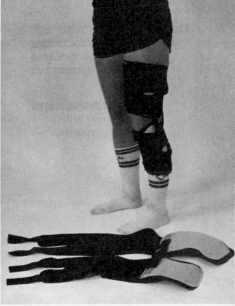

mits movement and yet offers support is desirable. Such material may consist of an elastic, rubberized fabric. In most cases of low back strain, supporting the abdominal viscera will alleviate considerable discomfort.

Shoulder Restraint Braces

The shoulder braces (Fig. 3-20) used in sports are essentially restraining devices for the chronically dislocated shoulder. Their purpose is to restrict the upper arm from being elevated more than 90 degrees and externally rotated, thus preventing it from being placed in a vulnerable position. Because of the ensuing limitation in range of motion of the arm, the athlete's capabilities are considerably reduced.

Other Elastic Pads and Supports

Elastic pads and supports are varied and can be suited to most body areas. Thigh, forearm, wrist, and elbow devices afford mild support and give protection from direct blows.

PADS AND ORTHOSES

Besides the various bandages and protective and supportive adhesive taping used in sports medicine, there are commercial and self-constructed devices designed to aid the injured athlete. Generally, these devices may be divided into pads and orthoses. Pads consist of various resilient materials that cushion against injury.

orthosis
Orthopedic device designed to support, align, prevent, or correct a deformity or to improve function

In sports medicine an **orthosis** is an orthopedic device designed to support, align, prevent, or correct a deformity or to improve the function of a movable body part. Sport medicine orthotics is fast becoming an important technique requirement for all coaches and trainers.

Types of Devices

Foot Pads

Figure 3-20

Shoulder braces used in sports are essentially restraining devices for the chronically dislocated shoulder.

Commercial foot pads are intended for use by the general public and are not usually designed to withstand the rigors of sports activities. Those commercial pads that are suited for sports are not durable enough for a limited budget. If money is no object, the ready-made commercial pad has the advantage of

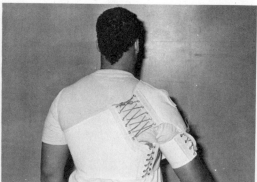

saving time. Commercial pads are manufactured for almost every type of common structural foot condition, ranging from corns and bunions to fallen arches. Indiscriminate use of these aids, however, may result in intensifying the pathological condition or delaying the athlete from seeing the team physician or team podiatrist for evaluation. Recently a yield material, Sorbothane II, has been developed. Made into a protective foot pad, it can dissipate over 90% of the energy that the foot produces and fully return to its original shape when the force is removed.[13]

Orthopedic Footwear and Orthotics

Devices that are built into or placed inside a shoe to permit proper functioning of the foot are defined as *orthopedic footwear* or *orthotics*. The athlete should never be allowed to wear special shoes or an orthosis without first consulting the team physician or team podiatrist (Fig. 3-21). It should be noted that any change in the configuration of a shoe or the application of an orthosis, if not warranted, can adversely affect the athlete's postural balance. In most cases in which a foot orthosis is needed to correct or prevent a deformity or to provide support, it is determined by a podiatrist. A plaster mold of the athlete's foot is made and a customized rigid or semirigid orthosis that can be inserted in the shoe is constructed.

Construction of Protective and Supportive Devices

Being able to construct protective and supportive devices is of considerable value in sports. The primary mediums used are sponge rubber, felt, adhesive felt or adhesive sponge rubber, gauze pads, cotton, lamb's wool, and plastic material. All these have special uses in athletic training.

Soft Materials

Sponge rubber (foam rubber) is resilient, nonabsorbent, and able to protect the body against shock. It is particularly valuable for use as a protective padding for bruised areas, and it can also serve as a supportive pad. Newly formulated foam rubber is currently being used extensively as inner soles in sports shoes. Covered by a synthetic leather sheet, this new material prevents blisters and calluses by absorbing vertical, front-to-back, and rotary forces. Sponge rubber generally ranges from 1/8 to 1/2 inch (0.3 to 1.25 cm) in thickness.

Felt is a material composed of matted wool fibers pressed into varying thicknesses that range from 1/4 to 1 inch (0.6 to 2.5 cm). Its benefit lies in its

Figure 3-21

Types of sports orthoses. **A**, Orthoplast with a foam rubber doughnut; **B**, Orthoplast splint; **C**, Orthoplast rib protector with a foam rubber pad; **D**, fiberglass material for splint construction; **E**, plaster of paris material for cast construction; **F** foam rubber pad; **G**, Aloplast foam moldable material for protective pad construction.

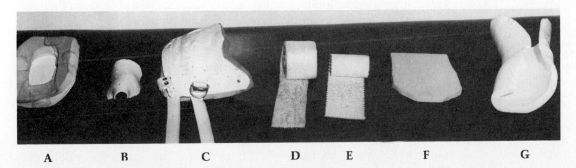

A   B   C   D   E   F   G

Heatforming plastics of the low-temperature variety are the most popular in athletic training.

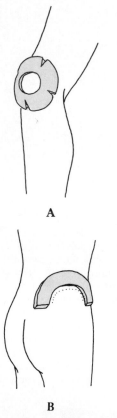

A

B

Figure 3-22

Protective pads can be of varying shapes and sizes and are cut to fit body contours. **A**, Doughnut shape. **B**, Horseshoe shape.

comfortable, semiresilient surface, which gives a firmer pressure than most sponge rubbers. Because felt will absorb perspiration, it clings to the skin, and it has less tendency to move about than sponge rubber. Because of its absorbent qualities it must be replaced daily.

Adhesive felt (moleskin) or *sponge rubber* is a felt or sponge rubber material containing an adhesive mass on one side, thus combining a cushioning effect with the ability to be held in a specific spot by the adhesive mass. It is a versatile material that is useful on all body parts.

Gauze padding is less versatile than other pad materials. It is assembled in varying thicknesses and can be used as an absorbent or protective pad.

Cotton is probably the cheapest and most widely used material in sports. It has the ability to absorb, to hold emollients, and to offer a mild padding effect.

Lamb's wool is a material commonly used on and around the athlete's toes when circular protection is required. In contrast to cotton, lamb's wool does not pack but keeps its resiliency over a long period of time.

Protective pads can be of varying shapes and sizes, cut to fit the body contours. In addition to the flat and variously shaped compression pads, pads of two other distinct shapes, the *doughnut* and the *horseshoe,* are often used (Fig. 3-22). Each is adapted so that pressure is placed around the perimeter of an injured area, leaving the injury free from additional pressure or trauma.

Rigid Materials

A number of plastic materials are becoming widely used in sports medicine for customized orthoses. They can brace, splint, and protect a body area. They may provide casting for a fracture, support for a foot defect, or a firm, nonyielding surface to protect a severe contusion.

Plastics used for these purposes differ in their chemical composition and reaction to heat. The three major categories are heatforming and heatsetting plastics and heatplastic foams.[16]

Heatforming plastics are of the low temperature variety and the most popular in athletic training. When heated to between 140° and 180° F (60° and 82.2° C), depending on the material, the plastic can be accurately molded to a body part. Aquaplast (polyester sheets) and Orthoplast (synthetic rubber thermoplast) are popular types.

Heatsetting plastics require relatively higher temperatures for shaping. They are rigid and difficult to form, usually requiring a mold rather than being formed directly to the body part.[16] High-impact vinyl (polyvinyl chloride), Kydex (polyvinyl chloride acrylic), and Nyloplex (heatplastic acrylic) are examples of the more commonly used heatforming plastics.

Heatplastic foams are plastics that have differences in density as a result of the addition of liquids, gas, or crystals. They are commonly used as shoe inserts and other body padding. Aloplast (polyethylene foam) and Plastazate (polyethylene foam) are two commonly used products.[16]

SUMMARY

It is essential that schools provide quality, well fitting protective sports equipment. All equipment must be properly maintained or, when beyond good maintenance, must be discarded. It is important that protective equipment come under close scrutiny for material durability and proper fitting.

Collision sports such as American football and ice hockey require special head protection. Football helmets must withstand repeated blows with low velocity, while ice hockey helmets must withstand forces having a higher impact. All football helmets must come under the standards established by the National Operating Committee on Standards for Athletic Equipment (NOCSAE).

Face protection is extremely important in sports that can produce injuries. They variously fall into the categories of full face guards, mouth guards, ear guards, and eye protection devices. Examples of sports positions requiring full face protection are the football player, the goalie in ice hockey, the lacrosse player, and the catcher in baseball. Many sports, such as football, require mouth guards to avoid injuring the teeth. Ear guards are worn by wrestlers, boxers, and water polo players. Eye protection should be required in sports with fast moving projectiles, such as racquetball and squash. The eye guards providing the most protection are those that are completely closed and cover the entire eye.

Many sports require protection of various parts of the athlete's body. American football players, ice hockey players, and baseball catchers are good examples of sports positions that require body protection. Commonly, the protection includes shoulder, chest, and thigh guards. The female breast should also be protected against injury from projectiles or abnormal movement from running and jumping activities.

Quality sports footwear properly fitted is essential to prevent injuries. Socks must be clean, without holes, and made of proper material. Shoes must be suited to the sport and fitted to the largest foot. The wide part of the foot matches the wide part of the shoe. If the shoe has cleats, they are positioned at the metatarsophalangeal joints.

Currently there are many pieces of specialized protective sports equipment on the market. These are designed to support weak ankles and protect the knee from lateral forces. There are supports for low back problems and braces that restrain the shoulder from dislocating. In addition to the specialized protective equipment commercially available, athletic trainers often construct customized equipment out of a variety of materials to pad injuries and to support the feet. Podiatrists are experts in devising orthopedic footwear and orthotic devices to improve the biomechanics of the foot. Many of the devices are made of heatforming plastics that can be molded and shaped at relatively low temperatures.

REVIEW QUESTIONS AND CLASS ACTIVITIES

1. What are the implications of groups such as the ASTM in the development of safe sports equipment?
2. Discuss the types of head protection necessary in various sports.
3. Invite an athletic trainer or equipment manager into the classroom to review football helmet and shoulder pad fitting.
4. Critically examine the types of face guards commonly used in various sports. What are the differences?
5. How does the properly fitted mouth guard protect against tooth injury and brain concussion?
6. What are the advantages and disadvantages of eye protection devices?
7. How does the Donzis pad protect against injury?

8. How can the female breast be protected against running and jumping injuries?
9. What should you look for when purchasing a running shoe or a football shoe?
10. Discuss the relative merits of commercial knee and ankle protective devices.

REFERENCES

1. American Society for Testing and Materials, Committee F-8 on Sports Equipment and Facilities: Member information packet, Philadelphia, 1978, The Society.
2. Bishop, P.J., et al.: The ice hockey helmet: how effective is it? Phys. Sportsmed. 7:96, 1979.
3. Bishop, P.J., et al.: Performance of eye protectors for squash and racquetball, Phys. Sportsmed. 10:62, March 1982.
4. Bishop, P.J., et al.: An evaluation of football helmets under impact conditions, Am. J. Sports Med. 12:233, May/June 1984.
5. Cain, T.E., et al.: Use of the air-inflated jacket in football, Am. J. Sports Med. 9:240, 1981.
6. Castaldi, C.R.: Injuries to the teeth. In Vinger, P.F., and Hoerner, E.F. (editors): Sports injuries: the unthwarted epidemic, Boston, 1981, John Wright, PSG, Inc.
7. Gardenswartz, A.: Equipment for sport. In Appenzeller, O., and Atkinson, R. (editors): Sports medicine, Baltimore, 1981, Urban & Schwarzenberg, Inc.
8. Gehlsen, G., and Albohm, M.: Evaluation of sports bras, Phys. Sportsmed. 8:89, 1980.

9. Goldsmith, W., and Kabo, J.M.: Performance of baseball headgear, Am. J. Sports Med., 10:31, 1982.
10. Hodgson, V.R., and Thomas, L.M.: Biomechanical study of football head impacts using a head model—condensed version; final report prepared for NOCSAE, 1973.
11. Houston, J.T.: Helmet makers seek better product, tests. In More, M. (editor): Football injury and equipment update, Phys. Sportsmed. 10:197, 1982.
12. Hulse, W.F.: Sports equipment standards. In Vinger, P.F., and Hoerner, E.F. (editors): Sports injuries: the unthwarted epidemic, Boston, 1981, John Wright, PSG, Inc.
13. Jahn, W.T.: Visco-elastic orthotics: Sorbothane II, J. Ortho. Sports Phys. Ther. 4:174, 1983.
14. Lester, R.A.: The coach as codefendant: football in the 1980's. In Appenzeller, H. (editor): Sports and law: contemporary issues, Charlotesville, V., 1985, The Michie Co.
15. Martin, M.: But does the shoe fit? The First Aider, p. 6, Feb. 1985, Cramer Products, Inc.
16. Peppard, A., and O'Donnell, M.: A review of orthotic plastics, Ath. Train. 18:77, 1983.

ANNOTATED BIBLIOGRAPHY

Adrian, M.S.: Difficulties of interfacing people and materials. In Vinger, P.F., and Hoerner, E.F. (editors): Sports injuries: the unthwarted epidemic, Boston, 1981, John Wright, PSG, Inc.
Presents the many difficulties inherent in making the "ideal" interfacing, or perfect linking, of protective equipment and the athlete.
Burns, D.: A manufacturer's perspective. In Vinger, P.F., and Hoerner, E.F. (editors): Sports injuries: the unthwarted epidemic, Boston, 1981, John Wright, PSG, Inc.
Discusses the major dilemmas manufacturers face when producing sports equipment.
Ellison, A.E. (chairman, editorial board): Athletic training and sports medicine, Chicago, 1984, American Academy of Orthopaedic Surgeons.
Three chapters detail protective devices: Chapter 10, "Principles of Protective Devices"; Chapter 11, "Upper and Lower Extremities"; and Chapter 12, "Other Protective Devices."

Morehouse, C.A.: Obsolescence in protective equipment. In Vinger, P.F. and Hoerner, E.T. (editors): Sports injuries: the unthwarted epidemic, Boston, 1981, John Wright, PSG, Inc.
Discusses the specific factors leading to obsolescence, such as becoming ineffective in injury prevention, becoming out of style, introducing an additional hazard, creating an unnecessary weight, and being too bulky.

Chapter 4

WOUND DRESSING, TAPING, AND BANDAGING

When you finish this chapter, you will be able to:

Dress wounds

Explain the principles of using athletic tape

Use the common types of bandages necessary in sports medicine

A major skill in athletic training is the proper application of wound dressing, athletic tape, and other types of bandages. Each of these skill areas requires a great deal of practice before a high level of proficiency can be attained. The following categories are basic to the athletic training/sports medicine program.

WOUND DRESSINGS

A **bandage**, when properly applied, can contribute decidedly to recovery from sports injuries. Bandages carelessly or improperly applied may cause discomfort, allow wound contamination, or even hamper repair and healing. In all cases bandages must be firmly applied—neither so tight that circulation is impaired nor so loose that the **dressing** is allowed to slip.

Skin lesions are extremely prevalent in sports; abrasions, lacerations, and puncture wounds are almost daily occurrences. It is of the utmost importance to the well-being of the athlete that open wounds be cared for immediately. All wounds, even those that are relatively superficial, must be considered to be contaminated by microorganisms and therefore must be cleansed, medicated (when called for) and dressed. Dressing wounds requires a sterile environment to prevent infections.[3]

Individuals who perform wound management in sports have often been criticized for not following good principles of cleanliness. It is obvious from the large number of athletes who acquire severe wound infections each year that this criticism is valid. To alleviate this problem one must adhere to standard procedures in the prevention of wound contamination.

bandage
A strip of cloth or other material used to cover a wound

dressing
Medicine applied to a material, such as gauze, and then applied to a wound

Wound Description

Abrasions are common conditions in which the skin is scraped against a rough surface. The top layer of skin is worn away, thus exposing numerous blood capillaries. This general exposure, with dirt and foreign materials scraping and penetrating the skin, increases the probability of infection unless the wound is properly debrided and cleansed (see Fig. 4-1 for illustrations of abrasions and the other wound descriptions listed here).

Figure 4-1

Wounds occurring in athletics can present a serious problem of infection. **A1**, and **A2**, Abrasion. **B**, Laceration. **C**, Puncture. **D**, Incision. **E1** and **E2**, Avulsion.

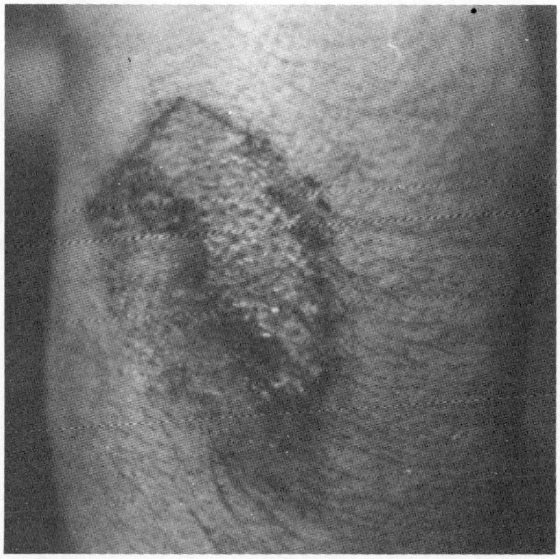

A1

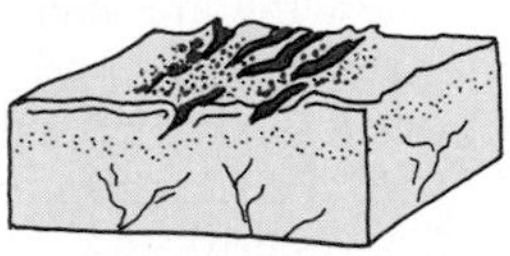

A2

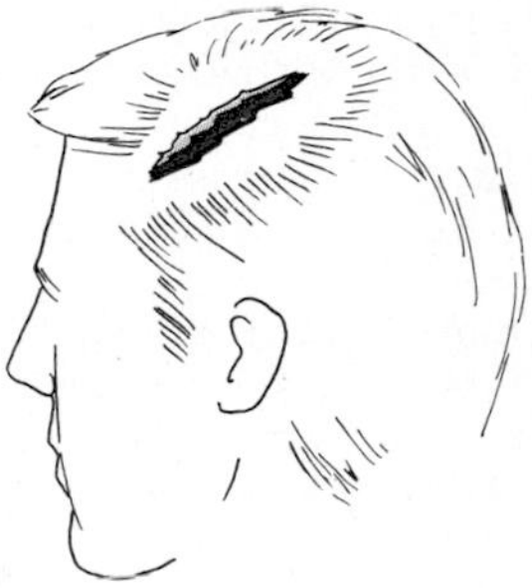

B

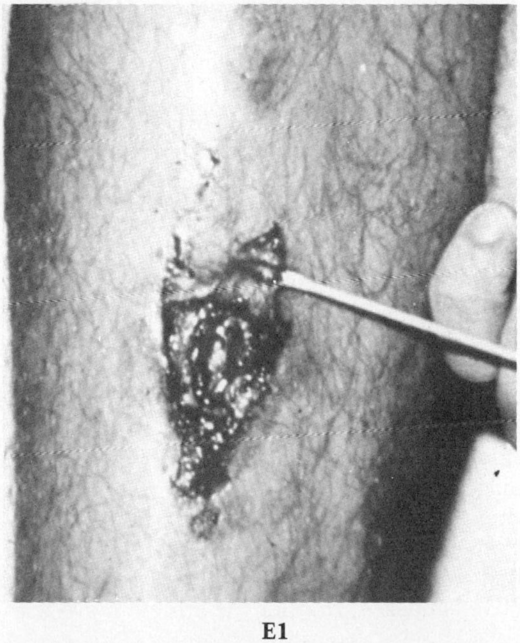

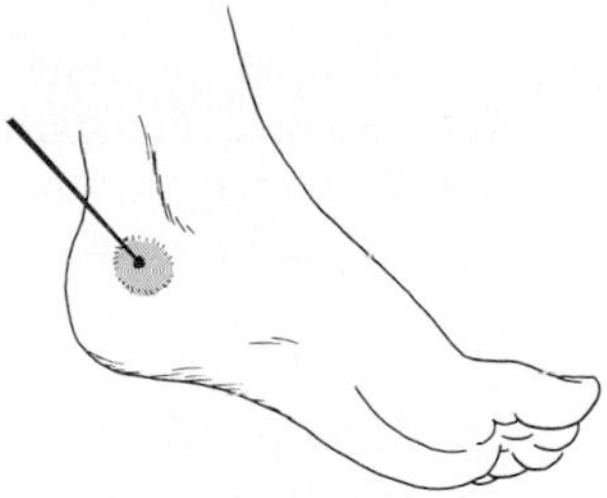

C

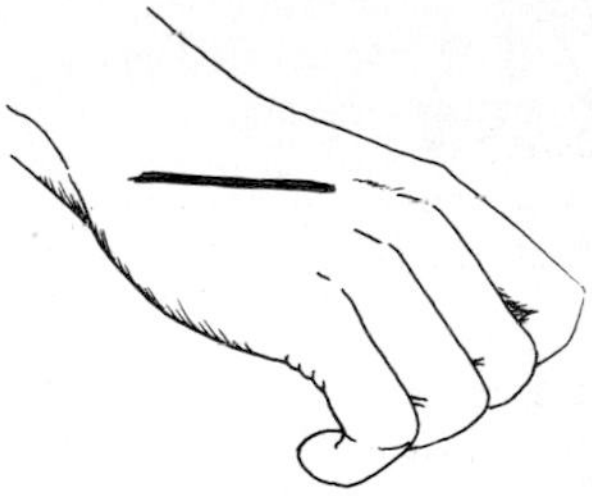

D

E1

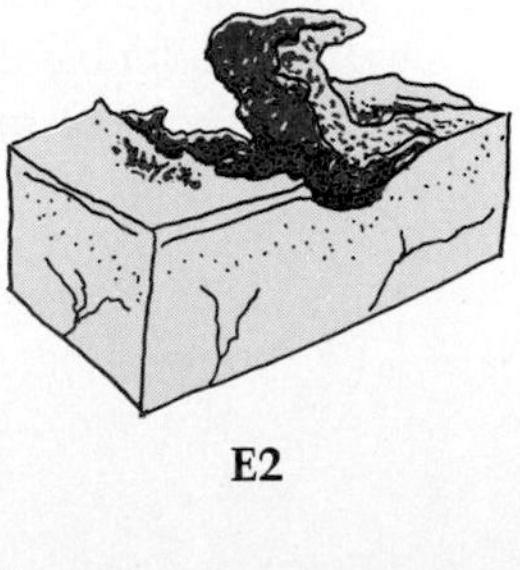

E2

Puncture wounds can easily occur during physical activities and can be fatal. Direct penetration of tissues by a pointed object such as a track shoe spike can induce the tetanus bacillus into the bloodstream, possibly making the athlete a victim of lockjaw. All puncture wounds and severe lacerations should be referred immediately to a physician.

Lacerations are also common in sports and occur when a sharp or pointed object tears the tissues, giving a wound the appearance of a jagged-edged cavity. As with abrasions, lacerations present an environment conducive to severe infection. The same mechanism that causes a laceration also can lead to a skin avulsion. In this case a piece of skin is ripped.

Incisions are clearly cut wounds that often appear where a blow has been delivered over a sharp bone or a bone that is poorly padded. They are not as serious as the other types of exposed wounds.

Avulsion wounds occur when skin is torn from the body and are frequently associated with major bleeding. The avulsed tissue should be placed on moist gauze, preferably saturated with saline solution.[3] It is then put into a plastic bag and immersed in cold water and taken along with the athlete to the hospital for reattachment.[3]

Training Room Practices in Wound Care

The following are suggested procedures to use in the training room to cut down the possibility of wound infections. See Table 4-1 for more specific suggestions regarding the care of external wounds.

1. Make sure all instruments used such as scissors, tweezers, and swabs are sterilized.
2. Clean hands thoroughly.
3. Clean a skin lesion thoroughly.
4. Place a nonmedicated dressing on a lesion if the athlete is to be sent for medical attention.
5. Avoid touching any parts of a sterile dressing that will come in contact with a wound.
6. Place medication on a pad rather than directly on a lesion.
7. Secure the dressing with tape or a wrap; always avoid placing pressure directly over a lesion.

Materials

Bandages peculiar to sports consist essentially of gauze, cotton cloth, and elastic wrapping. Plastics are also being used more frequently. Each material offers a specific contribution to the care of injuries.

Gauze Gauze materials are used in three forms: as sterile pads for wounds, as padding in the prevention of blisters on a taped ankle, and as a roller bandage for holding dressings and compresses in place.

Cotton cloth Cotton is used primarily for cloth ankle wraps and for triangular and cravat-type bandages. It is soft, is easily obtained, and can be washed many times without deterioration.

Elastic roller bandage The elastic bandage is extremely popular in sports because of its extensibility, which allows it to conform to most parts of the body. Elastic wraps are "active bandages" that let the athlete move with-

Eight basic uses for dressings and bandages:
  Protect wounds from infection
  Protect wounds from further insult and contamination
  Control external and internal hemorrhage
  Act as a compress over exposed or unexposed injuries
  Immobilize an injured part
  Protect an unexposed injury
  Support an injured part
  Hold protective equipment in place

All wounds must be considered to be contaminated by microorganisms.

out restriction. They also act as a controlled compression bandage, in which the regulation of pressure is graded according to the athlete's specific needs; however, they can cause dangerous constriction if not properly applied. A *cohesive elastic bandage* has been developed that exerts constant, even pressure. It is lightweight and contours easily to the body part. The bandage is composed of two layers of nonwoven rayon, which are separated by strands of Spandex material. The cohesive elastic bandage is coated with a substance that makes the material adhere to itself, eliminating the need for metal clips or adhesive tape for holding it in place.

Plastics Plastics are playing an increasing role in sports medicine. Spray plastic coatings are used to protect wounds. A variety of plastic adhesive tapes are also used because they are waterproof. A good practice is to use plastic food envelopes to insulate analgesic balm packs and to protect bandages and dressings from moisture. A common plastic pad used for wound dressing is the Telfa pad. Plastic materials that can be formed into a desired shape when heated are also becoming an integral part of the training room list of supplies.

TAPING IN SPORTS

The use of adhesive substances in care of the external lesions goes back to ancient times. The Greek civilization is credited with formulating a healing paste composed of lead oxide, olive oil, and water, which was used for a wide variety of skin conditions. This composition was only recently changed by the addition of resin and yellow beeswax and, even more recently, rubber. Since its inception, adhesive tape has developed into a vital therapeutic adjunct.[2]

Two types of tape are generally used in sports medicine—linen and elastic. Linen, the most commonly used, is only slightly yielding, if at all. Elastic tape, in comparison, is made to stretch. Where linen tape rigidly holds a dressing, bandage, or body part in place, elastic tape compresses and moves as the body moves. One possible reason for more extensive use of linen tape is its lower cost. Also, waterproof, hypoallergenic, plastic-backed tape is available for wound dressing, and a felt-backed tape is available for support and cushioning.[4]

When purchasing linen tape, consider:
  Grade of backing
  Mass
  Winding tension

Tape Usage

Injury Care

When used for sports injuries, adhesive tape offers a number of possibilities:
- Retention of wound dressings
- Stabilization of compression-type bandages that are used to control external and internal hemorrhaging
- Support of recent injuries to prevent additional insult that might result from the activities of the athlete

Injury Protection

Protecting against acute injuries is another major use of tape support. This can be achieved by limiting the motion of a body part or by securing some special device.

Linen Adhesive Tape Qualities

Modern adhesive tape has great adaptability for use in sports because of its uniform adhesive mass, adhering qualities, and lightness, as well as relative strength of the backing materials. All of these are of value in holding wound dressings in place and in supporting and protecting injured areas. It comes in a variety of sizes; 1-, 1 1/2-, and 2-inch (2.5, 3.75, and 5 cm) widths are commonly used in sports medicine. The tape also comes in tubes or special packs.

TABLE 4-1

Care of external wounds

Type of Wound	Action of Coach or Trainer	Initial Care	Follow-up Care
Abrasion	1. Provide initial care.	1. Cleanse abraded area with soap and water; debride with brush.	1. Change dressing daily and look for signs of infection.
	2. Wound seldom requires medical attention unless infected.	2. Apply a solution of hydrogen peroxide over abraded area; continue until foaming has subsided.	
		3. Apply a petroleum-based medicated ointment to keep abraded surface moist. In sports, it is not desirable for abrasions to acquire a scab. Place a nonadhering sterile pad (Telpha pad) over the ointment.	
Laceration	1. Cleanse around the wound. Avoid wiping more contaminating agents into the area.	1. Complete cleansing and suturing are accomplished by a physician; injections of tetanus toxoid may be required.	1. Change dressing daily and look for signs of infection.
	2. Apply dry, sterile compress pad and refer to physician.		
Puncture	1. Cleanse around the wound. Avoid wiping more contaminating agents into the area.	1. Complete cleansing and injections of tetanus toxoid, if needed, are managed by a physician.	1. Change dressing daily and look for signs of infection.
	2. Apply dry, sterile compress pad and refer to physician.		
Incision	1. Clean around wound.	1. Cleanse wound.	1. Change dressing daily and look for signs of infection.
	2. Apply dry, sterile compress pad to control bleeding and refer to physician.	2. Suturing and injections of tetanus toxoid are managed by a physician, if needed.	
Avulsion	1. Clean around wound; save avulsed tissue.	1. Wound is cleansed thoroughly; avulsed skin is replaced and sutured by a physician; tetanus toxoid injection may be required.	1. Change dressing daily and look for signs of infection.
	2. Apply dry, sterile compress pad to control bleeding and refer to physician		

Some popular packs provide greater tape length on each spool. When linen tape is purchased, factors such as cost, grade of backing, quality of adhesive mass, and properties of unwinding should be considered.

Tape Grade

Linen-backed tape is most often graded according to the number of longitudinal and vertical fibers per inch of backing material. The heavier and more costly backing contains 85 or more longitudinal fibers and 65 vertical fibers per square inch. The lighter, less expensive grade has 65 or fewer longitudinal fibers and 45 vertical fibers.

Adhesive Mass

As a result of improvements in adhesive mass, one should expect certain essentials from tape. It should adhere readily when applied and should maintain this adherence despite profuse perspiration and activity. In addition to having adequate sticking properties, the mass must contain as few skin irritants as possible and must be able to be removed easily without leaving a mass residue or pulling away the superficial skin.

Winding Tension

The winding tension that a tape roll possesses is quite important to the operator. Sports place a unique demand on the unwinding quality of tape; if tape is to be applied for protection and support, there must be even and constant unwinding tension. In most cases a proper wind needs little additional tension to provide sufficient tightness.

Tape Storage

When storing tape the following steps should be taken:
1. Store in a cool place, such as in a low cupboard.
2. Stack so that the tape rests on its flat top or bottom in order to avoid distortion.

Using Adhesive Tape in Sports

Preparation for Taping

Special attention must be given when applying tape directly to the skin. Perspiration and dirt collected during sport activities will prevent tape from properly sticking to the skin. Whenever tape is employed, the skin surface should be cleansed with soap and water to remove all dirt and oil. Hair should be removed by shaving to prevent additional irritation when the tape is removed. If additional adherence or protection from tape irritation is needed, a preparation containing rosin and a skin-toughening agent should be applied. Commercial benzoin or skin tougheners offer astringent action and dry readily, leaving a tacky residue to which tape will adhere firmly.

Taping directly on skin provides maximum support. However, applying tape day after day can lead to skin irritation. To overcome this problem many coaches and trainers sacrifice some support by using a protective covering on the skin. The most popular is a commercial, moderately elastic underwrap material that is extremely thin and fits snugly to the contours of the part to be taped. One commonly used underwrap material is polyester urethane foam, which is fine, porous, extremely lightweight, and resilient. Proper use of an underwrap requires the body part to be shaved and sprayed with a tape adherent. When taping the ankle it is desirable to place a protective greased pad anterior and posterior to the ankle in order to prevent tape cuts and secondary infection.

Proper Taping Technique

Selection of the correct tape width for the body part to be taped depends upon the area to be covered. The more acute the angles present, the narrower the tape width needed to fit the many contours. For example, the hands and feet usually require 1/2- or 1-inch (1.25 or 2.5 cm) tape, the ankles require 1 1/2-inch (3.75 cm) tape, and the larger skin areas such as thighs and back can accommodate 2- to 3-inch (5 to 7.5 cm) tape with ease. **NOTE:** Supportive tape improperly applied could aggravate an existing injury or disrupt the mechanics of a body part causing an initial injury to occur.

Tearing Tape

Coaches and athletic trainers use various techniques in tearing tape (Fig. 4-2). A method should be employed that permits the operator to keep the tape roll in hand most of the time. The following is a suggested procedure:
1. Hold the tape roll in the preferred hand with the index finger hooked through the center of the tape roll and the thumb pressing its outer edge.
2. With the other hand, grasp the loose end between the thumb and index finger.
3. With both hands in place, make a quick, scissorslike move to tear the tape.

When tearing is properly executed, the torn edges of the linen-backed tape appear to be relatively straight, without curves, twists, or loose threads sticking out. Once the first thread is torn, the rest of the tape tears easily. Learning to tear tape effectively from many different positions is essential for speed and efficiency. Many tapes other than the linen-backed type cannot be torn manually and require a knife, scissors, or razor blade cutter.

Rules for Tape Application

It is essential that important rules are observed in the use of adhesive tape.

1. If the part to be taped is a joint, *place it in the position in which it is to be stabilized* or, if the part is musculature, *make the necessary allowance for contraction and expansion.*

2. *Overlap the tape at least half the width of the tape below.* Unless tape is overlapped sufficiently, the active athlete will separate it, thus exposing the underlying skin to irritation.

3. *Avoid continuous taping.* Tape continuously wrapped around a body part may cause constriction. It is suggested that one turn be made at a time and that each encirclement be torn to overlap the starting end by approximately 1 inch (2.5 cm). This rule is particularly true of the nonyielding, linen-backed tape.

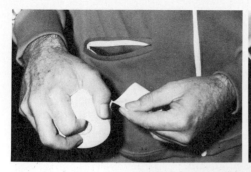

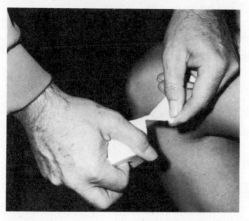

Figure 4-2

Methods of tearing linen-backed tape.

4. *Keep the tape roll in hand whenever possible.* By learning to keep the tape roll in the hand, seldom laying it down, and by learning to tear the tape, an operator can develop taping speed and accuracy.

5. *Smooth and mold the tape as it is laid on the skin.* To save additional time, tape strips should be smoothed and molded to the body part as they are put in place; this is done by stroking the top with the fingers, palms, and heels of both hands.

6. *Allow tape to fit the natural contour of the skin.* Each strip of tape must be laid in place with a particular purpose in mind. Linen-backed tape is not sufficiently elastic to bend around acute angles but must be allowed "to fall as it may," fitting naturally to the body contours. Failing to allow this creates wrinkles and gaps that can result in skin irritations.

7. *Start taping with an "anchor" piece and finish by applying a "lock" strip.* Taping should commence, if possible, by sticking the tape to an anchor piece that has loosely encircled the body part. This affords a good medium for the stabilization of succeeding tape strips, so that they will not be affected by the movement of the part.

8. *Where maximum support is desired, tape directly over skin surfaces.* In cases of sensitive skin other mediums may be used as tape bases. With the use of artificial bases, one can expect some movement between the skin and the base.

Removing Adhesive Tape

Tape usually can be removed from the skin by manual methods, by the use of tape scissors or tape cutters, or by chemical solvents.

Manual removal   When tape is pulled from the body, the operator must be careful not to tear or irritate the skin. Tape must not be wrenched in an outward direction from the skin but should be pulled in a direct line with the hair growth (Fig. 4-3).

Use of tape scissors or cutters   The characteristic tape scissors have a blunt nose that slips underneath the tape smoothly without gouging the skin. Precautions should be taken to avoid cutting the tape too near the site of the injury, lest the scissors aggravate the condition.

Use of chemical solvents   When an adhesive mass is left on the skin after taping, a chemical cleaning agent or alcohol should be used. Commercial cleaning solvents are often highly flammable. Extreme care must be taken to store these solvents in a cool place and in tightly covered metal containers. Alcohols can remove stubborn elastic tape residue. For hygienic reasons tape residue should be removed daily.

Adhesive Tape and Injury Prophylaxis

The value of adhesive tape as a prophylaxis is controversial.

Adhesive tape as a prophylaxis has routinely been applied to ankles for many years; however, recently there has been controversy as to the real benefits, if any, ankle taping provides.

ARGUMENTS AGAINST ROUTINE ANKLE TAPING

1. Tape is applied over movable skin.
2. Moisture collects under tape, increasing its looseness.
3. Constant taping for activity weakens supporting muscle tendons.
4. Tape support is reduced 40% after 10 minutes of vigorous activity.
5. Taping often replaces the practice of thoroughly exercising the ankle joint.
6. The tradition of taping is based on folklore rather than on facts.
7. Taping gives the athlete false security and soon becomes a psychological crutch.

ARGUMENTS FOR ROUTINE ANKLE TAPING

1. Wrapping or taping the ankles does not significantly hinder motor performance.
2. Properly applied tapings, even though they loosen during activity, provide critical support at the limits of ankle movement.
3. Because tapings do loosen in the initial period of activity, the midrange of ankle movement is allowed, thus removing adverse stress from the knee joint.
4. Players of high-risk sports, such as football, basketball, and soccer, should use ankle prophylaxis.
5. Athletes having a history of recent ankle injury or chronically weak ankles should be given every possible protection against further insult.
6. Statistics show that athletes who wear tape as an ankle prophylaxis have fewer injuries.
7. Pressure of tape on the peroneus brevis muscle stimulates it to contract.

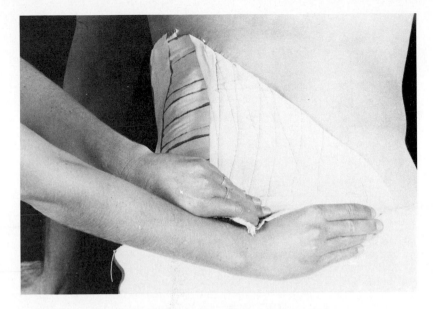

Tape as an Adjunct to Conditioning and Rehabilitation

Ankle taping to prevent injury should only be employed as an adjunct to proper and extensive exercise. Tape should never be applied indiscriminately, but under highly controlled conditions. The primary muscles of concern are the plantar muscles of the foot, the peroneal group, and the gastrocnemius-soleus complex. Special attention should be paid to stretching the heel cord. Heel cord (Achilles tendon) tightness may be a major cause of lateral ankle sprain. When the Achilles tendon is tight and the ankle is forced into plantar flexion, the subtalar joint is placed into a supinated position, causing an increased stress on the ankle's lateral capsule.

Athletes with normal or near-normal ankles should rely more on strengthening exercises than on artificial aids. When prophylaxis is needed in a high-risk sport, wraps may be preferable to rigid taping. Ankle taping should not become routine unless an honest effort at reconditioning has failed to adequately restore function to the ankle. One must remember that an improperly applied wrap or taping can compound an injury and may even create postural imbalances that could adversely affect other parts of the body.[2] Currently ankle braces are being increasingly used in cases in which there is weakness.

Ankle taping should only be used as an adjunct to proper and extensive exercise.

COMMON TYPES OF BANDAGES USED IN SPORTS MEDICINE

Triangular and cravat-type bandages, usually made of cotton cloth, may be used when roller types are not applicable or available. Figure-8 and spica bandages are also used in sports medicine.[1]

Triangular and Cravat Bandages

The triangular and cravat-type bandages are primarily used as first aid devices. They are valuable in emergency bandaging because of their ease and speed of

The principle use of the triangular bandage in athletic training is for arm slings.

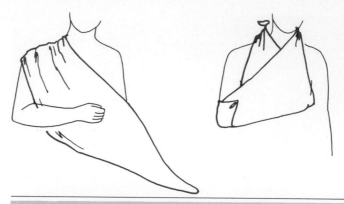

Figure 4-4

Cervical arm sling.

CERVICAL ARM SLING

The cervical arm sling is designed to support the forearm, wrist, and hand. A triangular bandage is placed around the neck and under the bent arm that is to be supported.

Materials needed: One triangular bandage and one safety pin.

Position of the athlete: The athlete stands with the affected arm bent at approximately a 70-degree angle. The arm will sit in the sling at rest.

Position of the operator: The operator stands facing the athlete.

Procedure: Fig. 4-4 illustrates the proper procedure for applying the cervical arm sling. **Note**: In cases in which greater arm stabilization is required than that afforded by a sling, an additional bandage can be swathed about the upper arm and body (Fig. 4-6).

application. In sports the more diversified roller bandages are usually available and lend themselves more to the needs of the athlete. The principal use of the triangular bandage in athletic training is for arm slings. There are two basic kinds of slings, the cervical arm sling and the shoulder arm sling, and each is applicable to different situations (Figs. 4-4 and 4-5). **NOTE:** *When applying either sling the athlete must stand in as erect a posture as possible. Also the circulation in the arm is periodically determined to be unimpaired.*

Sling and Swathe

The sling and swathe combination is desired to stabilize the arm securely in cases of shoulder dislocation or fracture (Fig. 4-6).

Roller Bandages

To apply a roller bandage, hold it in the preferred hand with the loose end extending from the bottom of the roll.

Roller bandages are made of many materials; gauze, cotton cloth, and elastic wrapping are predominantly used in the training room. The width and length vary according to the body part to be bandaged. The sizes most frequently used are the 2-inch (5 cm) width by 6-yard (5 1/2 m) length for hand, finger, toe, and head bandages; the 3-inch (7.5 cm) width by 10-yard (9 m) length for the extremities; and the 4-inch (10 cm) or 6-inch (15 cm) width by 10-yard (9 m) length for thighs, groin, and trunk. For ease and convenience in the application of the roller bandage, the strips of material are first rolled into a cylinder. When a bandage is selected, it should be a single piece that is free from wrinkles, seams, or any other imperfections that may cause skin irritation.

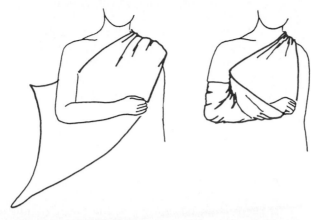

Figure 4-5

Shoulder arm sling.

SHOULDER ARM SLING

The shoulder arm sling is suggested for forearm support when there is an injury to the shoulder girdle or when the cervical arm sling is irritating to the athlete.

Materials needed: One triangular bandage and one safety pin.

Position of the athlete: The athlete stands with the injured arm bent at approximately a 70-degree angle.

Position of the operator: The operator stands facing the athlete.

Procedure: Fig. 4-5 illustrates the proper procedure for applying the shoulder arm sling.

Application

Application of the roller bandage must be executed in a specific manner to adequately achieve the purpose of the wrap. When a roller bandage is about to be placed on a body part, the roll should be held in the preferred hand with the loose end extending from the bottom of the roll. The back surface of the loose end is placed on the body part and held in position by the other hand. The bandage cylinder is then unrolled and passed around the injured area. As the hand pulls the material from the roll, it also standardizes the bandage pressure and guides it in the proper direction. To anchor and stabilize the bandage, a number of turns, one on top of the other, are made. Circling a body part requires the operator to alternate the bandage roll from one hand to the other and back again.

To acquire maximum benefits from a roller bandage, it should be applied uniformly and firmly, but not too tightly. Excessive or unequal pressure can hinder the normal blood flow within the part. The following points should be considered when using the roller bandage:

1. A body part should be wrapped in its position of maximum muscle contraction to ensure unhampered movement or circulation.
2. It is better to use a large number of turns with moderate tension than a limited number of turns applied too tightly.
3. Each turn of the bandage should be overlapped by at least one-half of the overlying wrap to prevent the separation of the material while en-

Figure 4-6

Sling and swathe.

Figure 4-7

Circular wrist bandage.

gaged in activity. Separation of the bandage turns tends to pinch and irritate the skin.

4. When limbs are wrapped, fingers and toes should be scrutinized *often* for signs of circulation impairment. Abnormally cold fingers or toes are signs of excessive bandage pressure.

The usual anchoring or roller bandages consist of several circular wraps directly overlying each other. Whenever possible, anchoring is commenced at the smallest circumference of a limb and is then moved upward. Wrists and ankles are the usual sites for anchoring bandages of the limbs. Bandages are applied to these areas in the following manner:

1. The loose end of the roller bandage is laid obliquely on the anterior aspects of the wrist or ankle and held in this position. The roll is then carried posteriorly under and completely around the limb and back to the starting point.
2. The triangle portion of the uncovered oblique end is folded over the second turn.
3. The folded triangle is covered by a third turn, thus finishing a secure anchor.

After a roller bandage has been applied, it is held in place by a *locking technique*. The method most often used to finish a wrap is that of firmly tying or pinning the bandage or placing adhesive tape over several overlying turns.

Once a bandage has been put on and has served its purpose, removal can be performed either by unwrapping or by carefully cutting with bandage scissors. Whatever method of bandage removal is employed, extreme caution must be taken to avoid additional injury.

Circular Bandage

In training procedures the circular bandage is used to cover a cylindrical area and to anchor other types of bandages. Fig. 4-7 illustrates the proper procedure for applying the circular bandage.

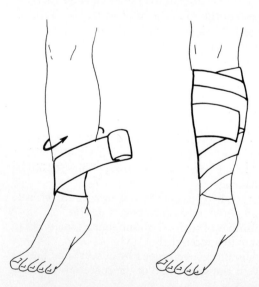

Figure 4-8

Spiral bandage.

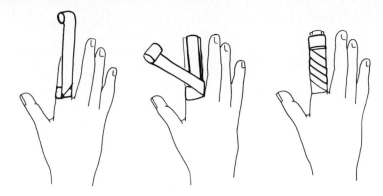

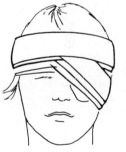

Figure 4-9

Recurrent finger bandage.

Spiral Bandage

The spiral bandage is widely used in sports for covering a large area of a cylindrical part. Fig. 4-8 illustrates the proper procedure for applying the spiral bandage.

A good example of the spiral bandage is the *recurrent finger bandage* (Fig. 4-9).

Eye Bandage

For cases in which a bandage is needed to hold a dressing on an eye, the procedure illustrated in Fig. 4-10 is suggested.

Jaw Bandage

Bandages properly applied can be used to hold dressings and to stabilize dislocated or fractured jaws as illustrated in Fig. 4-11.

Figure-8 and Spica Bandages

Figure-8 and spica bandages are readily applicable in athletic training. They are used both for support and for holding dressings in place near highly mova-

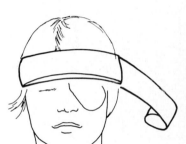

Figure 4-10

Eye bandage.

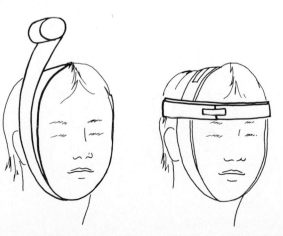

Figure 4-11

Jaw bandage.

ble joints. There is little difference between the two types. The spica has a larger loop on one end than does the figure-8.

The shoulder, elbow, hip, knee, and ankle joints are well suited for use of the figure-8 or the spica bandage.

Shoulder Spica

The shoulder spica, illustrated in Fig. 4-12, is used predominantly for the retention of wound dressings or analgesic balm packs, for holding cold packs in place, and for moderate muscular support. The axilla must be well padded to prevent skin irritation and constriction of blood vessels.

Hand and Wrist Figure-8

A figure-8 bandage, (Fig. 4-13) can be used for wrist and hand support as well as for holding dressings in place. The anchor is executed with one or two turns around the palm of the hand. The roll is then carried obliquely across the anterior or posterior portion of the hand, depending on the position of the wound, to the wrist, which it circles once; then it is returned to the primary anchor. As many figure-8s as needed are applied.

Elbow Figure-8

The elbow figure-8 bandage can be used to secure a dressing in the bend of the elbow or to restrain full extension in hyperextension injuries; when it is reversed, it can be employed for conditions on the posterior aspect of the elbow. Fig. 4-14 illustrates the proper procedure for applying the elbow figure-8.

Hip Spica

The hip spica (Fig. 4-15) serves two purposes in sports. It holds analgesic packs in place and offers a mild support to injured hip adductors or flexors.

Elastic wraps used for the hip should be double the length of the regular wrap.

NOTE: If movement restriction of the groin is needed, a hip spica wrap should be applied in reverse to Fig. 4-15 (see Fig. 12-14).

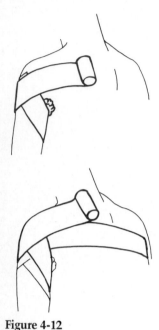

Figure 4-12

Shoulder spica.

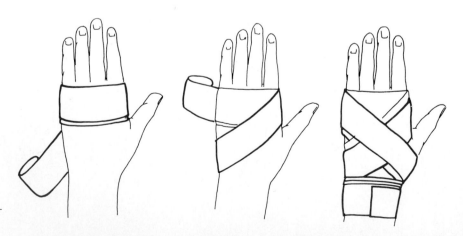

Figure 4-13

Hand and wrist figure-8.

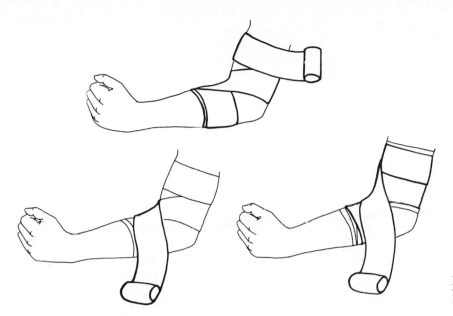

Figure 4-14

Elbow figure-8.

Ankle and Foot Spica

The ankle and foot spica bandage is primarily used in sports for the compression of new injuries, as well as for holding analgesic balm packs or wound dressings in place. Fig. 4-16 illustrates the proper procedure for applying the ankle and foot spica.

Arm or Leg Figure-8

As with other figure-8 bandages, the arm or leg type is used for keeping dressings in position, for holding splints in place, and for giving mild or moderate

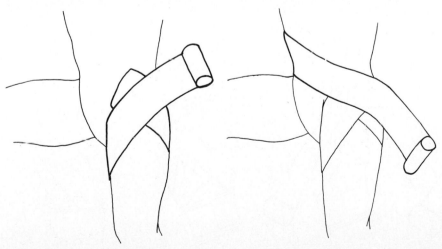

Figure 4-15

Hip spica.

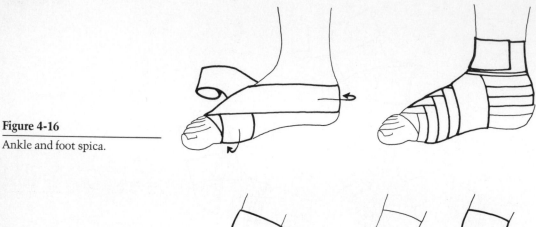

Figure 4-16

Ankle and foot spica.

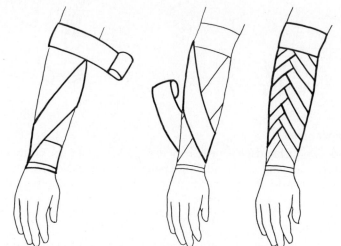

Figure 4-17

Arm or leg figure-8.

Figure 4-18

Demigauntlet bandage.

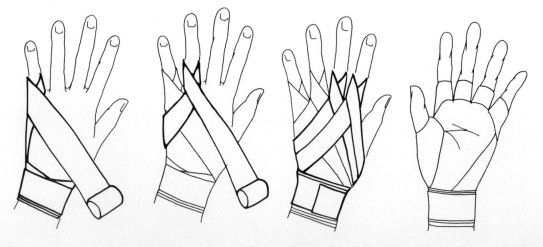

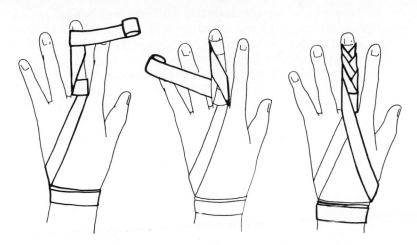

Figure 4-19

Finger bandage.

muscle support. Fig. 4-17 illustrates the proper procedure for applying the arm or leg figure-8.

Demigauntlet Bandage

The demigauntlet bandage (Fig. 4-18), has considerable versatility in sports. It holds dressings on the back of the hand, and it also offers support and protection to knuckles.

Finger Bandage

The finger bandage can be used to hold dressings or tongue depressor splints in place. Fig. 4-19 illustrates the proper procedure for applying the finger bandage.

SUMMARY

Bandages, when properly applied, can contribute decidedly to recovery from sports injuries. Wounds should be properly cared for immediately. Cleanliness is of major importance at all times in the training room and on the field. Materials commonly used for bandages and dressings in sports are gauze, cotton cloth, elastic material, and plastics.

Adhesive tape is used extensively in athletic training. The two most common types are the linen and elastic-backed. In the sports setting adhesive tape is used to hold wound dressings in place, to stabilize compression-type bandages, and to support recent injuries or to prevent injuries from occurring. Adhesive tape is composed of a backing and the adhesive mass. Tape grading is based on heaviness of its backing.

When taping directly over skin, the skin must be clean and shaved. Taping directly onto the skin is preferred; however, if done daily, to avoid irritation, an underwrap material is usually applied. In taping for support: (1) the tape should overlay at least one-half the width of the preceding piece, (2) continuous taping is to be avoided, and (3) tape is allowed to fit the normal contour of the skin.

Adhesive tape as a prophylaxis has routinely been applied to ankles for many years. Some coaches and trainers believe this is a waste of money; however, many others believe, based on data, that taping ankles can reduce sprains and, when a sprain occurs, lessen its severity.

Common types of bandages used in sports are the triangular, cravat, and roller types. Major uses of the triangular and cravat bandages are for first aid and for arm slings, of which the cervical and shoulder types are the most common. Probably the most common bandage used is the roller type.

Common roller bandages are gauze for wounds, cotton cloth for ankle wraps, and elastic wraps. Common roller bandage wrap patterns are circular, spiral, and figure-8.

REVIEW QUESTIONS AND CLASS ACTIVITIES

1. Demonstrate the correct way of dressing a wound.
2. Observe the athletic trainer in dressing wounds in the training room.
3. What aspects of backing, adhesive mass, and winding tension should be considered when purchasing athletic tape?
4. How should the skin be prepared when applying athletic tape?
5. Demonstrate proper use of the roller, triangular, and cravat bandages.

REFERENCES

1. Arnheim, D.D.: Modern principles of athletic training, ed. 6, St. Louis, 1985, Times Mirror/Mosby College Publishing.
2. Meissner, L.: Functional bandages. In Kuprian, W. (editor): Physical therapy for sports, Philadelphia, 1982, W.B. Saunders Co.
3. Parcel, G.S.: Basic emergency care of the sick and injured, ed. 3, St. Louis, 1986, Times Mirror/Mosby College Publishing.
4. Soos, T.H.: Taping the injured athlete. In Kulund, D.N. (editor): The injured athlete, Philadelphia, 1982, J.B. Lippincott Co.

ANNOTATED BIBLIOGRAPHY

Athletic training, National Athletic Training Association, P.O. Box 1865, Greenville, NC 27835-1865.
Each volume of this quarterly journal contains practical procedures in bandaging, taping, as well as orthotic application.
Ellison, A.D. (editor, chairman): Athletic training and sports medicine, Chicago, 1984, American Academy of Orthopaedic Surgeons.
Part 3, "Taping and Bandaging," offers three chapters that provide the readers with taping and bandaging foundations as well as important procedures common to athletic training/sports medicine.
First aider, Cramer Products, Inc. P.O. Box 1001, Gardner, Kans. 66030.
Published seven times throughout the school year, many of its volumes contain taping and bandaging techniques that have been submitted by readers.
Sports medicine digest, P.O. Box 2160, Van Nuys, Calif. 91404-2160.
Many volumes of this monthly paper dedicated to sports medicine discuss bandaging and taping techniques and major sports medicine problems.
Sports medicine guide, Mueller Sports Medicine, Inc., 1 Quench Dr., Prairie du Sac, Wis. 53578.
Published four times a year, this publication often presents, along with discussions on specific injuries, many innovative taping and bandaging techniques.

Chapter 5 | # EMERGENCY PROCEDURES IN SPORTS

When you finish this chapter, you will be able to:

Assess vital signs of an injured athlete

Perform basic lifesaving emergency procedures

Carry out emergency procedures and first aid for
  musculoskeletal sports injuries

Demonstrate proper emergency procedures for
  environmental emergencies

Most sports injuries do not result in life-or-death emergency situations, but when such situations do arise, prompt care is essential. Emergency is defined as "...an unforeseen combination of circumstances or the resulting state that calls for immediate action."[15] Time becomes the critical factor, and assistance to the injured must be based on knowledge of what to do and how to do it—how to carry out effective aid immediately. There is no room for uncertainty, indecision, or error.

The prime concern of emergency aid is to maintain cardiovascular function and, indirectly, central nervous system function, since failure of any of these systems may lead to death. The key to emergency aid is the initial evaluation of the injured athlete. Time is of the essence, so this evaluation must be done rapidly and accurately so that proper aid can be rendered without delay. In some instances these first steps not only will be lifesaving but also may determine the degree and extent of permanent disability.

Before discussing emergency procedures in sports, it is important for the coach or athletic trainer to understand the legal implications of school sports.

The legal liability of the coach or athletic trainer is not always well defined or thoroughly understood.

LEGAL IMPLICATIONS OF SCHOOL SPORTS

In recent years negligence suits against teachers, coaches, trainers, school officials, and physicians because of sports injuries have increased both in frequency and in the amount of damages awarded. An increasing awareness of the many risk factors present in physical activities has had a major effect on the coach and trainer in particular (Fig. 5-1). A great deal more care is now taken in following coaching and athletic training procedures that conform to the legal guidelines governing liability.

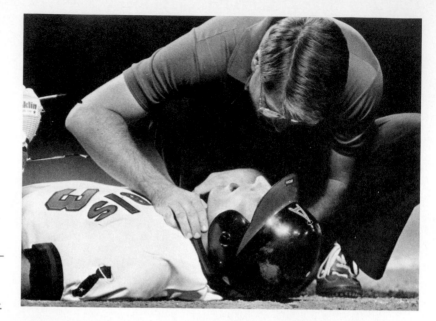

Figure 5-1

The coach, as well as the athletic trainer, must take a great deal of care when involved with an athletic injury.

liability
The legal responsibility to perform an act in a reasonable and prudent manner

Liability

Liability is the state of being legally responsible for the harm one causes another person.[15] It assumes that the coach or athletic trainer would act according to the standard of the reasonably prudent person. This standard requires that the coach or athletic trainer function as any reasonable person of ordinary prudence (with comparable education, skills, and training) would act in a comparable situation.[15] In most cases in which the charge has been negligence the key has been to compare the actions of a hypothetical, reasonably prudent person to the actions of the defendant. This is done to ascertain whether the course of action followed by the defendant was in conformity with the judgment exercised by such a reasonably prudent person. The key phrase has been "reasonable care." Individuals who have many years of experience, who are well educated in their field, and are certified or licensed, must act in accordance to this background. Negligence is the failure to use ordinary or reasonable care—care that persons of ordinary prudence would exercise in order to avoid injury to themselves or to others under similar circumstances. The standard assumes that the individual is neither the exceptionally skillful individual nor the extraordinarily cautious one, but rather is a person of *reasonable* and *ordinary* prudence. Put another way, it is expected that the individual will bring a common sense approach to the situation at hand and will exercise due care in its handling. An example might be a training situation in which the trainer, through improper or careless handling of a therapeutic agent, seriously burns an athlete. Another illustration, occurring all too often in sports, is one in which a coach or trainer moves a possibly seriously injured athlete from the field of play to permit competition or practice to continue and does so either in an improper manner or before consulting those

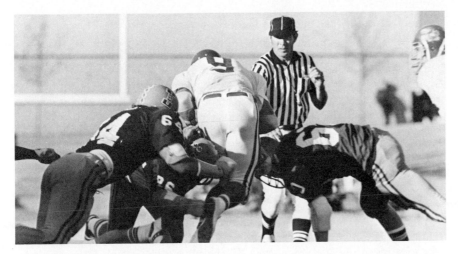

Figure 5-2

In terms of liability, the referee must consider the health and well-being of the athlete at all times.

qualified to know the proper course of action. Should a serious or disabling injury result, the coach or trainer is liable to suit. It should also be noted that a referee should at all times consider the health and well-being of the athlete (Fig. 5-2).

Assumption of Risk

The courts generally acknowledge that hazards are present in sports through the concept of "assumption of risk." In other words, the individual either by expressed or implied agreement assumes the danger and hence relieves the other individual of legal responsibility to protect him or her; by so doing he or she agrees to take his or her own chances. This concept, however, is subject to many and varied interpretations in the courts. This is particularly true when a minor is involved, since he or she is not considered able to render a mature judgment about the risks inherent in the situation. Although athletes participating in a sports program are considered to assume a normal risk, this in no way exempts those in charge from exercising reasonable care and prudence in the conduct of such activities or from foreseeing and taking precautionary measures against accident-provoking circumstances.

Torts

Torts are legal wrongs committed against the person or property of another.[15] Such wrongs may emanate from an act of *omission*, wherein the individual fails to carry out a legal duty, or from an act of *commission*, wherein he or she commits an act that is not legally his or hers to perform. In either instance, if injury results, the person can be held liable. In the case of omission a coach or trainer may fail to refer a seriously injured athlete for the proper medical attention. In the case of commission the coach or trainer performs a medical treatment not within his or her legal province and from which serious medical complications develop.

Negligence

The tort concept of negligence is held by the courts when it is shown that an individual (1) does something that a reasonably prudent person would not do or (2) fails to do something that a reasonably prudent person would do under circumstances similar to those shown by the evidence.

It is expected that a person possessing more training in a given field or area will possess a correspondingly higher level of competence than, for example, a student will. An individual will therefore be judged in terms of his or her performance in any situation in which legal liability may be assessed. It must be recognized that liability, per se, in all of its various aspects, is not assessed at a universal level nationally but varies in interpretation from state to state and from area to area. It is therefore well to know and acquire the level of competence expected in your particular area.

Medical Diagnoses

Medical diagnoses may be made *only* by a licensed physician.

Medical diagnoses may be made *only* by a licensed physician, and any final decisions regarding such diagnoses are the physician's alone. There is a fine line indeed between the recognition of an injury and its diagnosis. Debating this difference serves no useful purpose other than to further confound the distinction. In situations in which time is of the essence, as is often the case in sports injuries, the ability to evaluate quickly, accurately, and decisively is vitally important. In such situations the coach or trainer must remain within the limits of his or her ability and training and must act in full accord with professional ethics.

In summary the coach, to be reasonable and prudent, must at all times consider the athletes' health and welfare.[4,5] The coach must:
1. Warn the athlete of the potential dangers inherent in the sport.
2. Supervise constantly and attentively.
3. Properly prepare and condition the athlete.
4. Properly instruct the athlete in the skills of the sport.
5. Ensure that proper and safe equipment and facilities are used by the athlete at all times.

In case of an injury the coach or trainer must use reasonable care to obtain proper medical treatment for the injured athlete and to use reasonable care to prevent further injury until medical care is obtained.[6] Coaches and trainers must keep good records on injuries that occur.

RECOGNIZING VITAL SIGNS

The ability to recognize basic physiological signs of injury is essential to proper handling of critical injuries. When evaluating the seriously ill or injured athlete, there are nine response areas to be aware of: pulse, respiration, temperature, skin color, pupils, state of consciousness, movement, abnormal nerve stimulation, and blood pressure.

Pulse

Vital signs to watch for:
 Pulse
 Respiration
 Temperature
 Skin color
 Pupils
 State of consciousness
 Movement
 Abnormal nerve stimulation
 Blood pressure

The pulse is the direct extension of the functioning heart. In emergency situations it is usually determined at the carotid artery at the neck or the radial artery in the wrist (Fig. 5-3). A normal pulse rate per minute for adults ranges from 60 to 80 beats and in children from 80 to 100 beats. It should be noted,

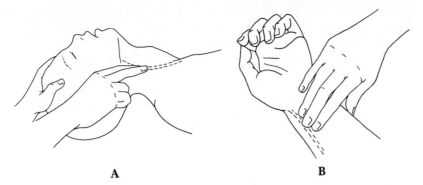

A   B

Figure 5-3

Pulse rate taken at the carotid artery (**A**) and radial artery (**B**).

however, that trained athletes usually have slower pulses than the typical population.

An alteration of a pulse from the normal may indicate the presence of a pathological condition. For example, a *rapid but weak pulse* could mean shock, bleeding, diabetic coma, or heat exhaustion. A *rapid and strong pulse* may mean heat stroke or severe fright, a *strong but slow pulse* could indicate a skull fracture or stroke, and *no pulse* means cardiac arrest or death.[10]

Respiration

The normal breathing rate per minute is approximately 12 breaths in adults and 20 to 25 breaths in children. Breathing may be shallow (indicating shock), irregular, or gasping (indicating cardiac involvement). Frothy blood from the mouth indicates a chest injury, such as a fractured rib, that has affected a lung. Look, listen, and feel: *look* to ascertain whether the chest is rising or falling; *listen* for air passing in and out of the mouth or nose or both; and *feel* where the chest is moving.

Temperature

Body temperature is maintained by water evaporation and heat radiation. It is normally 98.6° F (37° C). Temperature is measured with a thermometer, which is placed under the tongue, armpit, or in case of unconsciousness, in the rectum. Changes in body temperature can be reflected in the skin. For example, hot, dry skin might indicate disease, infection, or overexposure to environmental heat. Cool, clammy skin could reflect trauma, shock, or heat exhaustion, whereas cool, dry skin is possibly the result of overexposure to cold.

To convert Fahrenheit to centigrade (Celsius):
$$°C = (°F - 32) \div 1.8$$
To convert Celsius to Fahrenheit:
$$°F = (1.8 \times °C) + 32$$

Skin Color

For individuals who are lightly pigmented, the skin can be a good indicator of the state of health. In this instance three colors are commonly identified in medical emergencies: red, white, and blue. A red skin color may indicate heatstroke, high blood pressure, or carbon monoxide poisoning. A pale, ashen, or white skin can mean insufficient circulation, shock, fright, hemorrhage, heat exhaustion, or insulin shock. Skin that is bluish in color (cyanotic), primarily noted in lips and fingernails, usually means that circulating blood is poorly oxygenated. This may indicate an airway obstruction or respiratory insufficiency.

Assessing a dark-pigmented athlete is different from assessing a light-pigmented athlete. These individuals normally have pink coloration of the nail beds, inside the lips, mouth, and tongue. When a dark-pigmented person goes into shock, the skin around the mouth and nose will often have a grayish cast, while the tongue, the inside of the mouth, the lips, and the nail beds will have a bluish cast. Shock resulting from hemorrhage will cause the tongue and inside of the mouth to become a pale, grayish color instead of blue. Fever in these athletes can be noted by a red flush at the tips of the ears.[10]

Pupils

Some athletes normally have irregular and unequal pupils.

The pupils are extremely sensitive to situations affecting the nervous system. Although most persons have pupils of regular outline and of equal size, some individuals normally have pupils that may be irregular and unequal. This disparity requires the coach or athletic trainer as well as the physician to know which of their athletes deviate from the norm.

A constricted pupil may indicate that the athlete is using a central nervous system depressant drug. If one or both pupils are dilated, the athlete may have sustained a head injury, may be experiencing shock, heatstroke, or hemorrhage, or may have ingested a stimulant drug (Fig. 5-4). The pupils' response to light should also be noted. If one or both pupils fail to accommodate to light, there may be brain injury or alcohol or drug poisoning. When examining an athlete's pupils the presence of contact lenses or an artificial eye should be noted.

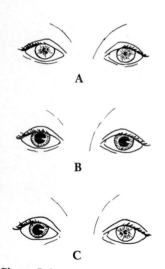

Figure 5-4

The pupils of the eye are extremely sensitive to situations affecting the nervous system. **A**, Normal pupils. **B**, Dilated pupils. **C**, Irregular pupils.

State of Consciousness

When recognizing vital signs the examiner must always note the athlete's state of consciousness. Normally the athlete is alert, aware of the environment, and responds quickly to vocal stimulation. Head injury, heatstroke, and diabetic coma can vary an individual's level of conscious awareness.

Movement

The inability to move a body part can indicate a serious central nervous system injury that has involved the motor system. An inability to move one side of the body could be caused by a head injury or cerebrovascular accident (stroke). Paralysis of an upper limb may indicate a spinal injury; inability to move the lower extremities could mean an injury below the neck; and pressure on the spinal cord could lead to limited use of the limbs.[10,17]

Abnormal Nerve Stimulation

The injured athlete's pain or other reactions to an adverse stimuli can provide valuable clues. Numbness or tingling in the limb with or without movement can indicate nerve or cold damage. Blocking of a main artery can produce severe pain, loss of sensation, or lack of a pulse in a limb. A complete lack of pain or awareness of serious but obvious injury may be caused by shock, hysteria, drug usage, or a spinal cord injury. Generalized or localized pain in the injured region probably means there is no injury to the spinal cord.[8]

Blood Pressure

Blood pressure, as measured by the sphygmomanometer, indicates the amount of force that is produced against the arterial walls. It is indicated at two pressure levels: systolic and diastolic. **Systolic pressure** occurs when the heart pumps blood, while **diastolic pressure** is the residual pressure present in the arteries when the heart is between beats. The normal systolic pressure for 15- to 20-year-old males ranges from 115 to 120 mm Hg. The diastolic pressure, on the other hand, usually ranges from 75 to 80 mm Hg. The normal blood pressure of females is usually 8 to 10 mm Hg lower than in males for both systolic and diastolic pressures. At the age of 15 to 20, a systolic pressure of 135 mm Hg and above may be excessive; also, 110 mm Hg and below may be considered too low. The outer ranges for diastolic pressure should not exceed 60 and 85 mm Hg, respectively. A lowered blood pressure could indicate hemorrhage, shock, heart attack, or internal organ injury.

systolic blood pressure
The pressure caused by the heart pumping

diastolic blood pressure
The residual pressure when the heart is between beats

EMERGENCY EVALUATION OF THE CONSCIOUS ATHLETE

There are two major considerations in emergency evaluation: first, control of life-threatening conditions and, second, management of non-life-threatening injuries.

1. Primary emergency evaluation
   a. Check 5 to 10 seconds for problems in breathing
   b. Check 5 to 10 seconds for abnormal or arrested pulse
   c. Check for external bleeding
   d. Check for shock
2. Secondary emergency evaluation
   a. Check for head injury
   b. Check for spinal injury
   c. Check for dislocation and function
   d. Check for skin wounds

EMERGENCY EVALUATION OF THE UNCONSCIOUS ATHLETE

The state of unconsciousness provides one of the greatest dilemmas in sports. Whether it is advisable to move the athlete and allow the game to resume or to await the arrival of a physician, ambulance, or emergency medical technicians is a question that too often is resolved hastily. Unconsciousness may be defined as a state of insensibility in which there is a lack of conscious awareness. This condition can be brought about by a blow to either the head or the solar plexus, or it may result from general shock. It is often difficult to determine the exact cause of unconsciousness.

Use the following procedures to recognize and evaluate the injury sustained by an unconscious athlete:

1. Understand the sequence of the accident, either by having witnessed the event or by questioning other players and spectators.
2. After learning how the accident occurred, decide what part of the body was most affected. Often no one is fully aware of just when or how the athlete was hurt. Therefore, the position or attitude in which the athlete was found may present an important key as to how the injury took place. It is a normal reaction for a person to pull away from an injuring force and to grasp at the painful area.

3. Do not move the unconscious athlete from the position found until a thorough examination has been made.
4. Make the examination as follows:
   a. Follow the ABCs of CPR
   b. Starting with the head, determine first whether there is bleeding or whether there is a straw-colored fluid coming from the nose, eyes, ears, or mouth. Look for bumps, lacerations, or deformities that may indicate a possible concussion or skull fracture.
   c. Check for shock.
   d. Moving down the body, check each part for deformities. Where possible, compare one side of the body to the other. Palpate for abnormal movements and uneven surfaces.

Ideally, although it is not always possible, the athlete should be fully conscious before one attempts removal from the field, so that the athlete can be questioned about where the pain is and can be asked to move fingers or toes to determine possible spinal fracture or paralysis. *Ammonia should **not** be used on an unconscious athlete, since it tends to elicit a jerk reflex, which may aggravate a cervical spine injury.* Transportation of the unconscious person from the playing field must be directed, ideally, by the physician or athletic trainer. When such transportation is necessary, it should always be carried out in the manner used for moving a person with a fractured spine (see Fig. 5-15).

Avoid placing ammonia under the nose of an unconscious athlete.

The First Steps of CPR*

All athletic personnel should have current CPR certification.

Establish unresponsiveness of the athlete by tapping or gently shaking his or her shoulder and shouting, "Are you okay?" Note that shaking should be avoided if there is a possible neck injury. If the athlete is unresponsive, call out for help, position the athlete for assistance, and then proceed with the ABCs of cardiopulmonary resuscitation (CPR).[16]

The ABC mnemonic of CPR is easily remembered and indicates the sequential steps utilized for basic life support:

A Airway opened
B Breathing restored
C Circulation restored

Frequently, when A is restored, B and C will resume spontaneously, and it is then unnecessary to carry them out. In some instances, the restoration of A and B obviates the necessity for step C. If the athlete is in a position other than supine, he or she must be carefully rolled over as a unit, avoiding any twisting of the body, since CPR can be administered only with the athlete lying flat on the back with knees straight or slightly flexed (see Fig. 5-15). When performing CPR for an adult victim, the following sequence should be followed:

Airway Opened

1. **NOTE**: A face mask may have to be cut away before CPR can be rendered (Fig. 5-5). Open the airway by using the head-tilt/chin-lift method. Lift chin with one hand while pushing down on victim's forehead with the other, a-

---

*The changes noted in CPR follow Standards and guidelines for cardiopulmonary resusitation and emergency cardiac care, J.A.M.A. 255–2841–3044, 1986. Because of the serious nature of this important area, updates should be routinely looked for by the American Red Cross and/or the American Heart Association.

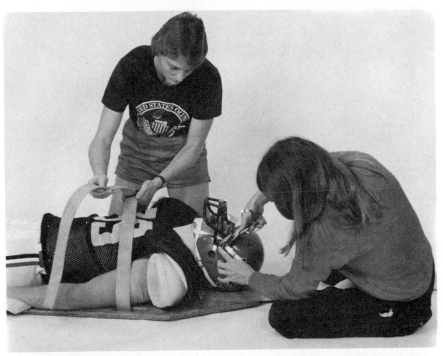

Figure 5-5

A face mask may have to be removed before CPR can be rendered.

voiding the use of excessive force. The tongue is the most common cause of respiratory obstruction; the forward lift of the jaw raises the tongue away from the back of the throat, thus clearing the airway. **NOTE:** In suspected head or neck injuries perform a modified jaw maneuver. In this procedure displace the jaw forward only, keeping the head in a fixed, neutral position.

2. In an unconscious individual, since the tongue often acts as an impediment to respiration by blocking the airway, it is necessary to use the chin-lift maneuver. Lift the chin by placing the fingers of one hand under the lower jaw near the chin, lifting and bringing it forward and thus supporting the jaw and lifting the tongue. Avoid compressing the soft tissue under the jaw, since this could obstruct the airway. Avoid completely closing the mouth. The teeth should be slightly apart. **Look** to see if the chest rises and falls. **Listen** for air passing in or out of the nose or mouth. **Feel** on the cheek whether air is being expelled, this should take 3 to 5 seconds.

3. If neither of the foregoing is sufficiently effective, additional forward displacement of the jaw can be effected by grasping each side of the lower jaw at the angles, thus displacing the lower mandible forward as the head is tilted backward. In executing this maneuver both elbows should rest on the same surface as that upon which the victim is lying. Should the lips close, they can be opened by retracting the lower lip with a thumb. In suspected neck injuries this is the maneuver that should be used, since it can be performed effectively without extending the cervical spine.

4. If necessary, clear the mouth of any foreign objects, such as vomitus, mouthpiece, dentures, or dislodged bridgework, but do not waste a great deal of time.

5. If opening the athlete's airway does not cause spontaneous breathing, proceed to step B.

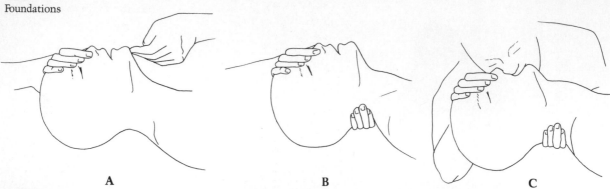

A   B   C

Figure 5-6

The procedure for conducting mouth-to-mouth resuscitation requires pinching the nose shut (**A**), moving the head back (if there is no neck injury) (**B**), and after taking a deep breath, placing the mouth over the victim's mouth (**C**), thereby forming an air-tight seal and blowing until the chest rises.

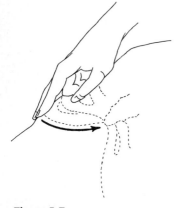

Figure 5-7

With the middle and index fingers of the hand closest to the waist, the lower margin of the victim's rib cage is located. The fingers are then run along the rib cage to the notch where the ribs meet the sternum. The middle finger is placed on the notch with the index finger next to it on the lower end of the sternum.

Breathing Restored

1. With the hand that is on the athlete's forehead, pinch the nose shut, keeping the heel of the hand in place in order to hold the head back (if there is no neck injury) (Fig 5-6). Taking a deep breath, place your mouth over the athlete's mouth, to provide an airtight seal, and give 2 slow breaths at 1 to 1 1/2 seconds per inflation. Observe chest rise. Remove your mouth and listen for the air to escape through passive exhalation.

2. Should the athlete still not be breathing, give 2 full breaths, then check the carotid artery for pulse. If pulse is present, continue rescue breathing at the rate of 12 times a minute (every 5 seconds). Recheck for continued pulse presence for 5 to 10 seconds after each series of 12 ventilations, or after 1 minute, when a single operator is functioning.

3. If no pulse is evident, then artificial circulation must be provided through cardiac compression coupled with the rescue breathing (step C).

Circulation Restored

1. Maintain open airway. Position yourself close to the side of the athlete's chest. With the middle and index fingers of the hand closest to the waist, locate the lower margin of the athlete's rib cage on the side next to you (Fig. 5-7).

2. Run the fingers up along the rib cage to the notch where the ribs meet the sternum.

3. Place the middle finger on the notch and the index finger next to it on the lower end of the sternum.

4. Next, the hand closest to the athlete's head is positioned on the lower half of the sternum next to the index finger of the first hand that located the notch; then the heel of that hand is placed on the long axis of the breast bone.

5. The first hand is then removed from the notch and placed on the top of the hand on the sternum so that the heels of both hands are parallel and the fingers are directed straight away from the coach or trainer (Fig. 5-8).

6. Fingers can be extended or interlaced, but they must be kept *off* of the chest.

7. Elbows are kept in a locked position with arms straight and shoulders positioned over the hands, enabling the thrust to be straight down.

8. In a normal-sized adult, enough force must be applied to depress the sternum 1 1/2 to 2 inches (4 to 5 cm). After depression there must be a com-

plete release of the sternum to allow the heart to refill. The time of release should equal the time of compression. For the single operator compression must be given at the rate of 80 to 100 times per minute, maintaining a rate of 15 chest compressions to two quick breaths, thus alternating B and C.

9. When two rescuers are available, they are positioned at opposite sides of the athlete (Fig. 5-9). The one providing the breathing does so by giving 1 breath after every five chest compressions, which are being administered by the other rescuer at the rate of 80 to 100 compressions per minute. The carotid pulse must be checked frequently by the ventilator during chest compression to ascertain the effectiveness of the compression. In the beginning check after 10 sets of 5:1 have been completed, after which ventilation and compression should be interrupted every few minutes of ventilation to determine whether spontaneous breathing and pulse have occurred. With the exception of inserting an airway and transporting, *never interrupt CPR for more than 5 seconds*. Adequate circulation must be maintained. Any interruption in compression permits the blood flow to drop to zero.

Every coach and trainer should be certified in CPR and should take a refresher examination at least once a year. It is wise to have all training assistants certified as well.

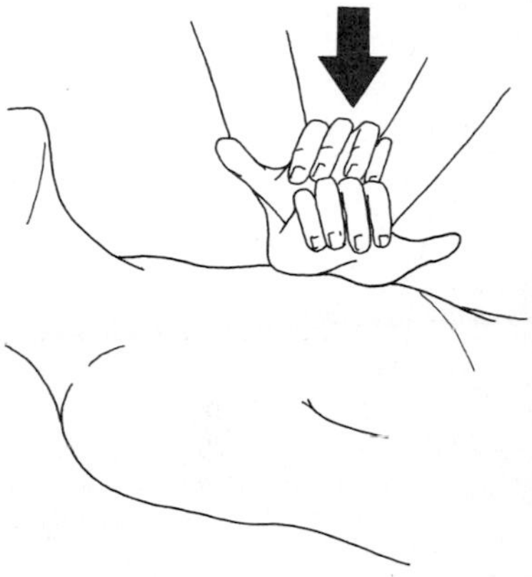

Obstructed Airway Management

Death by choking on foreign objects claims close to 3000 lives every year. Choking is a possibility in many sports activities; for example, an athlete may choke on a mouth guard, a broken bit of dental work, chewing gum, or even a "chaw" of tobacco. When such emergencies arise, early recognition and prompt, knowledgeable action are necessary to avert a tragedy. An uncon-

Figure 5-8

The heel of the headward hand is placed on the long axis of the lower half of the sternum next to the index finger of the first hand. The first hand is moved from the notch and placed on top of the hand on the sternum with fingers interlaced.

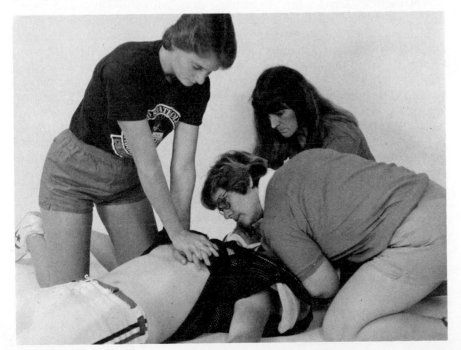

Figure 5-9

Cardiac compression, using two rescuers, interposes one breath for every five chest compressions. The third person in the photo is an instructor and observer.

Number of Rescuers	Ratio of Compressions to Breaths	Rate of Compressions
1	15:2	80-100 times/min
2	5:1	80-100 times/min

scious person can choke also — the tongue may fall back in the throat, thus blocking the upper airway. Blood clots resulting from head, facial, or dental injuries may provide an impediment to normal breathing, as may vomiting. When complete airway obstruction occurs, the individual is unable to speak, cough, or breathe. If the athlete is conscious, there is a tremendous effort made to breathe, the head is forced back, and the face initially is congested and then becomes cyanotic as oxygen deprivation is incurred. If partial airway obstruction is causing the choking, some air passage can be detected, but in a complete obstruction no air movement is discernible.[9]

To relieve airway obstruction caused by foreign bodies, two maneuvers are recommended: (1) Heimlich maneuver and (2) finger sweeps of the mouth and throat.

Heimlich Maneuver

There are two methods of obstructed airway management, depending on whether the victim is in an erect position or has collapsed and is either unconscious or too heavy to lift. For the conscious victim the Heimlich maneuver is applied until he or she is relieved or goes unconscious. In cases of unconsciousness, 6 to 10 maneuvers are applied, followed by a finger sweep with an attempt at ventilation.

Method A Stand behind the athlete. Place both arms around the waist just above the belt line, and permit the athlete's head, arms, and upper trunk to hang forward (Fig. 5-10, A) Grasp one fist with the other, placing the thumb side of the grasped fist immediately below the xiphoid process of the sternum, clear of the rib cage. Now sharply and forcefully thrust the fists into the abdomen inward and upward several times. This "hug" pushes up on the diaphragm, compressing the air in the lungs and creating forceful pressure against the blockage, thus usually causing the obstruction to be promptly expelled. Repeat the maneuver 6 to 10 times in each series.

Method B If the athlete is on the ground or on the floor, lay him or her on the back and straddle the thighs, keeping your weight fairly centered over your knees. Place the heel of your left hand against the back of your right hand and push sharply into the abdomen just above the belt line (Fig. 5-10, B). Repeat as many times as needed to expel the blockage. Care must be taken in either of these methods to avoid extreme force or applying force over the rib cage because fractures of the ribs and damage to the organs can result.

Finger Sweeping

If a foreign object, such as a mouth guard, is lodged in the mouth or the throat and is visible, it may be possible to remove or release it with the fingers. Care must be taken that the probing does not drive the object deeper into the throat. It is usually impossible to open the mouth of a conscious victim who is in distress, so the Heimlich maneuver technique should be put to use im-

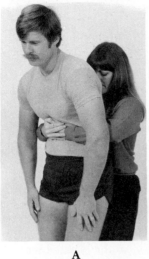 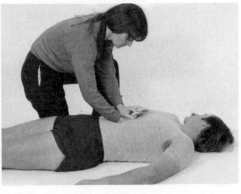

A   B

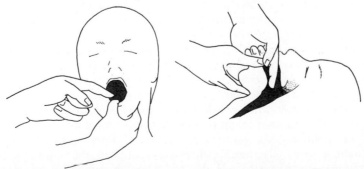

Figure 5-10

The Heimlich maneuver for an obstructed airway. **A**, Standing. **B**, Reclining.

mediately. In the unconscious athlete, turn the head either to the side or face up, open the mouth by grasping the tongue and the lower jaw, hold them firmly between the thumb and fingers and lift—an action that pulls the tongue away from the back of the throat and from the impediment. If this is difficult to do, the crossed finger method can usually be employed effectively. The index finger of the free hand (or, if both hands are employed, an assistant can probe) should be inserted into one side of the mouth along the cheek deeply into the throat; using a hooking maneuver, attempt to free the impediment, moving it into a position from which it can be removed (Fig. 5-11). Attempt to ventilate after each sweep until airway is open. Once the object is removed an attempt is made to ventilate the athlete, if he or she is not already breathing.

EMERGENCY CARE OF ACUTE MUSCULOSKELETAL INJURIES

Learning to intelligently evaluate the nature and extent of an injury is in the purview of a coach or trainer when a physician is not immediately available. At this time a decision may have to be made as to whether the athlete's continued participation would be detrimental, what first aid is necessary, and whether medical referral is necessary. To reach such decisions reasonably and

Figure 5-11

Finger sweeping of the mouth is essential in attempting to remove a foreign object from a choking victim.

prudently the responsible person must have a basic knowledge of sports injury characteristics.

Emergency care of musculoskeletal injuries stemming from sports activities requires: (1) recognition that there is an injury, (2) evaluation of the extent of injury, and (3) proper care.

Injury Recognition and Evaluation

By law coaches and trainers are not allowed to diagnose injuries; however, they can recognize the gross signs of injuries.

A logical process must be used to accurately evaluate the extent of a sport injury. One must be aware of the major signs that reveal the site, nature, and, above all, severity of the injury. Detection of these signs can be facilitated (1) *by understanding the mechanism or traumatic sequence of the injury* and (2) *by methodically inspecting the injury.* Knowledge of the mechanism of an injury is extremely important in finding the area of the body that is most affected. When the injury mechanism has been determined, the examiner proceeds to the next phase—physical inspection of the affected region. At this point information is gathered from what was seen, what was heard, and what was felt.

Initial On-site Injury Inspection and Evaluation

Symptoms and signs   When evaluating an injury, there must be a concern for symptoms and signs. A *symptom* is defined as an adverse change in the body that is subjectively described by the athlete. A *sign* is an objective indication of an injury determined by the examiner through seeing, hearing, and feeling.

To understand the mechanism of injury, a brief history of the complaint must be taken. Of course, this is dependent upon the consciousness of the athlete. The unconscious athlete must be treated as though there is a severe neck injury. The athlete is asked, if possible, about the events leading up to the injury and how it occurred. The athlete is further asked what was heard or felt when the injury took place. When examining the athlete for the possibility of a musculoskeletal injury, the greatest concern is for fractures; dislocations are second; subluxations are third; sprains are fourth; strains are fifth; and contusions are next. Do not move the athlete until the nature and extent of the injury have been determined. First, a *visual observation* is made of the injured body part, which is then compared to the uninjured body part. The initial visual examination can disclose obvious deformity, swelling, and skin discoloration. Next, *what was heard* at the time of the injury is determined. Sounds occurring at the time of the injury or during manual inspection yield pertinent information on the type and extent of pathology present. Such uncommon sounds as grating or harsh rubbing may indicate fracture. Joint sounds may be detected when either arthritis or an internal derangement is present. Areas of the body that have abnormal amounts of fluid may produce sloshing sounds when gently felt or moved. Such sounds as a snap, crack, or pop at the moment of injury often indicate a breaking of bone. Finally, the region of the injury is gently felt. *Feeling or palpating a body part* can, in conjunction with visual and audible signs, indicate the nature of the injury. As the examiner gently feels the injury and surrounding structures with the fingertips, several factors can be revealed: the extent of point tenderness, the extent of irritation (whether it is confined to soft tissue alone or extends to the bony tissue), and the determination of deformities that may not be detected by visual examination.

After a quick on-site injury inspection and evaluation, the following decisions are made:

1. The seriousness of the injury
2. The type of first aid and immobilization necessary
3. Whether or not the injury warrants immediate referral to a physician for further evaluation
4. The manner of transportation from the injury site to the sidelines, training room, or hospital

Off-site Injury Inspection and Evaluation

Once the athlete has been removed from the site of injury to a place of comfort and safety, further inspection and evaluation is made by the athletic trainer or physician. This process consists of six steps: (1) determination of major complaints, (2) general inspection, (3) bony palpation, (4) soft tissue palpation, (5) neurological evaluation, and (6) functional evaluation. *This same type of inspection and evaluation is given to athletes who are not in an initial or acute state of injury but who have a recurrent or chronic complaint.*

Because musculoskeletal injuries are extremely common in sports, a knowledge of their immediate care is necessary. Three areas of first aid are highly important: (1) control of hemorrhage, management of early inflammation, muscle spasm, and pain; (2) immobilization or splinting; and (3) handling and transportation.

Hemorrhage, Inflammation, Muscle Spasm, and Pain Management

Of major importance in musculoskeletal injuries is the initial control of hemorrhage, early inflammation, muscle spasm, and pain. The acronym for this process is ICE (ice, compression, and elevation). Added to this is the important factor of rest.

Ice, Compression, Elevation, and Rest (ICE-R)

Ice (cold application) Cold, primarily ice in various forms, has been found to be an effective first aid agent. As a constrictor of blood vessels, cold applied for 10 to 20 minutes decreases the swelling that usually occurs for 4 to 6 hours following injury. It also minimizes pain and muscle spasm. Cold makes blood thicker, lessens capillary seepage, and decreases the blood flow to the injured area.[13] Cold applied to a recent injury will lower metabolism and the tissue demands for oxygen and reduce hypoxia. This benefit extends to uninjured tissue, preventing injury-related tissue death from spreading to adjacent normal cellular structures.[13] However, it should be noted that prolonged application of cold may cause tissue damage.

For best results, ice packs (crushed ice and towel) should be applied directly to the skin. Frozen gel packs should not be used directly against the skin, because of the possibility of skin injury. A good rule of thumb is to apply a cold pack to a recent injury for a 20-minute period and repeat every 1 to 1 1/2 hours throughout the waking day. Depending on the severity and site of

ICE-R (ice, compression, elevation, and rest) are essential in the emergency care of musculoskeletal injuries.

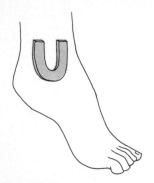

Figure 5-12

A horseshoe-shaped pad can be placed around the maleolus to reduce edema.

the injury, cold may be applied intermittently for 1 to 72 hours. For example, a mild muscle tear or strain will probably require one or two 20-minute periods of cold application, whereas a severe knee or ankle ligament sprain might need 3 days of intermittent cold. If in doubt as to the severity of an injury, it is best to extend the time that ICE-R is applied.

Compression　In most cases immediate compression of an acute injury is considered an important adjunct to cold and elevation and in some cases may be superior to them. Placing external pressure on an injury assists decreasing hemorrhage and hematoma formation. Fluid seepage into interstitial spaces is retarded by compression, and absorption is facilitated.[20] It should be noted, however, that application of compression to the anterior compartment syndrome would be contraindicated (see page 217).

Many types of compression are available. An elastic wrap that has been soaked in water and frozen in a refrigerator can provide both compression and cold when applied to a recent injury. Pads can be cut from felt or foam rubber to fit difficult-to-compress body areas. A horseshoe-shaped pad, for example, placed around the malleolus in combination with an elastic wrap and tape, provides an excellent way to prevent or reduce ankle edema (Fig. 5-12). Although cold is applied intermittently, compression should be maintained throughout the day. At night it is best to remove the wrap completely and elevate the body part above the heart to avoid pooling of fluids when the body processes slow down.

Elevation　Along with cold and compression, elevation reduces internal bleeding. By elevating the affected body part above the level of the heart, bleeding is reduced and venous return is encouraged, further reducing swelling.

Rest　Rest is essential for musculoskeletal injuries. This can be achieved by not moving the body part or can be guaranteed by the application of tape, wraps, splints, casts, and the assistance of a cane or crutches. Immobilization of an injury for the first 2 or 3 days after injury helps to ensure healing of the wound without complication. Too early movement will only increase the possibility of hemorrhage and the extent of disability, prolonging recovery.

An ICE-R Schedule

1. Evaluate the extent of injury.
2. Apply crushed ice in a moist towel pack on the injury.
3. Hold ice pack firmly to the injury site with an elastic wrap.
4. Elevate injured body part above the level of the heart.
5. After 20 minutes remove ice pack.
6. Replace ice pack with a compress wrap and pad.
7. Elevate injured body part.
8. Reapply ice pack in 1 to 1 1/2 hours and, depending on degree of injury, continue this rotation until injury resolution has taken place and healing has begun.
9. When retiring, remove elastic wrap.
10. Elevate injured part above the heart.
11. The next day, when arising, ICE-R is begun again and carried on throughout the day.
12. With second or third degree injury, continue this same process for 2 or 3 days.

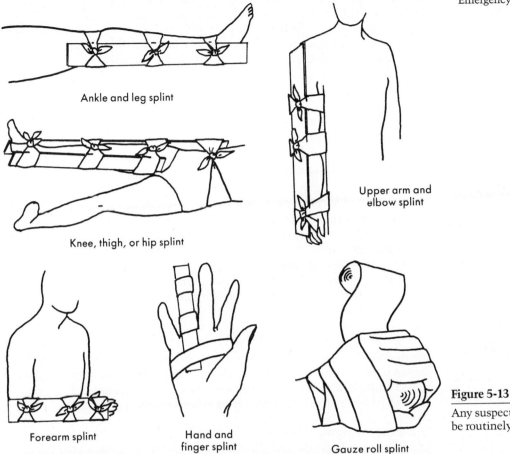

Ankle and leg splint

Knee, thigh, or hip splint

Upper arm and elbow splint

Forearm splint

Hand and finger splint

Gauze roll splint

Figure 5-13

Any suspected fracture should be routinely splinted.

Emergency Splinting

Any suspected fracture should always be splinted before the athlete is moved. Transporting a person with a fracture without proper immobilization can result in increased tissue damage, hemorrhage, and shock. Conceivably a mishandled fracture could cause death. Therefore, a thorough knowledge of splinting techniques is important (Fig. 5-13).

The application of splints should be a simple process through the use of emergency splints. In most instances the coach or trainer does not have to improvise a splint, since such devices are readily available in most sports settings. The use of padded boards is recommended. They are easily available, can be considered disposable, and are easy to apply. Commercial basswood splints are excellent, as are disposable cardboard and clear plastic commercial splints. The clear plastic splint is inflated with air around the affected part and can be used for extremity splinting, but its use requires some special training (Fig. 5-14). This provides support and moderate pressure to the body part and affords a clear view of the site for x-ray examination. It should be noted that the inflatable splint should not be used if it will alter a fracture deformity. For fractures of the femur the half-ring type of traction splint offers

Any suspected fracture should always be splinted before the athlete is moved.

Figure 5-14

The air splint provides excellent support as well as a clear site for x-ray examination.

An unconscious athlete must be treated as having a cervical fracture.

the best support and immobilization but takes considerable practice to master. Whatever the material used, the principles of good splinting remain the same. It should be noted that a compound fracture must be carefully dressed to avoid additional contamination. Two major concepts of splinting are to splint from one joint above to one joint below the fracture and to splint where the athlete lies. If at all possible, do not move the athlete until he or she has been splinted.

Splinting of Lower Limb Fractures

Fractures of the ankle or leg require immobilization of the foot and knee. Any fracture involving the knee, thigh, or hip needs splinting of all the lower limb joints and one side of the trunk.

Splinting of Upper Limb Fractures

Fractures about the shoulder complex are immobilized by a sling and swathe bandage, with the upper limb bound to the body securely. Upper arm and elbow fractures must be splinted with immobilization effected in a straight arm position to lessen bone override. Lower arm and wrist fractures should be splinted in a position of forearm flexion, supported by a sling. Hand and finger dislocations and fractures should be splinted with tongue depressors, gauze rolls, or aluminum splints.

Splinting of the Spine and Pelvis

Injuries involving a possible spine or pelvic fracture are best splinted and moved using a spine board (Figs. 5-15 and 5-16). When such injuries are suspected *the coach or trainer should not, under any circumstances, move the injured athlete except under the express direction of a physician.*

Handling the Injured Athlete

Moving, lifting, and transporting the injured athlete must be executed so as to prevent further injury. Emergency aid authorities have suggested that improper handling causes more additional insult to injuries than any other emergency procedure.[10,12,15] There is no excuse for poor handling of the injured athlete.

Moving the Injured Athlete

It is very important that an unconscious athlete or one believed to have a spinal fracture be moved like a "log." The athlete who is unconscious and unable to describe the injury in terms of sensation and site *must be treated as having a cervical fracture.*

Suspected spinal injury Suspected spinal injury requires extremely careful handling and is best left to properly trained ambulance attendants or certified paramedics who are more skilled and have the proper equipment for such transport. If such personnel are not available, moving should be done under the express direction of a physician or athletic trainer and using a spine board (Fig. 5-15, *A-E*). One danger inherent in moving an athlete with a suspected spinal injury, and in particular a cervical injury, is the tendency of the neck and head to turn because of the victim's inability to control his or her movements. Torque so induced creates considerable possibility of spinal cord or root damage when small fractures are present. The most important principle in transporting an individual on a spine board is *to keep the head and neck in alignment with the long axis of the body*. In such cases it would be best to have one individual whose sole responsibility would be to ensure and maintain proper positioning of the head and neck until head is secured to a backboard.

    Suspected severe neck injury   Once an injury to the neck has been recognized as severe, a physician and an ambulance should be summoned immediately. Primary emergency care involves maintaining normal breathing, treating for shock, and keeping the athlete quiet and in the position found until medical assistance arrives. Ideally, transportation be not be attempted until the physician has examined the athlete and given permission. The athlete should be transported while lying on the back with the curve of the neck supported by a rolled up towel or pad or encased in a stabilization collar. Neck stabilization must be maintained throughout transportation, first to the ambulance and then to the hospital, and throughout the hospital procedure. If stabilization is not continued, additional cord damage and paralysis may ensue.

These steps should be followed when moving an unconscious athlete:[7]

1. Establish whether the athlete is breathing and has a pulse.
2. Plan to move the athlete on a spine board.
3. If the athlete is lying prone, he or she must be turned over for CPR or to be secured to the spine board. *An unconscious athlete or one with a possible cervical fracture is transported face up. An athlete with a spinal fracture in the lower trunk area other than cervical is transported face down.*[10]

   a. Place all extremities in an axial alignment (Fig. 5-15, *A*).
   b. To roll the athlete over requires four or five persons with the "captain" of the team protecting the athlete's head and neck. The neck must be stabilized and not moved from its original position no matter how distorted it may appear.
   c. The spine board is placed close to the side of the athlete (Fig. 5-15, *B*)
   d. Each assistant is responsible for one of the athlete's body segments. One assistant is responsible for turning the trunk, another the hips, another the thighs, and the last the lower legs.
4. With the spine board close to the athlete's side, the captain gives the command to roll him or her onto the board as one unit (Fig. 5-15, *C*).
5. On the board, the athlete's head and neck continue to be stabilized by the captain (Fig. 5-15, *D*).
6. If the athlete is a football player, the helmet is not removed; however, the face guard is removed or lifted away from the face for possible CPR. **NOTE**: To move the guard, the plastic fasteners holding it to the helmet are cut.
7. The head and neck are next stabilized on the spine board by a chin strap secured to metal loops. Finally, the trunk and lower limbs are secured to the spine board by straps (Fig. 5-15, *E*).

    An alternate method of moving the athlete onto a spine board, if he or she is face up, is the *straddle slide method*. Five persons are used—a captain stationed at the athlete's head and three or four assistants. One assistant is in charge of lifting the athlete's trunk, one the hips, and one the legs. On the command "lift" by the captain, the athlete is lifted while the fourth assistant

Improper transportation procedures often cause additional insult to athletic injuries.

slides a spine board under the athlete between the feet of the captain and assistants (Fig. 5-16).

Transporting the Injured Athlete

As with moving, transporting the injured athlete must be executed so as to prevent further injury. There is no excuse for the use of poor transportation techniques in sports. Planning should take into consideration all the possible transportation methods and the necessary equipment to execute them. Capable persons, stretchers, and even an ambulance may be needed to transport the injured athlete. Four modes of assisting in travel are used: ambulatory aid, manual conveyance, stretcher carrying, and vehicular transfer.

Ambulatory aid Ambulatory aid (Fig. 5-17) is that support or assistance given to an injured athlete who is able to walk. Before the athlete is allowed to walk, he or she should be carefully scrutinized to make sure that the injuries are minor. Whenever serious injuries are suspected, walking should be pro-

Figure 5-15

A, When moving an unconscious athlete, first establish whether the athlete is breathing and has a pulse. *An unconscious athlete must always be treated as having a serious neck injury.* If lying prone, the athlete must be turned over for CPR or be secured to a spine board for possible cervical fracture. All of the athlete's extremities are placed in axial alignment with one coach or trainer stabilizing the athlete's neck and head. **B**, The spine board is placed as close to the athlete as possible. **C**, Each assistant is responsible for one of the athlete's segments. When the coach or trainer (captain) gives the command "roll," the athlete is moved as a unit onto the spine board. **D**, At all times, the captain continues to stabilize the athlete's neck. **E**, The head and neck are stabilized onto the spine board by means of a chin strap secured to metal loops, and finally the trunk and lower limbs are secured to the spine board by straps.

A

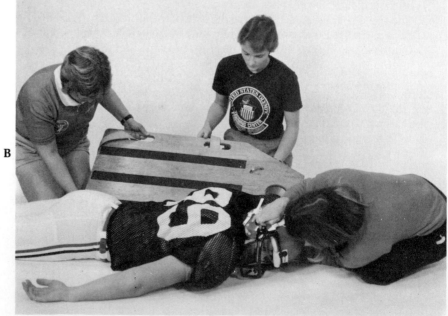
B

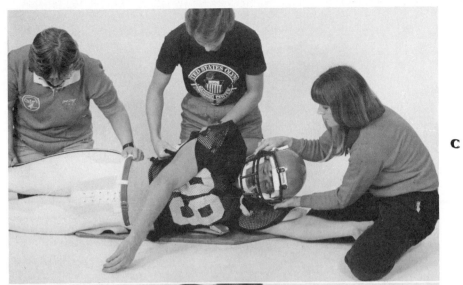

C

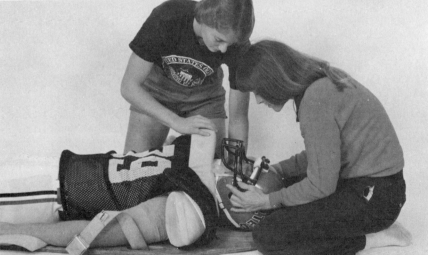

D

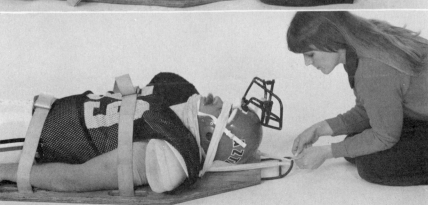

E

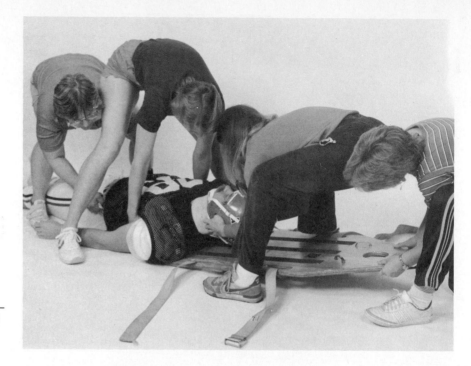

Figure 5-16

An alternate method of placing
the athlete on a spine board is
the straddle slide method.

hibited. Complete support should be given on both sides of the athlete. The athlete's arms are draped over the assistants' shoulders, and their arms encircle his or her back.

Manual conveyance Manual conveyance (Fig. 5-18) may be used to move a mildly injured individual a greater distance than could be walked with ease. As with the use of ambulatory aid, any decision to carry the athlete must be made only after a complete examination to determine the existence of potentially serious conditions. The most convenient carry is done by two assistants.

Stretcher carrying Whenever a serious injury is suspected, the best and safest mode of transportation for a short distance is by stretcher. With each segment of the body supported, the athlete is gently lifted and placed on the stretcher, which is carried adequately by four assistants, two supporting the ends of the stretcher and two supporting either side (Fig. 5-19). It should be noted that any person with an injury serious enough to require the use of a stretcher must be carefully examined before being moved.

When transporting a person with a limb injury, be certain the injury is splinted properly before transport. Athletes with shoulder injuries are more comfortably moved in a semisitting position, unless other injuries preclude such positioning. If injury to the upper extremity is such that flexion of the elbow is not possible, the individual should be transported on a stretcher with the limb properly splinted and carried at the side with adequate padding placed between the arm and the body.

Vehicular transfer If an injury demands vehicular transfer, an ambulance should be used if at all possible. Only in an extreme emergency should

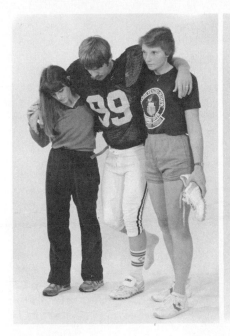 

Figure 5-17

The ambulatory aid method of transporting a mildly injured athlete.

Figure 5-18

Manual conveyance method of transporting a mildly injured athlete.

other modes of travel be considered. Because of the liability risks involved, it is unwise for coaches or trainers to use their own cars. Most vehicles other than ambulances are not equipped for carrying a stretcher patient. In cases of moderate injury, when it is inadvisable for an athlete to walk home, the parents should be notified so that they may make the necessary arrangements for proper medical attention.

SPECIAL EMERGENCY CONDITIONS

Three emergency situations may require special consideration: hemorrhage, shock, and environmental stress.

Hemorrhage

In any injury situation one must be constantly aware of the danger of hemorrhage. *Hemorrhage* is the escaping of blood through the walls of the blood vessels or through ruptured blood vessels. There are three basic types of hemorrhage: arterial, venous, and capillary. It is vitally important that hemorrhaging be promptly recognized.

1. *Arterial hemorrhage* is a condition in which an artery has been damaged or severed. There is a very rapid flow of bright red blood, usually escaping in a rhythmical spurting with each heartbeat. Because of the rapidity with which the blood is lost from the body, this type of hemorrhaging is considered the most dangerous. It requires immediate attention. The body part should be elevated promptly and a compress bandage applied directly over the site of the hemorrhage.

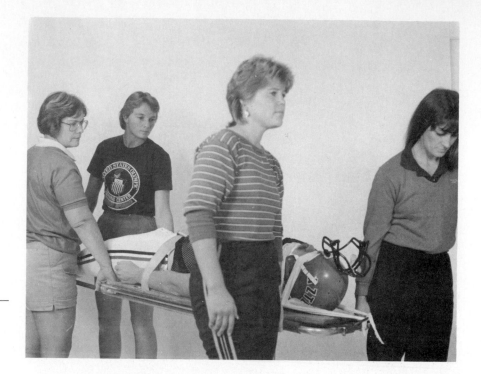

Figure 5-19

Whenever a serious injury is suspected, a stretcher is the safest method of transporting the athlete.

2. *Venous hemorrhage* is characterized by a rapid, steady escape of dark blood from the wounded area. It is controlled by elevation of the body part and application of direct pressure over the area.

3. *Capillary hemorrhage* is an oozing or very gradual seeping of blood from the wounded area and is easy to control through elevation of the body part and direct pressure on the sterile dressing that is placed directly over the wound.

As stated, elevation of the part and direct pressure are considered the best measures in controlling hemorrhage. When the injured area is raised above the level of the heart, there is a diminishing of the pulse pressure, resulting in a reduced amount of blood in the vessels.

Internal hemorrhage is unexposed and therefore invisible to the eye unless hemorrhaging is manifested through the body openings or is identified through x-ray or other diagnostic techniques. Its danger lies in the difficulty of diagnosis. When internal hemorrhaging occurs either subcutaneously or intramuscularly, the athlete may be moved without danger in most instances. However, the direction of bleeding within a body cavity such as the skull or thorax is of the utmost importance, since it could mean the difference between life and death. Because the symptoms are obscure, internal hemorrhage is difficult to diagnose properly. It has been said that as a result of this difficulty, internal injuries require hospitalization under complete and constant observation by a medical staff to determine the nature and extent of the injuries. All severe hemorrhaging will eventually result in shock and therefore should be treated on this premise.

Shock

In any injury shock is a possibility, but when severe bleeding, fractures, or deep internal injuries are present, the development of shock is assured. Shock occurs when there is a diminished amount of fluid available to the circulatory system. As a result there are not enough oxygen-carrying blood cells available to the tissues, particularly those of the nervous system. This occurs when the vascular system loses its capacity to hold the fluid portion of the blood within its system, because of a dilation of the blood vessels within the body and a disruption of the osmotic fluid balance (Fig. 5-20). When this occurs a quantity of plasma is lost from the blood vessels to the tissue spaces of the body, leaving the solid blood particles within the vessels and thus causing stagnation and slowing up the blood flow. With this general collapse of the vascular system there is widespread death of tissues, which will eventually cause the death of the individual unless treatment is given.

Certain conditions, such as extreme fatigue, extreme exposure to heat or cold, extreme dehydration of fluids and minerals, or illness, predispose an athlete to shock.

In a situation in which there is a potential shock condition, there are other signs by which the coach or trainer should assess the possibility of the athlete's lapsing into a state of shock as an aftermath of the injury. The most important clue to potential shock is the recognition of a severe injury. It may happen that none of the usual signs of shock is present. To avoid shock in cases of such injury it is vitally important that immediate care be given to the athlete. These steps should be followed in sequence:

1. *Bleeding,* because it is one of the conditions that causes shock, should receive first consideration. If the wound is of a disturbing nature, the athlete should not be permitted to see it.
2. *Body temperature* should be kept normal, 98.6° F (37° C), since extreme variations of temperature serve only to accentuate the condition of shock.
3. *Body position* should be arranged with the athlete's body flat and the head lower than the rest of the body. If there is no head or chest injury, the feet can be elevated 6 inches or more.

Signs of shock:
  Blood pressure is low
  Systolic pressure is usually
    below 90 mm Hg
  Pulse is rapid and very weak
  Athlete may be drowsy and
    appear sluggish
  Respiration is shallow and
    extremely rapid

Figure 5-20

In shock, blood vessels dilate, causing the osmotic fluid balance to be disrupted, allowing plasma to become lost into tissue spaces.

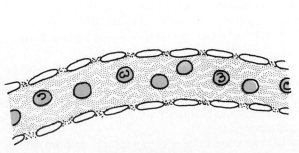

Normal capillary

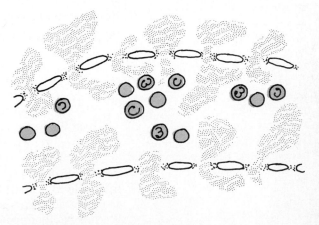

Dilated capillary

4. *Oxygen*, if available, can be administered to help restore starved tissues.
5. *Pain* is one of the causes of shock, and the athlete's physician will often administer sedation to enable the athlete to be more at ease.

Shock can also be compounded or initially produced by the psychological reaction of the athlete to an injury situation. Fear or the sudden realization that a serious situation has occurred can result in shock. In the case of a psychological reaction to an injury the athlete should be instructed to lie down and avoid viewing the injury. This athlete should be handled with patience and gentleness, but with firmness as well. Spectators should be kept away from the injured athlete. Reassurance is of vital concern to the injured individual. The person should be given immediate comfort through the loosening of clothing.

The Emergency Plan

To ensure the proper care of the seriously injured athlete all athletic programs must have an emergency plan. The following questions must be answered as part of the plan:

1. Are emergency phone numbers available?
2. Where is the nearest phone to be used in an emergency situation?
3. Who is designated to make the telephone call?
4. What information should be told to the ambulance personnel (e.g., type of situation, exact location of the emergency, where to enter the facility, name of person calling, phone number where you are calling from, etc.)?
5. Who will have access keys to gates or padlocks?
6. Have accident forms been devised to record all aspects of the emergency situation?
7. Has an emergency plan been written for all athletic fields, courts, and gymnasiums?
8. Have the coaches, trainers, athletic director, and other school personnel been apprised of the emergency plan? Do these individuals know what his or her emergency situation responsibilities are?

Environmental Stress

People concerned with sports are increasingly aware of the impact of environmental stress on the performer. One not only must be aware of the factors of temperature, humidity, and wind but must also be prepared to make appropriate changes in the types of uniforms or equipment to be worn, the length and number of practice sessions, and the weight loss of each athlete.

Heat Illness

In the United States heat illness is the second most frequent cause of sports death.

Concern is rising at the increase in causes of heat exhaustion and heatstroke in sports. Among football players and distance runners there have been a number of deaths in high school and college, all of which were directly attributable to heatstroke. Uniforms and helmets have been found to be major causative factors in the death of players.

It is vitally important to have knowledge of temperature and humidity in planning practice and game uniforming and procedures. One should familiarize oneself with the use of the sling psychrometer or the instrument used in establishing the WBGT Index (wet-bulb, globe temperature index). One should be able to determine not only relative humidity but also the danger zones; then one can advise the coaching staff and athletes with a reasonable degree of authority. In addition, one should become familiar with the clinical signs and treatment of heat stress (Fig. 5-21).

Body temperature regulation results almost entirely through cutaneous cooling from the evaporation of sweat. During exercise there is some respiratory heat loss, but the amount is relatively small. The effectiveness of sweat evaporation is strongly influenced by relative humidity and wind velocity and under the most ideal conditions does not exceed 70% to 80%.[11] When temperature exceeds 80° F (26.6° C), sweating is the only effective means that the body has of heat dissipation. However, when a high temperature is accompanied by high humidity, a condition with serious implications exists, since high humidity reduces the rate of evaporation *without* diminishing sweating. The stage is set for heat exhaustion or heatstroke unless certain precautionary measures have been observed (see Table 5-1). When a person's temperature reaches 106° F (41.1° C) the chances of survival are exceedingly slim.

An average runner may lose from 1.5 to 2.5 L/hr through active sweating; much greater amounts can be lost by football players in warm weather activity. Seldom is more than 50% of this fluid loss replaced, even though replacement fluids are taken ***ad libitum***, since athletes usually find it uncomfortable to exercise vigorously with a full stomach, which could interfere with the respiratory muscles. The problem in fluid replacement is how rapidly the fluid can be eliminated from the stomach into the intestine, from which it can enter the bloodstream. Cold drinks (45° to 55° F [7.2° to 12.8° C]) tend to empty more rapidly from the stomach than do warmer drinks and offer no particular threat to a normal heart or in inducing cramps.

Sweating occurs whether or not the athlete drinks water, and if the sweat losses are not replaced by fluid intake over a period of several hours, dehydration results.[9] Therefore, athletes must have unlimited access to water. Failure to permit *ad libitum* access will not only undermine their playing potentialities but also may be responsible for permitting a dangerous situation to develop that could conceivably have fatal consequences (Fig. 5-22).

Women are apparently more physiologically efficient in body temperature regulation than men. Although they possess as many heat-activated

ad libitum
The amount desired

Figure 5-21

A sling psychrometer is used to determine relative humidity.

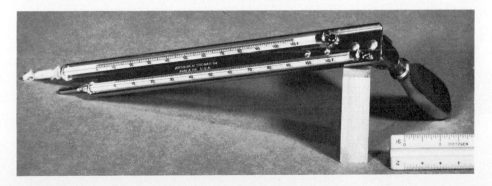

sweat glands as men, they sweat less and manifest a higher heart rate when working in heat.[19] Although slight differences exist, the same precautionary measures apply to both genders.

Body build must be considered when determining individual susceptibility to heat stress. Overweight individuals may have as much as 18% greater heat production than an underweight individual, since metabolic heat is produced proportionately to surface area. It has been found that heat victims tend to be overweight. Death from heatstroke increases at a ratio of approximately 4 to 1 as body weight increases.

Prevention   The following should be considered when planning a training-competitive program that is likely to take place during hot weather:

The prevention of heat illness involves:
  Gradual acclimatization
  Lightweight uniforms
  Routine weight record
    keeping
  Unrestricted fluid
    replacement
  Well-balanced diet
  Routine temperature/
    humidity readings

1. *Gradual acclimatization.* This is probably the single most effective method of avoiding heat stress. Acclimatization should involve not only becoming accustomed to heat but also becoming acclimatized to exercise in hot temperatures. A good preseason conditioning program, started well before the advent of the competitive season and carefully graded as to intensity, is recommended.[3]

2. *Uniforms.* Select uniforms on the basis of temperature and humidity. Initial practices should be conducted in short-sleeved T-shirts, shorts, and socks, moving gradually into short-sleeved net jerseys, lightweight pants, and socks as acclimatization proceeds.

3. *Weight records.* Careful weight records of all players must be kept. Weights should be taken both before and after practice. A loss of 3% to 5% of body weight will reduce blood volume and could be a serious health threat.[19]

4. *Pre-event hydration.* Drinking 8 to 12 ounces of water prior to competition may help to prevent heat illness.[4]

5. *Fluid replacement.* Intake of water should be carefully observed. Athletes should have unlimited access to cold water at all times. This means before, during, and after activity.

Text continued on p. 118.

Figure 5-22

Athletes must have unlimited access to water, especially in hot weather.

TABLE 5-1

Contrasting heatstroke and heat exhaustion

	Heatstroke	Heat Exhaustion
Cause	Inadequate or failure of heat loss	Excessive fluid loss
Symptoms	Headache, weakness, sudden loss of consciousness	Gradual weakness, nausea, anxiety, excess sweating, light-headedness
Signs	Hot, red, dry skin; little sweating; rapid pulse; very high temperature	Pale, grayish, clammy skin; weak, slow pulse; low blood pressure; faintness
Management	Rapid cooling by full body immersion in cold water, ice packs, fanning; immediate hospitalization	For syncope, head down, replace lost water and salt

ENVIRONMENTAL CONDUCT OF SPORTS: PARTICULARLY FOOTBALL

I. General warning
  A. Most adverse reactions to environmental heat and humidity occur during the first few days of training.
  B. It is necessary to become thoroughly acclimatized to heat to successfully compete in hot or humid environments.
  C. Occurrence of a heat injury indicates poor supervision of the sports program.

II. Athletes who are most susceptible to heat injury
  A. Individuals unaccustomed to working in the heat.
  B. Overweight individuals, particularly large linemen.
  C. Eager athletes who constantly compete at capacity.
  D. Ill athletes, having an infection, fever, or gastrointestinal disturbance.
  E. Athletes who receive immunization injections and subsequently develop temperature elevations.

III. Prevention of heat injury
  A. Take complete medical history and provide physical examination. Include:
    1. History of previous heat illnesses or fainting in the heat.
    2. Inquiry about sweating and peripheral vascular defects.
  B. Evaluate general physical condition.
    1. Type and duration of training activities for previous month.
      a. Extent of work in the heat.
      b. General training activities.
  C. Measure temperature and humidity on the practice or playing fields.
    1. Make measurements before and during training or competitive sessions.
    2. Adjust activity level to environmental conditions.
      a. Decrease activity if hot or humid.
      b. Eliminate unnecessary clothing worn when hot or humid.
  D. Acclimatize athletes to heat gradually.
    1. Acclimatization to heat requires work in the heat.
      a. Recommend type and variety of warm weather workouts for preseason training.
      b. Provide graduated training program for first 7 to 10 days—and other abnormally hot or humid days.
    2. Train in early morning or evening.
    3. Provide adequate rest intervals and water replacement during the acclimatization period.
  E. Body weight loss during activity in the heat.
    1. Body water should be replaced as it is lost.
      a. Allow additional water as desired by player.
      b. Provide salt on training tables (no salt tablets should be taken).
      c. Weigh each day before and after training or competition.
        (1) Treat athlete who loses excessive weight each day.
        (2) Treat well-conditioned athlete who continues to lose weight for several days.
  F. Clothing and uniforms
    1. Provide lightweight clothing that is loose fitting at the neck, waist, and sleeve. Use shorts and T-shirt at beginning of training.
    2. Avoid excessive padding and taping.
    3. Avoid use of long stockings, long sleeves, double jerseys, and other excessive clothing.
    4. Avoid use of rubberized clothing or sweatsuits.
    5. Provide clean clothing daily—all items.

Continued.

G. Provide rest periods to dissipate accumulated body heat.
  1. Rest in cool, shaded area with some air movement.
  2. Avoid hot brick walls or hot benches.
  3. Loosen or remove jerseys or other garments.
  4. Take water during the rest period.
IV. Trouble signs: stop activity!

Headache	Unconsciousness	Faintness
Nausea	Vomiting	Chill
Mental slowness	Diarrhea	Cyanotic appearance
Incoherence	Cramps	
Visual disturbance	Seizures	
Fatigue	Rigidity	
Weakness	Weak, rapid pulse	
Unsteadiness	Pallor	
Collapse	Flush	

6. *Salt intake and electrolyte beverages.* In maintaining an adequate salt content 1 tablespoon per day will satisfy most sports needs. It should be noted that excessive salt intake along with limited water intake causes cellular dehydration. Many commercial electrolyte drinks have high concentrations of salt that cause a fluid retention within the stomach and small intestines, producing an upper abdominal distress.[2]

7. *Diet.* A well-balanced diet is essential. Fat intake should be minimized.

8. *Temperature/humidity readings.* Dry-bulb and wet-bulb readings should be taken on the field before practice. The purchase of a sling psychrometer for this purpose is recommended. It is relatively inexpensive and uncomplicated to use. The relative humidity should be calculated. The suggestions below regarding temperature and humidity will serve as a guide.

Cold Stress

Cold weather is a frequent adjunct to many outdoor sports in which the sport itself does not require heavy protective clothing; consequently, the weather becomes a pertinent factor in injury susceptibility. In most instances the activity itself enables the athlete to increase the metabolic rate sufficiently to

Many sports played in cold weather do not require heavy protective clothing; thus weather becomes a factor in injury susceptibility.

Temp (°)	Humidity	Procedure
80°-90° F (26.7°-32.2° C)	Under 70%	Watch those athletes who tend toward obesity.
80°-90° F (26.7°-32.2° C)	Over 70%	Athletes should take a 10-minute rest every hour, and T-shirts should be changed when wet. All athletes should be under constant and careful supervision.
90°-100° F (32.2°-37.8° C)	Under 70%	
Over 100° F (37.8° C)	Over 70%	Under these conditions it would be well to suspend practice. A shortened program conducted in shorts and T-shirts could be established.

be able to function physically in a normal manner and dissipate the resulting heat and perspiration through the usual physiological mechanisms. An athlete may fail to warm up sufficiently or may become chilled because of relative inactivity for varying periods of time demanded by the particular sport either during competition or training; consequently, the athlete is exceedingly prone to injury. Low temperatures alone can pose some problems, but, when such temperatures are further accentuated by wind, the chill factor becomes critical. For example, a runner proceeding at a pace of 10 mph directly into a wind of 5 mph creates a chill factor equivalent to a 15 mph headwind.

During strenuous physical activity in cold weather, as muscular fatigue builds up, the rate of exercise begins to drop and may reach a level wherein the body heat loss to the environment exceeds the metabolic heat protection, resulting in definite impairment of neuromuscular responses and exhaustion. A relatively small drop in body core temperature can induce shivering sufficient to materially affect one's neuromuscular coordination. Shivering ceases below a body temperature of 85° to 90° F (29.4° to 32.2° C). Death is imminent if the core temperature rises to 107° F (41.6° C) or drops to between 77° and 85° F (25° and 29° C).

Apparel for competitors must be geared to the weather. The function of such apparel is to provide a semitropical microclimate for the body and prevent chilling. Such clothing should not restrict movement, should be as lightweight as possible, and should consist of material that will permit the free passage of sweat and body heat that would otherwise accumulate on the skin or the clothing and provide a chilling factor when activity ceases. Clothing should be layered, and outerwear should have zippers for ease of removal. Preliminary to exercise, during activity breaks or rest periods, and at the termination of exercise, a warm-up suit should be worn to prevent chilling. Because a major heat loss can occur from the head and hands, wearing a warm cap and mittens is important. Activity in cold, wet, and windy weather poses some problem, since such weather reduces the insulative values of the clothing worn, and, consequently, the individual may be unable to achieve energy levels equal to the subsequent body heat losses. Runners who wish to continue outdoor work in cold weather should use lightweight insulative clothing and, if breathing cold air seems distressful, should use ski goggles and a ski face mask or should cover the mouth and nose with a free-hanging cloth. Contrary to common belief, the breathing of cold air is not harmful to pulmonary tissues.

Overexposure to cold   Severe overexposure to a cold climate is less common than heat illness; however, it is still a major risk of winter sports, long-distance running in cold weather, and swimming in cold water.[9]

General body cooling   A core temperature that gets below 80° F (26.7° C) leads to unconsciousness. With a rectal temperature of 86.4° F (30.2° C), the athlete displays a slurring of speech, clumsy movement, pupils that respond sluggishly, shallow respiration, and a heartbeat that may be irregular and slow.[1,9] The skin appears pale; the tissue of the lips, around the nose, and underneath the fingernails is a bluish hue (cyanosis). Muscle tonus increases, causing the neck and limbs to become stiff and rigid. Metabolic pH changes also occur, leading to acidosis, liver necrosis, uremia, renal failure, and seizures.

Low temperatures accentuated by wind can pose major problems for athletes.

Cold injuries in sports include:
  Frostnip
  Superficial frostbite
  Deep frostbite
  Chilblains

Severe exposure to cold is a major medical emergency. The first concern is the maintenance of an airway. If the heart has stopped and the athlete's temperature is approximately 84° F (29° C) or less, it may be difficult to reestablish a heart rhythm. External rewarming should take place if the condition ranges from mild to moderate. Emergency rewarming at the site includes immersing the athlete's hands and forearms in water that is between 113 ° and 118° F (45° and 48° C). If the athlete is conscious, a hot drink may help in rewarming. Alcohol of any kind must be avoided because it vasodilates peripheral capillaries. In cases of severe cold exposure, rewarming too rapidly can cause the peripheral capillaries to become dilated, pulling blood and warmth from the core of the body. In a hospital setting, the athlete may be given warm enemas and warm intravenous solutions.

Local body cooling Local cooling of the body can result in tissue damage ranging from superficial to deep. Exposure to a damp, freezing cold causes mild or superficial frostbite (frostnip). In contrast, exposure to dry temperatures well below freezing will more commonly produce a deep freezing type of frostbite.

Prevention The primary preventive measures for local body cooling injuries are obvious but often disregarded. The athlete should wear non-constricting, multilayered clothing, including warm gloves and socks. Because so much heat is lost via an unprotected head, warm headgear is essential in cold climates. Local cold injuries that may be seen in athletes are frostnip, superficial frostbite, deep freezing frostbite, and chilblains.

Frostnip involves ears, nose, cheeks, chin, fingers, and toes. It is commonly seen when there is a high wind, severe cold, or both. The skin initially appears very firm, with cold, painless areas that may peel or blister in 24 to 72 hours. Affected areas can be treated early by firm, sustained pressure of the hand (without rubbing), by blowing hot breath on the spot, or, if the injury is to the fingertips, by placing them in the armpits.

Superficial frostbite involves only the skin and subcutaneous tissue. It appears pale, hard, cold, and waxy. Touching the injured area will reveal a sense of hardness but with yielding of the underlying deeper tissue structures. When rewarming, the superficial frostbite will at first feel numb, then will sting and burn. Later the area may produce blisters and be painful for a number of weeks.

Deep frostbite is a serious injury indicating tissues that are frozen. This is a medical emergency requiring immediate hospitalization. As with frostnip and superficial frostbite, the tissue is initially cold, hard, pale or white, and numb. Rapid rewarming is required, including hot drinks, heating pads, or hot water bottles that are 100° to 110° F (38° to 43° C). On rewarming, the tissue will become blotchy-red, swollen, and extremely painful. Later the injury may become gangrenous, causing a loss of tissue.

Chilblains result from prolonged and constant exposure to cold for many hours. In time there is skin redness, swelling, tingling, and pain in the toes and fingers. This adverse response is caused by problems of peripheral circulation and can be avoided by preventing further cold exposure.

Rewarming methods for cold stress Rewarming methods are usually listed under the headings of passive rewarming and active external rewarming.[15]

1. Passive rewarming

a. Remove from environmental exposure (e.g., wind, cold, etc.).
b. Replace wet clothing with dry.
c. Cover body with insulating material (e.g., blanket).
2. Active external rewarming
a. Gradually rewarm body part by immersion in heated water not to exceed 110° F (43° C).
b. Do not rub affected area.

SUMMARY

Recently negligence suits have increased in frequency and amount of damage awarded. The law assumes that a coach or trainer will act in a reasonable and prudent manner. One who does not is considered negligent.

Recognizing vital signs is essential in carrying out emergency care. Pulse rate, respiration, temperature, skin color, pupil size, state of consciousness, the ability to move, abnormal nerve stimulation or no stimulation, and blood pressure must be noted in emergency situations.

When evaluating conscious athletes, check for breathing, pulse rate, external bleeding, and shock. When evaluating the unconscious athlete, serious cervical injury should always be suspected.

The mnemonic of CPR is ABC: A—airway opened; B—breathing restored; C—circulation restored. When using one rescuer the ratio of compressions to breaths is 15:2 with 80-100 compressions per minute. When using two rescuers the ratio of compressions to breaths is 5:1 with 80-100 compressions per minute.

There are two steps for relieving an obstructed airway. They include the Heimlich maneuver, and a finger sweep of the throat.

ICE-R is the acronym for ice, compression, elevation, and rest. This procedure is used for acute musculoskeletal injuries. Cold constricts blood vessels, compression decreases hemorrhage and hematoma formation, and elevation reduces bleeding in the area of the injury.

Any suspected fracture should be immobilized by splinting. The clear plastic, inflatable splint is very popular in sports medicine. It affords compression and allows a clear view for x-ray.

A suspected spinal fracture requires extreme care in transporting, which should be accomplished by using a spine board. The athlete should be moved onto the spine board like a "log," meaning, the head and neck are kept in alignment with the long axis of the body.

All major athletic injuries, such as fractures, should be associated with shock. Shock occurs when there is a diminished amount of fluid available to the circulatory system.

Heat illness is a major problem in sports activities such as football and distance running. The primary indirect cause of death in football is heatstroke.

Cold weather is another environmental stressor that can adversely affect an athlete. With the addition of wind and cold the problems could be critical to the athlete's performance and health.

REVIEW QUESTIONS AND CLASS ACTIVITIES

1. What are the vital signs related to: pulse, respiration, temperature, skin color, pupils, state of consciousness, movement, abnormal nerve stimulation, and blood pressure?

2. What procedures must be followed in the emergency evaluation of the conscious athlete?

3. What procedures must be followed in the emergency evaluation of the unconscious athlete?

4. Identify the ABCs of CPR.

5. How can throat obstruction be remedied?

6. List the steps in providing emergency care for musculoskeletal injuries.

7. Describe how an athlete with a suspected cervical injury should be moved.

8. What steps should be taken in arterial hemorrhage?

9. How must shock be treated?

10. Compare the symptoms of heat exhaustion and heatstroke.

11. Practice and demonstrate proficiency in the following emergency skills:
    a. Recognize vital signs — practice taking pulse and respiration.
    b. Make a primary and secondary emergency evaluation of the conscious athlete.
    c. Evaluate the unconscious athlete.
    d. Perform CPR.
    e. Render first aid to the choking victim.
    f. Provide emergency care to acute musculoskeletal injuries, including:
       (1) ICE-R
       (2) The use of different types of splints
    g. Apply the spine board and transport a suspected lower spine and neck injury victim.
    h. Treat for shock from an acute musculoskeletal injury.
    i. Treat for heat exhaustion.
    j. Treat for suspected frostbite.

REFERENCES

1. Appenzeller, O., and Atkinson, R.: Temperature regulation and sports. In Appenzeller, O., and Atkinson, R. (editors): Sports medicine, Baltimore, 1981, Urban & Schwarzenberg, Inc.

2. Arnheim, D.D.: Modern principles of athletic training, ed. 6, St. Louis, 1985, Times Mirror/Mosby College Publishing.

3. Basic guidelines for beating the heart, The First Aider, p. 6, Summer 1985, Cramer Products, Inc.

4. Borkowski, R.P.: Lawsuit less likely if safety comes first, The First Aider, p. 11, October 1985, Cramer Products, Inc.

5. Borkowski, R.P.: Coaches and the courts, The First Aider, pp. 1, 4, Summer 1985, Cramer Products, Inc.

6. Drowatzky, J.N.: Legal duties and liability in athletic training, Ath. Train., 20:11, Spring 1985.

7. Emergency care and transportation of the sick and injured, Chicago, 1971, The Committee on Injuries, American Academy of Orthopaedic Surgeons.

8. Emergency care and transportation of the sick and injured, ed. 2, Chicago, 1977, American Academy of Orthopaedic Surgeons.

9. Gutmann, L.: Temperature-related problems in athletic and recreational activities. In Joynt, R.J. (editor): Seminars in neurology, vol. 1, no. 4, p. 242, 1981.

10. Hafen, B.Q.: First aid for health emergencies, ed. 2, St. Paul, Minn., 1981, West Publishing Co.

11. Hanson, P.G.: Heat injury to runners, Phys. Sportsmed. 7:91, 1979.

12. Henderson, J.: Emergency medical guide, ed. 4, New York, 1978, McGraw-Hill Book Co.

13. Knight, K.J.: ICE for immediate care of injuries, Phys. Sportsmed. 10:137, 1982.

14. Murphy, R.J.: Heat illness in the athlete, Am. J. Sports Med. **12**:258, July/August 1984.

15. Parcel, G.S.: Basic emergency care, ed. 3, St. Louis, 1986, Times Mirror/ Mosby College Publishing.

16. Standards and guidelines for cardiopulmonary resuscitation (CPR) and emergency cardiac care (ECC), J.A.M.A. **255**:2841-3044, 1986.

17. Stephenson, H.E., Jr. (editor): Immediate care of the acutely ill and injured, ed. 2, St. Louis, 1978, The C.V. Mosby Co.

18. Stone, B.: Dehydration and its effects upon endurance activity, Ath. J. **14**:64, 1982.

19. Wells, C.L.: Sexual differences in heat stress response, Phys. Sportsmed. **5**:78, 1977.

20. Wilkerson, G.B.: External compression for controlling traumatic edema, Phys. Sportsmed. **13**:96, June 1985.

ANNOTATED BIBLIOGRAPHY

Appenzeller, H. (editor): Sports and law, Charlottesville, Va., 1985, The Michie Co.
  Presents a number of topics relevant to the care and prevention of athletic injuries. Of particular relevance are: Chapter 1, "Sports Litigation—A Perspective"; 1.3, "Athletic Trainer" (by R. Kenan and P. Stokes); 1.5, "Coach" (by R. Borkowski); Chapter 2, "Administrative Issues"; 2.1, "Implications of the Seattle Decision" (by J. Adams); Chapter 3, "Coaching Issues"; and Chapter 5, "Sports Medicine Issues"; 5.1, "The Legal Status of the Athletic Trainer" (by B. Baker).

Bangs, C.C.: Cold injuries. In Strauss, R.H. (editor): Sports medicine, Philadelphia, 1984, W.B. Saunders Co.
  Discusses thermal regulations of heat production and heat loss. Also discusses the major problems of hypothermia, first aid, and hospital treatment.

Parcel, G.S.: Basic emergency care of the sick and injured, ed. 3, St. Louis, 1986, Times Mirror/Mosby College Publishing.
  Presents a wide coverage on the area of emergency. Of special interest are: Chapter 2, "Legal Considerations Involved in Emergency Care by Nonmedical Personnel" (by M.D. Helmet and M.E. Mackert) and Section III, Trauma Emergencies."

Sutton, J.R.: Heat illness. In Strauss, R.H. (editor): Sports medicine, Philadelphia, 1984, W.B. Saunders Co.
  Describes heat exhaustion, heat syncope, and heat stroke in detail. Also covers other components of environmental heat stress such as humidity, air movement, and radiant heat.

Part Two | # SPORTS INJURY CAUSATION, RESPONSE, AND MANAGEMENT

Part Two provides the introductory student with an understanding of how the body is susceptible to traumatic musculoskeletal injuries; how injuries are classified, recognized and evaluated; the tissue response to injury; and the foundation of therapy and rehabilitation.

PHYSICAL SUSCEPTIBILITY AND MECHANISMS OF SPORTS INJURIES

When you finish this chapter, you will be able to:

Identify the major structural characteristics of the body that predispose it to sports injuries

Specify the characteristics of soft tissue when mechanical stresses are applied

Designate the influences of faulty posture on the athlete's susceptibility to injury

Identify the relationship of faulty mechanics to sustaining microtraumas

Explain the relationship of postural malalignments to sustaining sports injuries

Explain why certain exercise movements should be avoided because of their injury-producing potential

The human body as a machine, using bony levers, is less than 25% efficient. In addition, more than one-half of the body's total weight is located in the upper part of the body and is supported by rather narrow bones.

Although the bones of the body are not primarily designed to withstand shock, the musculature does serve as a shock absorber by absorbing impact forces and distributing them over a relatively large area (Fig. 6-1). Areas with little or no overlying musculature, such as the shin and skull, have no such protection.

The fact that humans are posturally in an upright position makes them prone to various kinds of conditions. For example, there is greater strain on the lumbar vertebral curve due to the weight of the abdominal viscera in the bipedal position as opposed to the quadruped position. The upright position also places a great deal of stress on the small surface area that the two feet provide.

The head, weighing close to 14 pounds, is balanced almost precariously on top of seven small cervical vertebrae, which are sustained mainly by ligaments and muscles. The neck is particularly vulnerable to injury by excessive hyperflexion and hyperextension.

Mechanical causes of sports injuries to the musculoskeletal system may have hereditary, congenital, or acquired defects that may predispose an athlete to a specific type of injury. Defects in the anatomical structure or in a particular body build also may make an athlete prone to a particular injury.

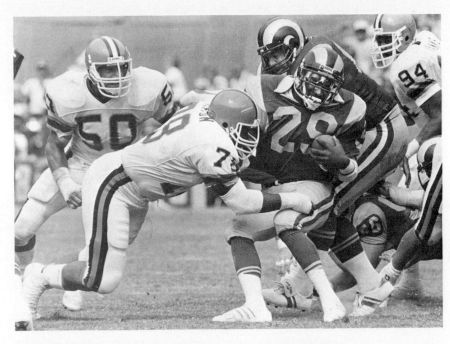

Figure 6-1

Although bones of the body are not primarily designed to withstand shock, the muscles do serve to absorb impact forces and distribute them over a relatively large area.

TISSUE AND BODY STRUCTURAL CHARACTERISTICS

Understanding the body's ability to resist sports injuries requires some knowledge of tissue and structural characteristics.

Soft Tissues

Excessive force applied to soft tissue will cause injury. The coach or trainer should have a clear understanding of the types of forces to which athletes are subjected. The three forces particularly significant to soft tissues are compression, tension, and shear[8] (Fig. 6-2). *Compression* is a force that, with enough energy, crushes tissue. Soft tissue can withstand and absorb compressional forces; however, when the force is excessive and can no longer be absorbed, a contusion, or bruise, occurs. Tissue crushing results in hemorrhage, muscle fiber disruption, and spasm. *Tension* is the force that pulls and extends tissue. *Shear* is a force that moves across the parallel organization of connective tissue fibers. Tendons and ligaments are designed to effectively withstand tension forces but do not resist shear or compressional forces well. Excessive compressional forces can cause contusions, and excessive tension or shear forces can result in injuries such as sprains (ligaments), or strains (musculotendinous units) of varying degrees of severity.

Major forces that can injure soft tissue are compression, tension, and shear.

Tendons

Basically, a muscle tendon attaches a muscle to a bone and concentrates a pulley force in a limited area. A tendon is commonly twice the strength of the muscle it serves. When a force is great enough to tear tendinous tissue the tear usually occurs at the muscle belly, musculotendinous junction, or bony attachment.[2] A constant, abnormal, prolonged tension on a tendon causes a gradual infiltration of scar tissue into the tendon, weakening it over a period of time.[1]

Ligaments and Capsules

Ligaments maintain anatomical integrity and structural alignment. Attaching bone to bone, ligaments are strongest in their middle and weakest at their ends.[1] When an intact ligament is traumatically stretched, the injury often produces an avulsion-type fracture or tear at the ends rather than in the middle.

Constant compression or
tension will cause ligaments to
deteriorate; intermittent
compression and tension will
increase strength and growth.

Constant compression or tension will cause ligaments to deteriorate, whereas intermittent compression and tension increase strength and growth, especially at the bony attachment.[1,7] Chronic inflammation of ligamentous, capsular, and **fascial** tissue causes a shrinkage of collagen fibers; therefore, repeated microtraumas over time make capsules and ligaments highly susceptible to major acute injuries.

Another unique characteristic of ligaments and capsules is that they generally heal slowly due to a poor blood supply. However, nerve innervation is plentiful and responds to injury with a high degree of pain.[5]

fascia
A thin layer of connective
tissue for supporting internal
organs or muscles

Joints

A freely moving (diarthrodial) joint is a union of two bones. Its movement depends on inherent structures, including shape, ligamentous restraint, atmospheric pressure created by the articular surfaces, the presence of an articular disk, and the muscles acting on it.[1] Table 6-1 indicates the relative strengths of selected joints in terms of sports participation.

Major Joints

Spine The spine, or vertebral column, consists of 26 articulated bone segments called vertebrae, which permit forward flexion, backward extension, lateral flexion, and rotation of the trunk. To achieve this considerable variety of movement, use is made of the intervertebral disks and a number of opposing curves in the anteroposterior plane. These two features permit flexi-

Figure 6-2

Mechanical forces that can
injure soft tissue.
A, Compression. **B**, Tension.
C, Shear.

TABLE 6-1

General strength grades in selected joints

Joint	Skeleton	Ligaments	Muscles
Ankle	Strong	Moderate	Weak
Knee	Weak	Moderate	Strong
Hip	Strong	Strong	Strong
Lumbosacral	Weak	Strong	Moderate
Lumbar vertebrae	Strong	Strong	Moderate
Thoracic vertebrae	Strong	Strong	Moderate
Cervical vertebrae	Weak	Moderate	Strong
Sternoclavicular	Weak	Weak	Weak
Acromioclavicular	Weak	Moderate	Weak
Glenohumeral	Weak	Moderate	Moderate
Elbow	Moderate	Strong	Strong
Wrist	Weak	Moderate	Moderate
Phalanges (toes and fingers)	Weak	Moderate	Moderate

bility and resilience. In addition to permitting a wide range of movement, the spine serves as a place of support and attachment for the ribs and muscles and for the pelvis and head. It also serves as a shock absorber, as a means of distributing body weight, and as a factor in locomotion (Fig. 6-3).

The pelvic girdle consists of three fused boxes: the ilium, ischium, and pubis. The pelvis articulates with the spine at the sacroiliac joint and is, to a limited degree, an extension of the spinal column. The only observable pelvic girdle movements are those of anterior and posterior tilt.

The pelvis plays an important role in the prevention of injuries to the spine. In sports in which there is a lifting action, force is conveyed to the pelvis, the abdominal muscles, and the thoracic spine, reducing the stress on the lumbosacral joint by as much as 30% and that on the lower thoracic spine by as much as 50%. Abdominal strength is essential to prevent lumbosacral injuries.

Shoulder complex The shoulder complex is composed of numerous joints of which the glenohumeral, acromioclavicular, and sternoclavicular can sustain sports injuries. The shoulder complex plays a critical role in many sports and is subject to many soft tissue and joint injuries. In many sports the other parts of the body play a somewhat secondary role. It is quite possible to identify certain derangements of the shoulder joint as being peculiar to a particular sport (Fig. 6-4).

The joints of the shoulder maintain their integrity through the ligamentous structures rather than through bony structures, making them susceptible to severe sprains and dislocations. Dislocations of the shoulder joint occur when the arm is forced backward well beyond its normal range in the position

Abdominal strength is essential to prevent lumbosacral injuries.

Figure 6-3

The spine and pelvis may be at risk in many collision and contact-type sports.

Figure 6-4

Wrestling severely stresses the
shoulder and other major joints.

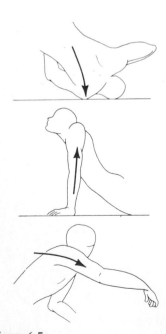

Figure 6-5

Common mechanisms of
shoulder injuries.

of throwing, forcing the proximal end of the humerus out of the shallow
shoulder socket and displacing it to a position under the coracoid process of
the scapula (Fig. 6-5).

Many shoulder injuries are caused by a descending force or impact that
drives the acromion downward and away from the clavicle, causing an acromioclavicular separation or dislocation. This is a somewhat common injury. In football it occurs when the shoulder is used as a driving force or when
the shoulder forcefully contacts the ground while it is in a position of forward
rotation. Another common mechanism of injury to the shoulder is falling on
the outstretched arm.

Soft tissue injuries can result from the repetitious dynamic contraction of
the muscle, as in pitching. The repeated microtraumas culminate in a chronic
injury. A sudden, all-out contraction of a muscle wherein the antagonist muscles fail to control the effort is another cause. Direct, forceful impact to the
muscle, as from a blow, is still another cause of soft tissue injury.

Elbow joint   The elbow is a complex hinge joint. Forcible extension, forcible hyperextension, and impact forces are the principle causes of injury to
this joint. Muscle strains resulting from forcible hyperextension are quite
common, as are capsular strains. They usually result either from a fall in
which the athlete lands on an extended and locked elbow joint or when the
arm and elbow are in an extended, supportive position and an impact force is
directed on the posterior aspect of the arm in the vicinity of the elbow joint.
Throwing, in which the arm is forcefully extended, can result in a painful
traumatic elbow injury (Fig. 6-6).

Wrist joint   The wrist joint offers a variety of movements. The freedom
of action of the wrist joint makes this area the most mobile of the body. Injuries to the wrist are common; most appear to be the result of force applied
when the wrist is in a hyperextended position, thus instituting a severe compression (Fig. 6-7).

Figure 6-6

Typical mechanism of an elbow injury.

Figure 6-7

Common mechanisms of wrist injuries.

Wrist injuries are common to many sports but achieve a considerable incidence and significance in wrestling and gymnastics. Compression injuries are fairly commonplace in the tumbling aspect of free exercise and long horse vault. In these activities speed is added to mass to increase the resultant force thrust against the hyperextended wrist. Rotary movements, as performed in tumbling, also create an additional hazard since a rotational shearing action is exerted on the hyperextended wrist if the hand is improperly placed. Severe sprains or fractures are usually the result.

Hip joint   The hip joint is a freely movable joint. The head of the femur is the main weight-bearing point of the body and, as such, is subjected to much force. Most hip injuries, which are relatively uncommon, occur when the athlete attempts a sudden change of direction and consequently subjects the neck of the femur to considerable torque. On occasion injuries occur because the joint is forced beyond the limits of its range of motion (Fig. 6-8).

Knee joint and related structures   The knee, a hinge joint, permits free flexion and extension, and in some instances a slight amount of rotation of the tibia. Although formed by the articulation of only two bones, the tibia and the femur, this is not only an exceedingly complex joint but also the largest articulation in the body.

The stress demands made on the knee joint in most sports are quite severe (Figs. 6-9 and 6-10). Because of the structure of the knee joint, ligamentous injuries are especially common despite the joint reinforcements. The knee is particularly vulnerable to forces delivered either laterally or medially when the joint is in a position of extension. Often the ligaments on the side of the knee, called *collateral ligaments*, are sprained or completely torn—the

Figure 6-8

Common mechanism of hip injuries.

most frequently injured being the medial collateral. This injury may occur as an isolated trauma. More commonly, however, it is associated with tears of the internal ligaments, called the *anterior* and *posterior cruciate ligaments*, and with injury to either or both of the cartilages (menisci) (Fig. 6-11). Such injury may involve various combinations. The menisci may be slit, severed, torn, avulsed, or broken into two or more pieces as the result of abnormal forces applied to the joint.

Repeated knee joint injuries can eventually lead to chronic problems. Such conditions are often reflected in muscle atrophy, constant pain, swelling, and a complaint of "catching" or "giving way."

The patella (kneecap) and related structures can present many problems in sports activities. The patella can be acutely fractured or dislocated. A common chronic condition is chondromalacia, a degeneration of the articular surface that leads to softening and the possibility of a degenerative arthritis. Another problem related to the patella and extensor mechanism is Osgood-Schlatter disease, a condition of the growth area of the tibial tubercle and a patellar or quadricep tendinitis that occurs from jumping or kicking.

Severe twisting of the knee is often encountered, particularly in those sports for which cleated shoes are worn. The amount of torque engendered

Figure 6-9

The demands on knee joints in football are severe.

Figure 6-10

Volleyball stresses the hands and knees.

when the foot is firmly fixed and the rest of the body continues to rotate longitudinally is of considerable magnitude; consequently, the knee ligaments are subjected to tremendous stress, especially the anterior cruciate ligament, and are frequently sprained. In those ball sports involving running and changes of direction as evasive maneuvers, cutting plays an important part and frequently provides the mechanism of injury to the knee and occasionally the ankle (Fig. 6-12).

Ankle joint The ankle joint is a freely movable hinge joint formed by the tibia and fibula articulating with the talus. The lower leg bones and ankle joint, comprised of the tibia and fibula, are strengthened by the interosseous membrane between the two bones and a complex of ligaments. These ligaments include the anterior and posterior tibiofibular and talofibular, deltoid, and interosseous ligaments. All these, together with the capsule that surrounds the joint, ensure its integrity. The strength of the joints is further augmented by the tendons of the long muscles of the lower leg, a number of

Figure 6-11

Mechanisms of knee sprains. Arrow in each case indicates direction of applied force.

Figure 6-12

Soccer places great stress on the knees and ankles.

which traverse the joint. The ankle joint has a range of motion from 75 to 80 degrees, moving from plantar flexion to dorsiflexion. The foot has about 50 to 70 degrees of movement from inversion to eversion, occurring at the subtalar and transverse tarsal articulations.

Sprains occur most often to the ankles and knees. Because of the inadequate support supplied by the muscles and ligaments, the ankle joint suffers frequent and often severe injury (Fig. 6-13).

Bone Structural Characteristics and Susceptibility to Fracturing

The student of athletic training should have some understanding of the long bone susceptibility to fracture. The skeleton varies in composition and structure, which affects its susceptibility to sports injury. Bones differ according to their type, location, and makeup. The type of bone may be designed for full body support, such as the tibia, or for dexterity and fine movements, such as the radius or ulna. Long bones are not uniform; they have different regions along their length that respond uniquely to stress.

Although long bones can bend slightly they are generally brittle and are poor shock absorbers. As tension is increased in a long bone it also becomes more brittle.

Many factors of bone structure affect its strength. Anatomical strength or weakness can be affected by a bone's shape and its changes in shape or direc-

Long bones are not uniform; they have different regions along their length that respond uniquely to stress.

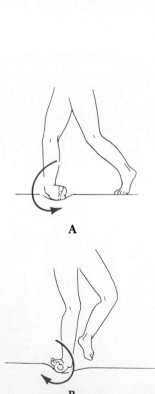

Figure 6-13

A and **B**, Common mechanisms of ankle injuries. **C**, Basketball produces a high number of serious ankle injuries.

tion. A hollow cylinder is one of the strongest structures for resisting both bending and twisting as compared to a solid rod that has much less resistance to such forces[3] (Fig. 6-14).

Stress forces become concentrated where a long bone suddenly changes shape and direction. Long bones that change shape gradually are less prone to injury than those that change suddenly. The clavicle, for example, is prone to fracture because it changes from round to flat at the same time that it changes direction.

Long bones can be stressed or loaded to fail by *tension, compression, bending,* and *twisting* (torsion). These forces, either singularly or in combination, can cause a variety of fractures. For example, spiral fractures are caused by twisting, whereas oblique fractures are caused by the combined forces of axial compression, bending, and torsion. Transverse fractures occur by bending.

Long bones can be stressed by tension, compression, bending, and twisting (torsion).

POSTURAL DEVIATIONS AND INJURY POTENTIAL

Postural deviations are often a primary source of injuries caused by either unilateral asymmetries, bone anomalies, abnormal skeletal alignments, or poor mechanics of movement. Many sports activities are unilateral, thus leading to considerable overdevelopment of a body segment. This resulting imbalance is manifested by a postural deviation as the body seeks to reestablish itself in relation to its center of gravity. Such imbalances may be a cause of injury.[4] For example, a consistent pattern of injury relationship to asymmetries within the pelvis and legs (short leg syndrome) has shown these to be factors in knee injury.[6] Unfortunately, not much in the form of remedial work is usually done; as a result, an injury often becomes chronic—sometimes to the point that continued participation in a sport must be halted. When possible, faulty postural conditions should be treated through proper exercise, working under

Postural deviations are often a primary source of injuries.

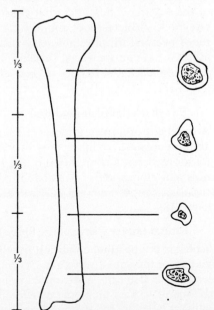

Figure 6-14

Anatomical strengths or weaknesses of a long bone can be affected by its shape, changes in direction, and hollowness.

the direction of an orthopedist or other qualified medical personnel. Remedial work of this type can complement the training program and in most instances may assist principally in maintaining sufficient bilateral development to minimize the more obvious undesirable effects of intensive unilateral development. Development of the muscles that counteract the actions of the prime moving muscles will reinforce and establish stability and assist in the development and maintenance of good muscular balance. A number of postural conditions offer genuine hazards to athletes by making them exceedingly prone to specific injuries.

Common Postural Problems

There are a number of postural problems that are commonly seen in athletes. These are knock-knees (genu valgum), bowlegs (genu varum), round back (kyphosis), swayback (lumbar lordosis), and lateral rotary curving deviation of the spine (scoliosis).

Knock-knees (Genu Valgum)

Knock-knees is an orthopedic disorder whereby the knee joint angles inward causing the body weight to be borne principally on the medial aspects of the articulating surfaces. The knee in this position is unstable and prone to injury (Fig. 6-15).

Bowlegs (Genu Varum)

Bowlegs are the opposite of knock-knees. In this situation extra stress is placed on the knee's lateral ligaments (Fig. 6-16).

Round Back (Kyphosis)

Round back is an accentuation of the thoracic spine's posterior curvature. This postural condition is often associated with a forward head, a winging out of the scapula bones, and a flat chest. It is also commonly combined with a swayback. Athletes with round backs typically have overly strong but shortened pectoral muscles and weaker upper back and shoulder muscles. Such athletes have an increased susceptibility, depending upon their sport, to anterior shoulder dislocation and muscle strain in the anterior shoulder region (Fig. 6-17).

Swayback (Lumbar Lordosis)

A swayback or lumbar lordosis refers to an accentuation of the lumbar spine's anterior curvature. This creates an abnormal tightening of the lower back's extensor muscles, a contraction of the low back fascia, and a subsequent weakness and elongation of the abdominal muscles. Athletes with this postural malalignment are subject to low back muscle strains and ligament sprains (Fig. 6-18).

Lateral Rotary Curve of the Spine (Scoliosis)

Scoliosis is a postural condition in which there is a rotary, lateral, curving deviation of the spinal vertebrae. Sports that are unilateral can cause this problem, but it also can be attributed to poor habits or structural weaknesses. As the result of this problem muscle and bone become asymmetric. Athletes with scoliosis are more prone to injury (Fig. 6-19).

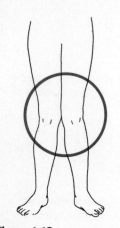

Figure 6-15

Genu valgum, knock-knees.

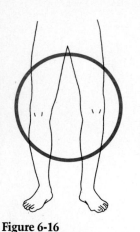

Figure 6-16

Genu varum, bowlegs.

ABNORMAL REPETITIVE STRESS AND MICROTRAUMAS

The problem of reinjury is a serious one in sports. Less severe injuries tend to occur and recur with increasing frequency and severity. This is usually the result of neglect or of inadequate treatment in terms of reconditioning.

There has always been an unfortunate tendency for many athletes to participate while hurt or before they have adequately recovered from an injury, thus exposing the condition to reinjury. This occurs in the mistaken belief that displaying fortitude in the presence of pain is traditionally not only the thing to do but also is heroic. Indeed, this is a misconception. Players who expose themselves to reinjury in this fashion do a disservice to themselves and to the team.

Pain tolerance is an individual matter, since no two people respond to pain in the same way. Some possess a very high tolerance, whereas others have a very low tolerance. The athlete who possesses a high tolerance will usually continue participation when injured or before completely recovered from a previous injury, thus increasing the chances for a reinjury perhaps more severe than the initial trauma. Many sports are predicated on violent physical contact, and a participant who is not up to par is almost certain to sustain additional injury.

Before an injured athlete is permitted to reenter training or competition a number of factors must be considered: the nature of the injury, the type of activity to be engaged in, the inherent risks, the age of the individual, and the personality of the athlete.

Injuries as a result of abnormal and repetitive stress that cause microtraumas fall into a class with certain identifiable syndromes. Such stress injuries frequently result in either limitation or curtailment of sports performance. Most of these injuries in athletes are directly related to the dynamics of running, throwing, or jumping. The injuries may result from constant and repetitive stresses placed on bones, joints, or soft tissues; from forcing a joint into an extreme range of motion; or from prolonged strenuous activity. Some of the injuries falling into this category may be relatively minor; still, they can prove to be quite disabling.

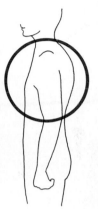

Figure 6-17

Kyphosis.

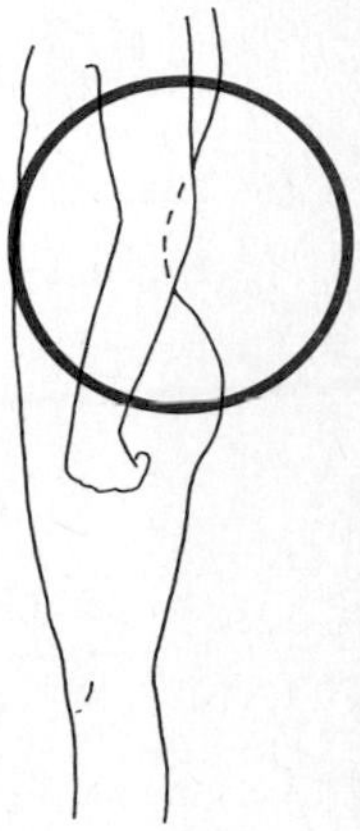

Figure 6-18

Lumbar lordosis.

SUMMARY

The human body, due to its mechanical inefficiency, may be prone to sports injuries. Added to this is the unique factor of functioning in the upright position.

Based on its use of levers the human body as a machine is less than 25% efficient. Added to this is the fact that humans basically function in a relatively unstable upright position making them more prone to sports injuries.

Both soft tissue and hard, bony tissues are subject to mechanical forces that can cause injury. Compression, tension, and shearing forces can adversely affect soft tissue; while tension compression, bending, and torsion can cause bone fractures.

A freely moving (diarthrodial) joint is the result of the union of two bones. This movement depends on inherent structures such as shape, ligamentous restraint, atmospheric pressure created by the articular surfaces, the presence of an articular disk, and the muscles that act on it.

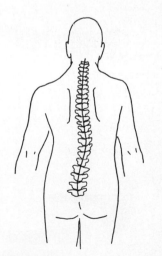

Figure 6-19

Scoliosis.

Text continued on p. 140.

Figure 6-20

Full squats.

Figure 6-21

Knee sitting.

Figure 6-22

Double leg lifts.

Figure 6-23

Straight-leg sit-ups.

Besides the numerous factors already discussed that make athletes susceptible to injury, many types of exercises currently in vogue should be avoided.

Full Squats

Exercises employing the full squat, especially involving heavy resistance, should not be performed. Engaging in a full squat places great strain on the cruciate ligaments that provide internal knee stability. Substituting either the quarter squat or half squat with the heels placed on a lift of 1 or 2 inches offers a safer alternative to the full squat (Fig. 6-20).

Knee Sitting

Knee sitting, like full squats, should be avoided, especially in those individuals who have heavy legs. Sitting on the lower legs may adversely open the knee joint, thereby stretching ligaments and producing joint instability. This position particularly should be avoided by those athletes having a history of knee injury (Fig. 6-21).

Double Leg Lifts

The double leg raise while in a long lying position can lead to serious low back injury or strain. This is particularly true for the athlete who has heavy legs or weak lower abdominal muscles. Lifting two straightened legs together can create an adverse tension in the iliopsoas muscles, thereby pulling the lumbar spine into an abnormal curve. This may be avoided *only* if the low back can be maintained in a flattened position throughout the movement (Fig. 6-22).

Straight-leg Sit-ups

Straight-leg sit-ups, like double leg lifts, should not be performed. These seriously strain the lower back by abnormally contracting hip flexors, primarily the iliopsoas muscles (Fig. 6-23).

Hands Behind the Neck Sit-ups

Sit-ups with the hands behind the neck should be avoided. In this position, the cervical spine can be adversely stressed (Fig. 6-24).

Head Bridge

Bridging up so that the weight of the trunk is supported on the top of the head can seriously compress the cervical vertebrae. Modified bridging, however, in which pressure is applied to the back of the head may be safe in selected situations (Fig. 6-25).

Back Hyperextension

Performing back hyperextensions can be dangerous. Such movements can abnormally compress the lumbar vertebrae and cause injury. A protective rule of thumb is not to arch the back more than raising the chest and head while keeping the abdomen in contact with the surface (Fig. 6-26).

Hurdler's Stretch

A recent addition to the list of contraindicated exercises is the hurdler's stretch. The position of the back legs places abnormal stress on the medial collateral ligament of the knee and should be avoided (Fig. 6-27).

Figure 6-24
Hands behind the neck sit-ups.

Figure 6-25
Head bridge.

Figure 6-26
Back hyperextension.

Figure 6-27
Hurdler's stretch.

The major freely movable joints of the body can be sprained or partially or completely dislocated while engaging in sports activities. The knee and ankle have very high incidences of such injuries.

Long bones, in terms of fracture, have relative strength based on their shape and whether or not they change direction. The clavicle is a good example of a bone prone to fracture because it changes from round to flat at the same time that it changes direction. The straight, round, hollow bone is a very strong structure. Although bones can bend slightly, they are brittle and are poor shock absorbers.

Postural deviations are often a primary source of injuries caused by either unilateral asymmetries, bone anomalies, abnormal skeletal alignments, or poor mechanics of movement. Postural deviations can lead to acute or overuse sports injuries. It is thought that correcting posture imbalances can help to prevent injury.

Most abnormal and repetitive stresses that produce microtraumas are related to the dynamics of running, throwing, or jumping. Injuries may stem from the constant stresses placed on bones, joints, or soft tissues.

A major problem in sports is one of reinjury. Less severe injuries tend to occur and recur with increasing frequency and severity. The tendency for athletes to play while hurt must be stopped.

One area of injury prevention that coaches can directly control is the athlete's avoidance of contraindicated exercises. Exercises to avoid are full squats, knee sitting, double leg lifts, straight-leg sit-ups, head bridges, back hyperextension, and the hurdler's stretch.

Contraindicated exercises in sports include:
Full squats
Knee sitting
Double leg lifts
Straight-leg sit-ups
Hands behind the neck sit-ups
Head bridge
Back hyperextension
Hurdler's stretch

REVIEW QUESTIONS AND CLASS ACTIVITIES

1. Is there a relationship between the body's mechanical inefficiency and sports injuries? Explain.
2. What mechanical forces injure soft tissue and bone?
3. Where do tendons normally tear?
4. What forces gradually weaken ligaments?
5. Why do ligaments heal slowly?
6. Discuss the susceptibility of the following joints to sports injuries: spine, shoulder complex, elbow, wrist, hip, knee, and ankle.
7. What types of forces can fracture a long bone?
8. There are a number of structural characteristics that make a long bone either strong or weak. Name them.
9. How may postural deviations be associated with sports injuries?
10. Discuss how microtraumas can occur.
11. Why are certain exercises injury producing?

REFERENCES

1. Cailliet, R.: Soft tissue pain and disability, Philadelphia, 1977, F.A. Davis Co.
2. Ciulo, J.V., and Zarins, B.: Biomechanics of the musculotendinous unit: relation to athletic performance and injury, Symposium on Olympic sports medicine, Clinics in sports medicine, vol. 2, p. 871, Philadelphia, 1982, W.B. Saunders Co.
3. Gozna, E.R.: Biomechanics of long bone injuries. In Gozna, E.R., and Harrington, I.J. (editors): Biomechanics of musculoskeletal injury, Baltimore, 1982, The Williams & Wilkins Co.
4. Grace, T.G.: Muscle imbalance and extremity injury, Sports Med., **2**:77, 1985.
5. Harrington, I.J.: Biomechanics of joint injuries. In Gozna, E.R., and Har-

rington, I.J., (editors): Biomechanics of musculoskeletal injury, Baltimore, 1982, The Williams & Wilkins Co.

6. Klein, J.: Developmental asymmetry of the weight-bearing skeleton and its implication on knee injury. In Scriber, K., and Burke, E.J. (editors): Relevant topics in athletic training, Ithaca, N.Y., 1978, Mouvement Publications.

7. Kotwick, J.E.: Biomechanics of the foot and ankle, Symposium on ankle and foot problems in the athlete, Clinics in sports medicine, vol. 1, p. 819, Philadelphia, 1981, W.B. Saunders Co.

8. Zarin, B.: Soft tissue and repair— biomechanical aspects, Int. J. Sports Med. (suppl. 1) 3:9, 1982.

ANNOTATED BIBLIOGRAPHY

Booher, J.M., and Thibodeau, G.A.: Athletic injury assessment, St. Louis, 1985, Times Mirror/Mosby College Publishing.

An in-depth study of the recognition and assessment of sports injuries.

Grace, T.G.: Muscle imbalance and extremity injury: a perplexing relationship, Sports Med. 2:77, March/April 1985.

Indicates that the relationship between muscle imbalance and extremity injury is perplexing and obscure. Much more research is needed in this area.

Subotnick, S.I.: The biomechanics of running: implications for the prevention of foot injuries, Sports Med., 2:144, March/April 1985.

Dr. Subotnick, a podiatrist, indicates that it is essential to understand the biomechanics of running in order for overuse injuries to be effectively treated. Good foot balance and biomechanics should be afforded when early signs of overuse injuries occur.

Chapter 7

CLASSIFYING EXPOSED AND UNEXPOSED SPORTS INJURIES

When you finish this chapter, you will be able to:

Categorize and define the major exposed and unexposed sports injuries

Explain the major characteristics of musculoskeletal sports injuries

Causative factors in sports injury[10]
Consequential (due to sports participation)
A. Primary
   1. Extrinsic
      (e.g., human,
      implemental,
      vehicular,
      environmental)
   2. Intrinsic (e.g.,
      instantaneous,
      overuse)
B. Secondary (e.g., early, late)

This chapter classifies and defines common skin and musculoskeletal injuries occurring in sports.

CAUSATIVE FACTORS OF SPORTS INJURIES

A primary injury is one that results directly from the stress imposed by a particular sport (Fig. 7-1). The injury can be externally caused, such as by body contact or by use of a piece of equipment. The use of some implement, such as a racquet or gymnastics equipment, can produce instantaneous trauma or overuse microtrauma from repeated stresses. Another extrinsic cause is through a vehicular accident, such as a motorcycle or racing car.[10] Environmental factors can also produce injury, such as accidents while engaged in mountaineering or water sports.

Intrinsic injuries are those occurring due to stresses created within the athlete. These can be instantaneous or chronically developed over a long period of time.

Secondary problems can arise from an injury, especially if it has not been properly treated initially or if the athlete has been allowed to return to competition too soon. An example of an early secondary problem after injury may be chronic swelling and weakness in a joint, whereas an example of later occurrence is arthritis that has developed in a joint many years after repeated sprains and improper care.

Nonconsequential causative factors refer to injuries or other problems that are not directly related to stress in a specific sport but adversely influence it. Periodic asthma attacks are an example of a nonconsequential causative factor that can adversely affect performance.

Figure 7-1

Falls are primary cause of
injury in athletics.

ACUTE ANATOMICAL FACTORS

Sports injuries also can be described according to the primary structure that
has been affected and the extent of trauma. The most external anatomy is the
skin. When it is wounded, the injury is highly visible. However, injuries affecting muscles, tendons, ligaments, joint capsules, cartilages, and bone are usually unexposed and internal.[2]

Exposed Skin Injuries

Exposed injuries can be classified primarily into five types of skin insults: abrasions, lacerations, avulsions, puncture, and incision wounds. The greatest
problem these conditions present is their vulnerability to infection because of
direct exposure to a contaminant (see Chapter 4, pp. 70-88).

Unexposed Injuries

Unexposed or closed wounds in sports include those internal injuries that do
not penetrate the top layer of skin.[8] Recognizing and caring for these conditions present a definite challenge, since one's actions can mean the difference
between a rapid or a prolonged period of recovery.

    A bruise or contusion is received because of a sudden traumatic blow to
the body. The intensity of a contusion can range from superficial to deep tissue compression and hemorrhage (Fig. 7-2).

    Interrupting the continuity of the circulatory system results in a flow of
blood and other fluids into the surrounding tissues. A blood tumor
(hematoma) is formed by the localization of internal bleeding into a clot,
which becomes encapsulated by a connective tissue membrane. The speed of
healing, as with all soft tissue injuries, depends on the extent of tissue damage and internal bleeding.

    Contusion or the crushing of soft tissue can penetrate to the skeletal
structures, causing a bone bruise. The extent to which an athlete may be hampered by this condition depends on the location of the bruise and the force of
the blow. Typical in cases of severe contusion are the following:

1. The athlete reports being struck a hard blow.
2. The blow causes pain and a transitory loss of function caused by pressure on and shock to the motor and sensory nerves.

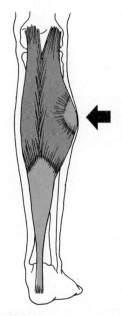

Figure 7-2

A contusion can range from a
superficial to a deep tissue
compression (*arrow*), injuring
cells and causing relative
amounts of hemorrhage.

3. Feeling often reveals a hard area, because of internal hemorrhage.
4. Ecchymosis or tissue discoloration (black and blue) may take place.

Strains

A strain, sometimes referred to as a muscle pull or tear, is a stretch, tear, or rip of a muscle (Fig. 7-3). The cause of muscle strain is often obscure. Most often a strain is produced by an abnormal muscular contraction. The cause of this abnormality has been attributed to many factors. One popular theory suggests that a fault in the reciprocal coordination of muscles takes place. The cause of this fault or incoordination is more or less a mystery. However, among the possible explanations are that it may be related to (1) a mineral imbalance caused by profuse sweating, (2) fatigue metabolites collected in the muscle itself, or (3) a strength imbalance between agonist and antagonist muscles.

A strain may range from a minute separation of connective tissue and muscle fiber to a complete tendinous avulsion or muscle rupture (graded as *first degree [mild], second degree [moderate], or third degree [severe]*). The resulting pathology is similar to that of the contusion or sprain, with capillary or blood vessel hemorrhage. Healing takes place in a similar fashion, with the organization of a **hematoma**, absorption of the hematoma, and finally the formation of a scar. Detection of the injury is accomplished by understanding how the injury occurred and the administration of a muscle stress test to determine the specific locality. The following are signs that a severe strain may have occurred:

1. Snapping sound when the tissue tears
2. Muscle fatigue and spasm before the strain occurred
3. Severe weakness and loss of function
4. A sharp pain immediately on the occurrence of injury
5. Spasmodic muscle contraction of the affected part
6. Extreme point tenderness on palpation
7. An indentation or cavity where tissues have separated or a bump indicating contracted tissue occurring immediately after injury

Continued overstretching of muscle tissue can lead to chronic inflammation. Some areas of the body, such as the elbow region and Achilles tendon, are more predisposed to chronic strain.

Muscle Cramps and Spasms

A cramp is usually a painful involuntary contraction of a skeletal muscle or muscle group. Cramps have been attributed to a lack of salt or other minerals or muscle fatigue. A reflex reaction caused by trauma of the musculoskeletal system is commonly called a *spasm*. The two types of cramps or spasms are the **clonic** type, with alternating voluntary muscular contraction and relaxation in quick succession, and the **tonic** type, with rigid muscle contraction that lasts over a period of time.

Sprains

The sprain, one of the most common and disabling injuries seen in sports, is a traumatic joint twist that results in stretching or totally tearing stabilizing connective tissues (Fig. 7-4). When a joint is forced beyond its normal anatom-

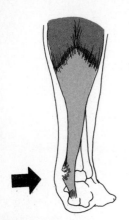

Figure 7-3

A strain can occur to any aspect of the musculotendinous unit. Depending on the amount of force, a strain can stretch or tear muscle fibers (*arrow*) or even avulse a tendon from a bone.

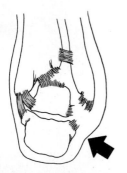

Figure 7-4

A sprain mainly involves ligamentous and capsular tissue (*arrow*); however, tendons also can be secondarily involved. A joint that is forced beyond its anatomical limits can stretch and tear tissue and, on occasion, avulse ligaments from their bony attachments.

ical limits, microscopic and gross pathologies occur. Specifically, there is injury to ligaments, to the articular capsule and synovial membrane, and to the tendons crossing the joint. According to the extent of injury, sprains are graded in three degrees. First degree (mild) indicates stretching of ligaments; second degree (moderate) indicates partial tearing, and third degree (severe) describes a complete severance or rupture of ligaments. Effusion of blood and synovial fluid into the joint cavity produces joint swelling, local temperature increase, pain or point tenderness, and skin discoloration (**ecchymosis**). According to statistics, the joints that are most vulnerable to sprains are the ankles, knees, and shoulders. Sprains occur least often to the wrists and elbows. Since it is often difficult to distinguish between joint sprains and tendon strains, the coach should expect the worst possible condition and manage it accordingly. Repeated joint twisting can eventually result in chronic inflammation, degeneration, and arthritis.

Dislocations

Dislocations are second to fractures in terms of disabling the athlete. The highest incidence of dislocations involves the fingers and, next, the shoulder joint. Dislocations, which result primarily from forces causing the joint to go beyond its normal anatomical limits, are divided into two classes: **subluxations** and **luxations**. Subluxations are partial dislocations in which an incomplete separation between two articulating bones occurs. Luxations are complete dislocations, presenting a total disunion of bone opposition between the articulating surfaces (Fig. 7-5).

　　Several factors are important in recognizing and evaluating dislocations:
1. There is a loss of limb function. The athlete usually complains of having fallen or of having received a severe blow to a particular joint and then suddenly being unable to move that part.
2. Deformity is almost always apparent. Since such deformity can often be obscured by heavy musculature, it is important for the examiner to feel the injured site to determine the loss of normal body contour. Comparison of the injured site with its normal counterpart often reveals distortions.
3. Swelling and point tenderness are immediately present.

　　At times, as with a fracture, x-ray examination is the only absolute diagnostic measure. First-time dislocations or joint separations may result in a rupture of the stabilizing ligamentous and tendinous tissues surrounding the joint and avulsion or pulling away from the bone. Trauma is often of such violence that small chips of bone are torn away with the supporting structures (avulsion fracture), or the force may separate growth epiphyses or cause a com-

Text continued on p. 148

ecchymosis
Black and blue skin coloration
due to hemorrhage

hematoma
A blood tumor

clonic muscle contraction
Alternating involuntary
muscular contraction and
relaxation in quick succession

tonic muscle contraction
Rigid muscle contraction that
lasts over a period of time

subluxation
Partial dislocation

luxation
Complete dislocation

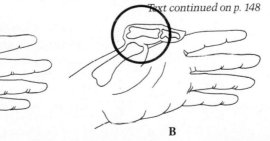

Figure 7-5

A joint that is forced beyond its
anatomical limits can become
partially dislocated (subluxated)
(**A**), or completely dislocated
(luxated) (**B**).

Comminuted fracture

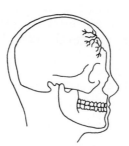

Depressed fracture

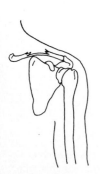

Greenstick fracture

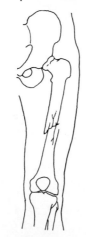

Impacted fracture

Fractures can be a partial or complete interruption in a bone's continuity and can occur without external exposure or can extend through the outer skin (compound fracture), creating a serious external wound. The fracture can be the result of a sudden traumatic event or a repetitive abnormal stress. Fractures are one of the most serious hazards in sports and should be routinely suspected in musculoskeletal injuries.

Comminuted fractures

consist of three or more fragments at the fracture site. These could be caused by a hard blow or a fall in an awkward position. From the physician's point of view, these fractures impose a difficult healing situation because of the displacement of the bone fragments. Soft tissues are often interposed between the fragments, causing incomplete healing. Such cases may need surgical intervention.

Depressed fractures

occur most often in flat bones such as those found in the skull. They are caused by falling and striking the head on a hard, immovable surface or by being hit with a hard object. Such injuries also result in gross pathology of soft areas.

Greenstick fractures

are incomplete breaks in bones that have not completely ossified. They occur most frequently in the convex bone surface, with the concave surface remaining intact. The name is derived from the similarity of the fracture to the break in a green twig taken from a tree.

Impacted fractures

can result from a fall from a height, which causes a long bone to receive, directly on its long axis, a force of such magnitude that the osseous tissue is compressed. This telescopes one part of the bone on the other.

Impacted fractures require immediate splinting by the coach or trainer and traction by the physician to ensure a normal length of the injured limb.

Longitudinal fractures

are those in which the bone splits along its length, often the result of jumping from a height and landing in such a way as to impact force or stress to the long axis.

Oblique fractures

are similar to spiral fractures and occur when one end receives sudden torsion or twisting and the other end is fixed or stabilized.

Serrated fractures,

in which the two bony fragments have a sawtooth, sharp-edged fracture line, are usually caused by a direct blow. Because of the sharp and jagged edges, extensive internal damage, such as the severance of vital blood vessels and nerves, often occurs.

Spiral fractures

have an S-shaped separation. They are fairly common in football and skiing, in which the foot is firmly planted and then the body is suddenly rotated in an opposing direction.

Transverse fractures

occur in a straight line, more or less at right angles to the bone shaft. A direct outside blow usually causes this injury.

Contrecoup fractures

occur on the side opposite to the part where trauma was initiated. Fracture of the skull is at times an example of the contrecoup. An athlete may be hit on one side of the head with such force that the brain and internal structures compress against the opposite side of the skull, causing a fracture.

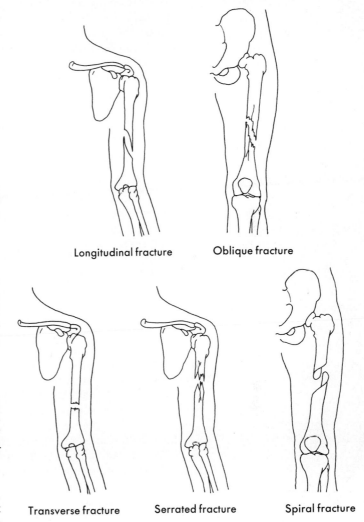

Longitudinal fracture   Oblique fracture

Transverse fracture   Serrated fracture   Spiral fracture

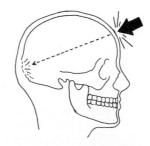

Contrecoup fracture

plete fracture of the neck in long bones. This indicates the importance of obtaining complete and thorough medical attention for first-time dislocations. It has often been said, "Once a dislocation—always a dislocation." In most cases this is true, since once a joint has been either subluxated or completely luxated the connective tissues that bind and hold it in its correct alignment are stretched to such an extent that the joint will be extremely vulnerable to subsequent dislocations. Chronic, recurring dislocations may take place without severe pain, because of the somewhat slack condition of the stabilizing tissues.

A first-time dislocation should
always be considered a possible
fracture.

A first-time dislocation should always be considered and treated as a possible fracture. Before the athlete is taken to a physician, the injury should be properly splinted and supported to prevent any further tissue damage.

Types of Fractures

Fractures can be a partial or complete interruption in a bone's continuity and can occur without external exposure or can extend though the outer skin (compound fracture), creating a serious external wound. The fracture can be the result of a sudden traumatic event or a repetitive abnormal stress. Fractures are one of the most serious hazards in sports and should be routinely suspected in musculoskeletal injuries.

Avulsion fractures   An avulsion fracture is a separation of a bone fragment from the larger bone by the pull of a ligament or tendon. This usually occurs as a result of a sudden, powerful twist or stretching force. An example of this situation is when the foot is suddenly twisted, causing the large medial ligament to avulse bone away from the internal malleolus. A good example of a tendinous avulsion is one that causes the kneecap to become fractured. This occurs when an athlete falls forward while suddenly bending a knee. The stretch of the patellar tendon pulls a portion of the kneecap apart (Fig. 7-6).

Signs of acute fractures   X-ray films can offer an accurate means of identifying an acute fracture. Whenever there is some question as to the possibility of a fracture having occurred, the athlete should be referred to a physician. An understanding of the gross fracture signs cannot be overemphasized. Coaches and trainers should familiarize themselves with these signs so as to be able to make the following examination at the time and place of injury.

1. Determine the mechanism of the injury:
   a. In what sport was the athlete engaged?
   b. How was the athlete hit?
   c. How did the athlete fall?
   d. Did the athlete feel a sudden pain when the injury occurred?
      NOTE: Often, immediate pain subsides and numbness is present for a period of 20 to 30 minutes.
2. Inspect the area of the suspected fracture:
   a. Deformity. Compare the corresponding part to determine the deformity.
   b. Swelling. Is rapid swelling taking place?
   c. Direct tenderness. Ascertain the presence of point tenderness, especially over bony structures.
   d. Indirect tenderness. By feeling the area around the injury site (palpation), determine whether pain can be elicited at the probable fracture point.

Figure 7-6

Mechanism of a tendinous
avulsion fracture caused by the
sartorius muscle being
abnormally stretched.

e. Bony deviations. Does palpation indicate any irregularity in the continuity of the bone?

f. Crepitus. On examining the body part, is there a grating sound apparent at the fracture site?

g. False joint. Is there an abnormal movement of the part, sometimes giving the appearance of an extra joint?

h. Discoloration. Is there discoloration around the site of injury? **NOTE**: Often, discoloration does not appear until several days after the injury has occurred.

i. What the athlete heard or felt.

Stress Fractures

Stress fractures have been variously called *march, fatigue,* and *spontaneous* fractures; the most commonly used term is stress fracture. The exact cause is not known, but there are a number of likely possibilities, such as an overload due to muscle contraction, an altered stress distribution in the bone accompanying muscle fatigue, a change in the ground reaction force, such as going from a wood surface to a grass surface, and performing a rhythmically repetitive stress leading up to a vibratory summation point.[4] The last possibility is favored by many authorities.[9] Rhythmic muscle action performed over a period of time at a subthreshold level causes the stress-bearing capacity of the bone to be exceeded, hence a stress fracture. A bone may become vulnerable to fracture during the first few weeks of intense physical activity or training. In the early period of conditioning weight-bearing bones undergo bone resorption and become weaker before they become stronger.

The most common sites of stress fracture are shown in Figure 7-7.

Typical responses for stress fractures in sports are as follows:

1. Coming back into competition too soon after an injury or illness
2. Going from one event to another without proper training in the second event
3. Starting initial training too quickly
4. Changing habits or the environment, such as running surfaces, the bank of a track, or shoes

Early detection of the stress fracture may be difficult. Because of the frequency of stress fractures in a wide range of sports, they always must be suspected in susceptible body areas that fail to respond to usual management. Until there is an obvious reaction in the bone, which may take several weeks, x-ray examination may fail to reveal any change. Although nonspecific, a bone scan can provide early indications in a given area.

Some basic signs of a stress fracture are swelling, local point tenderness, and pain. In the early stages of stress fracture the athlete may complain of pain when active, but not when at rest. Later the pain becomes constant with more intensity at night.

The major rule for the return of an athlete to full sports participation is not to return prematurely. *It is better to be held back 1 week longer than to return 1 week too early. If in doubt, hold longer.*

Guideline for return to participation:
Better to hold 1 week longer than to return 1 week too early.

Epiphyseal Conditions

Three types of epiphyseal growth site injuries can be sustained by children and adolescents performing sports activities. The most prevalent age range for

A musculoskeletal injury to a child or adolescent should always be considered a possible epiphyseal condition.

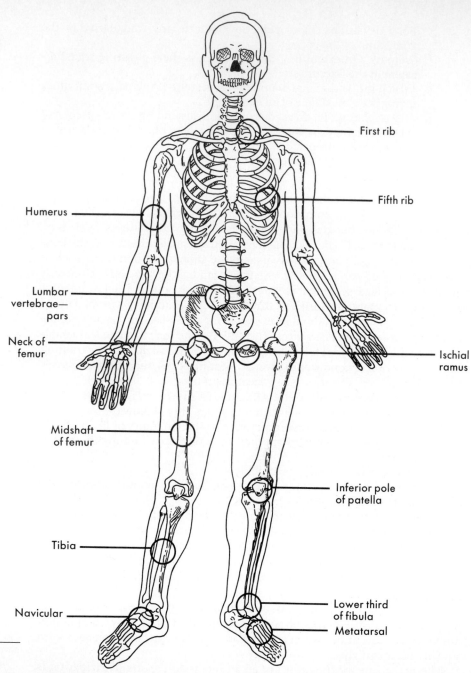

First rib

Fifth rib

Humerus

Lumbar
vertebrae—
pars

Neck of
femur

Ischial
ramus

Midshaft
of femur

Inferior pole
of patella

Tibia

Navicular

Lower third
of fibula

Metatarsal

Figure 7-7

The most common stress
fracture sites.

these injuries is from 10 to 16 years. They consist of injury to the epiphyseal
growth plate, articular epiphyseal injuries, and apophyseal injuries.

The epiphyseal growth plate The epiphyseal growth plate is a cartilaginous disk located near the end of each long bone (Fig. 7-8). Epiphyseal growth
plates are often less resistant to deforming forces than are ligaments of nearby
joints or the outer shaft of the long bones; therefore, severe twisting or a blow

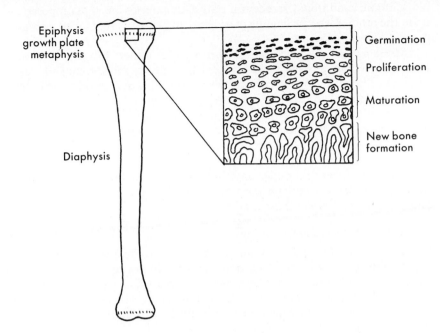

Epiphysis
growth plate
metaphysis

Germination

Proliferation

Maturation

New bone
formation

Diaphysis

Figure 7-8

The epiphyseal growth plate is
the cartilaginous disk located
near the end of each long bone.

to an arm or leg can result in a disruption of growth.[1,6,7] Injury could prematurely close the growth plate, causing a loss of length in the bone. Growth plate dislocation also could cause deformity of the long bone.

Articular epiphyseal injuries   The articular epiphyseal region at the end of the long bone is particularly vulnerable to injury in children and adolescents. Chronic joint disease may occur as a result of microtraumas, limb malalignments, or circulatory impairments.

Apophyseal injuries   The young, physically immature athlete is particularly prone to apophyseal injuries. The apophyses are "traction epiphyses" in contrast to the "pressure epiphyses" of the long bones. These apophyses serve as origins or insertion for muscles of growing bone that provide bone shape but not length. A common apophyseal avulsion condition found in sports is Osgood-Schlatter disease (see Chapter 11).

Chronic Conditions

The chronic condition is usually of long onset and duration, but acute injuries, if not properly managed, can soon become chronic. As in acute conditions, inflammation plays an important role in chronic injuries, although it does not necessarily present the classic stages of redness, swelling, pain, heat, and loss of function. Because of the constant presence of a low-grade inflammation, there is a proliferation of scar tissue. In sports a chronic condition may have any of several causal (etiological) factors: poor performance techniques, other acute injuries, or constant stress beyond physiological limits.

The use of improper performance technique places abnormal strain on joints and tendons, predisposing the athlete to a future chronic condition. Proper form must be stressed!

Chronic conditions can occur if traumatic injuries are superimposed one upon the other. Also, the healing of an acute injury, if delayed for some reason, may become chronic.

Stress beyond the physiological limits of the athlete (overuse syndrome) may occur either grossly, as in heat exhaustion, or, more frequently, as in small, insidious injuries occurring within muscles and joints. Such conditions are frequently difficult to detect as specific single traumatic episodes.

Generally, the care of chronic injuries in sports is the same no matter what area it is. Of prime importance are rest, immobilization, and heat applied to the injured body part. These procedures are often accompanied by the physician prescribing an anti-inflammatory medication.

A great number of chronic conditions are associated with sports participation. The student of athletic training should be familiar with some of the unique characteristics of these conditions.

Muscle and Tendon Conditions

Commonly, chronic tendon injuries are intrinsic and involve overuse.

Tendinitis Tendinitis has a gradual onset, diffuse tenderness because of repeated microtraumas, and degenerative changes. Obvious signs of tendinitis are swelling and pain that move as the tendon moves. Occasionally, tendinitis leads to deposits of minerals, primarily lime, within the tendon. This is known as *calcific tendinitis* (Fig. 7-9).

Tenosynovitis Tenosynovitis is inflammation of the sheath covering a tendon. In its acute state there is rapid onset, a crepitus as the tendon moves, and generalized swelling. In chronic tenosynovitis the tendons become eventually thickened, with pain and crepitus present on movement.

Bursitis The bursa is the fluid-filled sac found in places where friction might occur within body tissues. Bursae are predominantly located between bony prominences and muscles or tendons. Overuse of muscles or tendons at these prominences, as well as constant external compression or trauma, can result in bursitis. The signs and symptoms of bursitis include swelling, pain, and some loss of function. Repeated trauma may eventually lead to calcific deposits and degeneration of the internal lining of the bursa.[5]

ectopic calcification
Calcification occurring in an abnormal place

Ectopic calcification Voluntary muscles can become chronically inflamed, resulting in myositis. An *ectopic calcification* can occur in a muscle that directly overlies a bone. Tendinitis and tenosynovitis can be the result of or lead to calcium deposits within the tendon or synovial-lined sheath.

Atrophy and contracture Two complications of muscle and tendon conditions are atrophy and contracture. *Muscle atrophy* is the wasting away of muscle tissue. Its main cause in athletes is immobilization of a body part, inactivity, or loss of nerve stimulation. A second complication to sports injuries is *muscle contracture*, an abnormal shortening of muscle tissue where there is a great deal of resistance to passive stretch. Commonly associated with muscle injury, a contracture is associated with a joint that has developed unyielding and resisting scar tissue.

Joint Conditions

Two chronic conditions that are very common to athletes are the softening of the articular surface of a joint and traumatic arthritis.

 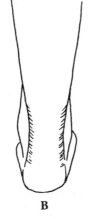 

A B C

Figure 7-9

Tenosynovitis is an
inflammation of the sheath
covering a tendon. **A**, Normal.
B, Strained. **C**, Chronic
tenosynovitis.

Osteochondrosis Osteochondrosis is a diseased state of a bone and its articular cartilage. A possible cause is a disruption of circulation due to repeated trauma.

Traumatic arthritis Traumatic arthritis is usually the result of micro-traumas. With repeated trauma to the articular joint surfaces, the bone and synovium thicken; and there is pain, muscle spasm, and joint crepitus on movement. Joint insult leading to arthritis can come from repeated sprains that leave a joint with weakened ligaments.

Nerve Responses

A number of abnormal nerve responses can be attributed to sports participation. Some of the more common conditions are referred pain and trigger points, numbness and tingling or increased sensitivity, nerve stretch or pinch injuries, and enuritis.

Pain that is felt at a point on the body other than its actual origin is known as *referred pain*. In the muscular system a common manifestation of referred pain is the *trigger point*, which is a center of irritation that when stimulated sets off pain to distant body areas.

Among the conditions affecting touch sensation, two are common to sports injuries: (1) a diminished sense of feeling or numbness with associated tingling or (2) an increased sensitivity to a stimulation. A variety of nerve injuries, such as nerve contusions and stretching, can lead to diminished or increased sensitivity as well as pain. Direct trauma to a nerve, such as a blow, can cause such symptoms as numbness, tingling, or muscle weakness. A sudden *nerve stretch* or *pinch* can lead to a sharp burning pain (a "burner") that radiates down the limb together with muscle weakness. If such conditions go untreated, they can lead to an eventual permanent loss of function.

Like other tissues in the body, nerves can become chronically inflamed from repeated irritation. *Neuritis* can be caused by the mechanical stresses of compression, direct blows, penetrating injuries, contusion, stretching, and nerve entrapment. Symptoms of neuritis can range from minor nerve involvement to paralysis.

SUMMARY

Sports injuries can occur directly from a sport or secondarily, such as coming back to a sport too soon after an injury has occurred. The injury can result from body contact, from a piece of equipment, or from within the athlete, such as an overuse situation.

Anatomically, injuries can be classified as exposed and unexposed. Examples of exposed injuries are skin lesions such as abrasions, lacerations, avulsions, punctures, and incisions. Unexposed or internal injuries consist of strains, sprains, dislocations, and fractures.

There are a number of fracture types. Those that are of the acute type are comminuted, depressed, greenstick, impacted, longitudinal, oblique, serrated, spiral, transverse, and contrecoup. Other fractures are avulsion, stress, epiphyseal, and apophyseal.

Chronic musculoskeletal conditions, unlike acute conditions, are defined as being of long onset and long duration. These conditions often occur from poor performance techniques, from other acute injuries, or from a constant stress that is beyond physiological limits.

REVIEW QUESTIONS AND CLASS ACTIVITIES

1. Compare the different ways sports injuries can be classified.
2. Differentiate the exposed injury from the unexposed injury.
3. Define strains, muscle spasms, sprains, dislocations, and types of fractures.
4. Why and how do stress fractures occur?
5. Differentiate an acute soft tissue injury from a chronic soft tissue injury, including mechanism, and the body's reaction to each.
6. How can major joints develop chronic conditions such as traumatic arthritis?
7. List types of nerve injuries that can be sustained in sports.

REFERENCES

1. Anthony, C.P., and Thibodeau, G.A.: Textbook of anatomy and physiology, ed. 11, St. Louis, 1983, The C. V. Mosby Co.
2. Arnheim, D.D.: Modern principles of athletic training, ed. 6, St. Louis, 1985, Times Mirror/Mosby College Publishing.
3. Booher, J.M. and Thibodeau, G.A.: Athletic injury assessment, St. Louis, 1985, Times Mirror/Mosby College Publishing.
4. Chamay, A.: Mechanical and morphological aspects of experimental overload and fatigue in bone, J. Biomech. 3:263, 1970.
5. Hafen, B.Q.: First aid for health emergencies, ed. 3, St. Paul, Minn., 1984, West Publishing Co.
6. Larson, R.L.: Physical activity and the growth and development of bone and joint structures. In Rarick, G.L. (editor): Physical activity: human growth and development, New York, 1973, Academic Press.
7. Micheli, L.J.: Sports injuries in children and adolescents. In Straus, R.H. (editor): Sports medicine and physiology, Philadelphia, 1979, W. B. Saunders Co.
8. Parcel, G.S.: Basic emergency care of the sick and injured, ed. 3, St. Louis, 1986, Times Mirror/Mosby College Publishing.
9. Stanitski, C.L., McMaster, J.H., and Scranton, P.E.: On the nature of stress fractures, Am. J. Sports Med. 6:391, 1978.
10. Williams, J.G.P.: Color atlas of injury in sport, Chicago, 1980, Year Book Medical Publishers, Inc.

ANNOTATED BIBLIOGRAPHY

Booher, J.M., and G.A. Thibodeau, Athletic injury assessment, St. Louis, 1985, Times Mirror/Mosby College Publishing.

An excellent guide to the classification, recognition, and evaluation of athletic injuries.

Standard nomenclature of athletic injuries, Monroe, Wis., 1976, American Medical Association.

An in-depth list of conditions found in the fields of athletic training and sports medicine. Each condition is described as to its etiology, symptoms, signs, complications, laboratory findings, x-ray findings, and pathology.

Williams, J.G.P.: Color atlas of injury in sport, Chicago, 1980, Year Book Medical Publishers, Inc.

An excellent visual guide to the area of sports injuries. It covers the nature and incidence of sport injury, types of tissue damage, and regional injuries caused by a variety of sports activities.

Chapter 8

HEALING AND REHABILITATION

When you finish this chapter, you will be able to:

List the major events in healing of acute soft tissue injuries

List the major events in healing of bone fractures

Describe the implications of pain to sports injuries

Identify the basic values and procedures in the use of superficial cold and heat therapy

Explain the various factors of exercise rehabilitation, including exercise and crutch walking

Individuals studying athletic training should have a basic knowledge of how tissue responds to acute and chronic injuries. Such knowledge establishes a foundation for immediate and follow-up injury care (Fig. 8-1). They also should have a basic knowledge of superficial cold and heat therapy, exercise rehabilitation, as well as crutch and cane fitting and walking.

HEALING

Soft Tissue

Soft tissue is considered to be all bodily tissues other than bone. The healing responses of soft tissue fall into three phases: the inflammatory phase, the repair phase, and the remodeling phase.[22]

Inflammatory Phase

Inflammation is the body's reaction to disease or injury. As the first phase of the healing response it is present during the first 3 or 4 days after an injury takes place. The major outward signs are redness, heat, swelling, pain, and in some cases a loss of function. In general, inflammation is designed to protect, localize, and rid the body of some injurious agent in preparation for tissue repair.

Acute trauma   At the time when trauma occurs and before inflammation begins the intact blood vessels in the region of the injury decrease in their diameter (vasoconstriction) and as a result decrease blood flow in the area. This lasts up to 10 minutes.[19] At the moment blood vessels constrict, coagulation begins to seal broken blood vessels. Key chemicals are also activated that will influence the next reactions.

Vasoconstriction is replaced by an increase in the diameter of the small blood vessels (**vasodilation**) in the area of injury. Associated with dilation is an

inflammatory phase:
Redness
Heat
Swelling
Pain
Loss of function

vasoconstriction
Decrease in the diameter of a blood vessel

156

Figure 8-1

Tissue healing and the causation of pain is not clearly understood. However, what is known must be studied as a foundation for proper injury management.

increase in blood thickness (viscosity), which leads to a slowing of blood flow and swelling. With dilation also comes serum seepage through the intact blood vessel lining in the injury area. This seepage lasts from a few minutes to 15 to 30 minutes depending on the severity of the injury.[1] In more severe trauma, seepage may become delayed.

When circulation is slowed, white cells (leukocytes) become concentrated mainly on the inner walls of the venules. The white cells then move through the walls of the venules through a process of ameboid action (diapedisis). These white cells then move to the injured body part and carry out the process of cleaning the area of debris. This process is known as **phagocytosis**.

vasodilation
Increase in the diameter of a blood vessel

Internal bleeding and swelling The amount of swelling associated with an injury is dependent on the extent of damaged vessels and hemorrhage and the amount of serum seepage that occurs through intact blood vessels. As stated earlier, bleeding begins to coagulate almost immediately after injury. Blood coagulation occurs in three stages: first, thromboplastin is formed; second, under the influence of thromboplastin plus calcium, prothrombin is converted into thrombin; third, thrombin changes from fibrinogen into the final fibrin clot.

phagocytosis
Process of ingesting microorganisms, other cells, or foreign particles, commonly by monocytes; a white blood cell

Repair Phase

In the beginning an injury is associated with tissue death from the initial trauma. Because circulation has been disrupted following trauma, cellular death may continue due to a lack of oxygen. Tissue death also is increased by

Cellular death continues after initial injury because:
　Disruption of circulation causes lack of oxygen
　Digestive enzymes of engulfing phagocytes spill over to kill normal cells

white cells spilling over their digestive enzymes to kill normal cells. Properly applied immediate care of the injury, including ice, compression, elevation, and rest (and immobilization when necessary), serves to decrease the potential of continued cellular death.

Repair is synonymous with initial healing and regeneration, the restoration of lost tissue. The healing period normally ranges from the inflammatory phase to about 3 weeks following injury.

During this stage two types of healing occur. *Primary healing,* healing by first intention, takes place in an injury that has even and closely opposed edges, such as a cut or incision. With this type of injury, if the edges are held in very close approximation, a minimum of granulation tissue is produced. *Secondary healing,* healing by secondary intention, results when there is a gaping lesion with large tissue loss that becomes replaced by scar tissue. External wounds, such as lacerations, and internal musculoskeletal injuries commonly heal by secondary intention.

It is always hoped that maximum restoration of destroyed tissue or regeneration takes place without undue scarring. This is dependent on the extent of injury, application of proper immediate care, and the type of tissue that predominates. For example, voluntary muscle tissue has limited regeneration capabilities, while bone and connective tissue readily regenerate.[21]

Remodeling Phase

Remodeling of the traumatized area overlaps that of repair and regeneration. Normally in acute injuries the first 3 weeks are characterized by increased production of scar tissue and the strength of its fibers. Strength of scar tissue continues to increase from 3 months to 1 year following injury. Ligamentous tissue has been found to take as long as a year to become completely remodeled. To avoid a rigid, nonyielding scar, there must be a physiological balance between **synthesis** and **lysis**. If there is excessive strain placed on the injury or if strain occurs too early, the healing process is extended. For proper healing of muscle and tendons, there must be careful consideration as to when to mobilize the site. Early mobilization can assist in producing a more viable injury site; however, too long a period of immobilization can delay healing.

Chronic inflammation The chronic muscle and joint problem is an ever-present concern in sports. It often results from repeated acute microtraumas and overuse. A prominent feature is constant low-grade inflammation causing the development of scar tissue and tissue degeneration.[4]

Fracture Healing

Those concerned with sports must fully realize the potential seriousness of a bone fracture (Fig. 8-2). Coaches often become impatient for the athlete with a fracture to return to competition before healing is complete. Time is required for proper bone union to take place. Like soft tissue healing, bone healing must go through a number of phases.[11]

Inflammatory Phase

Acute inflammation with proper immobilization usually lasts about 4 days. When a bone fractures there is injury to bony tissue and also to the surrounding tissue. There is hemorrhage and hematoma development. It is also accom-

synthesis
Build up

lysis
Break down

Chronic inflammation can stem from repeated acute microtraumas and overuse.

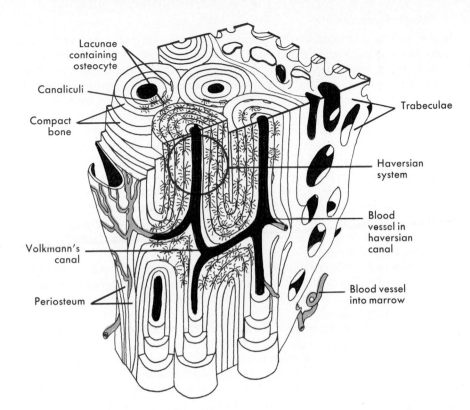

Lacunae containing osteocyte

Canaliculi

Compact bone

Volkmann's canal

Periosteum

Trabeculae

Haversian system

Blood vessel in haversian canal

Blood vessel into marrow

Figure 8-2

Bone is a complex organ in both growth and healing.

panied by a dying back of some uninjured bone due to a disruption of the intact blood circulation.

Repair Phase

As with a soft tissue injury, the hematoma begins to organize into a highly vascular granulated mass. This will gradually form a connective tissue junction between the fractured bone ends.

Soft and Hard Callus

Gradually the connective tissue junction forms into a soft callus. The soft callus is composed mostly of connective tissue and a network of woven bone. Beginning in 3 to 4 weeks after injury, and lasting 3 or 4 months, a hard callus forms. The hard callus is then replaced with mature bone. If the immobilization is unsatisfactory, cartilage tissue will be formed instead of mature bone.

Remodeling

When the hard callus has been resorbed and replaced with mature bone the remodeling process begins. It should be noted that remodeling may take years to be completed. Remodeling is considered finished when a fractured bone has been restored to its former shape or has developed a shape that can withstand major stresses.

Proper Fracture Care

In the treatment of fractures the bones must be immobilized completely until x-ray studies reveal that the hard callus has been replaced with mature bone. It is up to the physician to know the various types of fractures and the best form of immobilization for each specific fracture. During healing, fractures can keep an athlete out of participation for his or her particular sport for several weeks or months, depending on the nature, extent, and site of the fracture. During this period there are certain conditions that can seriously interfere with the healing process. Three such conditions are discussed below:

Conditions that interfere with fracture healing:
  Poor blood supply
  Poor immobilization
  Infection

1. If there is a *poor blood supply to the fractured area* and one of the parts of the broken bone is not properly supplied by the blood, that part will die and union or healing of the fracture will not take place. This condition is known as *aseptic necrosis* and can often be seen in the head of the femur, the navicular bone in the wrist, the talus in the ankle, or isolated bone fragments. The condition is relatively rare among vital, healthy, young athletes, except in the navicular bone of the wrist.

2. *Poor immobilization of the fracture site* resulting from poor casting by the physician and permitting motion between the bone parts, may not only prevent proper union but may also, in the event that union does transpire, cause deformity to develop.

3. *Infection* can materially interfere with the normal healing process, particularly in the case of a compound fracture, which offers an ideal situation for development of a severe streptococcal or staphylococcal infection. The increased use of modern antibiotics has considerably reduced the prevalence of these infections coincidental with or immediately following a fracture. The closed fracture is not immune to contamination, of course, since infections within the body or a poor blood supply can render it quite susceptible. If the fracture site should become and remain infected, the infection could interfere with the proper union of the bone. If soft tissue parts get caught between the severed ends of the bone—such as muscle, connective tissue, or other soft tissue immediately adjacent to the fracture—proper bone union may be unable to occur, often necessitating surgical cleansing of the area of soft tissues by a surgeon.

Pain Perception

Deep structural pain is contrasted to superficial pain because of its poor localization.

It is important to consider pain when discussing tissue response to injury. It is often described subjectively as "burning, sharp, dull, crushing, or piercing." Chusid[6] describes a painful stimulus as causing only two sensations—sharp or dull pain. These can be further described as being fast or slow pain.

The sensation of deep structural pain is contrasted to superficial pain because of its poor localization. Pain in the visceral structures is often associated with the autonomic system of sweating, blood pressure changes, and nausea. Deep visceral pain may also radiate to other body areas. If this occurs, the pain becomes referred to a body structure that was developed from the same embryonic segment or dermatome as the structure in which the pain originated (dermatomal rule).[6]

A number of theories on how pain is produced and perceived by the brain have been advanced. Only in the last two decades has science demonstrated that pain is both a psychological and physiological phenomenon and therefore is unique to each individual. Sports activities demonstrate this fact clearly. Through conditioning, an athlete learns to endure the pain of rigorous activity and to block the sensations of a minor injury.

As understanding of pain increases, there is a growing distinction between chronic and acute pain.[20] Acute pain protects the body against something harmful. On the other hand, chronic pain is a paradox that apparently serves no useful purpose. Bonica[3] indicates that acute pain is a disagreeable sensation and an emotional experience caused by tissue damage or a noxious stimulus. The real culprit in pain is the chemical called *bradykinin* which is considered the most pain-producing substance. It is a peptide, which is a fragment of a large protein molecule that circulates in the blood stream. When tissue is damaged in any way, tiny capillaries break releasing bradykinin into the surrounding region. Bradykinin in turn stimulates cells in the region of injury, which release another chemical—prostoglandin. Prostoglandin tells specialized nerve cells to relay the pain message to the brain.[5]

Referred Pain

One of the major areas of pain coaches and athletic trainers must be aware of is that produced from visceral injury. *Gray's Anatomy* states:

> Although most physiological impulses carried by visceral afferent fibers fail to reach consciousness, pathological conditions or excessive stimulation (e.g., trauma and inflammation) may bring into action those which carry pain. The central nervous system has a poorly developed power of localizing the source of such pain, and by some mechanism not clearly understood, the pain may be referred to the region supplied by the somatic afferent fibers whose central connections are the same as those of the visceral afferents.[9]

Visceral pain has a tendency to radiate and give rise to pain that becomes referred to the skin's surface.[5]

Psychological Aspects of Pain

Pain, especially chronic pain, is a subjective, psychological phenomenon. When painful injuries are treated, the total athlete must be considered, not just the pain or condition. Even in the most well-adjusted person, pain will create emotional changes. Constant pain will often cause self-centeredness and an increased sense of dependency.

Athletes, like nonathletes, vary in their pain thresholds. Some can tolerate enormous pain, while others find mild pain almost unbearable. Pain appears to be worse at night because persons are alone and more aware of themselves, plus being devoid of external diversions.[18] Personality differences can also cause differences in pain toleration. For example, athletes who are anxious, dependent, and immature have less toleration for pain than those who are relaxed and emotionally in control.

FOUNDATIONS OF SUPERFICIAL THERAPY

As an introductory text the major concern here is to present material that can be practiced by the nonprofessional in athletic training. This section is concerned with nonpenetrating therapeutics that do not require certification or licensure.

Cold and Heat

It has been known for centuries that cold and heat, when applied to the skin, have therapeutic capabilities. Both are currently used in athletic training in various ways depending on their availability and the philosophy of the user.

Cold as Therapy

As discussed in Chapter 5, the application of cold for the first aid of trauma to the musculoskeletal system is a well-accepted practice. When applied intermittently for 20 minutes every 1 1/2 waking hours it reduces many of the adverse aspects of the initial inflammatory phase that lasts from 3 to 4 days.

The major therapeutic value of cold is its ability to produce anesthesia, allowing pain-free exercise.

A major therapeutic value of cold used following the inflammatory phase is to produce anesthesia and allow the athlete to engage in pain-free exercise.[16] Another major factor is that cold application can reduce the muscle pain-spasm-pain cycle. When a muscle is injured it may generally go into spasm as a means of protecting itself against further injury. When spasm occurs it places pressure on nerve endings and produces more pain. With increased pain there is more spasm, therefore, the expression *pain-spasm-pain cycle*. By breaking this cycle more range of motion is allowed in a joint, muscles can be stretched more easily, and movement can be pain-free.[19]

Techniques for application of cold Cold as a first aid medium has been discussed in Chapter 5. It should be applied when hemorrhaging is under control and repair has started, usually 1 to 3 days after injury, based on the nature and extent of the condition. Depending on the body site and thickness of the subcutaneous fat, the following neuromuscular response has been suggested.[15]

Cold therapy can begin 1 to 3 days after injury.

The extent of cooling depends on the thickness of the subcutaneous fat layer.

Cryotherapeutic techniques:
Cryokinetics
Ice massage
Ice water immersion
Ice blanket/pack

Cryotherapy becomes an uncomfortable procedure during stage 2, when burning or aching occurs. This requires encouragement, especially during the first experience. When the athlete experiences the comfort of stage 3, little further encouragement is necessary.[14]

Cryokinetics The early work of Haden[13] and Grant[12] has clearly shown the value of cold when combined with passive or active movement for the treatment of painful musculoskeletal conditions. At stage 3, cold has depressed the excitability of free nerve endings and peripheral nerve fibers with a subsequent increase in the pain threshold. With the pain-spasm-pain diminished, greater pain-free motion is allowed. Although passive movement in the early stages of healing assists in developing more viable collagen tissue, voluntary active movement is preferred whenever possible. A variety of exercise techniques can be employed with cryotherapy.

Stage	Response	Time after Initiation
1	Cold sensation	0 to 3 min
2	Burning, aching	2 to 7 min
3	Local numbness, anesthesia; pain, reflex impulses stopped; pain-spasm-pain cycle interrupted	5 to 12 min

Ice massage Ice massage has been used in sports to some advantage. The technique calls for massaging the affected part with an ice cylinder obtained from freezing water in a styrofoam cup, which insulates the hand against the cold. Grasping the ice cylinder with a towel, it is moved in a circular manner over the affected area, continuing until the part progresses from an uncomfortable chill sensation to an ache and then numbness. This should take from about 5 to 10 minutes. When the body part is numb, gradual stretching and mobilization can be executed (Fig. 8-3). This technique is simple, inexpensive, and can be carried out at home.

Ice water immersion Immersion in 40° F (4° C) water is a simple means for treating a distal part. After analgesia, which occurs rapidly, the athlete is encouraged to move the part in a normal manner. A combination of cold water and the hydromassage action of a whirlpool has been found to reduce initial swelling and encourage healing.

Ice blanket or pack This is a convenient way to apply cold therapy. It may consist of plastic bags filled with crushed ice or simply toweling saturated with crushed ice. Exercise can begin after 6 to 12 minutes of chilling.

Adverse cold reactions and contraindications Even though superficial cold when carefully applied is usually safe, some individuals will have adverse reactions. Some athletes are allergic to cold and react with hives and joint pain or swelling. A few may have Raynaud's phenomenon in which arteries in the fingers and toes constrict in a vasospasm. Paroxysmal cold hemoglobinuria, a rarer disease, may lead to kidney dysfunction.

Heat as Therapy

The application of heat for disease and traumatic injuries has been used for centuries. Recently, however, its use in the immediate treatment phase of a musculoskeletal injury has been replaced with cold. As with cryotherapy, there are many unanswered questions as to how heat produces physiological responses, when it is best applied, and what types of heat-therapy are most ap-

Heat has the capacity to increase the extensibility of connective tissue.

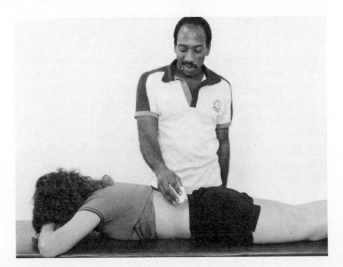

Figure 8-3

Ice massage is an excellent therapeutic modality in sports medicine.

propriate for a given condition. The desirable therapeutic effects of heat include (1) increasing the extensibility of collagen tissues, (2) decreasing joint stiffness, (3) reducing pain, (4) relieving muscle spasm, (5) reducing inflammation, edema, and exudates, and (6) increasing blood flow.[17]

Heat affects the extensibility of collagen tissue by increasing the viscous flow of collagen fibers and subsequently relaxing the tension. From a therapeutic point of view, heating contracted connective tissue permits an increase in muscle extensibility through stretching. Muscle contractions, a contracted joint capsule, and scars can be effectively stretched while being heated or just after the heat is removed.[17] An increase in extensibility does not occur unless the heat treatment is associated with stretching exercises.

Heat, like cold, can relieve pain but for different reasons. Whereas cold numbs the area, heat stimulates the nerves on the skin and stimulates key chemicals that aid in blocking pain sensations. Muscle spasm due to a reduction of blood supply can be relieved by heat. Heat is also believed to assist inflammation and swelling by a number of related factors, such as raising temperature, increasing metabolism, reducing oxygen tension, lowering the pH level, increasing the flow of fluids through the intact capillary walls, and releasing key hormones that cause vasodilation.

Heat treatments can be categorized as moist (e.g., from a whirlpool or water packs) or dry (e.g., from a heat lamp). Heat is provided through conduction, convection, or conversion. **Conduction** refers to direct contact with a hot medium such as a whirlpool or hot-water bath. **Convection** is indirect heat, or transfer of heat, caused by air or fluid circulating around the body. **Conversion** is the production of heat by other forms of energy. An example is diathermy, which produces heat from shortwave radio frequencies.

Contraindications for the use of superficial heat Superficial heat refers to a heat that mainly affects the surface of the skin. It is generally contraindicated to apply heat over a numb skin area. It is also contraindicated to apply heat over skin areas that have an inadequate blood supply. Such a situation can result in tissue death. Avoid applying heat over a hemorrhaging region, to gonads, or to a pregnant abdomen.[19] Important contraindications and precautions regarding the use of heat from any source are as follows:

1. Never apply heat when there is a loss of sensation.
2. Never apply heat immediately after an injury.
3. Never apply heat when there is a decreased arterial circulation.
4. Never apply heat directly over the eyes or genitals.
5. Never heat the abdomen during pregnancy.

Techniques for application of superficial heat Examples of superficial heat include moist hot packs, water soaks, whirlpool baths, contrast baths, paraffin baths, and analgesic balms and liniments.

Moist heat therapies Heated water is one of the most widely used therapeutic modalities in sports medicine. It is readily available for use in any sports medicine program. The greatest disadvantage of hydrotherapy is the difficulty in controlling the therapeutic effects. This is primarily caused by the rapid dissipation of heat, which makes maintaining a constant tissue temperature difficult.

For the most part moist heat aids the healing process in some local conditions by causing higher superficial tissue temperatures; however, joint and muscle circulation increase little in temperature. Superficial tissue is a poor

conduction
Heating by direct contact with a hot medium

convection
Heating indirectly through another medium, such as air or liquid

conversion
Heating by other forms of energy

thermal conductor, and temperature rises quickly on the skin surface as compared to the underlying tissues.

Hydrotherapy is best applied to postacute conditions of sprains, strains, and contusions. It produces mild healing qualities with a general relaxation of tense, spasmed muscles.

Each hydrotherapy modality has its own technique of application. Basically, the water temperature must be kept constant, within a range of 90° to 115° F (32.2° to 46.1° C), with variances based on the texture and pigmentation of the athlete's skin. A light-pigmented individual cannot, as a rule, withstand intense moist heat. Conversely, the dark-pigmented athlete is able to endure hotter temperatures.

General precautions The contraindications to and precautions for hydrotherapy are the same as for other types of heat devices. The following precautions must be considered:

1. Avoid overheating sensitive skin, the eyes, and the genitals.
2. Never apply heat to a recent injury until hemorrhage has subsided.
3. Use caution when the athlete is submerged in heated water, since light-headedness and even unconsciousness may result as blood is withdrawn from the head and centralized in other body areas.

Moist heat packs Commercial moist heat packs fall into the category of conductive heating. Silicate gel contained in a cotton pad is immersed in thermostatically controlled hot water at a temperature of 175° F (79.4° C). Each pad retains water and a constant heat level for 20 to 30 minutes. Six layers of toweling or commercial terry cloth are used between the packs and the skin. The usefulness of the moist heat pack lies in its adaptability; it can be positioned anywhere on the body.

The major value of the moist heat pack is in the general relaxation it brings and reduction of the pain-spasm-pain cycle (Fig. 8-4). There are limitations of the moist heat pack and all other superficial heating modalities: "the deeper tissues, including the musculature, are usually not significantly heated because the heat transfer from the skin surface into deeper tissues is inhibited by the subcutaneous fat, which acts as a thermal insulator, and by the increased skin flow, which cools and carries away the heat externally applied."[17]

To avoid burns the athlete should not lie on the pad. It has been estimated that the greatest heating occurs within 8 minutes of application and then steadily declines.[17]

Water immersion baths Water is a reasonably good conductor of heat with little heat loss to an immersed part. The most commonly used methods in sports are the whirlpool hydromassage bath and contrast bath.

Whirlpool bath A whirlpool bath is a combination therapy, giving the athlete both a massaging action and a hot water bath (Fig. 8-5). It has become one of the most popular heat-therapies used in sports medicine. Through water agitation and the heat transmitted to the injured area, local circulation can be increased, which is usually followed by a reduction in congestion, spasm, and pain. Table 8-1 describes a general treatment approach when using the whirlpool in sports.

When using the whirlpool soon after an injury the water jet should be directed toward the sides of the tank. Directing the stream of water on the injury will only aggravate the condition and perhaps cause additional bleeding.

Moist heat packs afford body part relaxation and reduction of the pain-spasm-pain cycle.

Figure 8-4

The commercial moist heat packs can retain heat for 20 to 30 minutes.

The whirlpool bath provides both heated water and massaging action.

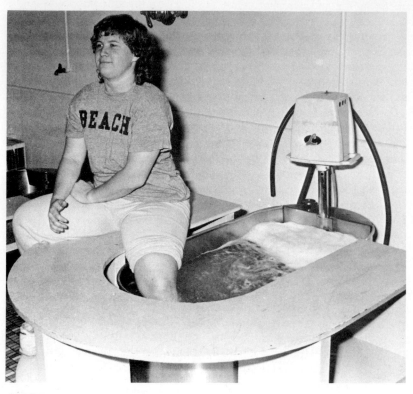

Figure 8-5

The whirlpool bath combines
massage and water at varied
temperatures.

TABLE 8-1

Sample whirlpool routine

Injury Progress	Water Temperature	Duration of Treatment
Step 2 of acute injury	40°F (4.4°C) (ice cold whirlpool)	5 min
Step 3 of acute injury	60°F (15.5°C)	10 min
Step 4 of acute injury	90° F (32.2° C)	10 min
Step 5 of acute injury	100°-102° F (37.8°-38.9° C)	10-20 min
Chronic injury	102°-105° F (38.9°-40.6° C)	10-20 min
To warm up before activity	100°-102° F (37.8°-38.9° C)	5 min
Full-body immersion	90°-100° F (32.2°-37.8° C)	5-10 min

Contrast bath procedure:
2 minutes immersion in ice
slush followed by 30 seconds
in tepid water (93° to 98° F
[33.9° to 36.7° C])

Contrast baths Contrast baths produce hyperemia in feet, ankles,
hands, and wrists of individuals who have a chronic inflammatory condition.
The following is a sequence of immersion time for each temperature:

The athlete is submerged for 10 minutes in water that is between 105°
and 110° F (40.6° and 43.3° C). After the initial soak, the athlete is submerged
for 1 minute in water that is between 59° and 68° F (15° and 20° C) and then is
shifted to the hot water for 4 minutes, alternating temperatures for a period of
30 minutes.[18]

A second method of contrast that has become popular in sports medicine
uses the concept of alternatively submerging the limb in an ice slush bath for

2 minutes and then in tepid water 93° to 98° F (33.9° to 37.7° C) for 30 seconds. The baths are alternated for 15 minutes, beginning and ending with cold immersion.[7]

EXERCISE REHABILITATION

Although it is often neglected, exercise is one of the most important therapeutic tools available to the coach and athletic trainer. Through a carefully applied exercise program in conjunction with other therapies and directed by a physician, an athlete often can be returned safely to competition after injury. The two major categories of exercise are conditioning and rehabilitation. *Exercise rehabilitation* is the restoration of an athlete to the level of preinjury fitness through a carefully planned and carried out program of therapeutic exercise. It is essential that the athlete return to competition with function fully restored. Too often athletes fail to regain full function and as a result perform at a subpar level, thereby risking permanent disability.

An injured athlete should be monitored throughout the entire convalescent and reconditioning periods. At no time should the immediate or future health of the athlete be endangered as a result of hasty decisions; at the same time the dedicated athlete should be given every possible opportunity to compete, provided that such competition does not pose undue risk. The final decision in this matter must rest with the team physician. The team physician must decide at what point the athlete can reenter competition without the danger of reinjury, as well as when the use of supportive taping or other aids is necessary to prevent further injury. It has been said that a good substitute is always more valuable than an injured star. There must be full cooperation between coach, trainer, and physician in helping to restore the athlete to the proper level of competitive fitness. Rehabilitation through exercise is considered one factor in the total therapy regimen.[10]

> The physician makes the final decision as to whether an athlete returns to competition.

Exercise rehabilitation after a sports injury is the combined responsibility of all individuals connected with a specific sport. To devise a program that is most conducive to the good of the athlete, basic objectives that consider his or her needs must be developed. In addition to maintaining a good psychological climate, the objectives are to (1) prevent deconditioning of the total body and (2) rehabilitate the injured part without hampering the healing process.

Preventing deconditioning involves keeping the body physically fit while the injury heals. In establishing a conditioning program, emphasis should be placed on maintaining strength, flexibility, endurance, and coordination of the total body. Whenever possible, athletes should engage in activities that will aid them in their sport but will not endanger recovery from the injury. When one limb is immobilized in a sling or cast, the opposite limb should be exercised if it can be done without pain or stress to the injured body part. In fact, all uninvolved body parts and joints should be exercised daily so as to maintain a reasonable degree of general strength and endurance.

Restoring the injured part to a preinjury state is so important that an exercise rehabilitation program must be started as soon as possible. An injured body part must be prevented from developing disuse degeneration. Disuse will result in atrophy, muscle contractures, inflexibility, and healing delay due to circulatory impairment. This is not to imply that sports injuries

should be "run off or worked through." Rather, a proper balance between resting and exercise should be maintained.

As in conditioning exercise, rehabilitation should follow the SAID principle. As in physical conditioning and in rehabilitation, the SAID principle refers to "specific *a*daptation to *i*mposed *d*emands." Through this process
strength, flexibility, endurance, proprioception, and coordination/agility of an
injured part is returned to a state of full recovery.

Muscular Strength and Endurance

Muscle Strength

Muscular strength allows the athlete to overcome a given resistance. It is one
of the most essential factors in restoring function after injury. Muscle size and
strength can be increased with use and can decrease in cases of disuse. Both
isotonic and isometric muscle contractions are used to advantage in rehabilitation. All movements and exercises should be carefully controlled and initially should be guided by pain. Pain-free motion should be a goal. Every effort
should be made to prevent atrophy and the loss of muscle tone when a body
part or joint is immobilized. As strength is slowly regained, weight bearing
may be introduced when the joint(s) is deemed capable of support. Isotonic
and isokinetic exercises are preferable because they increase function of a part
through a range of movement (Fig. 8-6). Isometric exercises involve no movement of the joints, but they develop strength primarily in the position exercised.

Immobilized parts may initially be carefully exercised through isometrics, while using a submaximal effort. Such exercise assists in preventing at-

Figure 8-6

Isokinetic exercising is often
preferable in the early stages of
limb rehabilitation because it
develops function through a
full range of motion.

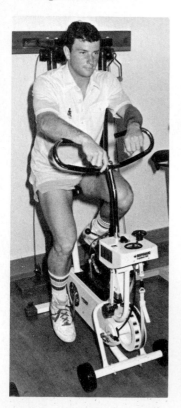

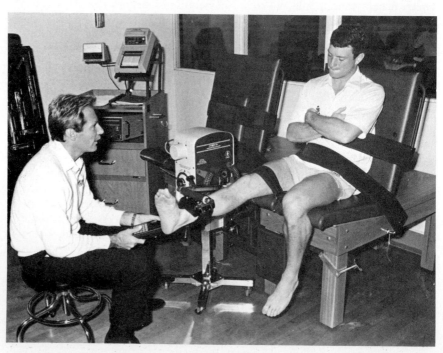

rophy and reduces loss of muscular strength until free movement can be executed. When at all possible a program designed to maintain cardiovascular endurance should accompany the program of musculoskeletal reconditioning.

After initial isometric exercises, as pain and swelling diminish or disappear, the athlete should begin a program of movement using either isotonic or isokinetic exercises to assist in the development of strength, endurance, and range of motion. Isokinetic exercises provide one of the best means of developing strength and endurance in the rehabilitative process, since they provide uniform strength demands and resistance throughout the full range of movement at a prescribed level of resistance. Isokinetic exercises assist the training experience by increasing the muscular force at all speeds of contraction. Rehabilitation is enhanced when the injured athlete is able to perform an exercise set at a specific speed and contractive force equal to his or her sport.

Classification of Isotonic Rehabilitative Exercise

Reconditioning exercises can be classified into four categories: (1) passive, (2) assistive, (3) active, and (4) resistive. Each can be used to advantage in restoring the athlete to a state of competitive fitness.

Passive exercise Passive exercise is the movement of an affected part by another person or by a device, without effort by the athlete. This technique can be used to advantage if an injury has hampered the range of joint motion or if the apprehensive athlete must be shown that the condition has been remediated and that there is no need for fear.

Assistive exercise Assistive exercise is movement of an injured part by the athlete with the assistance of another person.

Active exercise Active exercise is movement that is executed by the athlete without assistance. Exercises falling into this category are those used for general conditioning and those used remedially for restoring function to an injured part.

Resistive exercise Resistive exercise is movement that the athlete performs against a resisting force. Examples of resistive exercises include those performed with the use of free weights, manual resistance, and rubber surgical tubing.

Flexibility

Flexibility must be present if a part is to be functional. A part that is immobilized in a cast or brace or is not moved regularly through a full range of movement will eventually become inflexible. Important aspects of the athletic rehabilitation regimen are the stretching and muscle release techniques. These techniques are instituted only if they will not aggravate the injury.

Muscle Endurance

Muscle endurance, which is important to the restoration of the injured part, is the ability to sustain muscle contractions at a submaximal effort over a period of time. Muscle strength and endurance are indivisible parts of a continuum. For example, exercises employing progressive resistance at near maximal effort for four to six repetitions mainly affect strength; decreasing the resistance and increasing the number of repetitions require the ability to sustain a movement, thus increasing muscle endurance.

Figure 8-7

The highly motivated injured
athlete may become depressed
and begrudge time spent out of
action.

The athlete should avoid breath
holding when performing
strength and flexibility
exercises.

Proprioception

It is essential that an injured athlete redevelop the "feel" or "awareness" of where the body part is located at all times. Depending on the injury, this can be accomplished in many ways. The wobble or tilt board may be used for leg injuries. Other balance activities, such as standing on one foot or springing upward on a bouncer, can help proprioception. It is necessary that proprioception be restored before coordination/agility and speed activities are attempted.

Coordination/Agility and Speed of Movement

Exercise rehabilitation is concerned with reestablishing coordination and speed of movement. Before returning to a sport ready to resume full activity, an athlete must be able to perform at the same level of proficiency and have the same potential for delaying fatigue as before he or she became hurt. An athlete who is not at full capacity or who favors an injured part will most likely become reinjured or develop associated problems. Examples of coordination/agility exercises are zig-zag running, figure-8 running, and running and cutting.

Psychological Aspects of Exercise Rehabilitation

The highly motivated injured athlete may begrudge time spent out of action (Fig. 8-7). The coach and trainer must establish the fact that every person is unique as to healing and that everything is being done to assist the athlete's healing process. When an injury is serious, false hope should not be put forth for a fast "comeback." There should be a spirit of cooperation established between the athlete, coach, trainer, and physician.

Exercise Instruction

All rehabilitative exercises should be carefully taught to the athlete. The coach or athletic trainer first demonstrates the exercise, and the athlete repeats the exercise several times. It is important that the athlete fully understand the purpose of each exercise and know which muscles and body regions are primarily involved. Focusing on muscle action helps in synergy and keeps the exercise specific for a desired action. The athlete must be taught to perform at a given tempo. Isotonic exercise should be performed to four or more counts to ensure smooth movements. Two-count exercises produce jerky, arrhythmical movements.

Another major factor is to *avoid breath holding* in all strength and flexibility exercises. Breath holding creates general tension when relaxation is necessary.

The Exercise Rehabilitative Program

The proper selection and instruction in rehabilitative exercise cannot be overemphasized. All exercise forms should follow these principles:
1. Maintain a comfortable position involving the least strain possible.
2. Securely stabilize joints that are proximal to the injured part when exercising a specific body segment.
3. Perform all movements precisely and smoothly.
4. Conduct all movements within a pain-free range.

Exercise Overdosage

Engaging in exercise that is too intense or prolonged can be extremely detrimental to the progress of the athlete. The most obvious sign of overdosage is increased pain or discomfort lasting more than 3 hours. Other signs are decreased joint range of motion and decreased strength of the injured part. In most situations, early rehabilitation involves submaximal exercise performed in short bouts that are repeated many times daily. Exercise rehabilitation in the early stages of recovery is performed two or three times a day. As recovery increases, the intensity of exercise also increases, and the exercise is performed less often during the day and, ultimately, the week.

Rehabilitative Exercise Phases

Rehabilitative exercise in sports medicine can generally be categorized into six phases. A unique phase that comes before elective surgery is the presurgical phase. After the presurgical exercise phase, five additional phases can be identified: the postsurgical or acute exercise phase (phase 1), early exercise phase (phase 2), intermediate excrcise phase (phase 3), advanced exercise phase (phase 4), and the initial sports reentry phase (phase 5). Not all injured athletes experience all phases to achieve full rehabilitation. Depending on the type of injury and individual response to healing, phases may sometimes overlap.

Presurgical Exercise Phase

If surgery can be postponed, exercise may be used as a means to improve its outcome. By maintaining and in some cases increasing muscle tone and improving kinesthetic awareness, the athlete is prepared to continue the exercise rehabilitative program after surgery.

Exercise performed in the presurgical phase can often assist in recovery after surgery.

Postsurgical or Acute Injury Exercise Phase (Phase 1)

Exercise is often encouraged after surgery to the musculoskeletal system. The optimal time for commencement of therapeutic exercise is approximately 24 hours after surgery or injury. Exercise is employed to avoid muscle atrophy and to ensure return to sports participation as quickly as possible. Postsurgical exercise often repeats what was done presurgically. Commonly, the body part that was surgically repaired is immobilized by a cast, dressing, or sling. When immobilized, muscle tensing or isometrics may be employed to maintain muscle strength. Unless contraindicated, joints that are immediately adjacent (**distal** and **proximal**) to the immobilized part should be gently exercised to maintain their strength and mobility.

The postsurgical exercise phase should start 24 hours after surgery.

distal
Farthest from the point of attachment (opposite of proximal)

proximal
Nearest to the point of attachment (opposite of distal)

Early Exercise Phase (Phase 2)

The early exercise phase is a direct extension of the postsurgical, or acute injury, phase. The primary goals of this phase are to restore full muscle contraction without pain and to maintain strength in muscles surrounding the immobilized part. Muscle tensing is continued. Depending on the nature of the condition, isometric exercise against resistance may be added. Joints that are close to the injury are maintained in good condition by strengthening and mobility exercises.

Intermediate Exercise Phase (Phase 3)

When pain-free full muscle contraction has been achieved, the goals are to develop up to 50% range of motion of the unaffected part and 50% strength. A third goal is to restore near-normal neuromuscular coordination and proprioception.

Advanced Exercise Phase (Phase 4)

The ideal goals of the advanced phase of exercise are to fully restore power, flexibility, endurance, speed, and agility to the athlete.

The goals of phase 4 are to restore at least 90% of the athlete's range of motion and strength. Also the athlete is to undergo reconditioning for returning to his or her sport. The ideal goals in this phase are to fully restore power, flexibility, endurance, speed, proprioception, and agility of the injured part, as well as the entire body.

Initial Sports Reentry Phase (Phase 5)

Phase 5 of the exercise rehabilitation program involves returning to sports participation. In this phase the underlying factors are gradualness and avoiding having the athlete "overdo." In some cases this phase is a period in which muscle bulk is restored; in other instances the athlete carefully tests the results of the exercise rehabilitation process. It is essential that the athlete not return to competition before full range of movement, strength, and coordination have been attained and psychological readiness has been achieved.

The Exercise Rehabilitation Plan

The exercise rehabilitation plan must include:
  Injury situation
  Injury evaluation
  Exercise plan
  Criteria for full recovery
  Return to the sport

No exercise rehabilitation program can properly take place without a carefully thought out plan. It should contain four major elements: a clear understanding of the injury situation, an injury evaluation, an exercise plan, and criteria for recovery and returning to a specific sport.

Injury Situation

Persons responsible for carrying out exercise rehabilitation must have a complete and clear understanding of the injury. This should include (1) exactly how the injury was sustained, (2) careful inspection of the injury, and (3) the medical diagnosis, consisting of the major signs, symptoms, and anatomical structures affected.

Injury Evaluation

Before an exercise program is developed, an evaluation is made. It should include range of motion, muscle strength, and functional capacity of the part. The evaluation must take into consideration factors of swelling, pain, and movements or exercises that may be contraindicated.

Exercise Plan

When there is a clear understanding of the athlete's functional capacity, exercises are selected on a progressive basis. The exercises are grouped according to phases of rehabilitation. Criteria for progressing from one phase to another are established, as are criteria for ultimate recovery.

Criteria for Full Recovery

The athlete must successfully pass a functional evaluation before obtaining a release for competition. This means having recovered full range of motion, strength, and size of the injured body part. In addition, the athlete must demonstrate full-function capabilities that are sport specific, as well as a psychological readiness for returning to the sport.

FITTING AND USING THE CRUTCH OR CANE

The proper use of a crutch or cane is part of the rehabilitation process when necessary. When an athlete has a lower limb injury, weight bearing may be contraindicated. Situations of this type call for the use of a crutch or cane. Very often, the athlete is assigned one of these aids without proper fitting or instruction in their use. An improper fit and usage can place abnormal stresses on various body parts.[8] Constant pressure of the body weight on the crutch axillary pads can cause crutch palsy. The pressure on the nerves and blood vessels located in the arm pit can lead to temporary or even permanent numbness in the hands. Faulty mechanics in the use of crutches or canes can produce a chronic low back or hip strain.

Fitting the Athlete

The adjustable, wooden crutch is well suited to the athlete. For a correct fit the athlete should wear low-heeled shoes and stand with good posture and the feet close together. The crutch length is determined first by placing the tip 6 inches (15 cm) from the outer margin of the shoe and 2 inches (5 cm) in front of the shoe. The underarm crutch brace is positioned 1 inch (2.5 cm) below the fold of the underarm. Next, the hand brace is adjusted so that it is even with the athlete's hand, and the elbow is flexed at an approximate 30-degree angle (Fig. 8-8).

Fitting a cane to the athlete is relatively easy. Measurement is taken from the upper aspect of the femur to the floor while the athlete is wearing street shoes.

Walking with the Crutch or Cane

Many elements of crutch walking correspond with regular walking. The technique commonly used in sports injuries is the tripod method. In this method the athlete swings through the crutches without making any surface contact with the injured limb or by partially bearing weight with the injured limb. The following sequence is performed:
1. The athlete stands on one foot with the affected foot completely elevated or partially bearing weight.
2. Placing the crutch tips 12 to 15 inches (30 to 37.5 cm) ahead of the feet, the athlete leans forward, straightens the elbows, pulls the upper cross-

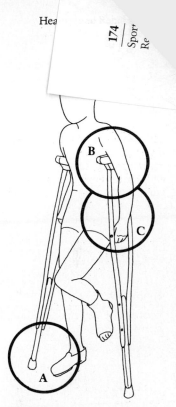

Figure 8-8

The crutch must be properly fitted to the athlete. **A,** The crutch tips are placed 6 inches (15 cm) from the outer margin of the shoe and 2 inches (5 cm) from the outer margin of the shoe and 2 inches (5 cm) in front of the shoe. **B,** The underarm crutch brace is positioned 1 inch (2.5 cm) below the anterior fold of the axilla. **C,** The hand brace is placed even with the athlete's hand, with the elbow flexed approximately 30 degrees.

Proper fitting of a crutch or cane is essential to avoid placing abnormal stresses on the body.

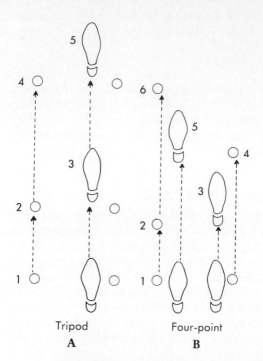

Figure 8-9

Crutch gait. **A**, Tripod method.
B, Four-point gait.

Tripod
A

Four-point
B

piece firmly against the side of the chest, and swings or steps between the stationary crutches (Fig. 8-9).

3. After moving through, the athlete recovers the crutches and again places the tips forward.

An alternate method is the four-point crutch gait. In this method the athlete stands on both feet. One crutch is moved forward, and the opposite foot is stepped forward. The crutch on the same side as the foot that moved forward moves just ahead of the foot. The opposite foot steps forward, followed by the crutch on the same side, and so on.

Once the athlete is able to move effectively on a level surface, negotiating stairs should be taught. As with level crutch walking, a tripod is maintained on stairs. When going upstairs the unaffected support leg moves up one step while the body weight is supported by the hands. The full weight of the body is transferred to the support leg followed by moving the crutch tips and affected leg to the step. When going downstairs the crutch tips and the affected leg move down one step followed by the support leg. If a handrail is available, both crutches are held by the outside hand, and a similar pattern is followed as with the crutch on each side.[2]

SUMMARY

The healing process of soft tissue consists of the inflammatory, repair, and remodeling phases. The inflammatory phase lasts 3 to 4 days and is designed to protect, localize, and prepare the tissue for repair. The phase is synonymous with healing and the restoration of lost tissue. Remodeling is the phase of healing that returns the injured tissue to full strength.

Fracture healing follows many of the steps of soft tissue healing, with the exception of the development of a soft and hard callus. The soft callus is composed mostly of connective tissue. The hard callus is composed of connective tissue and a network of woven bone that will slowly be replaced by mature bone. Fracture healing can be delayed if there is improper blood supply to the fractured area and poor immobilization.

Pain is both a psychological and physiological phenomenon. Pain perception is subjective and may be described as burning, sharp, dull, crushing, or piercing. Acute pain is designed to protect the body, while chronic pain serves no useful purpose. Chronic pain is believed to be caused by a noxious stimulus that affects the high-threshold nociceptors in skin, blood vessels, subcutaneous tissue, fascia, periosteum, viscera, and other pain-sensitive structures.

Both superficial cold and heat provide therapeutic benefits. Although for different reasons, they can break up the muscle pain-spasm-pain cycle and reduce swelling. Cold application produces a local anesthesia while increasing local circulation. Common superficial cold therapy techniques are ice massage, ice water immersion, and ice blanket packs. Superficial heat therapy techniques are moist heat packs, whirlpool baths, and contrast baths.

Exercise rehabilitation is a major approach in returning the injured athlete to his or her sport. Exercise rehabilitation, like physical conditioning, follows the SAID principle. It should be designed to prevent deconditioning and restore the injured part to a preinjury state. Isometric muscle contraction is commonly used to maintain strength of an immobilized part. When mobility is allowed, flexibility and isokinetic and isotonic strengthening exercises may be employed. Proprioception activities are engaged to restore balance. Coordination/agility and speed of movement activities follow the restoration of balance. Exercise overdosage must be avoided, with short bouts of submaximal exercise being performed in the early stages of rehabilitation. An exercise rehabilitation plan should include the injury situation, evaluation, exercise plan, and a criteria for full recovery.

The proper use of the crutch or cane when necessary is a major part of the rehabilitative process. Improper fitting or use of these devices can often aggravate an injury or create another physical problem.

REVIEW QUESTIONS AND CLASS ACTIVITIES

1. Name the outward signs of the inflammatory phase of healing.
2. Explain vasoconstriction and vasodilation in acute trauma.
3. How does blood coagulate?
4. Why does tissue continue to die after trauma ceases to occur?
5. What is the purpose of the remodeling phase?
6. Compare soft tissue and fracture healing.
7. What is the significance of "pain perception"?
8. Compare the body's reaction to cold and superficial heat.
9. Describe the typical ways of applying superficial cold and heat to a sports injury.
10. What does exercise rehabilitation do for an injured muscle or joint?
11. Why does overdosage of exercise occur? What are its signs?

12. Write a rehabilitation plan for a simulated injury situation.
13. Describe how to fit a pair of crutches and a cane.

REFERENCES

1. Anderson, W.A.D., and Scotti, R.M.: Synopsis of pathology, St. Louis, 1980, The C.V. Mosby. Co.
2. Aten, D.: Crutches: essential in caring for lower extremity injuries, Phys. Sportsmed. **8**:121, Nov. 1980.
3. Bonica, J.J.: Pathophysiology in pain. In: Current concepts of postoperative pain, New York, 1978, H.P. Publishing Co., Inc.
4. Bonta, I.L., and Parnham, M.J.: Prostaglandins and chronic inflammation, Biochem. Pharmacol. **27**:1611, 1978.
5. Boyd, C.E.: Referred visceral pain in athletics, Ath. Train. **15**:20, 1980.
6. Chusid, J.G.: Correlative neuroanatomy and functional neurology, ed. 17, Los Altos, Calif., 1979, Lange Medical Publications.
7. Cooper, D.L., and Fair, J.: Contrast baths and pressure treatment of ankle sprains, Phys. Sportsmed. **7**:143, April 1979.
8. Flood, D.K.: Proper fitting and use of crutches, Phys. Sportsmed. **11**:75, March 1983.
9. Goss, C.M.: Gray's Anatomy of the human body, Philadelphia, 1973, Lea & Febiger.
10. Gould, J.A., and Davies, G.J.: Orthopaedic and sports rehabilitation concepts. In Gould, J.A., and Davies, G.J. (editors): Orthopaedic and sports physical therapy, vol. 2, St. Louis, 1985, The C.V. Mosby Co.
11. Gradisar, I.A.: Fracture stabilization and healing. In Gould, J.A., and Davies, G.J. (editors): Orthopaedic and sports physical therapy, vol. 2, St. Louis, 1985, The C.V. Mosby Co.
12. Grant, A.E.: Massage with ice (cryokinetics) in the treatment of painful conditions of the musculoskeletal system, Arch. Phys. Med. Rehab. **44**:233, 1964.
13. Haden, C.A.: Cryokinetics in an early treatment program, Phys. Ther. **44**:990, 1964.
14. Hocutt, J.E., Jr.: Cryotherapy, Am. Fam. Physician **23**:141, 1981.
15. Hocutt, J.E., Jr., et al.: Cryotherapy in ankle sprains, Am. J. Sports Med. **10**:316, Sept./Oct. 1982.
16. Knight, J.L., and Londeree, B.R.: Comparison of blood flow in the ankle of uninjured subjects during therapeutic applications of heat, cold, and exercise, Med. Sci. Sports Exer. **12**:76, 1980.
17. Lehmann, J.F., and DeLateur, B.J.: Therapeutic heat. In Lehmann, J.F. (editor): Therapeutic heat and cold, ed. 3, Baltimore, 1982, The Williams & Wilkins Co.
18. Rusk, H.A.: Rehabilitation medicine, ed. 4, St. Louis, 1977, The C.V. Mosby Co.
19. Sherman, M.: Which treatment to recommend? Hot or cold? Am. Pharm. **NS20**:46, Aug. 1980.
20. Siracusano, G.: The physical therapist's use of exercise in the treatment of chronic pain, J. Ortho. Sports Phys. Ther. **6**:73, Sept./Oct. 1984.
21. van der Meulen, J.C.H.: Present state of knowledge on processes of healing in collagen structures, J. Sports Med. (suppl. 1) **3**:4, 1982.
22. Wilkerson, G.B.: Inflammation in connective tissue: etiology and management, Ath. Train. **20**:298, Winter 1985.

ANNOTATED BIBLIOGRAPHY

Blair, D.: Crutch use in athletics, Ath. Train. **19**:275, Winter 1984.
  Stresses the importance of properly fitting crutches to avoid unnecessary problems stemming from poor fitting and technique.

Guck, T.P.: Stress management for chronic pain patients, J. Ortho. Sports Phys. Ther. **6**:5, July/Aug. 1984.

An overview of stress management procedures for pain patients.

Harvey, J.S.: Symposium on rehabilitation of the injured athlete, Clinics in sports medicine, vol.4, Philadelphia, July 1985, W.B. Saunders Co.

Provides an in-depth discussion on the foundations of rehabilitation and the rehabilitation of specific sports injuries.

Kegerreis, S., Malone, T., and McCarroll, J.: Functional progressions: an aide to athletic rehabilitation, Phys. Sportsmed. **12**:67, Dec. 1984.

Stresses the importance of a planned, progressively difficult sequence of exercises for athletic rehabilitation.

Part Three | SPORTS CONDITIONS

P*art Three is concerned with presenting an introduction to those sports conditions that coaches commonly encounter. Chapters 9 through 16 present the prevention, immediate care, and general follow-up care of prevalent musculoskeletal conditions. Chapter 17 presents the problems and conditions other than those afflicting the musculoskeletal system.*

| # THE FOOT

When you finish this chapter, you will be able to:

Explain how to recognize the most common injuries
   sustained by the foot

Evaluate common foot injuries

Explain how to apply appropriate immediate and
   superficial follow-up care to the foot

The foot region has a high incidence of sports injuries. Dealing effectively
with these injuries at the coach's level is a major challenge.

THE FOOT

The human foot is a marvel of strength, flexibility, and coordinated movement. It transmits the stresses throughout the body when engaged in the activities of walking, running, and jumping. It is made up of 26 bones that are
held together by an intricate network of ligaments and fascia and moved by a
complicated group of muscles (Figs. 9-1 and 9-2).

Skin Trauma of the Foot

Many sports place demands on the feet that are far beyond the normal daily requirements. The skin of the feet becomes traumatized from abnormal
mechanical forces within the socks and shoes.

Prevention of Skin Trauma

Prevention of skin injury includes maintaining proper foot hygiene, wearing
properly fitting socks and shoes, and reducing abnormal stresses by correcting
faulty mechanics within the shoe. Some of the more common problems are
calluses, blisters, corns, and ingrown toenails.

Foot Calluses

Excessive callus development
must be avoided.

Foot calluses may be caused by shoes that are too narrow or too short. Calluses that develop from friction can become painful because the fatty layer
loses its elasticity and cushioning effect. The excess callus moves as a gross
mass, becoming highly vulnerable to tears, cracks, and ultimately infections.

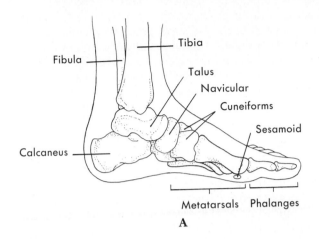

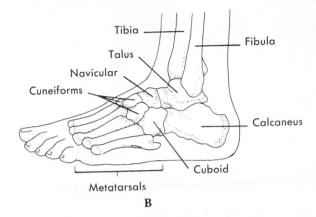

Fibula

Tibia

Talus

Navicular

Cuneiforms

Sesamoid

Calcaneus

Metatarsals Phalanges

A

Tibia

Talus

Navicular

Cuneiforms

Fibula

Calcaneus

Cuboid

Metatarsals

B

Figure 9-1

Bony structure of the foot. **A,**
Medial aspect, **B,** Lateral aspect.

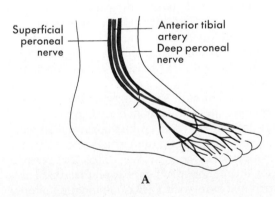

Superficial
peroneal
nerve

Anterior tibial
artery

Deep peroneal
nerve

A

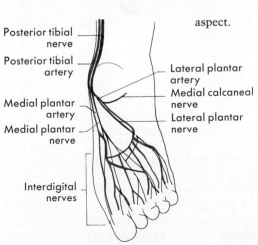

aspect.

Posterior tibial
nerve

Posterior tibial
artery

Medial plantar
artery

Medial plantar
nerve

Interdigital
nerves

Lateral plantar
artery

Medial calcaneal
nerve

Lateral plantar
nerve

B

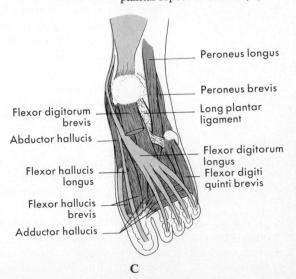

Peroneus longus

Peroneus brevis

Long plantar
ligament

Flexor digitorum
brevis

Abductor hallucis

Flexor hallucis
longus

Flexor hallucis
brevis

Adductor hallucis

Flexor digitorum
longus

Flexor digiti
quinti brevis

C

Figure 9-2

The major nerves of the foot (**A**
and **B**) and muscles of the
plantar aspect of the foot (**C**).

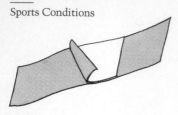

Figure 9-3

The direct means of preventing a blister is to "blank out" a piece of tape and fit it tightly over an irritated skin area.

Blisters can be prevented by:
 Dusting shoes and socks
  with talcum powder
 Applying petroleum jelly
 Wearing tubular socks or
  two pairs of socks

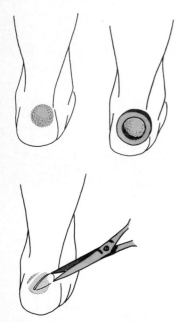

Figure 9-4

The conservative approach in caring for a blister should be taken whenever possible with a protective doughnut. If the blister is torn, a flap can be formed by cutting the skin half way around its perimeter to allow treatment of the underlying tissue.

Athletes whose shoes are properly fitted but who still develop heavy calluses commonly have foot mechanics problems that may require special orthotics. Special cushioning devices, such as wedges, doughnuts, and arch supports, may help to distribute the weight on the feet more evenly and thus reduce skin stress.[5] Excessive callus accumulation can be prevented by (1) wearing two pairs of socks, a thin cotton or nylon pair next to the skin and a heavy athletic pair over the cotton pair, or a single doubleknit sock; (2) wearing shoes that are the correct size and in good condition; and (3) routinely applying materials such as petroleum jelly to reduce friction.

Management of excess callosity   Athletes who are prone to excess calluses should be encouraged to use an emery callus file after each shower. Massaging small amounts of lanolin into devitalized calluses once or twice a week after practice may help maintain some tissue elasticity. The coach might have the athlete decrease the calluses' thickness and increase its smoothness by sanding or pumicing. **NOTE**: Great care should be taken not to totally remove the callus and the protection it affords at a given pressure point.

Blisters

Like calluses, blisters are often a major problem of sports participation, especially early in the season. As a result of horizontal shearing forces acting on the skin, fluid accumulates below the outer skin layer.[6] This fluid may be clear, bloody, or infected. Blisters are particularly associated with such sports as rowing, pole-vaulting, basketball, football, and weight events in track and field, such as the shot put and discus.

Blister prevention   Soft feet, coupled with shearing skin stress, can produce severe blisters. It has been found that a dusting of corn starch or the application of petroleum jelly can protect the skin against abnormal friction. Wearing tubular socks or two pairs of socks, as for preventing calluses, is also desirable, particularly for athletes who have sensitive feet or feet that perspire excessively. If, however, a friction area ("hot spot") does arise, the athlete has several options: (1) cover the irritated skin with a friction-proofing material such as petroleum jelly, (2) place a "blanked-out" piece of tape (Fig. 9-3) tightly over the irritated area, (3) cover the area with a piece of moleskin, or (4) apply ice to skin areas that have developed abnormal friction.

When blisters develop   When caring for a blister, one should be aware at all times of the possibility of severe infection from contamination. Whenever a blister appears to be infected it requires medical attention. In sports, two approaches are generally used to care for blisters: the conservative approach and the torn blister approach. The conservative approach should be followed whenever possible. Its main premise is that a blister should not be contaminated by cutting or puncturing but should be protected from further insult by a small doughnut until the initial irritation has subsided[5] (Fig. 9-4). If puncturing is necessary to prevent the blister from tearing, it should be done by introducing a sterilized needle underneath the epidermis, approximately 1/8 inch (0.3 cm) outside the diameter of the raised tissue. The blister should be opened wide enough that it does not become sealed. After the fluid has been dispersed a pressure pad is placed directly over the blister to prevent its refilling. When the tenderness has subsided in about 5 or 6 days, the loose skin is cut away. Conservative care of blisters is preferred for cases in which there is little danger of tearing or aggravation through activity. A product called "new skin" can be sprayed on blisters where raw skin is exposed to provide a protective coating.

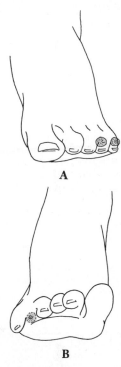

Figure 9-5
A, Hard corn. B, Soft corn.

CARING FOR A TORN BLISTER

1. Cleanse the blister and surrounding tissue with soap and water; rinse with an antiseptic.
2. Using sterile scissors, cut the torn blister halfway around the perimeter.
3. Apply antiseptic and a mild ointment, such as zinc oxide, to the exposed tissue.
4. Lay the flap of skin back over the treated tissue; cover the area with a sterile dressing.
5. Check daily for signs of infection.
6. Within 2 or 3 days, or when the underlying tissue has hardened sufficiently, remove the dead skin. This should be done by trimming the skin on a bevel and as close as possible to the perimeter of the blister.

Corns

The *hard corn (clavis durum)* is the most serious type of corn. It is caused by the pressure of improperly fitting shoes, the same mechanism that causes calluses. Hammer toes and hard corns are usually associated with the hard corns forming on the tops of the deformed toes (Fig. 9-5, *A*). Symptoms are local pain and disability, with inflammation and thickening of soft tissue. Because of the chronic nature of this condition, it requires a physician's care.[2]

The coach can aid the situation by issuing shoes that fit properly and then having athletes with such a condition soak their feet daily in warm, soapy water to soften the corn. To alleviate further irritation, the corn should be protected by a small felt or sponge rubber doughnut.

The *soft corn (clavis molle)* is the result of a combination of wearing narrow shoes and having excessive foot perspiration. Because of the pressure of the shoe coupled with the exudation of moisture, the corn usually forms between the fourth and fifth toes (Fig. 9-5, *B*). A circular area of thickened, white, **macerated skin** appears between the toes at the base of the proximal head of the phalanges, and there appears to be a black dot in the center of the corn. Both pain and inflammation are likely to be present.

macerated skin
Softening of the skin by soaking

Soft corn care When caring for a soft corn the best procedure is to have the athlete wear properly fitting shoes, keep the skin between the toes clean and dry, decrease pressure by keeping the toes separated with cotton or lamb's wool, and apply a **keratolytic** agent such as 40% salicylic acid in liquid or plasters.[5]

keratolytic
Loosening of the horny layer of the skin

Ingrown Toenails

An ingrown toenail is a condition in which the leading side edge of the toenail has grown into the soft tissue nearby, usually resulting in a severe inflammation and infection.

It is important that the athlete's shoes be of the proper length and width, since continued pressure on a toenail can lead to serious irritation or cause it

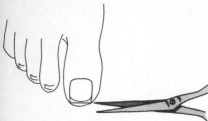

Figure 9-6

Prevention of ingrown toenails requires routine trimming so that the margins do not penetrate the skin on the side of the nail.

The athlete who is prone to heel bruises should routinely wear a padded heel cup.

Figure 9-7

Once an ingrown toenail occurs, proper management is necessary to avoid infection. **A,** A wisp of cotton being applied under the ingrown side; **B,** cutting a V in the center of the nail; **C,** shaving the top of the nail thin.

to become ingrown. The length of the sports socks is also at times a factor, since they can cause pressure on the toenails. It is important to know how to trim the nails correctly. Two things must be taken into consideration: first, the nail must be trimmed so that its margins do not penetrate the tissue on the sides (Fig. 9-6); second, the nail should be left sufficiently long that it is clear of the underlying tissue and still should be cut short enough that it is not irritated by either shoes or socks.

Acute Foot Injuries

Contusions

Two common contusions sustained in sports are to the heel and instep.

Heel bruise Of the many contusions and bruises that an athlete may receive, there is none more disabling than the heel bruise. Sport activities that demand a sudden stop-and-go response or sudden change from a horizontal to a vertical movement, such as basketball jumping, high jumping and long horse vaulting, are particularly likely to cause heel bruises. The heel has a thick, cornified skin layer and a heavy fat pad covering, but even this thick padding cannot protect against a sudden abnormal force directed to this area.

Immediate and follow-up care When injury occurs the athlete complains of severe pain in the heel and is unable to withstand the stress of weight bearing.[8]

A bruise of the heel usually develops into chronic inflammation of the periosteum. Follow-up management of this condition should be started 2 to 3 days after insult, involving a variety of superficial and deep-heat therapies. If

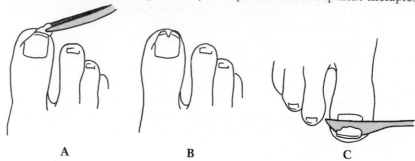

A   **B**   **C**

MANAGING THE INGROWN TOENAIL

1. Soak the toe in hot water (110° to 120° F [43.3° to 48.8° C]) for approximately 20 minutes, two or three times daily.
2. When the nail is soft and pliable, use forceps to insert a wisp of cotton under the edge of the nail and lift it from the soft tissue (Fig. 9-7).
3. Other methods of care include cutting a V in the center of the outer edge or shaving the toenail thin, both of which tend to pull the nail from the side.
4. Continue the chosen procedure until the nail has grown out sufficiently that it can be trimmed straight across. The correct trimming of nails is shown in Fig. 9-6.

An ingrown toenail can easily become infected. If this occurs it should be immediately referred to a physician for treatment.

the athlete recognizes the problem in its acute stage, the following procedures should be adhered to:

1. If possible, the athlete should not step on the heel for a period of at least 24 hours.
2. On the third and subsequent days warm whirlpool or ultrasound can be administered by the athletic trainer.
3. If pain when walking has subsided by the third day, the athlete may resume moderate activity — with the protection of a heel cup, protective doughnut, or protective taping (Fig. 9-8).

   NOTE: Because of the nature of the site of this condition, it may recur throughout an entire season.

   An athlete who is prone to or who needs protection from a heel bruise should routinely wear a heel cup with a foam rubber pad as a preventive aid. By surrounding the heel with a firm heel cup, traumatic forces are diffused.

Instep bruise   The bruised instep, like the bruised heel, can cause disability. These commonly occur by being stepped on or by being hit with a fast-moving, hard projectile, such as a baseball or hockey puck. Immediate application of cold compresses must be performed not only to control inflammation but most importantly to avoid swelling. Irritation of the tendons on the top of the foot can make wearing a shoe difficult. If the force is of great intensity, there is a good chance of fracture, requiring an x-ray.[4] Once inflammation is reduced and the athlete returns to competition a 1/8-inch (0.3 cm) pad protection should be worn directly on the skin over the bruise and a rigid instep guard should be worn external to the shoe.

Strains of the Foot

Insufficient conditioning of musculature, structural imbalance, or incorrect mechanics can cause the foot to become prone to strain. Common strains are to the metatarsal arch, the longitudinal arch, and the plantar fascia.

Metatarsal arch strain   The athlete who has acquired a fallen metatarsal arch or who has a high arch (pes cavus) is susceptible to this strain. In both cases malalignment of the forefoot subjects the flexor tendons on the bottom of the foot to increased tension (Fig. 9-9).

Longitudinal arch strain   Longitudinal arch strain is usually an early-season injury caused by subjecting the musculature of the foot to unaccustomed, severe exercise and forceful contact with hard playing surfaces. In this condition there is a flattening or depressing of the longitudinal arch while the foot is in the midsupport phase, resulting in a strain to the arch. Such a strain may appear quite suddenly, or it may develop rather slowly over a period of time.

As a rule, pain is experienced only when running is attempted and usually appears just below the inner ankle bone (medial malleolus) and the medial ankle tendons, accompanied by swelling and tenderness along the inner aspect of the foot. The flexor muscle of the great toe (flexor hallucis longus) often develops tenderness as a result of overuse in compensating for the strain on the medial arch ligaments.

Immediate and follow-up care   The management of a longitudinal arch strain involves immediate care of ICE-R followed by appropriate therapy, reduction of weight bearing, and exercise rehabilitation. Exercise and weight

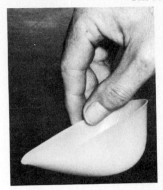

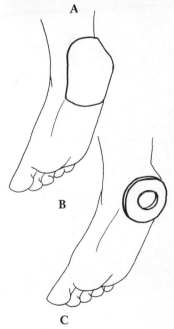

Figure 9-8

Heel protection through the use of heel cup (**A** and **B**) and protective heel doughnut (**C**).

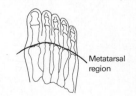

Metatarsal region

Figure 9-9

Bones comprising the metatarsal region.

Figure 9-10

Arch taping technique no. 1,
including an arch pad and
circular tape strips.

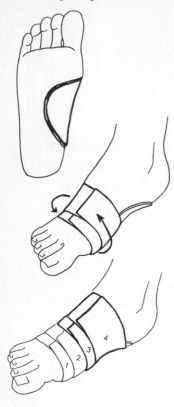

bearing must be performed pain free. Arch taping technique no. 1 or no. 2
might be used to allow earlier pain-free weight bearing (Figs. 9-10 and 9-11).

ARCH TAPING TECHNIQUE NO. 1

Arch taping with pad support. Arch taping with pad support employs the following procedures to strengthen weakened arches.
Materials needed: One roll of 1 1/2-inch (3.8 cm) tape, tape adherent, and a 1/8-
or 1/4-inch (0.3 to 0.6 cm) adhesive foam rubber pad cut to fit the longitudinal
arch.
Position of the athlete: The athlete lies face down on the table, with the foot
that is to be taped extending about 6 inches (15 cm) over the edge of the table.
To ensure proper position, allow the foot to hang in a relaxed position.
Position of the operator: The operator stands facing the sole of the affected foot.
Procedure: Fig. 9-10 illustrates the proper procedure for applying arch taping
technique no. 1.
CAUTION: Avoid putting on so many strips of tape as to hamper the action of
the ankle.

ARCH TAPING TECHNIQUE NO. 2

X taping for the longitudinal arch. When using the figure-8 method for taping
the longitudinal arch, the following steps are executed.
Materials needed: One roll of 1-inch (2.5 cm) tape and tape adherent.
Position of the athlete: The athlete lies face down on a table, with the affected
foot extending approximately 6 inches (15 cm) over the edge of the table. To
ensure proper position, allow the foot to hang in a relaxed natural position
Position of the operator: The operator faces the bottom of the foot.
Procedure: Fig. 9-11 illustrates the proper procedure for applying arch taping
technique no. 2.
NOTE: A variation of this method is to start and finish the X on each of the five
metatarsal heads (Fig. 9-12).

Figure 9-11

Arch taping technique no. 2 (X
taping).

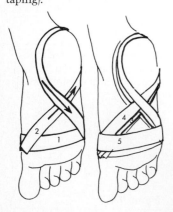

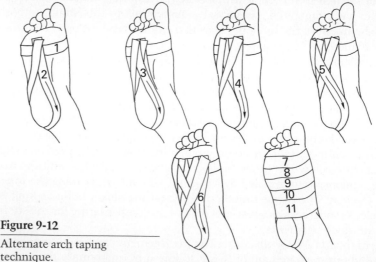

Figure 9-12

Alternate arch taping
technique.

The Sprained Great Toe

Sprains of the great toe are caused most often by kicking some nonyielding object. Sprains result from a considerable force applied in such a manner as to extend the joint beyond its normal range of motion ("jamming" it) or to impart a twisting motion to the toe, thereby twisting and tearing the supporting tissues. Symptoms of an acute injury appear. Care involves the following considerations:

1. The injury should be handled as an acute sprain.
2. The severity of the injury should be determined through palpation and, if there are signs of a fracture, through x-ray examination.
3. When a sprain is determined the athlete should wear a stiff-soled shoe.

TAPING FOR THE SPRAINED GREAT TOE

The following procedures are used for taping the great toe after a sprain.
Materials needed: One roll of 1-inch (2.5 cm) tape and tape adherent.
Position of the athlete: The athlete assumes a sitting position.
Position of the operator: The operator faces the sole of the affected foot.
Procedure: Fig. 9-13 illustrates the proper procedure for taping the sprained great toe.

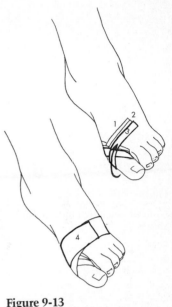

Figure 9-13

Taping for a sprained great toe.

Fractures and Dislocations of the Foot

Because of the foot's susceptibility to trauma in sports, fractures or dislocations can occur. Any moderate to severe contusion or twisting force must be suspected as being a fracture. X-ray examination should be routine in these situations.

Fractures and dislocations of the toes Fractures of the toes are usually the bone-crushing type such as may be incurred in kicking an object or stubbing a toe. Generally, they are accompanied by swelling and discoloration. Any suspected fracture of the great toe should be referred to a physician immediately. If the break is in the bone shaft, an adhesive taping is applied (Fig. 9-14). However, if more than one toe is involved, a cast may be applied for a few days. As a rule, 3 or 4 weeks of inactivity permits healing, although tenderness may persist for some time. A shoe with a wide toe box should be worn; in cases of a great toe fracture a stiff sole should be worn.

Fractures and dislocations of the toes are caused by kicking an object or by stubbing a toe.

Dislocation of the toes is less common than fractures. If one occurs, it is usually to the middle phalanx upper most joint. The mechanism of injury is the same as for fractures. Reduction is usually performed easily without anesthesia by the physician.

Fractures of the metatarsals Fractures of the metatarsals can be caused by direct force, such as being stepped on by another player, or by abnormal stress. They are characterized by swelling and pain. The most common acute fracture is to the *base of the fifth metatarsal (Jones fracture)*. It is normally caused by a sharp inversion and plantar flexion of the foot. It has all the appearances of a severe sprain. Care is usually symptomatic, with ICE-R employed to control swelling. Once swelling has subsided, a short leg walking cast is applied for 3 to 6 weeks. Ambulation is usually possible by the second week. A shoe with a large toe box should be worn.

Figure 9-14

Taping for a fracture of a toe.

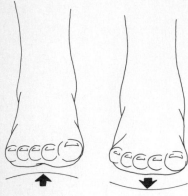

Figure 9-15

Normal and fallen metatarsal arches.

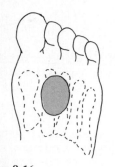

Figure 9-16

Metatarsal pad.

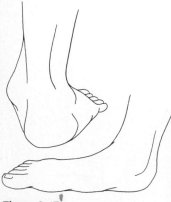

Figure 9-17

Fallen medial longitudinal arch.

Chronic and Overuse Foot Conditions

Lower extremity stress problems in sports very often begin in the foot region.

Arch Conditions

Painful arches are usually the result of improperly fitting shoes, an overweight condition, excessive activity on hard surfaces, overuse, faulty posture, or fatigue—any of which may cause a pathological condition in the supporting tissue of the arch. The symptoms in this case are divided into three degrees, each characterized by specific symptoms. The first degree shows itself as a slight soreness in the arch. The second degree is indicated by a chronic inflammatory condition that includes soreness, redness, swelling, and a slight visible drop in the arch. In the third degree a completely fallen arch is accompanied by extreme pain, immobility, and deformity.

Fallen metatarsal arch Activity on hard surfaces or prolonged stresses on the balls of the feet may cause weak or fallen anterior metatarsal arches (Fig. 9-15). When the supporting ligaments and muscles lose their ability to retain the metatarsal heads in a domelike shape, a falling of the arch results, thereby placing pressure on the nerves and blood vessels in the area. The athlete first notices an irritation and redness on the ball of the foot. As the condition progresses, pain, callus formation, toe cramping, and often a severe burning sensation develop. Care of fallen anterior metatarsal arch conditions should include hydrotherapy, light friction massage, exercise, and metatarsal pads (Fig 9-16).

Fallen medial longitudinal arch (flatfoot) Various stresses weaken ligaments and muscles that support the arch, thus forcing the navicular bone downward. The athlete may complain of tiredness and tenderness in the arch and heel. Ankle sprains frequently result from weakened arches, and abnormal friction sites may develop within the shoe because of changes in weight distribution. This condition may be the result of several factors: shoes that cramp and deform the feet, weakened supportive tissues, an overweight condition, postural anomalies that subject the arches to unaccustomed or unnatural strain, or overuse, which may be the result of repeatedly subjecting the arch to a severe pounding through participation on an unyielding surface. Commonly, the fallen medial longitudinal arch is associated with foot pronation (Fig. 9-17).

CARE FOR ARCH CONDITIONS

1. Shoes should be fitted properly.
2. Hydrotherapy, especially a whirlpool, should be given three or four times daily at a temperature of 105° F (40.6° C) until the initial inflammation has subsided.
3. Deep therapy, such as ultrasound, can be used when prescribed by a physician.
4. Arch orthoses may have to be used to ameliorate irritation of the weakened ligaments. If a pathological condition of the arch can be detected in the first or second degree, arch supports may be needed.
5. Weakened arches, if detected early, can be aided by an exercise program. If the arch is allowed to drop and the condition becomes chronic, exercising can offer little relief other than as a palliative aid.

ARCH TAPING TECHNIQUE NO. 3

The double X and forefoot support. As its name implies, this taping both supports the longitudinal arch and stabilizes the forefoot into good alignment.

Materials needed: One roll of 1-inch (2.5 cm) tape and tape adherent.

Position of the athlete: The athlete lies face down on a table, with the foot to be taped extending approximately 6 inches (15 cm) over the edge of the table.

Position of the operator: The operator faces the bottom of the foot.

Procedure: Fig. 9-18 illustrates the proper procedure for applying arch taping technique no. 3.

LOWDYE TECHNIQUE

The LowDye technique is an excellent method for managing the fallen medial longitudinal arch, foot pronation, arch strains, and plantar fasciitis. Moleskin is cut in 3-inch (7.5 cm) strips to the shape of the sole of the foot. It should cover the head of the metatarsal bones and the calcaneus bone (Fig. 9-19).

Materials needed: One roll of 1-inch (2.5 cm) tape, 1 roll of 2-inch (5 cm) tape, and moleskin.

Position of the athlete: The athlete sits with the foot in a neutral position and the great toe in plantar flexion.

Position of the operator: The operator faces the bottom of the foot.

Procedure
1. Apply the moleskin to the sole of the foot, pulling it slightly downward before attaching it to the calcaneus.
2. Grasp the fore foot with the thumb under the distal 2 to 5 metatarsal heads, pushing slightly upward, with the tips of the second and third fingers pushing downward on the first metatarsal head. While the foot is in this position, apply two or three 1-inch (2.5 cm) tape strips laterally, starting from the end of the fifth metatarsal bone and finishing at the end of the first metatarsal bone. Keep these lateral strips below the outer malleolus.
3. Secure the moleskin and lateral tape strip by circling the forefoot with four or five 2-inch (5 cm) strips. Start at the lateral dorsum of the foot, circle under the plantar aspect, and finish at the medial dorsum of the foot.

Figure 9-18

Arch taping technique no. 3 with double X and forefoot support.

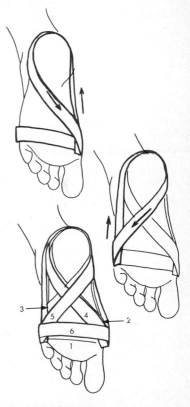

Figure 9-19

LowDye taping technique for the fallen medial longitudinal arch, foot pronation, arch strains, and plantar fasciitis.

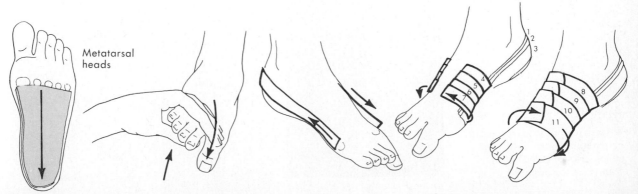

High arch (pes cavus)   Pes cavus (Fig. 9-20), commonly called claw foot, hollow foot, or an abnormally high arch, is not as common as pes planus, or flatfoot. In the rigid type of pes cavus, shock absorption is poor and can lead to problems such as general foot pain, painful metatarsal arch (metatarsalgia), and clawed or hammer toes. Pes cavus also may be without symptoms.

The accentuated high medial longitudinal arch may be congenital or indicate a neurological disorder. Commonly associated with this condition are clawed toes and abnormal shortening of the heel cord. The heel cord is directly linked with the plantar fascia. Also, because of the abnormal distribution of body weight, heavy calluses develop on the ball and heel of the foot.

Forefoot Conditions

A number of deformities and structural deviations affect the forefoot of many athletes.

Bunions   Bunions are one of the most frequent painful deformities of the great toe.

Causes   The reasons why a bunion develops are complex. Commonly, it is associated with a congenital deformity of the first metatarsal head, combined with wearing shoes that are pointed, too narrow, too short, or have high heels. The bursa over the side of the great toe becomes inflamed and eventually thickens. The joint becomes enlarged and the great toe becomes malaligned, moving medially toward the second toe, sometimes to such an extent that it eventually overlaps it. This type of bunion is also associated with the depressed or flattened transverse arch and a pronated foot.

The bunionette, or tailor's bunion, is much less common and affects the third joint of the fifth (little) toe. In this case the little toe angulates toward the fourth toe.

In all bunions both the flexor and extensor tendons of the toe become malpositioned, creating more angular stress on the joint.

In the beginning of a bunion there is tenderness, swelling, and enlargement of the joint. Poor-fitting shoes increase the irritation and pain. As the inflammation continues, angulation of the toe progresses, eventually leading to instability in the entire forefoot.

Figure 9-20

High arch (pes cavus).

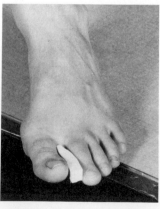

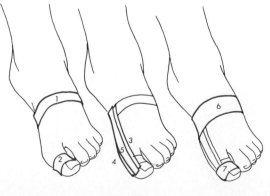

Figure 9-21

A, Wedging of the great toe can help reduce some of the abnormal stress of a bunion. **B,** Taping for the bunion.

A   B

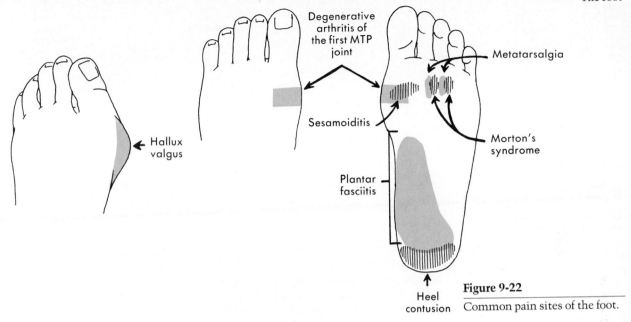

Degenerative arthritis of the first MTP joint

Metatarsalgia

Hallux valgus

Sesamoiditis

Morton's syndrome

Plantar fasciitis

Heel contusion

Figure 9-22

Common pain sites of the foot.

Care Each bunion has unique characteristics. Early recognition and care can often prevent increased irritation and deformity. Management procedures include the following:

1. Wear correctly fitting shoes with a wide toe box.
2. Place a felt or sponge rubber doughnut pad or lamb's wool over the medial side of the joint.
3. Wear a tape splint along with a resilient wedge placed between the great toe and the second toe (Fig. 9-21).
4. Apply superficial heat therapy to reduce inflammation.
5. Engage in daily foot exercises to strengthen both the extensor and flexor muscles of the toes.

If the condition progresses, a special orthotic device may help normalize foot mechanics. Surgery might be required in the later stages of this condition.

Metatarsalgia Although **metatarsalgia** is a general term to describe pain in the ball of the foot, it is more commonly associated with pain under the second and sometimes the third metatarsal head. A heavy callus often forms in the area of pain. Fig. 9-22 shows some of the more common pain sites in the foot.

Causes The most prevalent cause of this condition is the fallen metatarsal arch. Normally, the head of the first and fifth metatarsal bones bear slightly more weight than the second, third, and fourth. Normally, the first metatarsal head bears two sixths of the body weight, the fifth bears slightly more than one sixth, and the second, third, and fourth bear one sixth.[2] If the foot tends toward pronation, or if the metatarsal ligaments are weak, allowing the foot to abnormally spread (splayed foot), a fallen metatarsal arch is proba-

metatarsalgia
Pain in the metatarsal arch

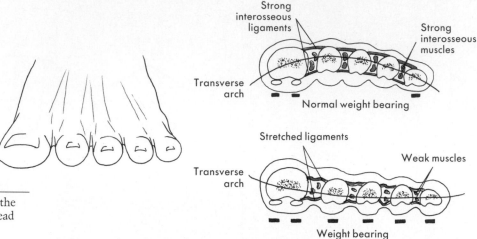

Figure 9-23

Normal weight bearing of the forefoot and abnormal spread (splayed foot).

ble (Fig. 9-23). As the transverse arch becomes flattened and the heads of the second, third, and fourth metatarsal bones become depressed, pain may result. A cavus deformity can also cause metatarsalgia.

Care Care of metatarsalgia usually consists of applying a pad to elevate the depressed metatarsal heads. **NOTE**: The pad is placed behind and not under the metatarsal heads.

A daily regimen of exercise should be practiced, concentrating on strengthening flexor and intrinsic muscles and stretching the heel cord.[1]

METATARSAL PAD SUPPORT

The purpose of the metatarsal pad is to reestablish the normal relationships of the metatarsal bones. It can be purchased commercially or constructed out of felt or sponge rubber (see Fig. 9-16).

Materials needed: One roll of 1-inch (2.5 cm) tape, a 1/8-inch (0.3 cm) adhesive felt oval cut to a 2-inch (5 cm) circumference, and tape adherent.

Position of the athlete: The athlete sits on a table or chair with the bottom surface of the affected foot turned upward.

Position of the operator: The operator stands facing the bottom of the athlete's foot.

Procedure

1. The circular pad is placed just behind the metatarsal heads.
2. About two or three circular strips of tape are placed loosely around the pad and foot.

Morton's syndrome Another foot deformity causing major forefoot pain is Morton's syndrome. Metatarsalgia is produced by an abnormally short first metatarsal bone. Weight is borne mainly by the second metatarsal bone, and there is hypermobility between the first and second proximal metatarsal joints (Fig. 9-24). The management is the same as that for foot pronation.

Hammer, or clawed, toes Hammer, or clawed, toes may be congenital, but more often the condition is caused by wearing shoes that are too short over a long period of time, thus cramping the toes. Hammer toe usually in-

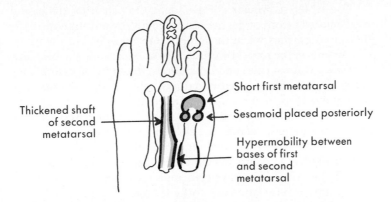

Thickened shaft
of second
metatarsal

Short first metatarsal

Sesamoid placed posteriorly

Hypermobility between
bases of first
and second
metatarsal

Figure 9-24

Morton's syndrome with an
abnormally short first
metatarsal bone.

volves the second or third toe, whereas clawed toes involve more than one toe. In both conditions the toe joints become malaligned, along with overly contracted flexor tendons and overly stretched extensor tendons. A deformity such as this eventually results in the formation of hard corns or calluses on the exposed joints. Quite often surgery is the only cure. However, proper shoes and protective taping (Fig. 9-25) can help prevent irritation.

Chronic and Overuse Syndromes

Because of the hard use that feet receive in many sports, they are prone to chronic and overuse syndromes. This is especially true if weight-transmission or biomechanical problems exist. Because distance running is becoming increasingly popular, musculoskeletal problems of the feet are also becoming more prevalent.

Bony outgrowths (exostoses) Exostoses are benign bony outgrowths from the surface of a bone and are usually capped by cartilage. Sometimes called *spurs*, such outgrowths occur principally at the head of the first metatarsal bone on the dorsum of the foot (Fig. 9-26). In certain instances what may at first appear to be an exostosis actually may be a partial dislocation (subluxation) of a midfoot joint. The causes of exostoses are highly variable. They include hereditary influences, faulty patterns of walking and running, excessive weight, joint impingements, and continual use of ill-fitting footwear.

Heel bursitis A common bursitis of the foot occurs to the bursa at the back of the heel located under the skin just above the attachment of the heel cord (Fig. 9-27). It often occurs because of pressure and rubbing of the upper edge of the sports shoe. Irritation produces an inflamed, swollen area. At the first sign of this condition a soft resilient pad should be placed over the bursa site. If necessary, larger shoes with a softer heel contour should be worn.

Heel spur syndrome (plantar fasciitis) Plantar fasciitis, or heel spur syndrome, is the most frequent hindfoot problem among distance runners.[9]

Causes Because of the stress that is placed on the calcaneus by the plantar soft tissue during repeated running or jumping activities, a chronic irritation and bone spur can occur. Athletes with a cavus deformity or pronated foot are susceptible to plantar fasciitis.

Most people will at some time in their lives develop foot problems.

exostoses
Benign bony outgrowths that protrude from the surface of a bone and are usually capped by cartilage

Figure 9-25

Taping for hammer, or clawed, toes.

Figure 9-26

Exostoses (bony outgrowths).

Figure 9-27

Heel bursitis.

The athlete complains of heel pain. On palpation the pain is usually located on the bottom of the heel and radiates toward the sole of the foot. Often the pain intensifies when the athlete gets out of bed in the morning and first puts weight on the foot; however, the pain lessens after a few steps.[9]

Care   Care of this condition follows the same procedures as for a chronic foot strain, including longitudinal arch support or LowDye arch support. Of major importance is a vigorous regimen of heel cord stretching, especially if the athlete's ankle cannot dorsiflex 10 to 15 degrees from a neutral position. Stretching should be conducted at least three times a day in the positions of straight-ahead, toe-in, and toe-out. The athlete should wear a shoe that is not too stiff and has a heel that is elevated 1/2 to 3/4 inch (1.3 to 1.9 cm) above the level of the sole.[9] The physician may prescribe an oral anti-inflammatory medication or an injection of a corticosteroid.

Foot Stress Fractures   Over 18% of all stress fractures in the body occur in the foot.[7] The most common stress of the foot occurs to one or more of the metatarsal bone shafts (Fig. 9-28).

Management of this stress fracture usually consists of 3 to 4 days of crutch walking or a short-leg walking cast for 1 to 2 weeks. Weight bearing may be resumed when pain has significantly subsided. Tape support and therapy for swelling and tenderness is given.[3] Running should be resumed very gradually for 3 to 4 weeks.

Foot tendinitis   Because of the many muscle tendons associated with the foot region, tendinitis is a common occurrence (Fig. 9-29). These problems are often caused by biomechanical foot imbalances coupled with overuse. Care of these difficulties include rest, heat or cold therapy, anti-inflammatory medications such as aspirin, and orthotics to alleviate biochemical problems.

Exercise Rehabilitation of the Foot

In most painful conditions of the foot, weight bearing is prohibited until pain has subsided significantly. During this period and until the athlete is ready to return to full activity, a graduated program of exercise can be instituted. Exercises are divided into two stages. Each exercise should be performed 3 times a day with 3 to 10 repetitions of each exercise and should progress to 2 or 3 sets.

Stage 1

In Stage 1 primary exercises are employed in the non-weight bearing or early phase of the condition. They include "writing the alphabet," picking up objects, ankle circumduction, and gripping and spreading.

1. *Writing the alphabet*—With the toes pointed, the athlete proceeds to write the complete alphabet in the air three times.
2. *Picking up objects*—The athlete picks up 10 small objects, such as marbles, with the toes and places them in a container.
3. *Ankle circumduction*—The ankle is circumducted in as extreme a range of motion as possible (10 circles in one direction and 10 circles in the other).
4. *Gripping and spreading*—Of particular value to toes, gripping and spreading is conducted up to 10 repetitions.

Stage 2

Stage 2 exercises are added to Stage 1 when the athlete is just beginning to bear weight. They include the "towel gather" and "scoop" exercises.

1. *Towel gathering*—A towel is extended in front of the feet. The heels are firmly planted on the floor, the forefoot on the end of the towel. The athlete then attempts to pull the towel with the feet without lifting the heels from the floor. As execution becomes easier, a weight can be placed at the other end of the towel for added resistance. Each exercise should be performed 10 times (Fig. 9-30).

2. *Towel scoop*—A towel is folded in half and placed sideways on the floor. The athlete places the heel firmly on the floor, the forefoot on the end of the towel. To ensure the greatest stability of the exercising foot, it is backed up with the other foot. Without lifting the heel from the floor, the athlete scoops the towel forward with the forefoot. As with the towel gather exercise, a weight resistance can be added to the end of the towel. The exercise should be repeated up to 10 times (Fig. 9-31).

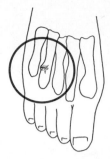

Figure 9-28

Stress fracture in the metatarsal region.

Figure 9-30

The towel gather exercise.

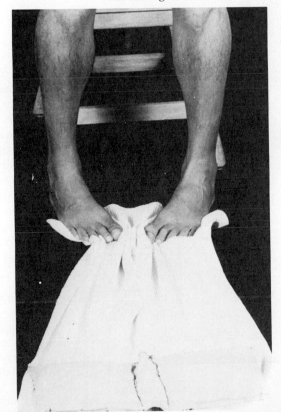

Figure 9-29

Common tendinitis of the foot and ankle region.

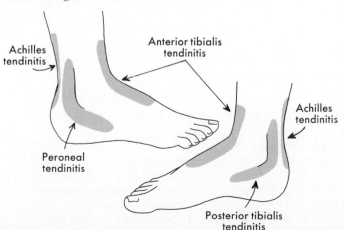

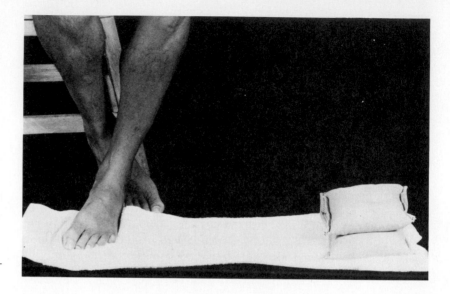

Figure 9-31

The towel scoop exercise.

SUMMARY

The human foot is a highly complicated structure requiring a great deal of strength, flexibility, and coordinated movement. The foot within the shoe can sustain forces that produce abnormal calluses, blisters, corns, and ingrown toenails. Common musculoskeletal injuries are bruises, metatarsal and longitudinal arch strains, fractures, and dislocations of the toes. Fractures, primarily stress fractures, are common to the metatarsal bones.

Painful arch conditions are often related to sports activities, the most common are metatarsal and longitudinal arch regions. Pain is commonly related to the falling of these arches.

Chronic and overuse foot conditions can lead to stress problems in the lower extremities. Common chronic problems occur to the arches of the foot, toes, and forefoot. The bunion, a common chronic condition, occurs when the great toe becomes deflected medially. Metatarsalgia also is a chronic conditions of the forefoot. Other problems include deformities such as hammer (clawed) toes, bony outgrowths, heel bursitis, heel spurs, tendinitis, and stress fractures.

REVIEW QUESTIONS AND CLASS ACTIVITIES

1. How can the foot be protected against skin trauma?
2. Discuss the steps in caring for a foot blister.
3. Why is the heel prone to bruising? How can heel bruises be prevented?
4. Compare the high longitudinal arch (pes cavus) to the low longitudinal arch (pes planus) in terms of associated injuries that may be produced.
5. Discuss the typical appearance of a dislocated and fractured toe.
6. Why do bunions and bunionettes occur? How can they be prevented?
7. How are the fallen metatarsal arch and metatarsalgia, related?

8. What kinds of foot deformities can be associated with the wearing of improperly fitting shoes?
9. Have a sports podiatrist talk to your class regarding (1) major sports injuries seen, (2) how are they treated, and (3) the role of orthotic devices in assisting biomechanical foot problems.

REFERENCES

1. Cailliet, R.: Foot and ankle pain, Philadelphia, 1968, F.A. Davis Co.
2. Gibbs, R.C.: Calluses, corns, and warts, Am. Fam. Physician **3**:4, 1971.
3. James, S.L., et al.: Injuries to runners, Am. J. Sports Med. **6**:2, 1978.
4. Kulund, D.N.: The injured athlete, Philadelphia, 1982, J.B. Lippincott Co.
5. Liteplo, M.G.: Sports-related skin problems. In Vinger, P.F., and Hoerner, E.F. (editors): Sports injuries: the unthwarted epidemic, Boston, 1982, John Wright, PSG, Inc.
6. Moschella, S.L.: Physically induced blisters. In Moschella, S.L., Pillsbury, D.M., and Hurley, H.J.: Dermatology, Philadelphia, 1975, W.B. Saunders Co.
7. Orava, S., et al.: Stress fractures caused by physical exercise, Acta Orthop. Scand. **49**:1, 1978.
8. Seder, J.I.: Heel injuries incurred in running and jumping. Phys. Sportsmed. **4**:10, 1976.
9. Waller, J.F.: Hindfoot and midfoot problems in the runner. In Mack, R.P. (editor): Symposium on the foot and leg in running sports, American Academy of Orthopaedic Surgeons, St. Louis, 1982, The C.V. Mosby Co.

ANNOTATED BIBLIOGRAPHY

McPoil, T.G., Jr., and Brocato, R.S.: The foot and ankle: biomechanical evaluation and treatment. In Gould, III, J.A., and Davies, G.J. (editors): Orthopaedic and sports physical therapy, vol. 2, St. Louis, 1985, The C.V. Mosby Co.
   Chapter 15 discusses normal and abnormal biomechanics of the foot and ankle. It provides an in-depth presentation in the area of biomechanical evaluation to detect faulty mechanics that can be corrected by the construction of an orthotic device.
Peterson, L. and Renstrom, P.: Sports injuries. Chicago, 1986, Year Book Medical Publishers, Inc.
   An overview of sports injuries that covers in-depth injuries to the foot.
Torg, J.S. (editor): Symposium on ankle and foot problems in the athlete, Clinics in sports medicine, vol. 1, no. 1, Philadelphia, March 1982, W.B. Saunders Co.
   Covers many important areas concerning the ankle and foot in sports including major topics such as incidence of injuries, biomechanics, surgical examination, injury management, adhesive strapping techniques, and athletic footwear.

Chapter 10

THE ANKLE AND LOWER LEG

When you finish this chapter, you will be able to:

Explain how to recognize the most common injuries
    sustained by the ankle and lower leg

Evaluate common ankle and lower leg injuries

Explain how to apply appropriate immediate and
    superficial follow-up care to the ankle and lower leg

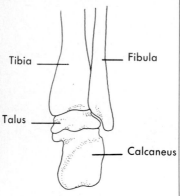

Tibia — — Fibula

Talus —

— Calcaneus

Figure 10-1

The ankle is a hinge-type joint
formed by the tibia, fibula, and
talus.

The regions of the ankle and lower leg have a high incidence of sports injuries. Dealing effectively with these injuries at the coach's level is a major
challenge.

THE ANKLE

The ankle is a hinge joint (ginglymus), formed by the articulation of two long
bones, the tibia and fibula, with the talus (Fig. 10-1). The ligamentous support
of the ankle (Fig. 10-2) further fortifies the bony arrangement. Laterally, the
most injured site, it is composed of relatively weak ligaments, the anterior
and posterior tibiofibular, the anterior and posterior talofibular, the lateral
talocalcaneal, and the posterior calcaneofibular. The stronger and less-injured
medial side contains the large deltoid ligament. The weakest aspect of the
ankle is its muscular arrangement, since the long muscle tendons that cross
on all sides of the ankle afford a maximum of muscle leverage but at the same
time provide poor lateral stability (Fig. 10-3).

Prevention of Ankle Injuries

Many ankle conditions, especially sprains, can be reduced by heel cord (Achilles tendon) stretching, strengthening of key muscles, proprioceptive training,
proper footwear, and in some cases proper taping (Fig. 10-4).

Heel Cord (Achilles Tendon) Stretching

An ankle that can easily dorsiflex at least 15 degrees or more is essential for
injury prevention. The athlete, especially one with tight Achilles tendons,
should routinely stretch before and after practice (Fig. 10-5).

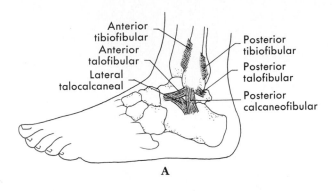

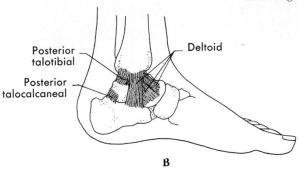

Figure 10-2

Major ligaments of the ankle.
A, Lateral aspect; and **B**, medial
aspect.

Figure 10-3

Muscles of the lower leg. **A**,
Anterior view; **B**, lateral view.
Continued on p. 200.

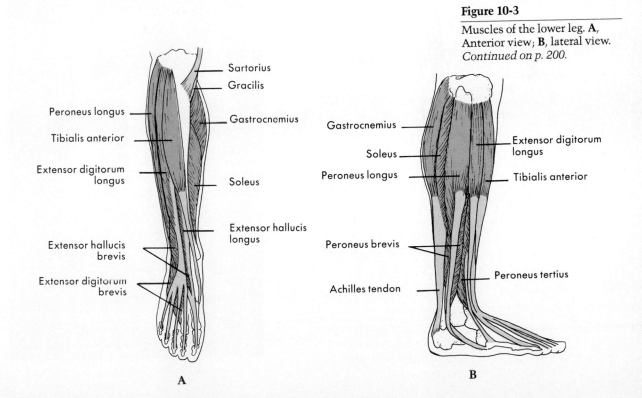

Figure 10-3, Continued

Muscles of the lower leg.
C, posterior view superficial
structures; **D**, posterior view
deep structures and **E**, blood
and nerve supply of the lower
leg.

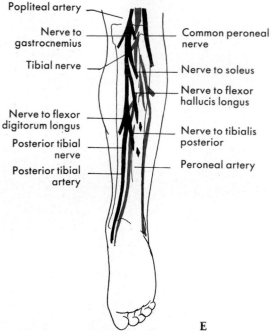

Gastrocnemius

Soleus

Peroneus longus

Peroneus brevis

Tibialis posterior

Flexor digitorum longus

Achilles tendon

C

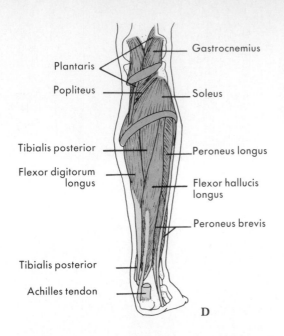

Plantaris

Popliteus

Tibialis posterior

Flexor digitorum longus

Gastrocnemius

Soleus

Peroneus longus

Flexor hallucis longus

Peroneus brevis

Tibialis posterior

Achilles tendon

D

Popliteal artery

Nerve to gastrocnemius

Tibial nerve

Nerve to flexor digitorum longus

Posterior tibial nerve

Posterior tibial artery

Common peroneal nerve

Nerve to soleus

Nerve to flexor hallucis longus

Nerve to tibialis posterior

Peroneal artery

E

Figure 10-4

The ankle has the highest
incidence of injury in
basketball.

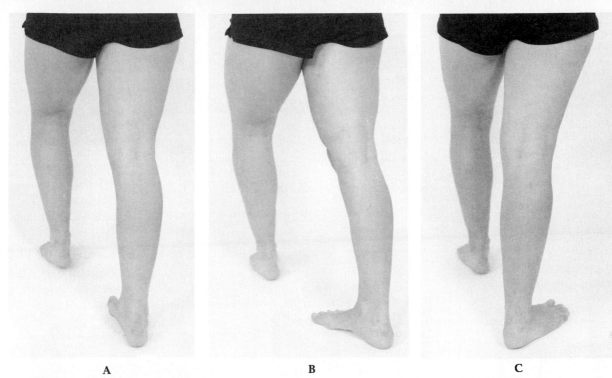

A   B   C

Figure 10-5

Stretching the Achilles tendon is essential for preventing ankle sprains. Stretching must be performed for all possible positions. **A**, Straight ahead. **B**, Adducted. **C**, Abducted.

Strength Training

Of major importance to ankle injury prevention is to achieve both static and dynamic joint stability (Fig. 10-6). A normal range of motion must be maintained, along with strength of the muscles that evert and invert the foot and those that permit plantar flexion and dorsiflexion of the ankle.[12]

Proprioceptive Ankle Training

Athletes who have ankle injuries or who spend most of their time on even surfaces may develop a proprioceptive deficiency.[10] Ankle ligamentous stability proprioception is also lost. The ankle and foot proprioceptive sense can be enhanced by locomotion over uneven surfaces or by spending time each day on a balance board (wobble board) (Fig. 10-7).

Footwear

As discussed in Chapter 3, proper footwear can be an important factor in reducing injuries to both the foot and ankle. Shoes should not be used in activities for which they were not intended—for example, do not wear running shoes designed for straight-ahead activity to play tennis, a sport demanding a great deal of lateral movement. Cleats on a shoe should not be centered in the middle of the sole but should be placed far enough on the border to avoid ankle sprains. High-top shoes, when worn by athletes with a history of ankle sprains, can offer greater support than low-top shoes.

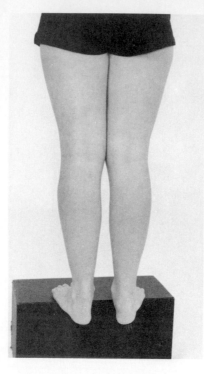
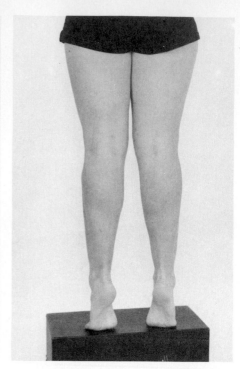

Figure 10-6

Strength training is essential for the prevention of ankle sprains.

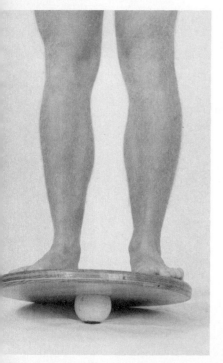

Figure 10-7

The wobble board is an excellent device for establishing ankle proprioception.

Preventive Ankle Wrapping, Taping, and Bracing

As discussed in Chapter 4, there is some doubt as to whether it is beneficial to routinely tape ankles that have no history of sprain. There is some indication that tape, properly applied, can provide some prophylactic protection. It is estimated that at least $100 million is spent in the United States each year for tape for high school football.[10] Poorly applied tape will do more harm than good. Tape that constricts soft tissue and blood circulation or disrupts normal biomechanical function can in time create serious physical problems. Although taping is preferred, a much cheaper cloth muslin wrap may provide limited protection.

Ankle bracing, another purported means to protection, can be constructed from orthoplast or Hecelite material or it can be purchased commercially. Braces may be effective in preventing lateral and inversion movement of the foot without inhibiting plantar flexion, however, research is needed to verify whether ankle braces are effective.[5]

Acute Ankle Injuries

Sprains

Because of their frequency and the disability that results, ankle sprains present a major problem for the coach, trainer, and team physician. It has been said that a sprained ankle can be worse than a fracture. Fractures are usually conservatively cared for, with immobilization and activity restriction,

ANKLE WRAP

Because tape is so expensive, the ankle wrap becomes an inexpensive and expedient means of protecting ankles.

Materials needed: Each muslin wrap should be 1 -1/2 to 2 inches (3.8 to 5 cm) wide and from 72 to 96 inches (180 to 240 cm) long to ensure complete coverage and protection. The purpose of this wrap is to give mild support against lateral and medial motion of the ankle. It is applied over a sock.

Position of the athlete: The athlete sits on a table, extending the leg and positioning the foot at a 90-degree angle. To avoid any distortion, it is important that the ankle be neither overflexed nor overextended.

Position of the operator: The operator stands facing the sole of the athlete's foot.

Procedure: Fig. 10-8 illustrates the proper procedure for applying the ankle wrap.

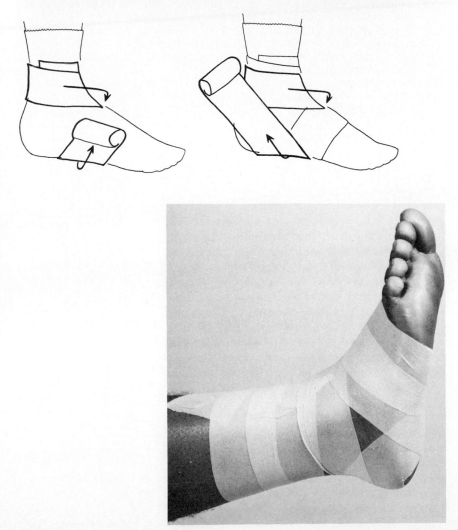

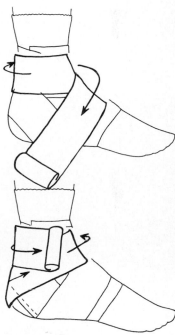

Figure 10-8

The ankle wrap.

Figure 10-9

Underwrap for ankle taping.

ROUTINE NONINJURY ANKLE TAPING

Ankle taping applied directly to the athlete's skin affords the greatest support; however, skin irritation will occur when applied and removed daily. To avoid this problem an underwrap material should be applied (Fig. 10-9). However, this will decrease the effectiveness of the taping technique. Before taping, follow these procedures:

1. Shave all the hair off the foot and ankle.
2. Apply a coating of a tape adherent to protect the skin and offer an adhering base. **NOTE:** It may be advisable to avoid the use of a tape adherent, especially in cases in which the athlete has a history of developing tape blisters. In cases of skin sensitivity the ankle surface should be thouroughly cleansed of dirt and oil and an underwrap material applied; or one could elect to tape directly to the skin.
3. If underwrap is not used, apply a gauze pad coated with friction-proofing material, such as grease, over the instep and to the back of the heel.
4. Do not apply tape if skin is cold or hot from a therapeutic treatment.

Materials needed: One roll of 1 1/2-inch (3.8 cm) tape and tape adherent.

Position of the athlete: The athlete sits on a table with the leg extended and the foot held at a 90-degree angle.

Position of the operator: The operator stands facing the foot that is to be taped.

Procedure: Fig. 10-10 illustrates the proper procedure for applying the routine noninjury ankle taping.

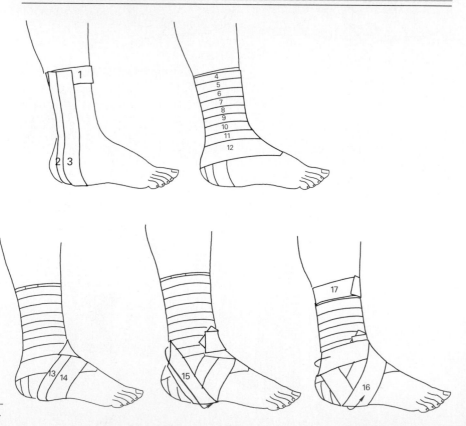

Figure 10-10

Routine noninjury ankle taping.

whereas the athlete with a sprained ankle is often rushed through management and returned to activity before complete healing has occurred. Incompletely healed, the ankle becomes chronically inflamed and unstable, eventually causing a major problem for the athlete.[8]

Mechanism of Injury

Ankle sprains are generally caused by a sudden lateral or medial twist. The inversion sprain, in which the foot turns inward, is the most common type of ankle sprain. This is because there is more bony stability on the lateral side, which tends to force the foot into inversion rather than eversion. If the force is great enough, inversion of the foot continues until the medial malleolus loses its stability and creates a fulcrum to further invert the ankle.[12] The peroneal or everting muscles resist the inverting force; and when they are no longer strong enough, the lateral ligaments become stretched or torn (Fig. 10-11, A).

Usually a lateral ankle sprain involves either one or two torn ligaments. If it is a single ligament tear, it usually involves the *anterior talofibular ligament*; however, if it is a double ligament tear with further inversion, the *calcaneofibular ligament* also tears (Fig. 10-11, B). The tight heel cord forces the foot into inversion, making it more susceptible to a lateral sprain. In contrast, a foot that is pronated, hypermobile, or has a depressed medial longitudinal arch is more susceptible to an eversion type of ankle sprain (Fig. 10-12).

The eversion sprain occurs less frequently than the inversion sprain. The usual mechanism is the athlete's having suddenly stepped in a hole on the playing field, causing the foot to evert and abduct and the planted leg to rotate externally. With this mechanism, the anterior tibiofibular ligament, interosseous ligament, and deltoid ligament may tear. With a tear of these ligaments, the ankle becomes unstable, leading to ultimate degeneration within the joint[2] (Fig. 10-13).

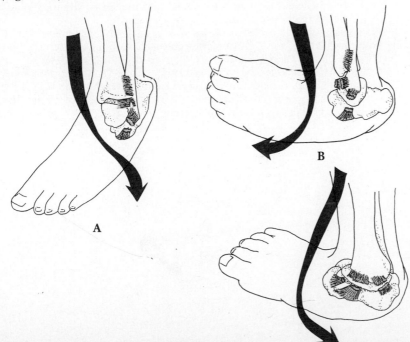

A

B

Figure 10-11

Mechanisms of an inversion ankle sprain.

Figure 10-12

Mechanism of an eversion ankle sprain.

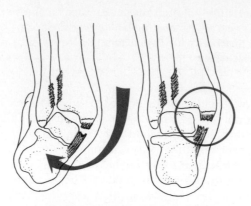

Figure 10-13

An eversion ankle sprain that creates an abnormal space between the medial malleolus and the talus.

A sudden inversion force could be of such intensity as to produce a fracture of the lower leg. An unexpected wrenching of the lateral ligaments could cause a portion of bone to be avulsed from the malleolus (Fig. 10-14).

General Immediate Care Considerations

In managing a sprained ankle these first aid measures should be followed:

1. Determine the extent of the injury. The main purpose of the ankle sprain examination is to estimate the injury's severity. **NOTE:** Swelling is not an indication of the severity of the injury.[4,17]

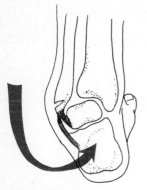

Figure 10-14

The same mechanism that produces an ankle sprain can also cause an avulsion fracture.

OPEN BASKETWEAVE TAPING TECHNIQUE

This modification of the closed basketweave or Gibney technique is designed to give freedom of movement in dorsiflexion and plantar flexion while providing lateral and medial support and giving swelling room. Taping in this pattern may be used immediately after an acute sprain in conjunction with a pressure bandage and cold applications, since it allows for swelling.

Materials needed: One roll of 1 1/2-inch (3.8 cm) tape and tape adherent.

Position of the athlete: The athlete sits on a table with the leg extended and the foot held at a 90-degree angle.

Position of the operator: The operator faces the sole of the athlete's foot.

Procedure: Steps 1 through 8 of the closed basketweave ankle taping (see Fig. 10-17) are first applied to the ankle. Fig. 10-15 illustrates the proper procedure for completion of the open basketweave taping technique.

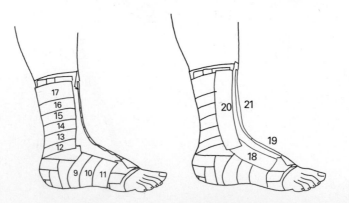

Figure 10-15

Open basketweave ankle taping.

2. Employ ICE-R.
   a. Apply an elastic pressure bandage around the perimeter of the malleolus at the site of the sprain to decrease internal bleeding.
   b. After the pressure bandage has been applied, decrease the temperature of the injured area by the use of ice packs. An elastic wrap that is thoroughly soaked in ice water and applied directly to the skin will cool faster when combined with an ice pack. Ice should be applied intermittently in 20-minute periods, five to six times a day. Do not expose the tissue to prolonged cooling. If a cold medium is not available, a horseshoe pad that is cut to fit around the malleolus and is held in place by an elastic wrap will help confine the internal hemorrhage (Fig. 10-16).
   c. Promptly elevate the injured limb, if at all practical, so that fluid pooling of the internal hemorrhage does not take place.
   d. The open basketweave taping technique can also be used in conjunction with cold application. **NOTE**: In most cases, joint swelling can be limited if the ICE-R routine is carefully followed for 24 hours.
3. If there is a possibility of fracture, splint the ankle and refer the athlete to the physician for x-ray examination and immobilization.
4. In most cases of moderate and severe ankle sprains continue cold applications through the second or even the third day.
5. Begin heat or cold therapy if hemorrhaging has stopped by the third day.
6. If there is edema present, electrical muscle stimulation may be beneficial.[18]

The extent of ankle swelling is *not* an indication of the severity of the injury.

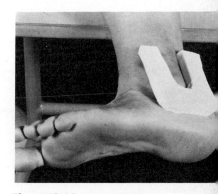

Figure 10-16

A horseshoe-shaped sponge rubber pad provides an excellent compress when held in place by an elastic wrap.

Inversion Ankle Sprains

Inversion ankle sprains are usually graded by the ligament or ligaments involved. In general, a first degree sprain is concerned with the anterior talofibular ligament, a second degree sprain with the calcaneofibular ligament, and a third degree sprain with the posterior talofibular ligament. In each instance of injury the foot is forcibly turned inward on the leg, as when a basketball player jumps and comes down on the foot of another player. Inversion sprains can also occur while an individual is walking and running on an uneven surface or suddenly steps into a hole.

First degree inversion ankle sprains The first degree ankle sprain is the most common type of sprain. Most result from an inversion stress with the foot in *mild* plantar flexion, usually stretching the anterior talofibular ligament.

There is mild pain and disability with point tenderness and in some cases localized swelling over the area of the anterior talofibular ligament. The anterior drawer test is negative with no discoloration and minimal loss of function.

Immediate and follow-up care ICE-R is used for 20 minutes every few hours for 1 to 2 days. It may be advisable for the athlete to limit weight-bearing activities for a few days. An elastic wrap might provide comfortable pressure when weight bearing begins. When the athlete's ankle is pain free and not swollen, a routine of circumduction is begun. The athlete is instructed to circle the foot first ten times in one direction then ten times in the other several times per day. When the athlete returns to weight bearing, application of tape may provide an extra measure of protection.

Second degree inversion ankle sprains Because it has a high incidence among sports participants and causes a great deal of disability with many days of lost time, the second degree ankle sprain is a major problem for the coach, athletic trainer, and physician.

The athlete usually complains that a tearing sensation was felt along with a pop or snap as the tissue gave way. Swelling is general along with a point tenderness at the sprain site. Some discoloration will occur 3 or 4 days after injury.

The second degree ankle sprain may completely tear the anterior talofibular ligament and stretch and tear the calcaneofibular ligament. Such an injury can produce a persistently unstable ankle that recurrently becomes sprained and later develops traumatic arthritis.

Immediate and follow-up care ICE-R therapy should be employed intermittently for 24 to 72 hours. X-ray examination should be routine for this degree of injury. The athlete should use crutches for 5 to 10 days to avoid bearing weight. A short-leg walking cast may be applied for 2 or 3 days. Plantar flexion and dorsiflexion exercises, if the athlete is pain free, may begin 48 hours after the injury occurs. Early exercise of this type helps to maintain range of motion and normal proprioception. After 1 or 2 weeks of non–weight bearing, when swelling and pain have decreased, weight bearing can be resumed.

Taping in the early inflammatory phase is of the open basketweave type (see Fig. 10-15), followed by the closed basketweave technique (see Fig. 10-17) when walking is resumed. The athlete must be instructed to avoid walking or running on uneven or sloped surfaces for 2 to 3 weeks after weight bearing has begun.

Once hemorrhage has subsided a therapy routine of superficial cold or heat should begin three times per day. Two or three weeks after the injury, circumduction exercises can be started. Exercises can progress gradually to resistive types.

Third degree inversion ankle sprains The third degree inversion ankle sprain is relatively uncommon in sports. When it does happen, it is quite disabling. Often the force causes the ankle to partially dislocate and then spontaneously reduce.

The athlete complains of severe pain in the region of the lateral malleolus. Swelling is general, with tenderness over the entire lateral area of the ankle.

Immediate and follow-up care Normally ICE-R is employed intermittently for 2 or 3 days. It is not uncommon for the physician to apply a short-leg walking cast, when the swelling has subsided, for 4 to 6 weeks. Crutches are usually given to the athlete when the cast is removed. Circumduction exercises are begun immediately after the cast is removed, followed by a progressive program of strengthening. In some cases surgery is warranted to stabilize the athlete's ankle for future sports participation.

Eversion Ankle Sprains

Eversion ankle sprains are less common than inversion sprains. Athletes who have hypermobile and/or pronated, or flat feet have a higher incidence of eversion sprains.

Depending on the degree of injury, the athlete complains of pain, sometimes severe, that occurs over the foot and lower leg. Usually the athlete is unable to bear weight on the foot. Most movement of the foot and ankle causes pain.

Ankle Fractures

There are two major situations in which ankle fractures occur: (1) when the foot is forcibly turned outward or inward, or (2) when the foot is fixed to the ground and the lower leg is either forcibly internally or externally rotated (Fig. 10-18).

A second or third degree eversion sprain can adversely affect the medial longitudinal arch.

CLOSED BASKETWEAVE (GIBNEY) TAPING TECHNIQUE

The closed basketweave technique offers strong tape support and is primarily used in athletic training for newly sprained or chronically weak ankles.

Materials needed: One roll of 1 1/2-inch (3.8 cm) tape and tape adherent.

Position of the athlete: The athlete sits on a table with the leg extended and the foot at a 90-degree angle.

Position of the operator: The operator faces the sole of the athlete's foot.

Procedure: Fig. 10-17 illustrates the proper procedure for applying the closed basketweave taping technique.

NOTE: When applying stirrups pull the foot into eversion for an inversion sprain and into a neutral position for an eversion sprain.

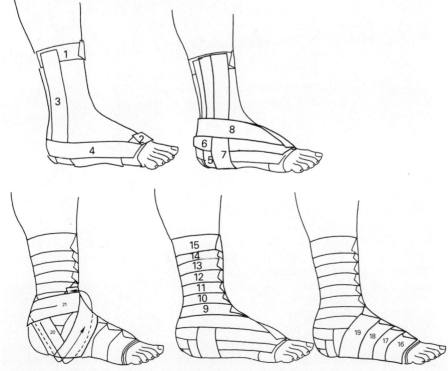

Figure 10-17

Closed basketweave ankle taping.

In most fracture cases, swelling and pain are extreme. There may be some or no deformity; however, if fracture is suspected, splinting is essential. ICE-R is employed as soon as possible to control hemorrhage and swelling. Once swelling is reduced, casting can take place, allowing the athlete to bear weight. Immobilization will usually last for at least 6 to 8 weeks.

Strains About the Ankle

A ruptured Achilles tendon usually occurs when inflammation has been chronic.

Heel cord (Achilles tendon) strain Achilles tendon strains are not uncommon in sports and occur most often as a result of a lack of coordination between the agonists and the antagonists, following ankle sprains or sudden excessive dorsiflexion of the ankle.

The resulting injury may range from mild to severe. The severe injury is usually thought of as a partial or complete avulsion or rupturing of the Achilles tendon. While receiving this injury, the athlete feels acute pain and extreme weakness when pointing the foot downward.

Immediate and follow-up care The following are first aid measures to be applied:

1. As with other acute conditions, pressure is first applied with an elastic wrap together with cold application.

Figure 10-18

Ankle fractures or dislocations can be a major sports injury.

2. Unless the injury is minor, hemorrhage may be extensive, requiring ICE-R over an extended period of time.
3. After hemorrhaging has subsided, an elastic wrap can be lightly applied for continued pressure, and the athlete can be sent home. Follow-up care should begin the following day.

NOTE: The tendency for Achilles tendon trauma to readily develop into a chronic condition requires a conservative approach to therapy and in many cases referral to a physician.

Follow-up care should be initiated in the following manner:
1. Hydromassage is used until soreness has subsided, beginning on the third day and continuing on subsequent days.
2. Both heels, affected or unaffected, should be elevated by placing a sponge rubber pad in the heel of each street shoe. Elevation decreases the extension of the tendon and thereby relieves some of the irritation.
3. In a few days the athlete will be able to return to activity. The Achilles tendon should be restricted by a tape support and a sponge rubber heel lift placed in each sports shoe. Heel lifts should be placed in both shoes or taped directly on the bottoms of both heels to avoid leg length asymmetry and subsequent adverse muscle and skeletal stresses.

HEEL CORD (ACHILLES TENDON) TAPING

Achilles tendon taping is designed to prevent the Achilles tendon from over-stretching.

Materials needed: One roll of 3-inch (7.5 cm) elastic tape, one roll of 1 1/2-inch (3.8 cm) linen tape, and tape adherent.

Position of the athlete: The athlete kneels or lies face down, with the affected foot hanging relaxed over the edge of the table.

Position of the operator: The operator stands facing the plantar aspect of the athlete's foot.

Procedure: Fig. 10-19 illustrates the proper procedure for applying the heel cord taping.

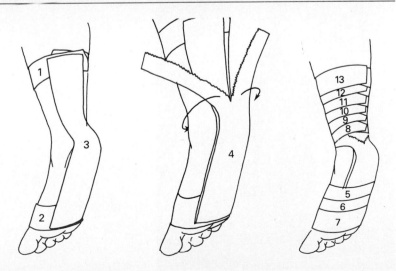

Figure 10-19

Achilles tendon taping.

Figure 10-20

Achilles tendon rupture.

Heel cord (Achilles) tendinitis   Achilles tendinitis usually occurs from overstretching, which causes a constant inflammation. This condition may develop gradually over a long period of time and may require weeks or even months to heal completely. Rest and the application of heat are the most important factors in healing. Heel lifts in shoes will relieve tension on the tendon. Gentle heel cord stretching is an adjunct to heat.

Heel cord (Achilles tendon) rupture   A rupture of the Achilles tendon (Fig. 10-20) is a possibility in sports that require stop-and-go action.[6] Although most common in athletes who are 30 years of age or older, rupture of the Achilles tendon can occur in athletes of any age. It usually follows a history of chronic inflammation and gradual degeneration caused by microtears. The ultimate insult normally is the result of sudden pushing-off action of the forefoot with the knee being forced into complete extension.

When the rupture occurs the athlete complains of a sudden snap or that something hit him or her in the lower leg.[5] Severe pain, point tenderness, swelling, discoloration, and loss of ability to point the toes are usually associated with the trauma. The major problem in the Achilles tendon rupture is accurate diagnosis. Often a partial rupture is thought to be a sprained ankle. Any acute injury to the Achilles tendon should be suspected as being a rupture. Signs indicative of a rupture are obvious indentation in the tendon site or a positive result to a Thompson test. The Thompson test (Fig. 10-21) is performed by simply squeezing the calf muscle while the leg is extended and the foot is hanging over the edge of the table. A positive Thompson sign is one in which squeezing the calf muscle does not cause the heel to move or pull upward or in which it moves less when compared to the uninjured heel.

Figure 10-21

The Thompson test to determine an Achilles tendon rupture is performed by simply squeezing the calf muscle while the leg is extended. A positive result to the test is one in which the heel does not move.

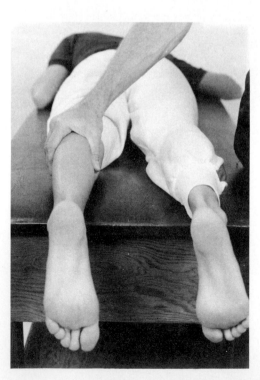

Care Usual care of a complete Achilles tendon rupture is surgical repair. On occasion, however, the physician may decide on a conservative approach.[13,16]

Chronic Ankle Injuries

The second degree sprain, with its torn and stretched ligaments, tends to have a number of serious complications. Because of laxity there is a tendency to twist and sprain the ankle repeatedly. This recurrence over a period of time can lead to joint degeneration and traumatic arthritis. Once a second degree sprain has occurred, there must be a concerted effort to protect the ankle against future trauma.

An eversion sprain of second degree or more severity can produce significant joint instability. Because the deltoid ligament is involved with supporting the medial longitudinal arch, a sprain can cause weakness in this area. Repeated sprains could lead to flatfoot (pes planus).

THE LOWER LEG

That portion of the anatomy that lies between the knee and the ankle is considered the lower leg. It is comprised of the thicker tibia bone, the more slender fibula bone, and the soft tissues that surround them. The soft tissue of the leg is organized in four compartments bounded by fascia or bone. The compartments are named for their various locations: anterior, lateral, superficial posterior, and deep posterior (Fig. 10-22).

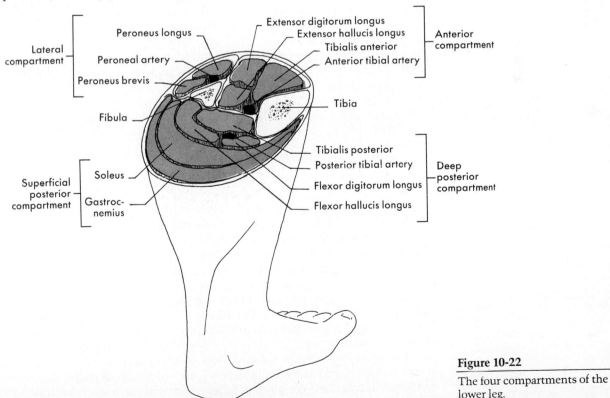

Figure 10-22

The four compartments of the lower leg.

Acute Leg Injuries

The leg is prone to a number of acute conditions, of which contusions and strains are most common. Although less common, fractures can occur in relation to direct trauma, such as being struck by a blow or through torsional forces with the foot fixed to the ground.

Leg Contusions

The shin bruise The shin, lying just under the skin, is exceedingly vulnerable and sensitive to bruising. Because of the absence of muscular or fat padding here, blows are not dissipated as they are elsewhere, and the covering of the bone, the periosteum, receives the full force of any impact delivered to the shin. Severe blows to the tibia often lead to a chronic inflammatory state. The shin is an extremely difficult area to heal, particularly the lower third, which has a considerably smaller blood supply than the upper position. An inadequately cared for injury to the periosteum may develop into a serious condition that results in the destruction and deterioration of bony tissue, known as *osteomyelitis*.

In sports in which the shin is particularly vulnerable, such as football and soccer, adequate padding must be provided. All injuries in this area are potentially serious and should never be permitted to go untended.

Muscle contusions Contusions of the leg, particularly in the area of the calf muscle, are common in sports. A bruise in this area can produce an extremely handicapping injury. Such a bruising blow to the leg will result in pain, weakness, and some loss of function.

When this condition occurs it is advisable to stretch the muscles in the region immediately to prevent spasm and then, for approximately 1 hour, to apply a compress bandage and cold packs to control internal hemorrhaging.

If cold therapy or other superficial therapy such as massage and whirlpool do not return the athlete to normal activity within 2 to 3 days, the use of ultrasound may be warranted. An elastic wrap or tape support will serve to stabilize the part and permit the athlete to participate without aggravation of the injury.

Leg Spasms and Muscle Strains

Muscle spasms Spasms are sudden, violent, involuntary contractions of one or several muscles and may be either clonic or tonic (see Chapter 7). How and why muscle spasms happen to athletes is often difficult to ascertain. Fatigue, excess loss of fluid through perspiration, and inadequate reciprocal muscle coordination are some of the factors that may predispose an individual to a contracture. The leg, particularly the gastrocnemius muscle, is prone to this condition. It is usually difficult to predict the occurrence of spasm, since only the aforementioned criteria can be used as a guide.

Care When a muscle goes into spasm there is severe pain and considerable apprehension on the part of the athlete. Care in such cases includes putting the athlete at ease and relaxing the contracted site. Firmly grasping the contracted muscle, together with a mild gradual type stretching, has been found to relieve most acute spasms. Vigorously rubbing an extremity during spasm will often increase its intensity. In cases of recurrent spasm the coach or trainer should make certain that fatigue or abnormal mineral loss through perspiring is not a factor, since the loss of salt or other minerals can result in abnormal motor nerve impulses to skeletal muscles.

Calf strain ("tennis leg")   Sports that require quick starts and stops, such as tennis, can cause a calf strain. Usually the athlete makes a quick stop with the foot planted flatfooted and suddenly extends the knee, placing stress on the medial head of the gastrocnemius (Fig. 10-23). In most cases it can be prevented by a regular routine of gradually stretching the calf region and exercising the antagonist and agonist muscles.[14] If the pain is sustained, immediate application of ICE-R is necessary, followed by a gentle, gradual stretch routine. Follow-up care should include a regimen of cold, heat, and mild exercise, together with walking in low-heeled shoes, accentuating a heel-toe gait.[16]

Leg Fractures

Fractures received during sports participation occur most often to the fingers, hand, face, and legs. Of leg fractures, the small fibula bone has the highest incidence and occurs principally to the middle third of the leg. Fractures of the larger tibia bone occur predominantly to the lower third.

Fractures of the shaft of the tibia and fibula result from either direct or indirect trauma during active participation in sports (Fig. 10-24). There is often a marked bony displacement with deformity, as a result of a strong pull of mus-

Figure 10-23

"Tennis leg" calf strain.

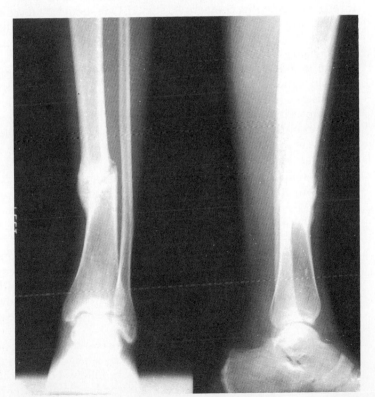

Figure 10-24

Fracture of the tibia.

cles in the region. Crepitus and a temporary loss of limb function are usually present.

Chronic Leg Injuries

A number of problems of the leg can be attributed to repetitive use and overuse. Three of these conditions are medial shin stress syndrome (shinsplints), compartment syndrome, and stress fracture.

Medial Shin Stress Syndrome (Shinsplints)

Shinsplints is a general term applied to a variety of conditions that seasonally plague many athletes. It is characterized by pain and irritation in the shin region of the leg and is usually attributed to an inflammation localized primarily in the tendon of the posterior tibial muscle or long flexor muscles of the toes. How or why inflammation is produced in this area is a mystery. It has been believed that chronic medial shin pain was a compartment syndrome; however, recent studies have discounted this view. Speculations advanced as to the cause include faulty posture alignment, falling arches, muscle fatigue, overuse stress, body chemical imbalance, or a lack of proper reciprocal muscle coordination between anterior and posterior aspects of the leg. All these factors, in various combinations or singly, may contribute to shinsplints.

This condition is regarded as a muscle or bone inflammation that occurs either acutely, as in preseason preparation, or chronically, developing slowly throughout the entire competitive season. One should approach this situation through deductive thinking. First, all information as to why a certain athlete may have acquired shinsplints must be gathered—examples include changing from a hard gymnasium floor activity to a soft field sport or exhibiting general fatigue after a strenuous season. Second, one should examine the athlete for possible structural body weaknesses. From this information an empirical analysis can be made as to the probable cause of shinsplints. However, persistent shin irritation and incapacitation must be referred to the physician for further examination. Conditions such as stress fractures, muscle herniations, or a severe swelling within the anterior fascia chamber may resemble the symptoms of shinsplints.

Jackson[9] suggests four grades of pain that can be attributed to shinsplints: grade I pain occurring after athletic activity; grade II pain occurring before and after activity but not affecting performance; grade III pain occurring before, during, and after athletic activity and affecting performance; and grade IV pain, so severe that performance is impossible.

Care   Care of shinsplints is as varied as its causes. Constant heat in the form of whirlpools, analgesic balm packs, and ultrasound therapy, with prescription by a physician, give positive results and, together with supportive taping and gradual stretching, afford a good general approach to the problem. It should be noted that a stress fracture must be ruled out before ultrasound is used.

Ice massage to the shin region and taking two aspirins have been found to be beneficial before a workout.[9] Ice massage is applied for 10 minutes or until redness takes place. Ice application should be followed by a gradual stretch to both the anterior and posterior aspects of the leg directly after the massage.

Static stretching should be a routine procedure before and after physical activity for all athletes who have a history of shinsplints. Exercise must also accompany any therapy program, with special considerations of the calf muscle and the plantar flexion and dorsiflexion movements of the foot.

Compartment Syndromes

Acute compartment syndrome The acute compartment syndrome resulting from exercise is much less common than the chronic or recurrent type. It is usually caused by performing unaccustomed exercise, such as running a long distance.[15] This is a very serious condition and needs to be promptly referred to a physician.

As an acute condition, the compartment continues to show signs of compression of nerves and blood vessels after the athlete stops exercising. The following signs are characteristic of anterior compartment syndrome, by far the most common form: (1) Weakness of foot dorsiflexion or extension of the great toe and (2) numbness (paresthesia) or tingling of the web between the first and second toe or over the foot's entire dorsal region.[19]

If by chance there is an acute posterior compartment **syndrome**, there is (1) weakness in plantar flexion, (2) weakness of great toe and little toe flexion, and (3) paresthesia of the sole of the foot.

Care An acute compartment syndrome requires immediate decompression by the surgical release of the fascia covering the area.[12] The incision may be left open and the leg splinted for a week.

Exercise-induced compartment syndrome The exercise-induced compartment compression syndrome is most frequently seen among runners and in sports such as soccer, which involve extensive running.[7,11] The compartments most often affected are the anterior and deep posterior, with the anterior having by far the highest incidence. On occasion, the lateral compartment may be involved.

The compartment compression syndrome occurs when the tissue fluid pressure has increased because of the confines of fascia or bone adversely compressing muscles, blood vessels, and nerves. With the increase in fluid pressure, muscle blood circulation is impeded, which could lead to permanent disability.[15]

The exercise-induced compartment compression syndrome is classified as acute or chronic (recurrent). The first type is an acute syndrome and a medical emergency, requiring immediate decompression to prevent permanent damage. The acute exercise-induced compartment compression syndrome resembles a fracture or a severe contusion.

The second type is one that is chronic or recurrent. Internal pressures rise slowly during exercise and subside after discontinuance of exercise. If exercise is not stopped in time, an acute emergency may occur. In chronic exercise-induced compartment compression syndrome, there is a constriction of blood vessels, producing ischemia and pain, but seldom neurological involvement.

Tibia or Fibular Stress Fractures

Stress fractures to the tibia or fibula are a common overuse stress condition, especially among distance runners.[3] Like many other overuse syndromes, athletes who have biomechanical foot problems are more prone to stress frac-

syndrome
Group of typical symptoms or conditions that characterize a deficiency or a disease

Exercise-induced compartment compression syndromes are most commonly seen in runners and soccer players.

The athlete with hypermobile
and/or pronated feet is more
susceptible to fibular stress
fracture. The athlete with rigid
pes cavus is more susceptible
to tibial fractures.

tures of the lower leg. Athletes who have hypermobile and/or pronated, or flat feet are more susceptible to fibular stress fracture, whereas those with rigid pes cavus are more prone to tibial stress fractures.[10] Runners frequently develop a stress fracture in the lower third of the leg; ballet dancers more commonly acquire one in the middle third.

The athlete complains of pain in the leg that is more intense on activity but relieved when resting. There is usually point tenderness, but it may be difficult to discern the difference between bone pain and soft tissue pain.

Detection of a stress fracture may be extremely difficult. X-ray examination may not determine a bone defect, which means more definitive testing by the physician would be required.

Care   The following regimen may be used for a stress fracture of the leg:
1. Discontinue running or other stressful locomotor activities for at least 6 weeks.
2. When pain is severe, use crutch walking or wear a cast.
3. Weight bearing may be resumed as pain subsides.
4. Bicycling may be used before returning to running.
5. After at least 6 weeks and a pain-free period for at least 2 weeks, running can begin again.[1]
6. Biomechanical foot correction may be necessary.

EXERCISE REHABILITATION OF THE ANKLE AND LOWER LEG

Too often athletes are permitted
to return to their sport
before adequate recovery has
taken place, causing the ankle
joint to become chronically
inflamed.

Rehabilitation exercises of the ankle and lower leg should be performed 2 to 3 times daily, progressing from 1 to 3 sets of ten repetitions. The athlete must consider all the major muscles associated with the foot, ankle, and lower leg. A program of three stages might include the following:

Stage 1—Early rehabilitation (all exercises must be conducted pain free).

1. *Writing the alphabet*—With toes pointed, 3 times.
2. *Picking up objects* one at a time with the toes, such as ten marbles, and placing them in a container.
3. *Gripping and spreading toes*—ten repetitions.
4. *Ankle circumduction*—ten circles in one direction and ten circles in the other.
5. *Flatfooted Achilles tendon stretching*—With foot flat on the floor, the Achilles tendon is stretched first with foot straight ahead, then adducted, and finally abducted. Each stretch is maintained for 20 to 30 seconds and repeated 2 to 3 times.
6. *Toe raises*—Standing flat on floor, the athlete rises onto toes as far as possible, with toes pointed straight ahead, pointed in, and finally pointed out; ten repetitions, 2 or 3 times.
7. *Walking on toes and heels*—The athlete walks ten paces forward on toes and ten paces backward on heels. Repeated 2 or 3 times.

Stage 2—Intermediate rehabilitation
1. *Towel gather*—ten repetitions, 2 or 3 times.
2. *Towel scoop*—ten repetitions, 2 or 3 times.
3. *Achilles tendon stretching and toe raise*—The athlete stands with toes on a raised area, such as a step, with heels over the edge. The heels are raised as far as possible and then returned to stretch the Achilles tendon as much as possible. This is performed with toes pointed straight ahead, pointed in, and then pointed out; ten repetitions, 2 or 3 times.
4. *Resistance*—Exercise anterior, lateral, and medial leg muscles against a resistance, such as surgical tubing or an inner tube strip. The rubber is attached around a stationary table or chair leg. The athlete then places the tubing

around the foot and pulls the forefoot into dorsiflexion, eversion, then reverses position and exercises the foot in plantar flexion inversion; ten repetitions, 3 or 4 times.

5. *Manual resistance* — Manual resistance can be applied by the trainer or another person. The exercise is performed in a complete range of motion and in all four ankle movements. Exercise is performed until fatigue or pain is felt.

6. *Proprioceptive ankle training* — The athlete spends 3 to 5 minutes daily on a balance board (wobble board) to reestablish ankle proprioception.

Stage 3 — Advanced rehabilitation

1. *Rope jumping* — 5 to 10 minutes daily.

2. *Heel-toe and then on-toe running* — The athlete starts with heel-toe jogging until a mile distance can be performed easily. Jogging is then shifted to jogging 50 yards and on-toe running 50 yards, graduating to all on-toe running for 1 mile.

3. *Zigzag running* — The athlete runs a zigzag pattern graduating from slow to full speed without favoring the leg.

4. *Backward running* — A final exercise for returning full ankle and lower leg function is running backward in an on-toe manner.

SUMMARY

The ankle has a high incidence of injury in sports activities. Although the ankle has relatively strong bony arrangement in terms of its supportive soft tissue, it is very weak laterally. Despite susceptible to injuries, preventive procedures can be taken. Through heel cord stretching, strength training, wearing of proper footwear and the application of appropriate taping or wrapping, many injuries can be prevented.

A second or third degree sprained ankle should have immediate care consisting of ICE-R. Cold is applied 20 minutes intermittently 5 to 6 times per day and lasting for 2 or 3 days. Compression is applied by an elastic wrap. The ankle is elevated above the level of the heart whenever possible. Weight bearing should be eliminated by the use of crutches.

The same mechanisms that strain a heel cord also can cause rupture. The Thompson test is standard for the suspected heel cord rupture. Repeated minor heel cord tears can cause tissue degeneration and subsequently a rupture.

The lower leg is subject to bruises, acute and chronic strain, and, on occasion, fractures. Chronic strain can lead to shinsplints or the more serious exercise-induced compartment syndrome.

REVIEW QUESTIONS AND CLASS ACTIVITIES

1. Discuss the relative strengths and weaknesses of the ankle joint.
2. How can ankle sprains be prevented?
3. Discuss the events leading to a typical inversion and eversion ankle sprain.
4. Discuss all steps in the immediate care of a second degree sprained ankle.
5. Establish two student committees consisting of three or more students to debate the advantages and disadvantages of routine ankle taping.
6. Indicate steps taken in caring for a second degree sprain.
7. Why is an eversion ankle sprain usually more serious than the inversion type?
8. Describe the ways an ankle can be fractured.

9. Describe an exercise rehabilitation program for a seriously injured ankle. Begin the program with the earliest exercise allowed and continue through to the time the athlete is allowed to return to basketball competition.
10. Describe the characteristics of a heel cord (Achilles tendon) rupture.
11. Contrast shinsplints from an exercise-induced compartment syndrome. How should they be managed?

REFERENCES

1. Birnbaum, J.S.: The musculoskeletal manual, New York, 1982, Academic Press, Inc.
2. Cailliet, R.: Foot and ankle pain, Philadelphia, 1968, F.A. Davis Co.
3. Conley, L.M.: Stress fractures, Ath. Train. **20**:16, Spring 1985.
4. Cox, J.S., and Brand, R.L.: Evaluation and treatment of lateral ankle sprains, Phys. Sportsmed. **2**:6, 1977.
5. Cutting, V.J.: Development of a student handbook for prevention of athletic injuries, an unpublished masters thesis, San Diego, 1985, San Diego State University.
6. Distenfano, V.J., and Nixon, J.E.: Ruptures of the Achilles tendon, J. Sports Med. **1**:4, 1973.
7. Galstad, U.A.: Anterior tibial compartment syndrome, Ath. Train. **17**:3, 1979.
8. Hoerner, E.F.: Foot and ankle injuries. In Vinger, P.F., and Hoerner, E.F. (editors): Sports injuries: the unthwarted epidemic, Boston, 1982, John Wright, PSG, Inc.
9. Jackson, D.W.: Shinsplints: an update, Phys. Sportsmed. **6**:10, 1978.
10. Kulund, D.N.: The injured athlete, Philadelphia, 1982, J.B. Lippincott Co.
11. Leach, R.E., and Corbett, M.: Anterior tibial compartment syndrome in soccer players, Am J. Sports Med. **7**:4 1979.
12. Mack, R.P.: Ankle injuries in athletics. In Torg, J.S. (editor): Symposium on ankle and foot problems in the athlete, Clinics in sports medicine, vol. 1, no. 1, Philadelphia, March 1982, W.B. Saunders.
13. Maron, B.R.: Orthopedic aspects of sports medicine. In Appenzeller, O., and Atkinson, R. (editors): Sports medicine, Baltimore, 1981, Urban & Schwarzenberg, Inc.
14. Millar, A.P.: Strains of the posterior calf musculature ("tennis leg"), Am. J. Sports Med. **7**:2, 1979.
15. Mubarak, S., and Hargens, A.: Exertional compartment syndromes. In Mack, R.P. (editor): Symposium on the foot and leg in running sports, American Academy of Orthopaedic Surgeons, St. Louis, 1982, The C.V. Mosby Co.
16. O'Donoghue, D.H.: Treatment of injuries to athletes, ed. 4, Philadelphia, 1984, W.B. Saunders Co.
17. Roy, S.P.: Evaluation and treatment of the stable ankle sprain, Phys. Sportsmed. **5**:8, 1977.
18. Voight, M.L.: Reduction of post traumatic ankle edema with high voltage pulsed galvanic stimulation, Ath. Train. **19**:279, Winter 1984.
19. Wallensten, R., and Eriksson, E.: Is medical lower leg pain (shinsplint) a chronic compartment syndrome? In Mack, R.P. (editor): Symposium on the foot and leg in running sports, American Academy of Orthopaedic Surgeons, St. Louis, 1982, The C.V. Mosby Co.

ANNOTATED BIBLIOGRAPHY

Fahey, T.D.: Athletic training: principles and practice, Palo Alto, Calif., 1986, Mayfield Publishing Co.
An overview of athletic training with an in-depth coverage of ankle and lower leg injuries.
Kessler, R.M.: The ankle and hindfoot. In Kessler, R.M., and Hertling, D. (editors): Management of common musculoskeletal disorders, Philadelphia, 1983, Harper & Row.
This chapter provides a good anatomy and biomechanics review of the ankle and hindfoot. It also details the management of acute and chronic ankle sprains.

Chapter 11

THE KNEE AND RELATED STRUCTURES

When you finish this chapter, you will be able to:

Describe the most common knee injuries and injuries to its related structures

Identify the most common knee injuries

Explain how to apply appropriate immediate and superficial follow-up care to a knee injury

Muscles and ligaments provide the main source of stability in the knee.

Major actions of the knee:
Flexion
Extension
Gliding
Rotation

The knee joint is considered one of the most complex joints in the human body. Because so many sports place extreme stress on the knee, it is also one of the most traumatized joints in sports. The knee is commonly considered a hinge joint (ginglymus). Medial and lateral rotations of the tibia are possible but only to a limited degree. Since the knee is extremely weak in terms of its bony arrangement, compensation is provided through the firm support of ligaments and muscles (Figs. 11-1, 11-2, 11-3, 11-4, 11-6, and 11-7). The knee is designed primarily for stability in weight bearing and mobility in locomotion; however, it is especially unstable laterally and medially.

The primary actions of the knee are flexion, extension, gliding, and rotation. Secondary movements consist of a slight internal (medial) and external (lateral) rotation of the tibia. The movements of flexion and extension take place above the menisci, a crescent-shaped fibrocartilage, whereas rotation is performed below the menisci. Rotation is caused mainly by the greater length of the medial condyle of the femur, which rolls forward more than the lateral condyle does.

Ligaments and the deeper capsular structures serve to stabilize the knee. Those that stabilize the knee laterally and medially are commonly known as the tibial (medial) collateral ligament and the fibular (lateral) collateral ligament. Internal stability is also provided by the cruciate ligaments. The anterior cruciate ligament attaches to the front of the tibia's upper surface between the two menisci passing to the medial aspect of the lateral condyle of the femur (see Fig. 11-1). In contrast, the posterior cruciate ligament attaches to the back of the tibia's upper surface passing forward to the lateral aspect of the medial condyle of the femur. In general, the anterior cruciate ligament stops excessive external rotation, stabilizes the knee in full extension, and

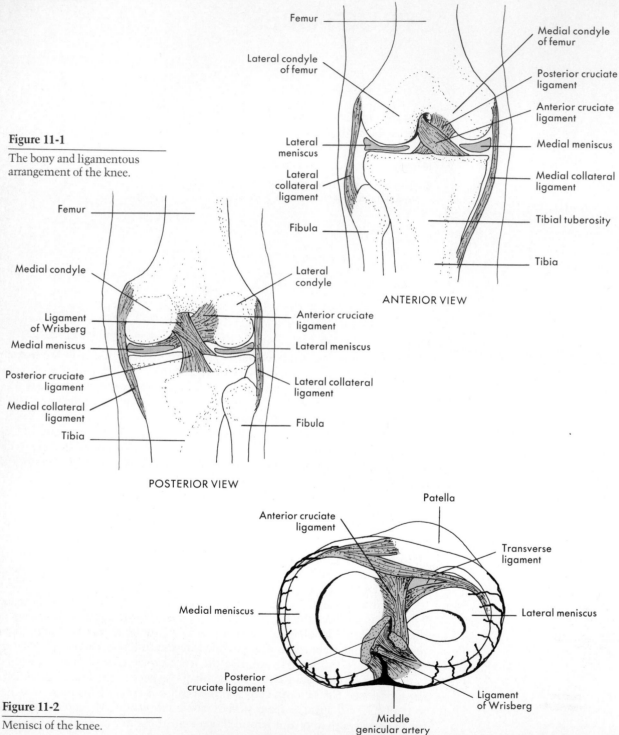

Figure 11-1

The bony and ligamentous arrangement of the knee.

Femur

Lateral condyle
of femur

Lateral
meniscus

Lateral
collateral
ligament

Fibula

Medial condyle
of femur

Posterior cruciate
ligament

Anterior cruciate
ligament

Medial meniscus

Medial collateral
ligament

Tibial tuberosity

Tibia

ANTERIOR VIEW

Femur

Medial condyle

Ligament
of Wrisberg

Medial meniscus

Posterior cruciate
ligament

Medial collateral
ligament

Tibia

Lateral
condyle

Anterior cruciate
ligament

Lateral meniscus

Lateral collateral
ligament

Fibula

POSTERIOR VIEW

Patella

Anterior cruciate
ligament

Transverse
ligament

Medial meniscus

Lateral meniscus

Posterior
cruciate ligament

Ligament
of Wrisberg

Middle
genicular artery

Figure 11-2

Menisci of the knee.

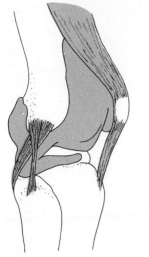

Figure 11-3

Synovial membrane of the
knee.

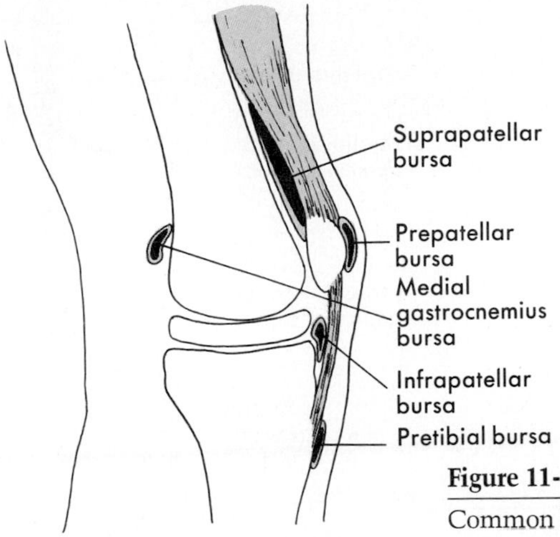

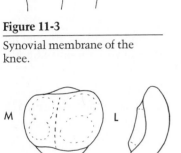

Posterior   Lateral

Figure 11-5

Patella.

Suprapatellar
bursa

Prepatellar
bursa

Medial
gastrocnemius
bursa

Infrapatellar
bursa

Pretibial bursa

Figure 11-4

Common bursae of the knee.

Figure 11-6

Musculature of the knee.

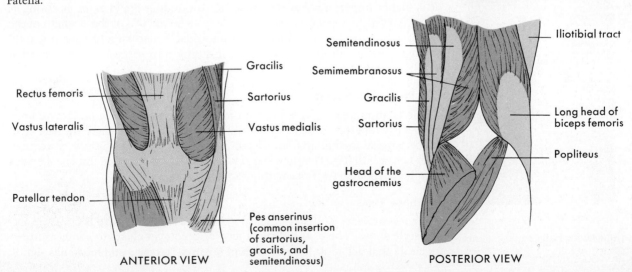

Rectus femoris

Vastus lateralis

Patellar tendon

Gracilis

Sartorius

Vastus medialis

Pes anserinus
(common insertion
of sartorius,
gracilis, and
semitendinosus)

ANTERIOR VIEW

Semitendinosus

Semimembranosus

Gracilis

Sartorius

Head of the
gastrocnemius

Iliotibial tract

Long head of
biceps femoris

Popliteus

POSTERIOR VIEW

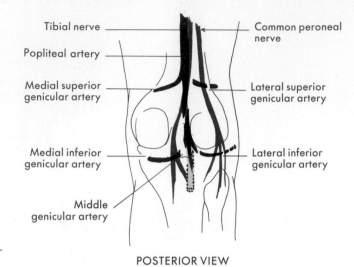

Tibial nerve

Popliteal artery

Medial superior
genicular artery

Medial inferior
genicular artery

Middle
genicular artery

Common peroneal
nerve

Lateral superior
genicular artery

Lateral inferior
genicular artery

POSTERIOR VIEW

Figure 11-7

Knee blood and nerve supply.

prevents hyperextension. The posterior cruciate ligament prevents internal rotation, guides the knee in flexion, and acts as a drag during the initial glide phase of flexion.

NOTE: It is beyond the intent of this text to provide a detailed discussion of the knee's anatomy. Anatomical drawings are provided as reference when certain structures are mentioned.

Prevention of Injuries

Knee injuries, especially in football, can be prevented by increasing muscle strength, using protective bracing, and wearing proper shoes.

Muscle Strength

It is highly important that the muscles surrounding the knee be as strong as possible. The hamstring muscles should have 60 to 70% of the strength of the quadriceps muscles. The gastrocnemius muscle also should have maximal strength. Although maximizing muscle strength may prevent some injuries, it fails to prevent rotary-type injuries.

Protective Bracing

There is an increasing trend toward football players wearing protective knee braces to avoid injury. Devices such as the Losse knee brace and the McDavid brace provide medial and lateral protection but not rotary injury protection. The Lenox Hill (Fig. 11-8) and Pro-Am braces (Fig. 11-9) are examples of braces that help stabilize the knee with rotary problems.[10]

Shoe Type

Over recent years, collision-type sports such as football have been using soccer-style shoes. The change from a few long, conical cleats to a large number of cleats that are short (no longer than 1/2 inch [1.3 cm]) and broad has signifi-

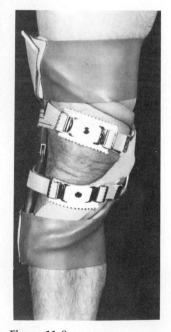

Figure 11-8

The Lenox Hill derotation knee brace.

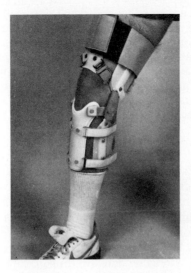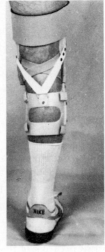

Figure 11-9

The Pro-Am knee brace.

cantly cut down on knee injuries in football. The higher number and shorter cleats are better because the foot does not become fixed to the surface and the shoe still allows for controlled running and cutting.

Acute Conditions

Contusions

A blow struck against the bony tissue and muscles crossing the knee joint can result in a very handicapping condition. Bruises to the medial aspect of the quadriceps region (vastus medialis) produce all the appearances of a knee sprain, including severe pain, loss of movement, and signs of acute inflammation. Such bruising is often manifested by swelling and discoloration caused by the tearing of muscle tissue and blood vessels. If adequate first aid is given immediately, the knee will usually return to functional use 24 to 48 hours after the trauma.

Bruising to the region of the knee joint is often to the deep bone. A traumatic compressive force delivered to the knee joint causes bleeding and results in profuse fluid swelling into the joint cavity and surrounding spaces. Swelling often takes place slowly and almost imperceptibly. It is advisable to prevent the athlete from engaging in further activity for at least 24 hours after receipt of a joint bruise. Activity causes an increase in circulation and may cause extensive joint swelling.

Immediate and follow-up care   Care of a bruised knee depends on many factors. However, management principally depends on the location and severity of the contusion. The following procedures are suggested:

1. Apply compression bandages and cold along with elevation until hemorrhage has stopped.
2. Have the athlete rest for 24 hours.
3. If swelling occurs, continue cold application for 72 hours. If swelling and pain are intense, refer the athlete to the physician.

4. Once the acute stage has ended and the swelling has diminished to little or none, cold application with active range of motion exercises should be conducted within a pain-free range. If a gradual use of heat is elected, great caution should be taken to avoid swelling.
5. Allow the athlete to return to normal activity, with protective padding, when pain and the initial irritation have subsided.
6. If swelling is not resolved within a week, a chronic condition may exist, indicating the need for further rest and medical attention.

Bursitis

Where tissue such as a tendon moves in relation to a bone, a fluid cushion, known as a *bursa*, develops. A bursa has an outer coat of dense fibrous tissue with a soft lining that secretes a small amount of fluid. When this lining becomes irritated a bursitis occurs. Bursitis in the knee can be acute, chronic, or recurrent. Any one of numerous knee bursae can become inflamed.

Bursae (see Fig. 11-4) often become inflamed from continued kneeling or from overuse of the patellar tendon. Swelling in the knee posteriorly may indicate an irritation of one of the bursae in this region. Swelling in the back of the knee (popliteal fossa) could be a sign of *Baker's cyst* (Fig. 11-10), which is an irritation of the bursa associated with the calf and hamstring muscles (gastrocnemius-semimembranous bursae). Baker's cyst is commonly painless, causing no discomfort or disability. Some inflamed bursae may be painful and disabling because of the swelling and should be treated accordingly.

Care Care usually follows a pattern of eliminating the cause, prescribing rest, and reducing inflammation. Contrast baths may help to reduce swelling. When the bursitis is chronic or recurrent and the synovium has thickened, aspiration and a steroid injection may be warranted.

Figure 11-10

Baker's cyst in the popliteal fossa.

Collateral Ligament and Capsular Injuries

Ligament and capsular sprains are the most frequently reported injury among the knee injuries that occur in sports. Many knee sprains involve the medial collateral ligament either by a direct blow from the lateral side in a medial direction or by a severe outward twist. Greater injury results from medial sprains than from lateral sprains because of their more direct relation to the articular capsule and the medial meniscus. Medial and lateral sprains appear in varying degrees, depending on knee position, previous injuries, the strength of muscles crossing the joint, the force and angle of the trauma, fixation of the foot, and conditions of the playing surface.

The position of the knee is important in establishing its vulnerability in traumatic sprains. Any position of the knee, from full extension to full flexion, can result in injury if there is sufficient force. Full extension tightens both lateral and medial ligaments. However, flexion affords a loss of stability to the lateral ligament but maintains stability in various portions of the broad medial ligament.[6] Medial collateral ligament sprains occur most often from a violently adducted and internally rotated knee. The most prevalent mechanism of a lateral collateral ligament or capsular sprain is one in which the foot is turned inward and the knee is forced laterally outward.

Speculation among medical authorities is that torn menisci seldom happen as the result of an initial trauma; most occur after the collateral ligaments have been stretched by repeated injury. Many mild to moderate sprains leave the knee unstable and thus vulnerable to additional internal derangements. The strength of the muscles crossing the knee joint is important in assisting the ligaments to support the articulation. These muscles should be conditioned to the highest possible degree for sports in which knee injuries are common. With the added support and protection of muscular strength, a state of readiness may be developed through proper training.

Evaluation of the Injured Knee Joint

The force and angle of the trauma usually determine the extent of injury that takes place. Even after having witnessed the occurrence of a knee injury, it is difficult to predict the amount of tissue damage. The most revealing time for determining the extent of knee joint injury is immediately after injury, before blood and other fluids in the joint mask the extent of trauma.

It should be noted that there are a number of knee ligament stability tests available to the qualified athletic trainer and physician. Coaches should be concerned with the obvious symptoms and signs of injury so that prompt medical referral may be made.

Figure 11-11

Constant stress on the medial aspect of the knee could make the medial collateral ligament and deeper capsular ligaments susceptible to an acute sprain.

valgus
Bent outward

varus
Bent inward

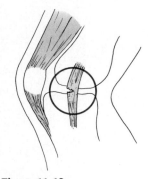

Figure 11-12

First degree medial collateral ligament sprain.

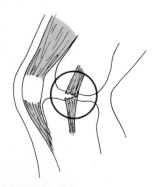

Figure 11-13

Second degree medial collateral ligament sprain.

hemarthrosis
Blood in a joint cavity

Acute Medial Knee Sprains

Medial injuries of the knee can involve the medial collateral or deeper capsular ligaments (Fig. 11-11).

First Degree Medial Collateral Ligament Sprain

A first degree medial collateral ligament injury of the knee has the following characteristics (Fig. 11-12):
1. A few ligamentous fibers are torn and stretched.
2. The joint is stable in valgus stress tests.
3. There is little or no joint swelling.
4. There may be some joint stiffness and point tenderness just below the medial joint line.
5. Even with minor stiffness, there is almost full passive and active range of motion.

Care Immediate care consists of ICE-R for at least 24 hours. After immediate care, the following procedures should be undertaken:
1. Crutches are prescribed if the athlete is unable to walk without a limp.
2. Follow-up care may involve cryokinetics, including 5 minutes of ice pack treatment preceding exercise or a combination of cold and compression or ultrasound.
3. Proper exercise is essential (see the knee joint reconditioning discussion on pp. 238-239).

Isometrics and straight-leg exercises are important until the knee can be moved without pain. The athlete then graduates to stationary bicycle riding or a high-speed isokinetic program. This helps the athlete to progress to knee muscle contraction that is nearing that of a particular running sport.

The athlete is allowed to return to full participation when the knee has regained normal strength, power, flexibility, endurance, and coordination. Usually 1 to 3 weeks is necessary for recovery. On returning to activity the athlete may require tape support for a short period.

Second Degree Medial Collateral Ligament Sprain

A second degree medial collateral ligament knee sprain indicates both microscopic and gross disruption of ligamentous fibers (Fig. 11-13). The only structures involved are the medial collateral ligament and the medial capsular ligament. It is characterized by the following:
1. A complete tear of the deep capsular ligament and partial tear of the superficial layer of the medial collateral ligament or a partial tear of both areas.[13]
2. There is no general joint instability, however, there may be a minimal or slight laxity in full extension, and as much as 5 to 15 degrees of movement when given a stress test with the knee in a 30° flexed position.
3. Swelling is slight or absent unless the meniscus or anterior cruciate ligament has been torn. An acutely torn or pinched synovial membrane, subluxated or dislocated patella, or an osteochondral fracture can produce extensive swelling and **hemarthrosis**.
4. Moderate to severe joint tightness with an inability to fully and actively extend the knee. The athlete is unable to place the heel flat on the ground.

5. Definite loss of passive range of motion.
6. Pain in the medial joint line, with general weakness and instability.

Care   The following steps should be followed when caring for a second degree medial collateral ligament strain:

1. ICE-R for 48 to 72 hours.
2. Crutches are used with a three-point gait until the acute phase of injury is over and the athlete can walk without a limp.
3. Depending on the severity and possible complications, a full-leg cast or postoperative knee immobilizing splint may be applied by the physician (Fig. 11-14).
4. Cryokinetics or other therapeutic modalities are employed three or four times daily.
5. Isometric exercise along with exercise to all the adjacent joints is performed three or four times daily.
6. Depending on the extent of injury and swelling, the immobilizing splint is removed and gentle range of movement may be performed.
7. Taping may be appropriate to provide some support and confidence to the athlete.

Third Degree Medial Collateral Ligament Sprain

Third degree medial collateral ligament sprain means a complete tear of the supporting ligaments. The following are major signs (Fig. 11-15):

1. Complete loss of medical stability
2. Minimal to moderate swelling

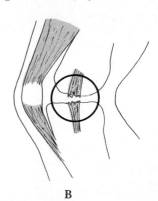

Figure 11-14

Knee immobilizer after a ligamentous injury.

A

B

Figure 11-15

A, A knee injury that results in both a medial collateral and anterior cruciate ligament tear. **B**, Third degree medial collateral ligament sprain.

3. Medial pain and point tenderness
4. Loss of range of motion because of effusion and hamstring spasm
5. The valgus stress test reveals some joint opening at full extension and significant opening at 30 degrees of flexion.

An anterior cruciate ligament tear or medial meniscus disruption may be present and should be tested for.

Immediate and follow-up care   Immediately refer the athlete to a physician. ICE-R for 20 minutes every 2 hours during the waking day should be performed for at least 72 hours. In many cases such an injury is surgically re-

---

TAPING FOR COLLATERAL LIGAMENT KNEE INJURIES

As with ankle instabilities the athlete with an unstable knee should never use tape and bracing as a replacement for proper exercise rehabilitation. If properly applied, taping can help protect the knee and become an aid in the rehabilitation process.[9]

Materials needed: One roll of 2-inch (5 cm) linen tape, one roll of 3-inch (7.5 cm) elastic tape, a 1-inch (2.5 cm) heel lift, and skin adherent.

Position of the athlete: The athlete stands on a 3-foot (90 cm) table with the injured knee held in a moderately relaxed position by means of a 1-inch (2.5 cm) heel lift. The hair is completely removed from a point 6 inches (15 cm) above to 6 inches (15 cm) below the kneecap.

Procedure

1. A circular, 2-inch (5 cm) linen tape anchoe strip is placed lightly around the thigh and leg at the hairline.
2. Twelve elastic tape strips are precut, each about 9 inches (22.5 cm) long. Stretched to their utmost, they are applied to the knee as indicated in Fig. 11-16.
3. Finally, elastic tape is applied as locks for the basketweave. Two or three strips of tape are cut to encircle the thigh and the leg. Some individuals find it advantageous to complete a knee taping by wrapping loosely with an elastic wrap, thus providing an added precaution against the tape becoming loose from perspiration.

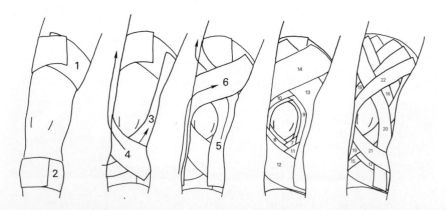

Figure 11-16

Taping for knee collateral ligament injuries.

paired as soon as possible after the acute inflammatory phase of 3 or 4 days after injury.

Acute Lateral Knee Sprains

Lateral knee sprains are due to an outward force to the lateral capsule and collateral ligament. The most common situation for injury is when the lower leg is internally rotated and the knee is suddenly forced outward. If the force is great enough, bony fragments can be pulled from the bone.[13]

The major signs include the following:

1. Pain and point tenderness along the joint line.
2. Depending on the degree of injury, there is usually some joint instability with joint opening on the varus stress test at 30 degrees of knee flexion.
3. Swelling is usually minimal because of bleeding into joint spaces.
4. The greater the ligamentous injury, the less pain is felt on the varus stress test.

Care of the lateral collateral ligament injury should follow procedures similar to those described for medial collateral ligament injuries.

Internal Knee Joint Conditions

The most common internal knee joint conditions are injuries to the cruciate ligament and to the meniscus.

Acute Anterior Cruciate Ligament Tear

Until recently the medial collateral ligament tear was considered much more prevalent than the complete anterior cruciate ligament tear. Today the anterior cruciate is considered the most commonly disrupted ligament in the knee.[11]

The anterior cruciate ligament tear is extremely difficult to diagnose. The earlier the determination the better, because swelling often will mask the full extent of injury. Besides swelling, this injury is associated with joint instability, and a positive drawer sign may be present. Therefore, ligament stress tests should be employed as soon as possible by the trainer or physician.[7]

The athlete often experiences a "pop," followed by immediate disability. The athlete complains that the knee feels like it is "coming apart." Although the tear may be isolated, it can be associated with a meniscus or medial collateral ligament tear (Fig. 11-17). The anterior cruciate ligament can be injured in a number of ways, including internal rotation of the thigh with the knee flexed while the foot is planted and forced hyperextension. Forced hyperflexion could conceivably injure both the anterior and posterior cruciate ligaments.

Immediate and follow-up care Even with proper first aid and immediate ICE-R, swelling begins within 1 to 2 hours and becomes a notable hemarthrosis within 4 to 6 hours.[3] The athlete typically cannot walk without help.

If a clinical evaluation is inconclusive, an arthroscopic examination may be warranted to make a proper diagnosis.

Figure 11-17

A cutting motion in football can often produce an isolated tear of the anterior cruciate ligament.

Anterior cruciate ligament injury could lead to serious knee instability; an intact anterior cruciate ligament is necessary for a knee to function in high-performance running and jumping situations. Controversy exists among physicians as to how best to treat an acute anterior cruciate ligament rupture and when surgery is warranted. It is well accepted that an unsatisfactorily treated anterior cruciate ligament rupture will eventually lead to major joint degeneration.[14] Therefore, a decision for or against surgery must be based on the athlete's age, the type of stress applied to the knee, and the amount of instability present, as well as the techniques available to the surgeon.[3]

The routine use of braces such as the Lenox Hill derotation brace, along with rotary and hyperextension taping, can provide some protection during activity.

Meniscal Lesions

A knee that locks and unlocks during activity may indicate a fractured meniscus.

The medial meniscus has a much higher incidence of injury than the lateral meniscus.[2] The higher number of medial meniscus tears is basically a result of the coronary ligament attaching the meniscus peripherally to the tibia and

---

ROTARY INJURY KNEE TAPING

The rotary taping method is designed to provide the knee with support when it is unstable from injury to the medial collateral and anterior cruciate ligaments.
Materials needed: One roll of 3-inch (7.5 cm) elastic tape, skin adherent, 4-inch (10 cm) gauze pad, and scissors.
Position of the athlete: The athlete sits on a table with the affected knee flexed 15 degrees.
Position of the operator: The operator stands facing the side of the athlete's flexed knee.
Procedure: Fig. 11-18 illustrates the proper procedure for applying the rotary injury knee taping.

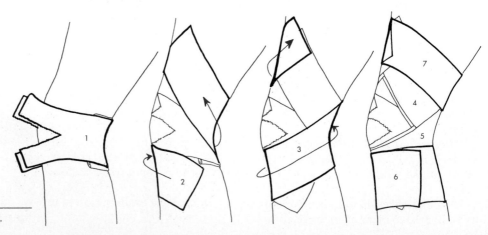

Figure 11-18
Rotary injury knee taping.

HYPEREXTENSION TAPING

Hyperextension taping is designed to prevent the knee from hyperextending.

Materials needed: One roll of 2 1/2-inch (5.5 cm) tape or 2-inch (5 cm) elastic tape, cotton or a 4-inch (10 cm) gauze pad, tape adherent, underwrap, and a 2-inch (5 cm) heel lift.

Position of the athlete: The athlete's leg should be completely shaved above midthigh and below midcalf. The athlete stands on a 3-foot (90 cm) table with the injured knee flexed by means of a 2-inch (5 cm) heel lift.

Position of the operator: The operator stands facing the back of the athlete's knee.

Procedure: Fig. 11-19 illustrates the proper procedure for applying the hyperextension taping. When the taping is finished, lock the supporting strips in place by applying two or three overlapping circles around the thigh and leg.

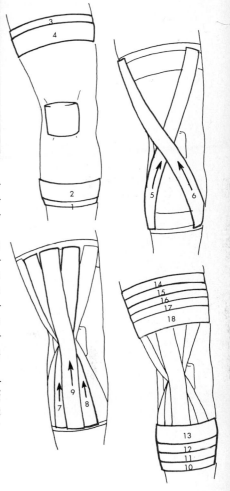

also to the capsular ligament. The lateral meniscus does not attach to the capsular ligament and is more mobile during knee movement. Because of the attachment to the medial structures, the medial meniscus is prone to disruption from inward and rotary tears.

A blow from the lateral side directed inward can often tear or stretch the medial collateral ligament and pull the medial meniscus out of its bed. Repeated mild sprains reduce the strength of the knee to a state favorable for a cartilage tear through lessening its normal ligamentous stability. A large number of medial meniscus injuries are the outcome of a sudden, strong internal rotation of the femur with a partially flexed knee while the foot is firmly planted. As a result of this action, the cartilage is pulled out of its normal bed and pinched between the femoral condyles. Tears that occur within the cartilage fail to heal due to lack of adequate blood supply[1,13] (Fig. 11-20).

Diagnosing a cartilage injury can be difficult. To determine the possibility of such an injury, a complete history should be obtained, which consists of information about past knee injury and an understanding of how the present

Figure 11-19

Hyperextension taping.

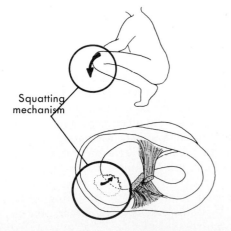

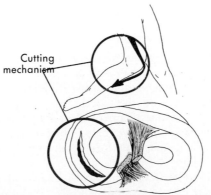

Figure 11-20

Common mechanisms of injury to the meniscus.

injury occurred. Diagnosis of menisci injuries should be made immediately after the injury has developed and before muscle spasm and swelling obscure the normal shape of the knee.

A meniscal tear may or may not result in the following:

1. Severe pain and loss of motion
2. A locked knee with inability to fully flex or extend
3. Pain in the area of the tear

Care The knee that is locked by a displaced cartilage may require unlocking under anesthesia so that a detailed examination can be conducted. If discomfort, disability, and locking of the knee continue, surgery may be required. For the nonlocking acute meniscus tear, immediate care should follow a second or third degree sprain care routine. The knee is cared for by splinting, crutch walking, muscle setting, and isometric exercise followed by gradual range of movement (ROM) and progressive resistance exercises.

Chronic injuries Once a knee cartilage has been fractured, its ruptured edges harden and may eventually atrophy. Occasionally, portions of the meniscus may become detached and wedge themselves between the articulating surfaces of the tibia and femur, thus imposing a locking, "catching," or "giving way" of the joint. Chronic meniscus lesions also may display recurrent swelling and obvious muscle atrophy about the knee. The athlete may complain of an inability to perform a full squat or to change direction quickly when running without pain, a sense of the knee collapsing, or a "popping" sensation. Such signs usually warrant surgical intervention. **NOTE**: Symptomatic meniscus tears can eventually lead to serious articular degeneration with major impairment and disability.

Loose bodies within the knee ("joint mice") Because of repeated trauma to the knee in sports activities, loose bodies can develop within the joint cavity. Loose bodies can stem from fragments from the menisci, pieces of torn synovial tissue, a torn cruciate ligament, or osteochondritis dissecans. The loose body may move around in the joint space and become lodged, causing locking, popping, and giving way. When the loose body becomes wedged between articulating surfaces, irritation can occur. If not surgically removed, the loose body can create conditions that lead to joint degeneration.

KNEECAP (PATELLAR) AND RELATED CONDITIONS

The position and function of the patella and surrounding structures expose it to a variety of traumas and diseases related to sports activities.

Patellar Fracture

Fractures of the patella can be caused by either direct or indirect trauma. Most fractures are the result of indirect violence in which a severe pull of the patellar tendon occurs against the femur when the knee is semiflexed. This position subjects the patella to maximal stress from the quadriceps tendon and the patellar ligament. Forcible muscle contraction may then fracture the patella at its lower half. Direct injury most often produces fragmentation with little displacement. Falls, jumping, or running may result in a fracture of the patella.

The fracture causes hemorrhage and joint effusion, resulting in a generalized swelling. Indirect fracture causes capsular tearing, separation of bone fragments, and possible tearing of the quadriceps tendon. Direct fracture involves little bone separation.

Care   Diagnosis is accomplished by use of the medical history, the palpation of separated fragments, and an x-ray confirmation. As soon as the examiner suspects a patellar fracture, a cold wrap should be applied, followed by an elastic compression wrap and splinting. The coach or athletic trainer should then refer the athlete to the team physician. The athlete normally will be immobilized for 2 to 3 months.

Acute Patellar Subluxation or Dislocation

When an athlete plants his or her foot, decelerates, and simultaneously cuts in an opposite direction from the weight-bearing foot, the thigh rotates internally while the lower leg rotates externally, causing a forced knee valgus. The quadriceps muscle attempts to pull in a straight line and as a result pulls the patella laterally—a force that may dislocate the patella. As a rule, displacement takes place outwardly with the patella resting on the lateral condyle.

An athlete who has a subluxated patella will complain that the knee catches or gives way. The knee may be swollen and painful. Pain is due to swelling, but also because the medial capsular tissue has been stretched and torn. Because of blood in the joint, the knee is restricted in flexion and extension.

The Dislocated Patella

An acute patellar dislocation is often associated with sudden twisting of the body while the foot or feet are planted. The athlete experiences a complete loss of knee function, pain, and swelling, with the patella resting in an abnormal position. The physician immediately puts the patella back in place (reduces the dislocation). If a period of time has elapsed before reduction, a general anesthesia may have to be used. After removal of the blood from the joint, ice is applied and the joint is splinted. A first-time patellar dislocation is always associated with a fracture. X-ray evaluation is performed before and after reduction.[13]

Care   After reduction the knee is immobilized in extension for 4 weeks or longer, and the athlete is instructed to use crutches when walking. During immobilization isometric exercises are performed at the knee joint. After immobilization the athlete should wear a horseshoe-shaped felt pad that is held in place around the patella by an elastic wrap or is sewn into an elastic sleeve that is worn while running or performing in sports (Fig. 11-21). Commercial braces are also available.

Muscle rehabilitation should be concerned with all the musculature of the knee, thigh, and hip. Knee exercise should be confined to straight leg raises.[9] This exercise starts with the athlete statically contracting the quadriceps muscle and holding it for 6 to 10 seconds. When this can be achieved pain free many times throughout the day, straight leg raising (SLR) can begin. The quadriceps muscle is contracted, then the leg is raised slowly as high as possible. This may be repeated several times per day. When SLR can be accomplished many times per day without pain, resistance (sand bags) is applied to the ankle in increments of 2 or fewer pounds. When weight is added, the DeLorme overload procedure is followed. The straight-leg-raise concept is also

Knees that "give way" or "catch" can have a number of possible pathological conditions:
Subluxating patella
Meniscus tear
Anterior cruciate ligament tear
Hemarthrosis

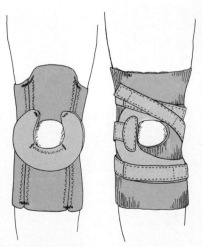

Figure 11-21

Special pads for the dislocating patella.

applied to the posterior aspect of the leg. The athlete performs SLRs face down. Progressions are the same as with the quadricep muscles.

Pain Related to the Kneecap and Femoral Groove

The patella, in relation to the femoral groove, can be subject to direct trauma or disease, leading to chronic pain and disability. Of major importance among athletes are those conditions that stem from abnormal patellar tracting within the femoral groove; the two most common of which are chondromalacia and degenerative arthritis.

Chondromalacia

Occurring most often among teenagers and young adults, chondromalacia is a gradual degenerative process. Cailliet[5] describes chondromalacia as undergoing three stages:

Stage 1 — Swelling and softening of the articular cartilage

Stage 2 — Fissuring of the softened articular cartilage

Stage 3 — Deformation of the surface of the articular cartilage due to fragmentation

The exact cause of chondromalacia is unknown. As indicated earlier, abnormal patellar tracting could be a major etiological factor. However, individuals with normal tracting have acquired chondromalacia, and some individuals with abnormal tracting are free of it.[5]

The athlete may experience pain in the anterior aspect of the knee while walking, running, ascending and descending stairs, or squatting. There may be recurrent swelling around the kneecap and a grating sensation on flexing and extending the knee.

On palpation there may be pain around the borders of the patella or when the patella is compressed within the femoral groove while the knee is passively flexed and extended. The athlete may have one or more lower limb alignment deviations.

In general, the care of chondromalacia involves rest for at least 6 weeks. A physician may prescribe anti-inflammatory medication and a regime of straight leg raising.

Other Extensor Mechanism Problems

Many other extensor mechanism problems can occur in the physically active individual. They can occur in the immature knee or through jumping and running.

The Immature Extensor Mechanism

Osgood-Schlatter disease is a condition of the tibial tuberosity growth region under the general classification of osteochondritis. To call this condition a *disease* is misleading because it is a number of conditions related to the growth center of the tibial tuberosity. The tibial tuberosity is an apophysis for the attachment of the patellar tendon.

The most commonly accepted cause is the repeated pull of the patellar tendon at the epiphysis of the tibial tubercle. Complete pulling away of the tibial tuberosity by the patellar tendon is a major complication of Osgood-Schlatter disease.

Repeated irritation causes swelling, hemorrhage, and gradual degeneration of the growth region due to impaired circulation. The athlete complains of pain on kneeling, jumping, and running. There is point tenderness over the tibial tuberosity (Fig. 11-22).

Larsen-Johannson disease is similar to Osgood-Schlatter disease but it occurs at the bottom of the kneecap. It is commonly caused by repeated muscle contraction (see Fig. 11-22).

Care Care is usually conservative and includes the following:

1. Stressful activities should be decreased until the epiphyseal union occurs, within 6 months to 1 year.
2. Severe cases may require a cylindrical cast.
3. Ice should be applied to the knee before and after activities.
4. Quadriceps and hamstring muscles should be isometrically strengthened.
5. Only in the most severe cases should surgery be performed.

Jumper's and Kicker's Knee Problems

Jumping, as well as kicking or running, may place extreme tension on the knee extensor muscle complex.[8] As a result of either one or more commonly repetitive injuries, tendinitis occurs in the patellar or quadriceps tendon. On rare occasions a patellar tendon may completely fail and rupture.

Patellar or quadriceps tendinitis Sudden or repetitive forceful extension of the knee may begin an inflammatory process that will eventually lead to tendon degeneration.[4]

Patellar or quadriceps tendinitis can be described in three stages of pain:

Stage 1—Pain after sports activity

Stage 2—Pain during and after activity (the athlete is able to perform at the appropriate level)

Stage 3—Pain during activity and prolonged after activity (athletic performance is hampered) may progress to constant pain and complete rupture

Care Any pain in the extensor mechanism must preclude sudden explosive movement such as that characterized by heavy plyometric-type exercis-

Conditions that may be mistaken for one another:
    Osgood-Schlatter disease
    Jumper's or kicker's knee

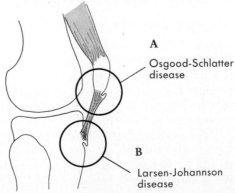

A
Osgood-Schlatter disease

B
Larsen-Johannson disease

Figure 11-22

Two conditions of the immature extensor mechanism. **A,** Osgood-Schlatter disease. **B,** Larsen-Johannson disease.

ing. Athletes with first- or second-stage tendinitis should carefully warm the tendons for 5 to 10 minutes in a whirlpool at 100° to 102° F (37.7° to 38.8° C) before performing an activity. Moist heat packs can be used instead of the whirlpool. After warming, a gradual static stretch should be applied as the tendons return to normal pre-exercise temperature. A gradual exercise warm-up should follow. The athlete should cease all activity at once if there is pain during exercise. An ice massage or pack should follow exercise. Third stage jumper's knee should be rested until it is symptom free.

Patellar or quadriceps tendon rupture An inflammatory condition of the knee extensor mechanism over a period of time can cause degeneration and weakness at the tendon attachment.[12] Seldom does a rupture occur in the middle of the tendon, but usually it is torn from its attachment. The quadriceps tendon ruptures from the superior pole of the patella, whereas the patellar tendon ruptures from the inferior pole of the patella. Proper conservative care of jumper's knee is essential to avoid such a major injury.[12]

Runner's and Cyclist's Knee

Runner's or cyclist's knee is a general description of many repetitive and overuse conditions that occur primarily to distance runners and cyclists. Many of these problems originally stem from structural asymmetries of the foot and lower leg as well as a leg-length discrepancy. Besides problems of patellar tendinitis, two common conditions are iliotibial band tendinitis and pes anserinus tendinitis or bursitis. A chronic pain occurs on the outer or inside aspect of the runner's knee. There may be a dull ache to a sharp pain.

Care Care of runner's or cyclist's knee includes correcting foot or leg malalignments. Rest and superficial therapy, such as cold packs may also be necessary. Athletes must warm-up properly and avoid aggravating the problem by running on inclines.

The Collapsing Knee

The most common causes of frequent knee collapse include a weak quadriceps muscle; chronic instability of the medial collateral ligament, anterior cruciate ligament, or posterior capsule; a torn meniscus; loose bodies within the knee; and a subluxating patella. Chondromalacia and a torn meniscus have also been known to cause the knee to give way.

RECONDITIONING OF THE KNEE REGION

Exercise programs for the knee fall basically into three categories: preoperative, postoperative, and preventive. When examination reveals torn ligaments or a torn meniscus, early surgical repair may be warranted. The preoperative program is concerned with increasing the strength and tone of the muscles surrounding the knee. A well-conditioned knee will undergo surgery with fewer negative effects than will one that is deconditioned.

The muscles that surround the knee, particularly the quadriceps and the hamstrings of the thigh, atrophy readily after a knee injury. Joint movement should be avoided until pain has subsided and initial healing is complete. While the knee joint is immobilized, the athlete should engage in isometric or static muscle contractions known as "quad setting" and graduate to straight leg raises, from both the sitting position with hip flexion and a prone position. The athlete can also execute toe raises to exercise the gastrocnemius muscle. During the period of immobilization, a graduated program of isometric contractions can be initiated by applying sandbag weights to the extended leg to afford resistance for periods of 6 to 10 seconds. Each isometric contraction should be followed by a period of complete relaxation, allowing the muscle tissue to receive a full complement of fresh blood. Active bending of the knee should be avoided until initial pain and soreness have diminished. A gradual program of leg swinging in the pain-free range combined with static stretching of the hamstrings can commence following removal from immobilization. A program of progressive resistance isotonic exercises is usually not begun until pain is minimal and healing has begun. **NOTE**: Caution must be observed when the athlete uses foot weights for resistance. Heavy objects fastened to the foot for resistance purposes may serve to stretch already extended internal structures. Support, therefore, should be given to the leg when it is hanging over the edge of the table. The athlete should begin with light resistance exercises executed several times per day. As strength and range of movement increase, resistance may also be increased.

Often the hamstring muscles and gastrocnemius are neglected in reconditioning of the knee. It should be remembered that these muscles contribute a considerable amount of support and stability to the knee; therefore, they should be conditioned along with the quadriceps.

When the athlete has reconditioned the knee to the point at which strength and flexibility are adequate for activity, light jogging graduating to running at half-speed straight ahead and then to figure-8 patterns may commence.

The criteria for an athlete returning to his or her sport depends a great deal on the requirements of the specific sport. In general, the athlete must have muscle strength equal to or greater than the normal leg. The muscles of greatest concern are the quadriceps, hamstrings, and gastrocnemius. The range of motion of the knee must be equal to or greater than the nonaffected side. It is also important that the circumference of the thigh 3 inches (7.5 cm) above the top of the patella be no less than 90% of the other thigh. A final test for a safe return to a running sport should be the ability to run full-speed in a figure-8 pattern around obstacles such as goalposts, first in one direction and then in the other, placing stress equally on each side of the knee.

SUMMARY

The knee is one of the most, if not *the* most, complex joints in the human body. As a hinge joint that also glides and has some rotation, it is also one of the most traumatized joints in sports. Three structures are most often injured: medial and lateral collateral capsules and ligaments, the menisci, and cruciate ligaments.

Prevention of knee injuries involves maximizing muscle strength, wearing protective bracing when needed, and wearing appropriate shoes.

Acute knee conditions include superficial conditions such as contusions and bursitis. Ligament and capsular sprains occur frequently to the medial aspect of the knee and less often to the lateral aspect. The most common ligament injury is to the anterior cruciate ligament.

The immediate care of a knee sprain requires ice, compression, and elevation (ICE) for 20 minutes intermittently every 1 1/2 hours during waking periods. ICE may be extended for several days depending on the extent of the injury. Rest is also essential during this inflammatory phase.

A meniscus can be injured in a variety of ways, including a rotary force to the knee with the foot planted, a sudden valgus or varus force, or a sudden flexion or extension of the knee. There may be severe pain and loss of motion, a locking of the knee, and pain in the area of the tear.

Chronic knee joint problems can occur when the articular cartilage is disrupted. Sometimes pieces of cartilage or bone become loose bodies in the knee joint. These floating pieces can cause chronic knee inflammation, locking, catching, or a giving way of the joint.

The kneecap and surrounding area can develop a variety of injuries from sports activities. Some of these are fracture, dislocation, and chronic articular degeneration such as chondromalacia. Other conditions in the region include Osgood-Schlatter disease or the jumper's knee.

REVIEW QUESTIONS AND CLASS ACTIVITIES

1. Explain the major structural and functional anatomical features of the knee.
2. How can knee injuries be prevented? What types of knee injuries are most difficult to prevent?
3. Describe the immediate care of first, second, and third degree medial collateral ligament sprains.
4. Demonstrate a collateral ligament knee taping.
5. Demonstrate a rotary knee taping.
6. Discuss loose bodies within the knee.
7. Why do kneecaps become subject to subluxations or dislocations?
8. What are some of the reasons for pain in the vicinity of the kneecap?
9. Describe Osgood-Schlatter disease.
10. Discuss major concepts of reconditioning the knee region.

REFERENCES

1. Arnoczky, S.P., and Warren, R.F.: Microvasculature of the human meniscus, Am. J. Sports Med. **10**:90, March/April 1982.
2. Baker, B.E., et al: Review of meniscal injury and associated sports, Am. J. Sports Med. **13**:1, Jan./Feb. 1985.
3. Berfeld, J.A.: Injury to the anterior cruciate ligament, Phys. Sportsmed. **10**:47, Nov. 1982.
4. Black, J.E., and Aten, S.R.: How I manage infrapatellar tendinitis, Phys. Sportsmed. **12**:86, Oct. 1984.
5. Cailliet, R.: Knee pain and disability, ed. 2, Philadelphia, 1983, F.A. Davis Co.
6. Derscheid, F.L., and Garrick, J.G.: Medial collateral ligament injuries in football, Am. J. Sports Med. **9**:365, Nov./Dec. 1981.
7. DiStefano, V.J.: The enigmatic anterior cruciate ligament, Ath. Train. **16**:244, 1981.
8. Ferretti, A., et al: Jumper's knee: an epidemiological study of volleyball players, Phys. Sportsmed. **12**:97, Oct. 1984.
9. Handling, K.A.: Taping procedure for an unstable knee, Ath. Train. **16**:248, Winter 1981.
10. Hofmann, A.A., et al: Knee stability in orthotic knee braces, Am. J. Sports Med. **12**:371, Sept./Oct. 1984.
11. Johnson, R.J.: The anterior cruciate: a dilemma in sports medicine, Int. J. Sports Med. **2**:71, May 1982.
12. Kelly, D.W., et al: Patellar and quadriceps tendon ruptures—jumper's knee, Am. J. Sports Med. **12**:375, Sept./Oct. 1984.

13. Maron, B.R.: Orthopedic aspects of sports medicine. In Appenzeller, O., and Atkinson, R. (editors): Sports medicine, Baltimore, 1981, Urban & Schwarzenberg, Inc.

14. McDaniel, J.W., and Dameron, T.B.: Untreated ruptures of the anterior cruciate ligament: a follow-up study, J. Bone Joint Surg. **62A**:696, 1980.

ANNOTATED BIBLIOGRAPHY

Cailliet, R.: Knee pain and disability, ed. 2, Philadelphia, 1983, F.A. Davis Co.

Presents an excellent overview of the knee's structural and functional anatomy as well as discussing in an easy-to-read manner the conditions that produce disability and pain.

Larson, R.L. (editor): Symposium on the knee, Clinics in sports medicine, vol. 4, no. 2, Philadelphia, April 1985, W.B. Saunders Co.

Covers in detail the areas of knee screening for athletics, diagnosis of knee injuries, acute and chronic injuries, and their treatment and rehabilitation.

Wallace, L.A., et al: The knee. In Gould III, J.A., and Davis, G.J. (editors): Orthopaedic and sports physical education, St. Louis, 1985, The C.V. Mosby Co.

Provides an excellent overview of knee anatomy, mechanisms of injury, injury prevention, physical examination, and treatment protocols.

Chapter 12

THE THIGH, HIP, AND PELVIS

When you finish this chapter, you will be able to:

Identify injuries to the thigh, hip, and pelvis

Administer immediate care to thigh, hip, and pelvic injuries

Administer follow-up care to thigh, hip, and pelvic injuries

Although the thigh, hip, and pelvis have relatively lower incidences of injury than the knee and lower limb, they still receive considerable trauma from a variety of sports activities. Of major concern are thigh strains and contusions and chronic and overuse stresses affecting the thigh and hip.

THE THIGH REGION

The thigh is generally considered that part of the leg between the hip and the knee. Several important anatomical units must be considered in terms of their relationship to sports injuries: the shaft of the femur, musculature, nerves and blood vessels, and the fascia that envelops the thigh (see Figs. 12-1 to 12-4 for more detailed anatomy).

Thigh Injuries

Injuries to the thigh muscles are among the most common in sports. Contusions and strains appear most often, with the former having the higher incidence.

Quadriceps Contusions

The quadriceps group is continually exposed to traumatic blows in a variety of vigorous sports. Contusions of the quadriceps display all the classic symptoms of most muscle bruises. They usually develop as the result of a severe impact to the relaxed thigh, compressing the muscle against the hard surface of the femur. At the instant of trauma, pain, a transitory loss of function, and immediate capillary effusion usually occur. The extent of the force and the degree of thigh relaxation determine the depth of the injury and the amount of structural and functional disruption that take place.

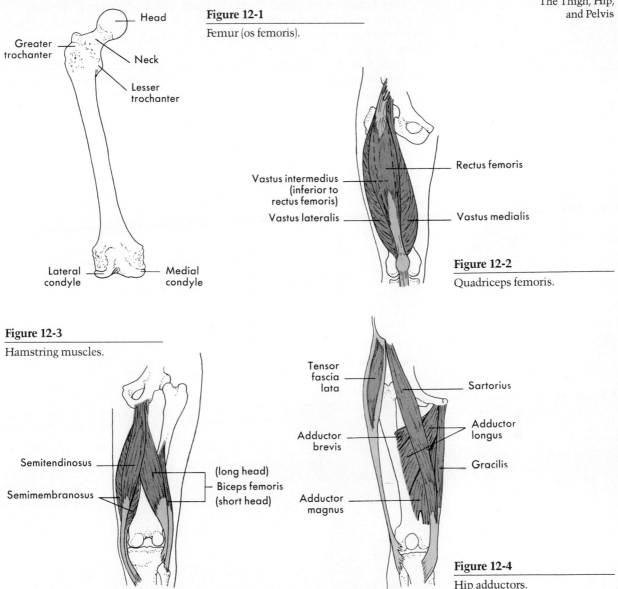

Figure 12-1

Femur (os femoris).

Figure 12-2

Quadriceps femoris.

Figure 12-3

Hamstring muscles.

Figure 12-4

Hip adductors.

Early detection and avoidance of profuse internal hemorrhage are vital, both in effecting a fast recovery by the athlete and in preventing widespread scarring. Detection of the thigh contusion or "charley-horse" is based on a history of injury, palpation, and a muscle function test. The athlete usually describes having been hit by a sharp blow to the thigh, which produced an intense pain and weakness. Palpation may reveal a circumscribed swollen area that is painful to the touch. A function test is given to the quadriceps muscle. Injury to the quadriceps produces varying degrees of weakness and a decreased range of motion.

First degree contusions   The first degree quadriceps contusion causes little pain or swelling and mild point tenderness at the site of trauma. There is little restriction of range of motion, with the athlete able to flex the knee 90 degrees or more.[1]

Second degree contusions   The moderate quadriceps contusion causes pain, swelling, and limited range of knee flexion. Range of knee motion is restricted to less than 90 degrees. An obvious limp is present.

Third degree contusions   The severe quadriceps contusion represents a major disability. A blow may have been so intense as to split the fascia lata, allowing the muscle to protrude through (muscle herniation) (Fig. 12-5). Pain is severe, and swelling may lead to hematoma. There is severely restricted movement of the knee.

Immediate and follow-up care   Compression by pressure bandage and the application of a cold medium can help control superficial hemorrhage, but it is doubtful whether pressure and cold will affect a deep contusion (Fig. 12-6). Rest is very important. This condition is cared for in three stages:

Stage 1—Minimizing hemorrhaging through the ICE-R procedure, combined with performing isometric exercises for the quadriceps muscle. Crutches may be warranted in second or third degree contusions. Gentle passive stretching is done while a cold pack is applied.

Stage 2—Employing hydromassage, deep thermal therapy, or cryotherapy and stretching to regain normal range of movement.

Stage 3—Increasing to full function by a graduated program of resistive exercise and sports participation.

Figure 12-5

Quadriceps contusion.

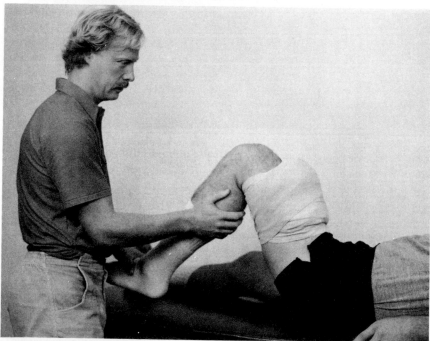

Figure 12-6

Immediate care of the thigh contusion; applying cold pack with a pressure bandage along with a mild stretch may provide some relief.

Generally, the rehabilitation of a thigh contusion should be handled conservatively. Cold packs combined with gentle stretching may be a preferred treatment. If heat therapy is employed, it should not be initiated until the acute phase of the injury has clearly passed. An elastic bandage should be worn to provide constant pressure and mild support to the quadriceps area. Manual massage and hydromassage are best delayed until resolution of the injury has begun. Exercise should be graduated from mild stretching of the quadriceps area in the early stages of the injury to swimming, if possible, and then to jogging and running. Exercise should not be conducted if it produces pain.

Medical care of a thigh contusion may include surgical repair of a herniated muscle or removal by hypodermic needle (aspiration) of a hematoma. Some physicians administer enzymes either orally or through injection for the dissolution of the hematoma.

Once an athlete has sustained a second or third degree thigh contusion, great care must be taken to avoid sustaining another one. The athlete should routinely wear a protective pad held in place by an elastic wrap while engaged in sports activity.

Myositis Ossificans Traumatica

A severe blow or repeated blows to the thigh, usually the quadriceps muscle, can lead to ectopic bone production. It commonly follows bleeding into the quadriceps muscle and a hematoma.[5] The contusion to the muscle causes a disruption of muscle fibers, capillaries, fibrous connective tissue, and periosteum of the femur. Acute inflammation follows resolution of hemorrhage. The irritated tissue may then produce tissue formations resembling cartilage or bone. In 2 to 4 weeks, particles of bone may be noted under x-ray examination. If the injury is to a muscle belly, complete absorption or a decrease in size of the formation may occur. This is less likely, however, if calcification is at a muscle origin or insertion. In terms of bone attachment some formations are completely free of the femur, while one is stalklike and another is broadly attached (Fig. 12-7).

Improper care of a thigh contusion can lead to *myositis ossificans traumatica*, bony deposits or ossification in muscle. The following can initially cause the condition or, once present, can aggravate it, causing it to become more pronounced:

1. Attempting to "run off" a quadriceps contusion
2. Too vigorous treatment of a contusion—for example, massage directly over the contusion, ultrasound therapy, or superficial heat to the thigh

Care Once myositis ossificans traumatica is apparent, treatment should be extremely conservative. If the condition is painful and restricts motion, the formation may be surgically removed after 1 year with much less likelihood of its return. Too early removal of the formation may cause it to return. Recurrent myositis ossificans may indicate a blood clotting problem such as hemophilia, which is a very rare condition.[4]

Thigh Strains

The two major areas for thigh strains are the quadriceps and hamstring groups.

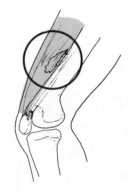

Figure 12-7

Myositis ossificans.

Myositis ossificans traumatica can occur from:
   A single severe blow
   Many blows to a muscle area
   Improper care of a contusion

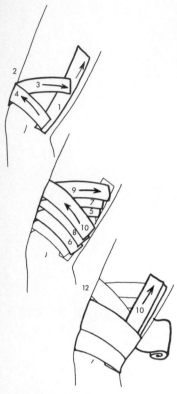

Figure 12-8

Quadriceps tape support.

In order of incidence of sports injury to the thigh, quadriceps contusions rank first, and hamstring strains rank second.

QUADRICEPS TAPE SUPPORT

The taping of the quadriceps muscle group is designed to give support against the pull of gravity. In cases of moderate or severe contusions or strains, taping may afford protection or mild support and give confidence to the athlete. Various techniques fitted to the individual needs of the athletes can be used.

Materials needed: One roll of 2- or 1 1/2-inch (5 or 3.75 cm) tape, skin toughener, and a 6-inch (15 cm) elastic bandage.

Position of the athlete: The athlete stands on the massage table with leg extended.

Position of the operator: The operator stands facing the anterior aspect of the athlete's injured thigh.

Procedure: Fig. 12-8 illustrates the proper procedure for applying the quadriceps tape support. **NOTE**: To ensure more effective stability of the quadriceps taping, it is suggested that the entire thigh be encircled by either a 3-inch (7.5 cm) elastic tape or a 6-inch (15 cm) elastic bandage.

Quadriceps muscle strain Quadriceps tendon strain was discussed under jumper's problems in Chapter 11. However, the rectus femoris muscle occasionally will become strained by a sudden stretch (e.g., falling on a bent knee) or a sudden contraction (e.g., jumping in volleyball or kicking in soccer). Usually it is associated with a muscle that is weakened or one that is overly constricted.

A tear in the region of the rectus femoris muscle may cause partial or complete disruption of muscle fibers. The incomplete tear may be located centrally within the muscle or more peripheral to the muscle.

A peripheral quadriceps femorus tear causes fewer symptoms than the deeper tear. In general, there is less point tenderness and development of a hematoma.[8] A more centrally located partial muscle tear causes the athlete more pain and discomfort than the peripheral tear. With the deep tear there is a great deal of pain, point tenderness, spasm and loss of function but with little discoloration from internal bleeding. In contrast, complete muscle tear of the rectus femoris muscle may leave the athlete with little disability and discomfort but with some deformity of the anterior thigh.

Immediate and follow-up care Immediate care involves employing ice, compression, and elevation (ICE) and proper rest. The extent of the tear should be ascertained as soon as possible before swelling, if any, masks the degree of injury. Crutches may be warranted for the first, second, and third days. After the acute inflammatory phase has progressed to resolution and healing has begun, a regimen of isometric muscle contraction, within pain-free limits, can be initiated along with cryotherapy. Other therapy approaches, such as cold whirlpool and ultrasound, also may be employed. Gentle stretching should not be begun until the thigh is pain free.

Hamstring strains Hamstring strains rank second in incidence of sports injuries to the thigh; of all the muscles of the thigh that are subject to strain, the hamstring group ranks the highest.

The exact cause of hamstring strain is not known. It is speculated that a quick change of the hamstring muscle from one of knee stabilization to that of extending the hip when running could be a major cause of strain (Fig. 12-9).

Figure 12-9

There is a high incidence of
hamstring strain in the sprint
event of track and field.

What leads to this muscle failure and deficiency in the complementary action of opposing muscles is not clearly understood. Some possible reasons are muscle fatigue, sciatic nerve irritation, faulty posture, leg-length discrepancy, tight hamstrings, improper form, or imbalance of strength between hamstring muscle groups.

In most athletes the hamstring muscle group should be 60% to 70% of the strength of opposing the quadriceps group. Stretching after exercise is imperative to avoid muscle contraction.[7]

Hamstring strain can involve the muscle belly or bony attachment. The extent of injury can vary from the pulling apart of a few muscle fibers to a complete rupture or an avulsion fracture (Fig. 12-10).

Capillary hemorrhage, pain, and immediate loss of function vary according to the degree of trauma. Discoloration may occur 1 or 2 days after injury.

A first degree hamstring strain usually is evidenced by muscle soreness on movement, accompanied by point tenderness. These strains are often difficult to detect when they first occur. Irritation and stiffness do not become apparent until the athlete has cooled down after activity. The soreness of the mild hamstring strain in most instances can be attributed to muscle spasm rather than to the tearing of tissue.

A second degree strain of a hamstring muscle represents partial tearing of muscle fibers, identified by a sudden snap or tear of the muscle accompanied by severe pain and a loss of function of knee flexion.

Third degree hamstring strains constitute the rupturing of tendinous or muscular tissue, involving major hemorrhage and disability.

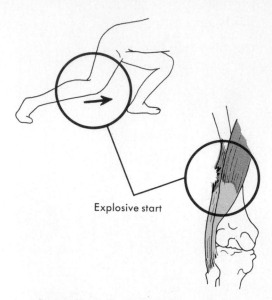

Explosive start

Figure 12-10

Hamstring tear.

Immediate and follow-up care Initially an ice pack, with crushed ice, and compression by an elastic wrap should be employed. Activity should be cut down until soreness has been completely alleviated. Ballistic stretching and explosive sprinting must be avoided.

In first degree hamstring strain, as with the other degrees, before the athlete is allowed to resume full sports participation, complete function of the injured part must be restored.

Second and third degree strains should be treated very conservatively. For second degree strains ICE-R should be used for 24 to 48 hours; for third degree strains ICE-R should be used for 48 to 72 hours. Athletes with third degree hamstring strains should be sent to a physician immediately. After the early inflammatory phase of injury has stabilized, a treatment regimen of isometric exercise, cryotherapy, and ultrasound may be beneficial. In later stages of healing gentle stretching within pain limits, jogging, stationary cycling, and isokinetic exercise at high speeds may be beneficial. Following elimination of soreness the athlete may begin isotonic knee curls. Full recovery may take from 1 month to a full season.

Strains are always a problem to the athlete, because they tend to recur as a result of their sometimes healing with inelastic, fibrous scar tissue. The higher the incidence of strains at a particular muscle site, the greater the amount of scar tissue and the greater the likelihood of further injury. The fear of "another pulled muscle" becomes to some individuals almost a neurotic obsession, which is often more handicapping than the injury itself.

Acute Femoral Fracture

In sports, fractures of the femur occur most often in the shaft rather than at the bone ends and are almost always caused by a great force, such as falling from a height or being hit directly by another participant. A fracture of the shaft most often takes place in the middle third of the bone because of the anatomical curve at this point, as well as the fact that the majority of direct

Femoral stress fractures are becoming more prevalent because of the increased popularity of repetitive, sustained activities, such as distance running.

HAMSTRING TAPING

It is extremely difficult to completely relieve the injured hamstring muscles by any wrapping or taping technique, but some stabilization can be afforded by each. The hamstring taping technique is designed to stabilize the moderately to severely contused or torn hamstring muscles, enabling the athlete to continue to compete.

Materials needed: One roll of 2- or 1 1/2-inch (5 or 3.75 cm) tape, skin toughener, and a roll of 3-inch (7.5 cm) elastic tape or a 6-inch (15 cm) elastic wrap.

Position of the athlete: The athlete lies face down or may stand on the table, with the affected limb flexed at about a 15-degree angle at the knee, so the hamstring muscle is relaxed and shortened.

Position of the operator: The operator stands at the side of the table, facing the athlete's injured thigh.

Procedure: Fig. 12-11 illustrates the proper procedure for applying the hamstring taping. When the taping is complete a 3-inch (7.5 cm) elastic tape or a 6-inch (15 cm) elastic wrap may be placed around the thigh to aid in holding the crisscross taping in place.

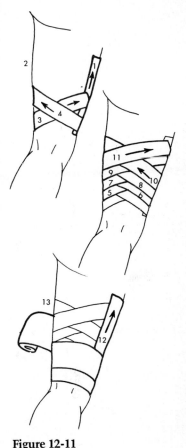

blows are sustained in this area. Shock generally accompanies a fracture of the femur because of the extreme amount of pathology and pain associated with this injury. Bone displacement is usually present as a result of the great strength of the quadriceps, which causes an overriding of the bone fragments. Direct violence produces extensive soft tissue injury with lacerations of the vastus intermedius, hemorrhaging, and muscle spasms.

A fractured femur is recognized by the classic signs of (1) deformity, with the thigh rotated outward; (2) a shortened thigh, caused by bone displacement; (3) loss of function; (4) pain and point tenderness; and (5) swelling of the soft tissues.

To prevent danger to the athlete's life and to ensure adequate reconditioning, immediate immobilization and referral to a physician must be made.

Thigh Rehabilitative Exercise

In general, exercise rehabilitation of the thigh is primarily concerned with the quadriceps and hamstring muscles. Hip adductors and abductor muscles are discussed in the hip exercise rehabilitation section. (Because of the relationship of thigh rehabilitation to the knee region, the reader is reminded to review Chapter 11). Normally, the progression for strength begins with muscle setting and isometric exercise until the muscle can be fully contracted, followed by active isotonic contraction and then by isotonic progressive resistance exercise or isokinetic exercise. Flexibility exercises include gently passive stretching followed by gradual static stretching. Relaxation methods or more vigorous manual stretching may also be employed. As with strengthening, flexibility exercises are performed within pain-free limits.

THE HIP AND PELVIC REGION

The pelvis is a bony ring formed by the two innominate bones, the sacrum, and the coccyx (Fig. 12-12). The innominate bones are each made up of an ilium, ischium, and pubis. The functions of the pelvis are to support the spine and trunk and to transfer their weight to the lower limbs. In addition to pro-

Figure 12-11

Hamstring taping.

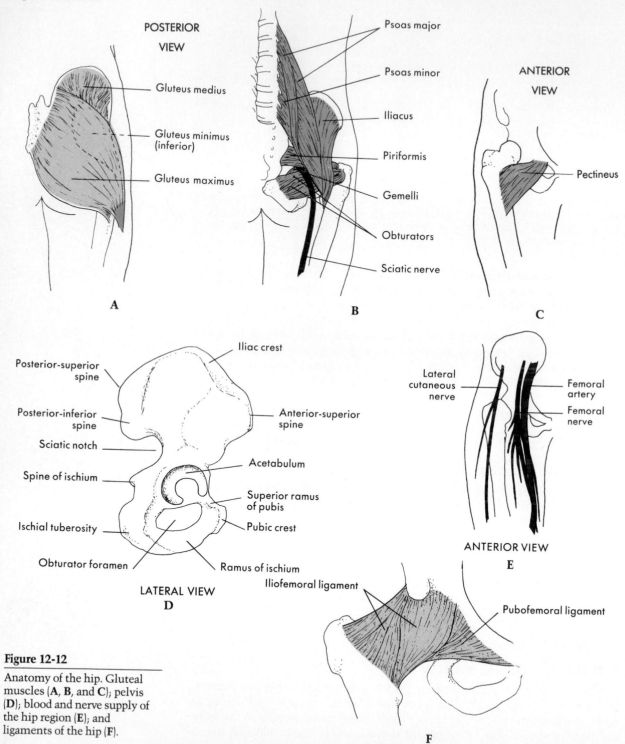

POSTERIOR VIEW

Gluteus medius

Gluteus minimus (inferior)

Gluteus maximus

A

Psoas major

Psoas minor

Iliacus

Piriformis

Gemelli

Obturators

Sciatic nerve

B

ANTERIOR VIEW

Pectineus

C

Posterior-superior spine

Posterior-inferior spine

Sciatic notch

Spine of ischium

Ischial tuberosity

Obturator foramen

Iliac crest

Anterior-superior spine

Acetabulum

Superior ramus of pubis

Pubic crest

Ramus of ischium

LATERAL VIEW
D

Lateral cutaneous nerve

Femoral artery

Femoral nerve

ANTERIOR VIEW
E

Iliofemoral ligament

Pubofemoral ligament

F

Figure 12-12

Anatomy of the hip. Gluteal muscles (**A**, **B**, and **C**); pelvis (**D**); blood and nerve supply of the hip region (**E**); and ligaments of the hip (**F**).

viding skeletal support, the pelvis serves as a place of attachment for the trunk and thigh muscles and a protection for the pelvic viscera. The basin formed by the pelvis is separated into a false and a true pelvis. The false pelvis is composed of the wings of the ilium; the true pelvis is made up of the coccyx, the ischium, and the pubis.

Groin Strain

The groin is the depression that lies between the thigh and the abdominal region. The musculature of this area includes the iliopsoas, the rectus femoris, and the adductor group (the gracilis, pectineus, adductor brevis, adductor longus, and adductor magnus). Any one of these muscles can be torn in sports activity and elicit what is commonly considered a groin strain (Fig. 12-13). Any overextension of the groin musculature may result in a strain. Running, jumping, or twisting with external rotation can produce such injuries. Contrary to some opinions, the adductor group is more often torn than is the iliopsoas.

The groin strain presents one of the most difficult injuries to care for in sports. The strain can appear as a sudden twinge or feeling of tearing during an active movement, or it may not be noticed until after termination of activity. As is characteristic of most tears, the groin strain also produces pain, weakness, and internal hemorrhage. If it is detected immediately after it occurs, the strain should be treated by intermittent ice, pressure, and rest for 48 to 72 hours.

Rest been found to be the best treatment for groin strains. Daily whirlpool therapy and cryotherapy are palliative; ultrasound offers a more definite approach. Exercise should be delayed until the groin is pain free. Exer-

Figure 12-13

Many sports that require a severe stretch of the hip region can cause a groin strain.

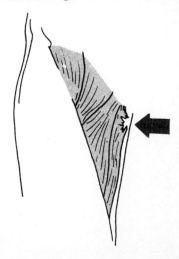

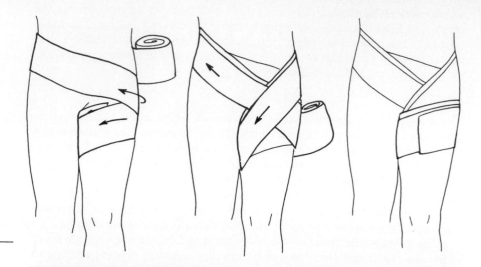

Figure 12-14

Groin support wrap.

GROIN SUPPORT WRAP (HIP SPICA)

The following procedure is used to support the groin strain.

Materials needed: One roll of extra long 6-inch (15 cm) elastic bandage, a roll of 1 1/2-inch (3.75 cm) adhesive tape, and nonsterile cotton.

Position of the athlete: The athlete stands on a table with weight placed on the uninjured leg. The affected limb is relaxed and internally rotated.

Position of the operator: The operator stands facing the anterior aspect of the injured limb.

Procedure: A piece of nonsterile cotton is placed over the injured site. Fig. 12-14 illustrates the proper procedure for applying the groin support wrap (hip spica).

---

cise rehabilitation should emphasize gradual stretching and restoring the normal range of motion. Until normal flexibility and strength are developed, a protective spica bandage should be applied. It should be noted that a pelvic stress fracture may produce groin pain. Therefore, distance runners, particularly, should be referred to a physician for examination when they suffer severe groin pain.[6]

Trochanteric Bursitis

Trochanteric bursitis is a relatively common condition of the greater trochanter of the femur. Although commonly called *bursitis*, it also could be an inflammation at the gluteus medius insertion site or at the iliotibial band as it passes over the trochanter. It is most common among women runners. Care should include elimination of running on inclined surfaces and correction of faulty running form and leg-length discrepancy. Cold packs or ice massage together with gentle stretching and rest with anti-inflammatory medication may be helpful.

Conditions of the Hip Joint

The hip joint, the strongest and best protected joint in the human body, is seldom seriously injured during sports activities.

Sprains of the Hip Joint

The hip joint is substantially supported by the ligamentous tissues and muscles that surround it, so any unusual movement that exceeds the normal range of motion may result in tearing of tissue. Such an injury may occur as the result of a violent twist, either produced through an impact force delivered by another participant or by forceful contact with another object; or such an injury may be sustained in a situation in which the foot is firmly planted and the trunk forced in an opposing direction. A hip sprain displays all the signs of a major acute injury but is best revealed through the athlete's *inability to circumduct* the thigh.

Dislocated Hip Joint

Dislocation of the hip joint rarely occurs in sports, and then usually only as the end result of traumatic force directed along the long axis of the femur. Such dislocations are produced when the knee is bent. The most common displacement is one posterior to the acetabulum and with the femoral shaft adducted and flexed.

The luxation presents a picture of a flexed, adducted, and internally rotated thigh. Palpation will reveal that the head of the femur has moved to a position posterior to the acetabulum. A hip dislocation causes serious pathology by tearing capsular and ligamentous tissue. A fracture is often associated with this injury, accompanied by possible damage to the sciatic nerve.

Immediate and follow-up care   Medical attention must be secured immediately after displacement, or muscle contractures may complicate the reduction. Immobilization usually consists of 2 weeks of bed rest and the use of a crutch for walking for a month or longer.

Complications   Complication of the posterior hip dislocation is likely. Such complications include muscle paralysis due to nerve injury in the area and a later development of a degeneration of the head of the femur (osteoarthritis).

Immature Hip Joint Problems

The coach or athletic trainer working with a child or adolescent should understand two major problems stemming from the immature hip joint. They are: (1) Legg-Perthe's avascular necrosis of the femoral head (coxa plana) and (2) a slipping of the femoral head called slipped capital femoral epiphysis.

Legg-Perthe's Disease (Coxa Plana)

Legg-Perthe's disease is avascular necrosis of the femoral head (Fig. 12-15). It occurs in children ages 3 to 12 and in boys more often than in girls. The reason for this condition is not clearly understood. It is listed under the broad heading of osteochondroses. Because of a disruption of circulation at the head of the femur, articular cartilage becomes necrotic and flattens.

The young athlete commonly complains of pain in the groin that sometimes is referred to the abdomen or knee. Limping is also typical. The condition can have a rapid onset, but more often it comes on slowly over a number of months.[3] Examination may show limited hip movement and pain.

Care   Care of this condition could mean complete bed rest to alleviate synovitis. A special brace to avoid direct weight bearing on the hip may have

A young athlete complaining of pain in the groin, abdomen, or knee and walking with a limp may display signs of Legg-Perthe's disease or a slipped capital femoral epiphysis.

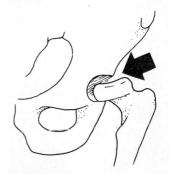

Figure 12-15

Legg-Perthes disease (coxa plana). Arrow indicates avascular necrosis of the femoral head.

Figure 12-16

Slipped capital femoral epiphysis (*see arrow*).

Figure 12-17

Sports that include violent extension of the body can produce serious pelvic injuries.

to be worn. If treated in time, the head of the femur will revascularize and regain its original shape.

Complications If the condition is not treated early enough, the head of the femur will become ill shaped, creating problems of osteoarthritis in later life.

Slipped Capital Femoral Epiphysis

The problem of a slipped capital femoral epiphysis (Fig. 12-16) is found mostly in boys between the ages of 10 and 17 who are characteristically very tall and thin or are obese. Although the cause is unknown, it may be related to the effects of a growth hormone. In one quarter of these cases both hips are affected.

As with Legg-Perthe's disease, the athlete has a pain in the groin that comes on suddenly as a result of trauma or over weeks or months as a result of prolonged stress. In the early stages of this condition signs may be minimal; however, in its most advanced stage there is hip and knee pain on passive and active motion, limitations of abduction, flexion, medial rotation, and a limp. X-ray examination may show femoral head slippage backward and downward.

Care In cases of minor slippage rest and non–weight bearing may prevent further slipping. Major displacement usually requires corrective surgery.

Complications If the slippage goes undetected or if surgery fails to properly restore normal hip mechanics, severe hip problems may occur in later life.

Snapping Hip Phenomenon

The snapping hip phenomenon is common among dancers, gymnasts, and hurdlers. It stems from habitual movements that cause muscles surrounding the hip to become imbalanced in strength. It commonly occurs when the participant laterally rotates and flexes the hip joint repeatedly, causing the hip joint and associated soft tissues to become unstable. The individual complains of a snapping, mainly when balancing on one leg. Care of this condition involves avoiding the action that causes snapping, stretching tight musculature, and strengthening weakened musculature. If there is pain, the athlete should be referred to a physician.

Pelvic Conditions

Athletes who perform activities involving violent jumping, running, and collisions can sustain serious acute and overuse injuries to the pelvic region (Fig. 12-17).

Contusion (Hip Pointer)

Iliac crest contusion, commonly known as *hip pointer*, occurs most often in contact sports. The hip pointer results from a blow to the inadequately protected iliac crest. The hip pointer is considered one of the most handicapping injuries in sports and one that is difficult to manage. A direct force to the unprotected iliac crest causes a severe pinching action to the soft tissue of that region.

Such an injury produces immediate pain, spasms, and transitory paralysis of the soft structures. As a result the athlete is unable to rotate the trunk or to flex his thigh without pain.

ILIAC TAPE SUPPORT

Iliac crest adhesive taping is designed to support, protect, and immobilize the soft tissue surrounding the iliac crest.

Materials needed: One roll of 2-inch (5 cm) adhesive tape, a 6-inch (15 cm) bandage, skin toughener, and tape adherent.

Position of the athlete: The athlete stands on the floor, bending slightly laterally toward the injured side.

Position of the operator: The operator faces the injured side of the athlete.

Procedure: Fig. 12-8 illustrates the proper procedure for applying the iliac tape support. When the taping is completed, a 6-inch (15 cm) elastic bandage is applied to additionally secure the tape and to prevent perspiration from loosening the taping.

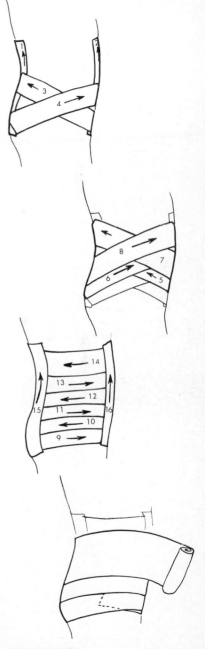

Immediate and follow-up care   Cold and pressure should be applied immediately after injury and should be maintained intermittently for at least 48 hours. In severe cases bed rest for 1 to 2 days will speed recovery. It should be noted that the mechanisms of the hip pointer are the same as those for an iliac crest fracture or epiphyseal separation.

Referral to a physician must be made and an x-ray examination given. A variety of treatment procedures can be employed for this injury. Ice massage and ultrasound have been found to be beneficial. Initially the injury site may be injected with a steroid. Later, oral anti-inflammatory agents may be used. Recovery time usually ranges from 1 to 3 weeks. When the athlete resumes normal activity, a protective pad must be worn to prevent reinjury.

Osteitis Pubis

Since the popularity of distance running has increased, a condition known as *osteitis pubis* has become more prevalent. It is also caused by the sports of soccer, football, and wrestling. As the result of repetitive stress on the pubic symphysis and adjacent bony structures by the pull of muscles in the area, a chronic inflammatory condition is created (Fig. 12-19). The athlete has pain in the groin region and area of the symphysis pubis. There is point tenderness on the pubic tubercle and pain when movements such as running, sit-ups, and squats are performed.[2]

Care   Follow-up care usually consists of rest and an oral anti-inflammatory agent. A return to activity should be gradual.

Hip Rehabilitative Exercise

When considering the reconditioning of the hip and groin region, one must consider its major movements: internal rotation, external rotation, adduction, abduction, extension, flexion, and the combined movement of internal and external circumduction. Because of the wide variety of possible movements, it is essential that exercise be conducted as soon as possible after injury, without aggravating the condition. When exercise is begun it should be practiced within a pain-free range of movement. A program should be organized to start with free movement leading to resistive exercises. A general goal is to perform 10 to 15 repetitions of each exercise, progressing from one set to three sets two or three times daily (Fig. 12-20).

Figure 12-18

Iliac tape support.

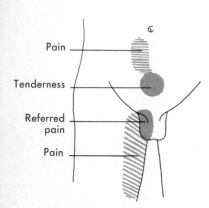

Pain

Tenderness

Referred
pain

Pain

Figure 12-19

Osteitis pubis and other pain
sites in the region of the pelvis.

Figure 12-20

Some basic exercises for hip
rehabilitation. **A**, Hip flexion.
B, Hip abduction. **C**, Abduction
against resistance. **D**, Hip
adduction. **E**, Combining
abduction and adduction. **F**,
Stretching the iliopsoas. **D**, Hip
adduction. **E**, Combining
abduction and adduction. **F**,
Stretching the iliopsoas.

F

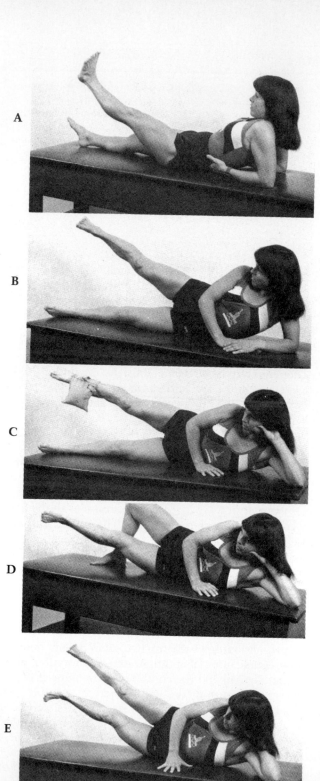

A

B

C

D

E

SUMMARY

The thigh is composed of the femoral shaft, musculature, nerves and blood vessels, and the fascia that envelops the soft tissue. It is considered that part of the leg between the hip and the knee.

The quadriceps contusion and hamstring strain represent the most common sports injuries to the thigh, with the quadriceps contusion having the highest incidence.

Of major importance in acute thigh contusion is early detection and the avoidance of internal bleeding. One major complication to repeated contusions is myositis ossificans.

Jumping or falling on a bent knee can strain the quadriceps muscle. A more common strain is that of the hamstring muscle. It is not clearly known why hamstring muscles become strained. Strain occurs most often to the short head of the biceps femoris.

The groin is the depression that lies between the thigh and abdominal region. Groin strain can occur to any one of a number of muscles located in this region. Running, jumping, or twisting can produce a groin strain.

A common problem of women runners is trochanteric bursitis. An irritation occurs in the region of the greater trochanter of the femur.

The hip joint, the strongest and best protected joint in the human body, has a low incidence of acute sports injuries. More common are conditions stemming from an immature hip joint. These include the conditions of Leggs-Perthe's disease (coxa plana) and the slipped capital femoral epiphysis.

A common problem in the pelvic region is the hip pointer. This condition results from a blow to the inadequately protected iliac crest. The contusion causes pain, spasm, and malfunction of the muscles in the area.

REVIEW QUESTIONS AND CLASS ACTIVITIES

1. Describe the major injuries to the thigh; include how contusions and strains are sustained and cared for.
2. Indicate the mechanism, formation, and basic care of a myositis ossificans in the quadriceps region.
3. Hamstring strains represent a major problem in sports. How may they be prevented? Describe a program for managing this problem.
4. Indicate the signs and immediate care of a femoral fracture.
5. Write an exercise rehabilitation program for a thigh injury.
6. How is a groin strain typically cared for?
7. Contrast a hip sprain from a subluxation or dislocation. Contrast signs and basic care.
8. Coxa plana and a slipped capital femoral epiphysis represent problems in the immature hip joint. Indicate their similarities and differences.
9. Describe how hip pointers can be prevented and when they occur. How can they be cared for?

REFERENCES

1. Cooper, D.L., and Fair, J.: Trainer's corner, treating the charley horse, Phys. Sportsmed. **7**:157, 1979.
2. Hanson, P.G., et al.: Osteitis pubis in sports activities, Phys. Sportsmed. **6**(10):111, 1978.
3. Jacobs, B.: Legg-Calvé-Perthe's disease, the "obscure affliction," Contemp. Surg. **10**:62, 1977.
4. Jokl, P., and Federico, J.: Myositis ossificans traumatica with hemophilia

(factor XI deficiency) in a football player, J.A.M.A. **237**:2215, 1977.

5. Lipscomb, A.B.: Treatment of myositis ossificans traumatica in athletics, Am. J. Sports Med. **4**:61, 1976.

6. Noakes, T.D., et al: Pelvic stress fractures in long distance runners, Am. J. Sports Med. **13**:120, 1985.

7. Oakes, B.W.: Hamstring muscle injuries, Aust. Fam. Physician, **13**:587, August 1984.

8. Sperryn, P.N.: Sport and medicine, Boston, 1983, Butterworth (Publishers), Inc.

ANNOTATED BIBLIOGRAPHY

Cailliet, R.: Soft tissue pain and disability, Philadelphia, 1977, F.A. Davis Co.
Provides an excellent overview of soft tissue pain throughout the body. One chapter is set aside to detail hip joint pain.

Sammarco, G.J.: The dancer's hip. In Sammarco, G.J. (editor): Symposium on injuries to dancers, Clinics in sports medicine, vol. 2, no. 3, Philadelphia, Nov. 1983, W.B. Saunders Co.
Covers the conditions of the dancer's hip. It includes conditions caused by poor training, normal use, and overuse and includes tendinitis and myositis.

| # THE ABDOMEN, THORAX, AND LOW BACK

When you finish this chapter, you will be able to:

Identify and care for the major abdominal injuries

Identify and provide immediate care for a spleen rupture and kidney contusion

Identify and care for major injuries of the thorax

Identify major low back conditions

This chapter deals with major sports injuries to the trunk region—specifically, the abdomen, thorax, and low back. Although lower in incidence when compared to injuries of the lower limbs, injury in the trunk region could be life threatening or could cause major long-term disability.

THE ABDOMEN

The abdominal cavity lies between the diaphragm and the pelvis and is bounded by the margin of the lower ribs, the abdominal muscles, and the vertebral column. Lying within this cavity are the abdominal **viscera**, which include the stomach and the lower intestinal tract, the urinary system, the liver, the kidneys, and the spleen (Figs. 13-1 and 13-2).

viscera
Internal organs

Abdominal Injuries

The abdominal area is particularly vulnerable to injury in all contact sports. A blow may produce superficial or even deep internal injuries, depending on its location and intensity.[11] Strong abdominal muscles give good protection when they are tensed, but when relaxed they are easily damaged. It is very important to properly protect the trunk region against the traumatic forces of collision sports. Good conditioning is essential, as is proper protective equipment and application of safety rules. Any suspected internal injury must be referred immediately to a physician.[10]

Injuries to the Abdominal Wall

Contusions Compressive forces that injure the abdominal wall are not common in sports. When they do happen, more often they are in collision sports such as football or ice hockey; however, any sports implements or high-

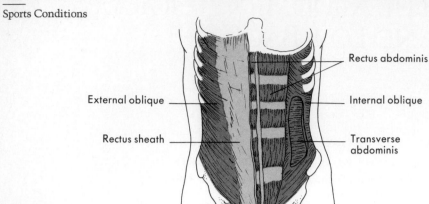

External oblique

Rectus sheath

Rectus abdominis

Internal oblique

Transverse abdominis

Figure 13-1

The abdominal musculature.

Figure 13-2

Abdominal viscera and the genitalia.

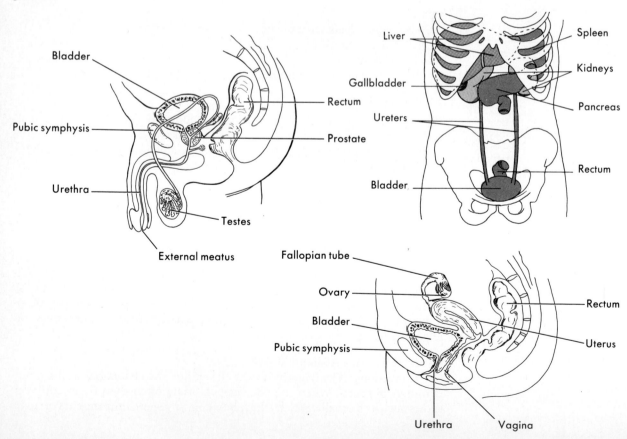

Bladder

Pubic symphysis

Urethra

Rectum

Prostate

Testes

External meatus

Liver

Gallbladder

Ureters

Bladder

Spleen

Kidneys

Pancreas

Rectum

Fallopian tube

Ovary

Bladder

Pubic symphysis

Rectum

Uterus

Urethra

Vagina

velocity projectiles can injure. Hockey goalies and baseball catchers would be very vulnerable to injury without their protective torso pads. Contusion may occur superficially to the abdominal skin or subcutaneous tissue or much deeper to the musculature. The extent and type of injury will vary depending on whether the force is blunt or penetrating.[10]

A contusion of the rectus abdominis can be very disabling. A severe blow can cause a hematoma that develops under the fascial tissue surrounding the rectus abdominis muscle. The pressure that results from hemorrhage causes pain and tightness in the region of the injury. A cold pack and a compression elastic wrap should be applied immediately after injury. An examination for signs of possible internal injury should be conducted.

Abdominal muscle strains   A sudden twisting of the trunk or reaching overhead can tear an abdominal muscle. These types of injuries have the potential to be very incapacitating, with severe pain and hematoma formation. Ice and an elastic wrap compress should be employed initially. Treatment should be conservative, with exercise staying within pain-free limits. Rest is essential.

Hernia   The term *hernia* refers to the protrusion of abdominal viscera through a portion of the abdominal wall. Hernias may be congenital or acquired. A congenital hernial sac is developed before birth, and an acquired hernia is developed after birth. Structurally a hernia has a mouth, a neck, and a body. The mouth, or hernial ring, is the opening from the abdominal cavity into the hernial protrusion; the neck is the portion of the sac that joins the hernial ring and the body; the body is the sac that protrudes outside the abdominal cavity and contains portions of the abdominal organs.

The acquired hernia occurs when a natural weakness is further aggravated by either a strain or a direct blow. Athletes may develop this condition as the result of violent activity. An acquired hernia may be recognized by the following:

1. Previous history of a blow or strain to the groin area that has produced pain and prolonged discomfort
2. Superficial protrusion in the groin area that is increased by coughing
3. Reported feeling of weakness and pulling sensation in the groin area

The danger of a hernia in an athlete is the possibility that it may become irritated by falls or blows. In addition to the aggravations caused by trauma, a condition may arise, commonly known as a *strangulated hernia*, in which the inguinal ring constricts the protruding sac and occludes normal blood circulation. If the strangulated hernia is not surgically repaired immediately, gangrene and death may ensue.

Hernias resulting from sports most often occur in the groin area; inguinal hernias (Fig. 13-3), which occur in men (over 75%), and femoral hernias, most often occurring in women, are the most prevalent types. Externally the inguinal and femoral hernias appear similar because of the groin protrusion, but a considerable difference is indicated internally. The inguinal hernia results from an abdominal enlargement of the opening of the inguinal canal through which the vessels and nerves of the male reproductive system pass. In contrast to this, the femoral hernia arises in the canal that transports the vessels and nerves that go to the thigh and lower limb.

Under normal circumstances the inguinal and femoral canals are protected against abnormal opening by muscle control. When intra-abdominal

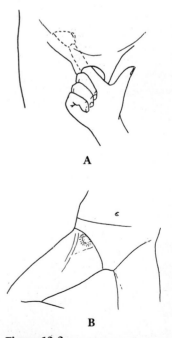

A

B

Figure 13-3

A, Inguinal hernia. **B**, Femoral hernia.

tension is produced in these areas, muscles produce contraction around these canal openings. If the muscles fail to react or if they prove inadequate in their shutter action, abdominal contents may be pushed through the opening. Repeated protrusions serve to stretch and increase the size of the opening. Most physicians think that any athlete who has a hernia should be prohibited from engaging in hard physical activity until surgical repair has been made.

The treatment preferred by most physicians is surgery. Mechanical devices such as trusses, which prevent hernial protrusion, are for the most part unsuitable in sports because of the friction and irritation they produce. Exercise has been thought by many to be beneficial to a mild hernia, but such is not the case. Exercise will not affect the stretched inguinal or femoral canals positively.

Intra-abdominal Conditions

idiopathic
Cause unknown

Stitch in the side   A "stitch in the side" is the name given an **idiopathic** condition that occurs in some athletes. It is best described as a cramplike pain that develops on either the left or right side of the trunk during hard physical activity. Sports that involve running apparently produce this condition.

The cause is obscure, although several hypotheses have been advanced. Among these are the following:

1. Constipation
2. Intestinal gas
3. Overeating
4. Diaphragmatic spasm as a result of poor conditioning
5. Lack of visceral support because of weak abdominal muscles
6. Distended spleen
7. Faulty breathing techniques leading to a lack of oxygen in the diaphragm
8. Ischemia of either the diaphragm or the intercostals

Immediate care of a stitch in the side demands relaxation of the spasm, for which two methods have proved beneficial. First, the athlete is instructed to stretch the arm on the affected side as high as possible. If this is inadequate, flexing the trunk forward on the thighs may prove beneficial.

Athletes with recurrent abdominal spasms may need special study. The identification of poor eating habits, poor elimination habits, or an inadequate training program may explain the athlete's particular problem. It should be noted that a stitch in the side, although not considered serious, may require further evaluation by a physician if abdominal pains persist.

Blow to the solar plexus   A blow to the sympathetic celiac plexus (solar plexus) produces a transitory paralysis of the diaphragm (often referred to as "having the wind knocked out"). Paralysis of the diaphragm stops respiration and leads to anoxia. When the athlete is unable to inhale, hysteria because of fear may result; it is necessary to allay such fears and instill confidence in the athlete.

Care   In dealing with an athlete who has had his or her wind knocked out, the coach or athletic trainer should adhere to the following procedures:

1. Help the athlete overcome apprehension by talking in a confident manner.
2. Loosen the athlete's belt and the clothing around the abdomen; have the athlete bend the knees.

3. Encourage the athlete to relax by initiating short inspirations and long expirations.

Due to a fear of not being able to breathe, the athlete may hyperventilate, which means breathing at an abnormal rate. Hyperventilation results in too much oxygen being delivered to the circulatory system and causes a variety of physical reactions to occur, such as dizziness, a lump in the throat, pounding heart, and fainting.[6]

There should always be some concern that a blow hard enough to knock the wind out could also cause internal organ injury.

Ruptured spleen Every year there are reports of athletes who suddenly die—hours, days, or even weeks after a severe blow received in a sports event. These deaths are often attributed to delayed hemorrhage of the spleen—the organ most often injured by blunt trauma.

Injuries to the spleen usually result from a fall that jars or a direct blow to the left upper quadrant of the abdomen (Fig. 13-4).

Infectious mononucleosis commonly enlarges and weakens the spleen predisposing it to injury from a blunt external blow to the trunk. An athlete with mononucleosis must not engage in jarring sports activities.

The gross indications of a ruptured spleen must be recognized so that an immediate medical referral can be made. Indications include a history of a severe blow to the abdomen and possibly signs of shock, abdominal rigidity, nausea, and vomiting. There may be a reflex pain occurring about 30 minutes after injury, called *Kehr's sign*, which radiates to the left shoulder and one-third of the way down the left arm.

Complications The great danger in a ruptured spleen lies in its ability to splint itself and then produce a delayed hemorrhage. Splinting of the spleen is formed by a loose hematoma formation and the constriction of the supporting and surrounding structures. Any slight strain may disrupt the splinting effect and allow the spleen to hemorrhage profusely into the abdominal cavity, causing the athlete to die of internal bleeding days or weeks after the injury. A ruptured spleen must be surgically removed.

Hollow viscus organ injuries When compared to hollow organs, the solid organs are more often injured in sports; however, on rare occasions a severe blunt blow to the abdomen may cause rupture or laceration of the duodenum or other structures of the small intestine.

Injuries to the Genitourinary System

Kidney contusion The kidneys are seemingly well protected within the abdominal cavity. However, on occasion, contusions and even ruptures of these organs occur. The kidney may be susceptible to injury because of its normal distention by blood. A severe outside force, usually one applied to the back of the athlete, will cause abnormal extension of an engorged kidney, which results in injury. The degree of renal injury depends on the extent of the distention and the angle and force of the blow. An athlete who has received a contusion of the kidney may display signs of shock, nausea, vomiting, rigidity of the back muscles, and blood in the urine (hematuria). As with other internal organs, kidney injury may cause referred pain to the outside of the body. Pain may be felt high on the back and may radiate forward around the trunk into the lower abdominal region. Any athlete who reports having re-

An athlete with mononucleosis must not engage in any jarring activities.

Athletes who complain of external pain in the shoulders, trunk, or pelvis following a severe blow to the abdomen or back may be describing a referred pain from an injury to an internal organ.

Solid internal organs are more at jeopardy from an injury than are hollow organs.

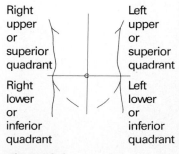

Figure 13-4

Abdominal quadrants.

ceived a severe blow to the abdomen or back region should be instructed to urinate two or three times and to look for the appearance of blood in the urine. If there is any sign of blood in the urine, immediate referral to a physician must be made.

Medical care of the contused kidney usually consists of a 24-hour hospital observation with a gradual increase of fluid intake. If the hemorrhage fails to stop, surgery may be indicated. Controllable contusions usually require 2 weeks of bed rest and close surveillance after activity is resumed. In questionable cases, complete withdrawal from one active playing season may be required.

Blow to the testicles   A severe blow to the testicles can produce an accumulation of fluid. After trauma the athlete complains of pain, swelling in the lower abdomen, and nausea. Cold packs should be applied to the scrotum, and referral to the physician should be made. A contusion to the scrotal region causes testicular spasms that add to the athlete's discomfort. A good technique to relieve such spasms is to have the athlete lie on his back and instruct him to flex his thighs to his chest. This position helps to relieve pain and relax the muscle spasm (Fig. 13-5).

Gynecological injuries   In general, the female reproductive organs have a low incidence of injury in sports; however, a woman water-skier may injure her vulva when water is forced into the vagina and fallopian tubes, later causing infection. On occasion the external genital organs (vulva) of the female may become contused, resulting in hematoma.

Other reasons for abdominal pain   A number of other abdominal pain sites can be disabling to the athlete. The coach or athletic trainer should be able to discern the potentially more serious pain sites and refer the athlete accordingly. Indigestion or dyspepsia commonly causes pain just below the sternum. Appendicitis, typically when the appendix is in a normal position

Pain at McBurney's point may indicate that the athlete is having an appendicitis attack.

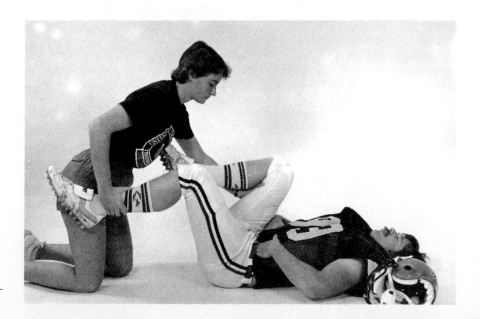

Figure 13-5

Reducing testicular spasm.

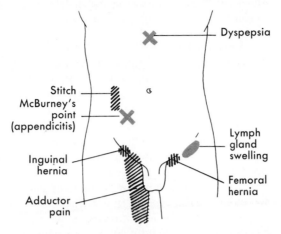

Dyspepsia

Stitch

McBurney's
point
(appendicitis)

Inguinal
hernia

Adductor
pain

Lymph
gland
swelling

Femoral
hernia

Figure 13-6

Common sites of abdominal
pain.

creates pain at McBurney's point, which is one-third the distance between the anteriosuperior iliac spine and the umbilicus. Fig. 13-6 shows some of the pain sites in the abdomen.

THE THORAX

That region of the body that lies between the neck and abdomen and is bounded by the ribs is known as the *thorax* (Fig. 13-7).

Thoracic Injuries

The chest is vulnerable to a variety of soft tissue injuries, depending on the nature of the sport.

Breast Problems

It has been suggested that many women athletes can have breast problems in connection with their sports participation.[12] Violent up-and-down and lateral movements of the breasts, such as are encountered in running and jumping, can bruise and strain the breast, especially in large-breasted women. Constant uncontrolled movement of the breast over a period of time can stretch Cooper's ligament, which supports the breast at the chest wall, leading to premature sagging of the breasts.[5]

Wearing a well-designed bra that has minimal elasticity and allows little vertical or horizontal breast movement is most desirable (see Fig. 3-13). Breast injuries usually occur during physical contact with either an opponent or equipment. In sports such as fencing or field hockey, women athletes must be protected by wearing plastic cup-type brassieres.

Rib Contusions

A blow to the rib cage can contuse intercostal muscles or, if severe enough, produce a fracture. Because the intercostal muscles are essential for the breathing mechanism, when they are bruised, both expiration and inspiration become very painful. Characteristically, the pain is sharp on breathing, and there is point tenderness. X-ray examination should be routine in such an in-

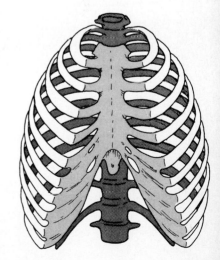

Figure 13-7

The thorax.

jury. ICE-R and anti-inflammatory agents are commonly employed. As with most rib injuries, contusions to the thorax are self-limiting, responding best to rest and cessation of sports activities.

Rib Fractures

A rib fracture is usually indicated by a severe, sharp pain on breathing.

Rib fractures are not uncommon in sports and have their highest incidence in contact sports, particularly in wrestling and football (Fig. 13-8).

Fractures can be caused by either direct or indirect traumas and can, infrequently, be the result of violent muscular contractions. A direct injury is the type caused by a kick or a well-placed block, with the fracture developing at the site of forced application. An indirect fracture is produced as a result of a general compression of the rib cage, such as may occur in football or wrestling.

The structural and functional disruption sustained in rib fractures varies according to the type of injury that has been received. The direct fracture causes the most serious damage, since the external force fractures and displaces the ribs inwardly. Such a mechanism may completely displace the bone and cause an overriding of fragments. The jagged edges of the fragments may cut, tear, or perforate the tissue of the delicate tissue surrounding the lump (pleurae), causing hemothorax, or they may collapse one lung (pneumothorax). Contrary to the pattern with direct violence, the indirect type usually causes the rib to spring and fracture outward, which produces an oblique or transverse fissure.

The rib fracture is usually quite easily detected. The medical history informs the coach or athletic trainer of the type and degree of force to which the rib cage has been subjected. After trauma, the athlete complains of having a

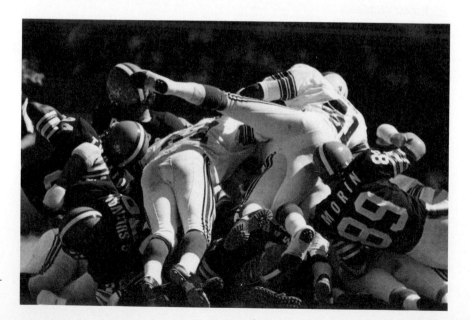

Figure 13-8

Collision sports can produce serious trunk injuries.

severe pain on inspiration and has point tenderness. A fracture of the rib will be readily evidenced by a severe sharp pain and possibly crepitus on palpation.

Care   The athlete should be referred to the team physician for x-ray examination if there is any indication of fracture.

An uncomplicated rib fracture is often difficult to identify on x-ray film. Therefore the physician plans the treatment according to the symptoms presented. The rib fracture is usually managed with support and rest. Simple transverse or oblique fractures heal within 3 to 4 weeks. A rib brace can offer the athlete some rib cage stabilization and comfort (Fig. 13-9).

Sternal Fracture

Fracture of the sternum occurs infrequently in sports. It can develop from a direct blow to the sternum, from a violent compression force applied posteriorly, or from hyperflexion of the trunk. The most frequently affected area of the sternum is the manubrium. This fracture results in sharp chest pain that occurs particularly on inhalation and is localized over the sternum, and as the result of this injury the athlete assumes a position in which the head and shoulders are dropped forward.

Palpation indicates mild swelling and, possibly, displaced fragments. An x-ray film must be taken to determine the extent of displacement.

The treatment may require bed rest for 2 to 3 weeks along with immobilization or the use of a sand weight over the fracture site. After activity is resumed, a posterior figure-8 bandage is applied to maintain the shoulders in an erect position.

Costochondral Separation and Dislocation

The rib is connected to the sternum or breast bone by cartilage. This cartilage connection can be separated or even be dislocated from its attachment by

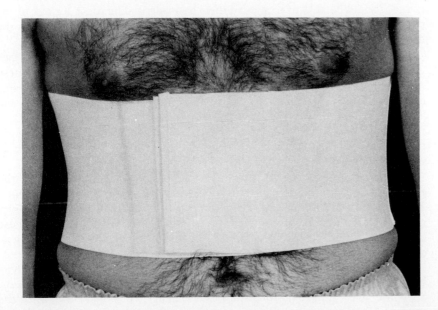

Figure 13-9

A commercial rib brace can provide moderate support to the thorax.

Figure 13-10

Costochondral separation.

traumas. In sports activities the costochondral separation or dislocation has a higher incidence than fractures. This injury can occur from a direct blow to the athlete's chest or indirectly from a sudden twist or a fall on a ball, compressing the rib cage. The costochondral injury displays many signs similar to the rib fracture, with the exception being that pain is localized in the junction of the rib cartilage and rib (Fig. 13-10).

The athlete complains of sharp pain on sudden movement of the trunk, with difficulty in breathing deeply. There is point tenderness with swelling. In some cases there is a rib deformity and a complaint that the rib makes a crepitus noise as it moves in and out of place.

Care As with a rib fracture, the costochondral separation is managed by rest and immobilization by tape or a rib brace. Healing takes anywhere from 1 to 2 months, precluding any sports activities until the athlete is symptom free.

Muscle Conditions of the Thorax

The muscles of the thorax are the intercostals and the erector spinae, latissimus dorsi, trapezius, serratus anterior, serratus posterior, and pectoralis major—all of which are subject to contusions and strains in sports. The intercostal muscles are especially susceptible. Traumatic injuries occur most often from direct blows or sudden torsions of the athlete's trunk. Care of such injuries requires immediate pressure and applications of cold for approximately 1 hour; after hemorrhaging has been controlled, immobilization should be employed.

Internal Complications

Internal complications in the thorax resulting from sports trauma are rare. They pertain principally to injuries of the lung, pleurae, and/or intercostal arteries. Because of the seriousness of internal injuries, the coach or athletic trainer should be able to recognize their basic signs. The most serious of the conditions are (1) pneumothorax, (2) hemothorax, (3) hemorrhaging into the lungs, (4) traumatic asphyxia, and (5) heart contusion.

Pneumothorax Pneumothorax is a condition in which the pleural cavity becomes filled with air that has entered through an opening in the chest. As the negatively pressured pleural cavity fills with air, the lung on that side collapses. The loss of one lung may produce pain, difficulty in breathing, and **anoxia.**

Hemothorax Hemothorax is the presence of blood within the pleural cavity. It results from the tearing or puncturing of the lung or pleural tissue involving the blood vessels in the area.

Hemorrhaging into the lungs A violent blow or compression of the chest without an accompanying rib fracture may cause a *lung hemorrhage.* This condition results in severe pain on breathing, difficult breathing (dyspnea), the coughing up of frothy blood, and signs of shock and cyanosis. If these signs are observed, the athlete should be treated for shock and immediately referred to a physician.

Traumatic asphyxia Traumatic asphyxia occurs as the result of a violent blow to or a compression of the rib cage, causing a cessation of breathing. Signs include a purple discoloration of the upper trunk and head, with the mucous membrane which lines the eye (conjunctivae) displaying a bright red

anoxia

A lack of oxygen

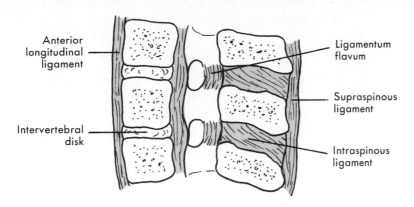

Anterior longitudinal ligament

Intervertebral disk

Ligamentum flavum

Supraspinous ligament

Intraspinous ligament

Figure 13-11

Major ligaments of the lumbar spine.

color. A condition of this type demands immediate mouth-to-mouth resuscitation and medical attention.

Heart contusion A heart contusion may occur when the heart is compressed between the sternum and the spine by a strong outside force, such as being hit by a pitched ball or bouncing a barbell off the chest in a bench press. This injury produces severe shock and heart pain. Death may ensue if emergency attention is not given immediately.

THE LOW BACK

The low back must be considered in the context of the entire spine. The lumbar, sacral, and coccygeal portions of the spine will be discussed in this chapter (Figs. 13-11 to 13-13).

Preventing Initial Low Back Injuries in Sports

All conditioning programs in sports should include work for the prevention of back injuries. Prevention involves:
1. Correction, amelioration, or compensation of functional postural deviations
2. Maintenance or increase of trunk and general body flexibility
3. Increase of trunk and general body strength

One should be aware of any postural anomalies that the athletes possess; with this knowledge, one should establish individual corrective programs. Basic conditioning should include an emphasis on trunk flexibility. Every effort should be made to produce maximum range of motion in rotation and both lateral and forward flexion. Strength should be developed to the ultimate, with stress placed on developing the spinal extensors (erector spinae) and on developing abdominal strength to ensure proper postural alignment (see Chapter 6).

Mechanisms of Low Back Pain in the Athlete

Back afflictions, particularly those of the lower back, are second only to foot problems in order of incidence to humans throughout their lives. In sports, back problems are relatively common and are most often the result of congenital, mechanical, or traumatic factors. Congenital back disorders are conditions that are present at birth. Many authorities think that the human back is

Considerations in preventing low back injuries:

Postural deviations must be corrected or compensated for.

A balance of strength and flexibility in the trunk and pelvis must be maintained.

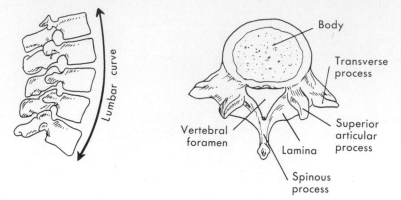

Figure 13-12

The lumbar vertebrae.

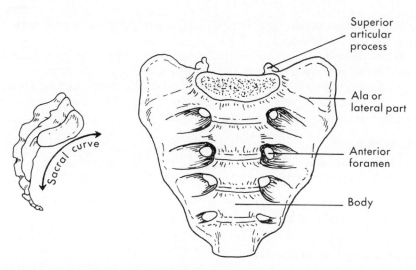

Figure 13-13

The sacrum, anterior view.

still undergoing structural changes as a result of upright position and therefore that humans are prone to slight spinal defects at birth, which later in life may cause improper body mechanics.

Physical defects in bony development are the underlying cause of many back problems in sports. Such conditions would remain undiscovered if not for a blow or sudden twist that creates an abnormal stress in the area of the **anomaly**.[7] The most common of these anomalies are excessive length of the transverse process of the fifth lumbar vertebra, incomplete closure of the neural arch (*spina bifida occulta*), nonconformities of the spinous processes, atypical lumbosacral angles or articular facets, and incomplete closures of the vertebral laminae. All these anomalies may produce mechanical weaknesses that make the back prone to injury when it is subjected to excessive postural strains.

An example of a congenital defect that may develop into a more serious condition when aggravated by a blow or a sudden twist in sports is the condition of *spondylolisthesis*. Spondylolisthesis is a forward slipping of the body of a vertebra, usually a lower lumbar vertebrae (see page 273).

anomaly
Deviation from the normal

Mechanical Defects of the Spine

Mechanical back defects are caused mainly by faulty posture, obesity, or faulty body mechanics — all of which may affect the athlete's performance in sports. Traumatic forces produced in sports, either directly or indirectly, can result in contusions, sprains, or fractures. Sometimes even minor injuries can develop into chronic and recurrent conditions, which may have serious implications for the athlete. To aid fully in understanding a back complaint, a logical investigation should be made into the history and the site of an injury, the type of pain produced, and the extent of impairment of normal function.

Maintaining proper segmental alignment of the body during standing, sitting, lying, running, jumping, and throwing is of utmost importance for keeping the body in good condition. Habitual violations of the principles of good body mechanics occur in many sports and produce anatomical deficiencies that subject the body to constant abnormal muscular and ligamentous strain. In all cases of postural deformity the coach or athletic trainer should determine the cause and attempt to rectify the condition through proper strength and mobilization exercises.

Back Trauma

Every football season there are stories of athletes who become paralyzed due to mishandled spine fractures. Such conditions would not occur if field officials, coaches, and athletic trainers would use discretion, exercise good judgment, and be able to identify certain gross indications of serious spine involvement.

Conditions Causing Low Back Pain

Soft Tissue Injuries

Soft tissue injuries of the back most often occur to the lower back. Those that occur in sports are produced by acute twists, direct blows, or chronic strains resulting from faulty posture or from the use of poor body mechanics in the sport. Tearing or stretching of the supporting ligamentous tissue with secondary involvement of the musculature occurs. Repeated strains or sprains cause the stabilizing tissues to lose their supporting power, thus producing tissue laxity in the lower back area.

Back contusions Back contusions rank second to strains and sprains in incidence. Because of its large surface area the back is quite susceptible to bruising in sports; football produces the greatest number of these injuries. A medical history indicating a violent blow to the back could indicate an extremely serious condition. Contusion of the back must be distinguished from a vertebral fracture; in some instances this is possible only by means of an x-ray examination. The bruise causes local pain, muscle spasm, and point tenderness. A swollen area may be visible also. Cold and pressure should be applied immediately for about 24 hours or longer, followed by rest and a gradual introduction of various forms of superficial heat. If the bruise handicaps the movement of the athlete, a penetrating therapy may hasten recovery. Ice massage combined with gradual stretching has been found to benefit soft tissue injuries in the lower back region. The time of incapacitation usually ranges from 2 days to 2 weeks.

Lower back strain and sprain   The mechanism of the typical lower back strain or sprain in sports activities usually occurs in two ways.[4] The first happens from a sudden, abrupt, violent extension contraction on an overloaded, unprepared, or underdeveloped spine, primarily in combination with trunk rotation. The second is the chronic strain commonly associated with faulty posture, usually excessive lumbar lordosis; however, conditions such as flat lower back or scoliosis also can predispose one to strain or sprain.[4]

Ideally, evaluation of the lower back strain or sprain is performed immediately after trauma has occurred. First, the possibility of fracture must be ruled out. Discomfort in the low back may be diffused or localized in one area and, as a rule, there is usually pain just in the low back region. There is also no neurological involvement to cause muscle weakness or sensation impairment.

Immediate and follow-up care   In the acute phase of this injury it is essential that cold packs or ice massage be used intermittently throughout the day to decrease muscle spasm. Injuries of moderate to severe intensity may require complete bed rest to help break the pain–muscle spasm cycle. The physician may prescribe oral analgesic medication.

Cryotherapy, ultrasound, and an abdominal support is often beneficial following the acute phase. A graduated program begins slowly in the subacute stage. Exercise must not cause pain.

Recurrent and chronic low back pain condition   Once an athlete has a moderate to severe episode of acute back strain or sprain there is high probability that it will occur again. With each subsequent episode the stage is set for the common problem of chronic low back pain. Recurrent or chronic low back pain can have many possible causes. Many episodes of strain or sprain can produce vertebral malalignment or eventually produce a disk disease that later causes nerve compression and pain. Gradually this problem could lead to muscular weakness and impairments in sensation. The older the athlete, the more prone he or she is to lower back injury. Incidence of this injury at the high school level is relatively low but becomes progressively greater at college and professional levels.[8] In most cases, because of postural anomalies and numerous small injuries, a so-called acute back condition is the culmination of a progressive degeneration of long duration that is aggravated or accentuated by a blow or sudden twist. The injury is produced as the result of an existing anatomical vulnerability. The trunk and vertebral column press downward on the sacrum, while the lower limbs and pelvis force upward; thus an abnormal strain can be exerted when the athlete's trunk is twisted in one direction, while the hamstring muscles pull downward on the pelvis on the opposite side. Such stress, if applied to an inelastic, structurally deformed, or muscularly weak lower back, will produce pathology.

Lumbar disk disease (intervertebral disk syndrome)   The lumbar disk is subjected to constant abnormal stresses stemming from faulty body mechanics, trauma, or both, which over a period of time can cause degeneration, that is, tears and cracks in the annulus fibrosus.

The area most often injured is the lumbar spine, particularly the disk lying between the fourth and fifth lumbar vertebrae. In sports, the mechanism of a disk injury is the same as for the lumbosacral sprain—a sudden twist that places abnormal strain on the lumbar region. Besides injuring soft tissues,

Individuals with lumbar disk disease should avoid performing forward-bending activities.

such a strain may herniate an already degenerated disk by increasing the size of the crack and allowing the nucleus pulposus to spill out (Fig. 13-14). This protrusion of the nucleus pulposus may place pressure on the cord of spinal nerves, thus causing radiating pains similar to those of sciatica.

The movement that produces a herniation or bulging of the nucleus pulposus may be excessive, and pain may be minimal or even absent. However, even without severe pain the athlete may complain of numbness along the nerve root and muscle weakness in the lower extremity.

Immediate and follow-up care Treatment of disk disease as directed by a physician usually includes:[2,3]

1. Strict bed rest for 1 to 2 weeks
2. Progressive ambulation
3. Anti-inflammatory agent and on occasion muscle relaxants
4. Analgesics and cryotherapy to break the pain–muscle spasm cycle (heat may be of value for its ability to relax muscles)

A condition that leads to a progressive bladder or bowel malfunction or severe paresis is considered a medical emergency. When symptom free, the athlete begins a daily program of exercise rehabilitation and postural education.

Spondylolisthesis The condition of spondylolisthesis is a forward slippage of a vertebra on the one below stemming from a degeneration of an articular process. It has the highest incidence in the lumbar region (Fig. 13-15). The athlete with this condition will usually have a swayback postural impairment. A direct blow or sudden twist or chronic low back strain may cause the defective vertebra to displace itself forward on the sacrum. When this happens, the athlete complains of localized pain or a pain that radiates into both buttocks, stiffness in the lower back, and increased irritation after physical activity.[9] The athlete with serious spondylolisthesis displays a short torso, heart-shaped buttocks, low rib cage, high iliac crest, and vertical sacrum; tight hamstring muscles and restricted hip extension may also be present. For the most part, these symptoms are the same for the majority of lower back problems; therefore, an x-ray film should be made to enable the physician to diagnose accurately. Discovery of a defective vertebra may be grounds for medical exclusion from collision and contact-type sports.[1]

Conservative care of acute problems usually consists of bed rest and flexion of the lumbar spine.[3] Casting to reduce hyperlordosis may also be employed. A slippage of 50% or more may cause a medical emergency, requiring surgical fusion of the spine.

Coccyx Injuries

Coccyx or tailbone injuries in sports are prevalent and occur primarily from such direct blows as those that are received in forcibly sitting down, falling, or being kicked by an opponent. Most injuries to the coccyx are the result of contusions.

Persistent pain in the coccyx region should be referred to a physician for x-ray and rectal examination. Pain in the coccygeal region is often prolonged and at times chronic. Such conditions are identified by the term *coccygodynia* and occur as a result of an irritation to the coccygeal plexus.

Text continued on p. 276.

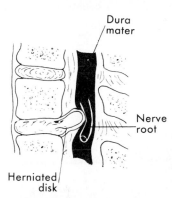

Figure 13-14

Intervertebral disk syndrome.

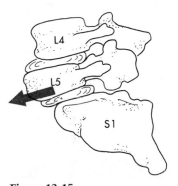

Figure 13-15

Spondylolisthesis.

Figure 13-16

Relax.

Figure 13-17

Pelvic tilt.

Figure 13-18

Knee to chest.

The Williams flexion series is an example of progressive exercises designed to stretch and strengthen the low back region.

The following exercises should be avoided if the back is hurting. Start with 3 repetitions and increase by 1 every 3 days. Repeat twice daily.

1. *Relax* (Fig. 13-16) — While lying on a firm surface (back flat and knees bent, feet flat, hands behind head), breathe in and out slowly, relaxing as much as possible.

2. *Pelvic tilt* (Fig. 13-17) — Tighten the abdomen and buttocks and press the low back against the floor. Hold for 5 seconds, then relax.

3. *Knee to chest* (Fig. 13-18) — Grab behind the knee of one leg and gently pull it toward the chest. Stretch for 10 seconds; slowly release and return leg to its original position. Repeat with the other leg.

4. *Both knees to chest* (Fig. 13-19) — While lying on your back, grasp both hands behind both knees and pull toward the chest. Stretch for 10 seconds; slowly release and return to the original position.

5. *Leg raise* (Fig. 13-20) — Flatten the back and grasp behind one knee. Bring it to the chest, then point the leg upward as much as possible. Hold for 10 seconds before lowering. Repeat with the other leg. **NOTE**: This exercise must be avoided if the athlete has numbness or weakness in the muscles of the leg.

Figure 13-19

Both knees to chest.

Figure 13-20

Leg raise.

6. *Erect pelvic tilt* (Fig. 13-21) — Stand 6 to 12 inches away from a wall facing outward. Press and flatten the low back against the wall. Hold for 10 seconds and relax.

7. *Uncurling the trunk* (Fig. 13-22) — From a full trunk curl, lean back slightly from a flexed knee position until tension is felt in the abdominal muscles. Return to the full curled position. Repeat 3 to 10 times.

8. *Hamstring stretch* (Fig. 13-23) — If hamstrings are tight, they should be stretched one at a time. Extend the leg to be stretched straight ahead; flex the other leg. As the extended leg is gradually stretched, rotate the flexed leg outward and reach forward with both arms. Hold for 30 seconds.

9. *Heel cord stretch* (Fig. 13-24) — Stand erect and lean toward the wall with one foot forward. Keep the back leg extended with the foot kept flat against the floor. As the body leans toward the wall, the heel cord is stretched. Keep the back straight at all times. Repeat with the other leg.

10. *Hip flexion stretch* (Fig. 13-25) — Lie supine on a table or bench with both legs dangling over the end. With the low back flat, grasp behind the knee of one leg and pull the thigh to the chest, keeping the opposite thigh flat on the table. Stretch the opposite leg. Hold for 30 seconds.

Figure 13-21

Erect pelvic tilt.

Figure 13-22

Uncurling the trunk.

Figure 13-23

Hamstring stretch.

Figure 13-25

Hip flexion stretch.

Figure 13-24

Heel cord stretch.

Care consists of analgesics and a ring seat to relieve the pressure on the coccyx while sitting. Palliative measures such as sitz baths or whirlpool in warm water might serve to alleviate some of the pain. It should be noted that pain with a fractured coccyx may last for many months. Once a coccygeal injury has healed, the athlete should be protected against reinjury by appropriately applied padding.

Rehabilitation of Low Back Conditions That Cause Pain

The following treatment procedures are emplcyed to a greater or lesser degree, depending on the type and extent of the pathological condition:
1. Limitation of activity
2. Anti-inflammatory and muscle relaxant medications
3. Cold or heat application and ultrasound
4. Passive exercise
5. Active progressive exercise
6. Relaxation training
7. Transcutaneous electrical nerve stimulation (TENS) application
8. Education for proper back usage
9. Use of a stiff mattress and proper sleeping positions

Where there is low back pain, the major concerns are to recondition proper strength and flexibility, improve body mechanics, and avoid engaging in harmful movements.

Rules for Back Care

The following are some general rules for back care:
1. Sleep on a firm mattress.
2. Sleep on the side with legs curled up or on the back with a pillow placed under the knees.
3. Sit so that the thighs are slightly elevated.
4. Stand with back flat and knees slightly bent.
5. Sit with back firmly against the back of a chair.
6. Do not bend over without bending the knees.
7. Do not twist trunk when placing a load down.
8. Carry heavy or bulky objects close to the body.
9. Lift heavy objects from the floor by keeping the back straight and bending the knees.
10. Avoid carrying unbalanced loads.

SUMMARY

The abdominal region can sustain a superficial or deep internal injury from a blow. Good conditioning that strengthens the abdominal muscles is essential to prevent contusions and strains.

Of the two common hernias, inguinal and femoral, the most prevalent is the inguinal. These conditions can be congenital or acquired. The major danger in each occurs when the protruding sac becomes constricted and circulation is impeded.

Two additional abdominal problems are the "stitch in the side" and a blow to the solar plexus. The causes of the cramplike stitch in the side are obscure, although poor eating habits and elimination habits or inadequate training habits are possibilities. A blow to the solar plexus produces a transitory paralysis of the diaphragm, which stops breathing for a short while.

The two major internal organs that can be injured in sports are the spleen and the kidney. A direct blow to the abdomen or a jarring fall can rupture the spleen. Shock, abdominal rigidity, nausea, and vomiting are signs of spleen injury. Although well protected, the kidney can be contused by a severe blow to the athlete's back. Signs of contusion are shock, nausea, vomiting, and rigidity of the back muscles.

The region of the thorax can sustain a number of different sports injuries such as rib contusions, fractures, separations, and dislocations. Internal thoracic complications include pneumothorax, hemothorax, traumatic asphyxia, and even heart contusions.

The low back can sustain a number of different injuries from sports activities. Prevention of low back injuries includes correcting or compensating for postural deviations, maintaining or increasing trunk and general body flexibility, and increasing trunk and general body strength.

Many low back problems stem from congenital defects such as spina bifida occulta or spondylolisthesis. Faulty posture is commonly the cause of mechanical defects in the spine. Faulty mechanics of the low back could eventually lead to a serious condition of lumbar disk disease. As with any musculoskeletal region, the low back can sustain traumatic sports injuries such as contusions, strains, and sprains.

REVIEW QUESTIONS AND SUGGESTED ACTIVITIES

1. Explain how the abdominal region sustains superficial injuries from sports activities. How may they be prevented?
2. What are the major signs of a hernia? How can a hernia be life threatening?
3. Describe the signs of a "stitch in the side."
4. What procedures would you take to aid an athlete who has had his or her wind knocked out?
5. Contrast the signs of a ruptured spleen to a severely contused kidney.
6. Describe the immediate care of an athlete with a hard blow to his testicles.
7. What are the dangers to a large-breasted woman who opts not to wear a bra in the sport of basketball?
8. Differentiate between the signs of a rib contusion and a rib fracture.
9. Differentiate between the signs of a sternal fracture and a costochondral separation.
10. Compare the signs of pneumothorax, hemothorax, and traumatic asphyxia.
11. Set up a low back injury preventive exercise program.
12. Perform a posture screening to detect body malalignments.
13. How are low back injuries sustained? Include in your answer traumatic events and congenital anomalies.

REFERENCES

1. Arnheim, D.D., and Sinclair, W.A.: Physical education for special populations, Englewood Cliffs, N.J., 1985, Prentice-Hall.
2. Birnbaum, J.S.: The musculoskeletal manual, New York, 1982, Academic Press.
3. Cailliet, R.: Low back pain, ed. 3, Philadelphia, 1981, F.A. Davis Co.
4. Cantu, R.C.: Low back injuries. In Vinger, P.F., and Hoerner, E.F. (editors): Sports injuries: the unthwarted epidemic, Boston, 1982, John Wright, PSG, Inc.

5. Gehlsen, G., and Albohm, M.: Evaluation of sports bras, Phys. Sportsmed. **8**:89, 1980.

6. Hafen, G.Q.: First aid in health emergencies, ed. 3, New York, 1984, West Publishing Co.

7. Jackson, D.W.: Low back pain in young athletes: evaluation of stress reaction and discogenic problems, Am. J. Sports Med. **7**:364, 1979.

8. Keene, J.S., and Drummond, D.S.: Back pain in the athlete—disk and vertebral injuries, Sports Med. Digest, **7**:5-6, Nov. 1985.

9. Leach, R.E.: Disc disease, spondylolysis and spondylolisthesis, Ath. Train. **12**:13, 1977.

10. Moncure, A.C., and Wilkins, E.W.: Injuries involving the abdomen, viscera, and genitourinary system. In Vinger, P.F., and Hoerner, E.F. (editors): Sports injuries: the unthwarted epidemic, Boston, 1982, John Wright, PSG, Inc.

11. O'Donoghue, D.H.: Treatment of injuries in athletes, Philadelphia, 1984, W.B. Saunders Co.

12. Schuster, K.: Equipment update: jogging bras hit the streets, Phys. Sportsmed. **7**:125, 1979.

ANNOTATED BIBLIOGRAPHY

Cailliet, R.: Low back pain syndrome, ed. 3, Philadelphia, 1981, F.A. Davis Co.

A complete monograph on low back problems. It covers anatomy, mechanical defects, and other more common low back disorders.

Gilabert, R.: Dancers spinal syndrome, J. Ortho. Sports Phys. Ther. **7**:180, January 1986.

A practical article concerning the causation of spinal syndromes in dancers. Also includes important information on injury prevention.

Kulund, D.N.: The injured athlete, Philadelphia, 1982, J.B. Lippincott Co.

Chapter 14, the torso, hip and thigh, provides an in-depth discussion of chest, abdominal, genitourinary, and low back injuries.

Micheli, L.J.: Back injuries in gymnastics. In Weiker, G.G. (editor): Symposium on gymnastics, Clinics in sports medicine, vol. 4, no. 1, Philadelphia, Jan. 1985, W.B. Saunders Co.

Discusses low back pain complaints in adolescent gymnasts as well as the evaluation and treatment of such injuries.

Chapter 14

THE UPPER SPINE, HEAD, AND FACE

When you finish this chapter, you will be able to:

Identify and provide proper immediate care of upper spine injuries

Identify and provide proper immediate care of head and face injuries

Sports injuries to the upper spine, head, or face could have major consequences for the athlete. A serious facial injury could lead to disfigurement or loss of sight or might even be life threatening. Injury to the head could result in major cerebral involvement, whereas an upper spinal injury could result in paralysis (Fig. 14-1).

THORACIC SPINE

The thoracic spine consists of 12 vertebrae. The first through the tenth thoracic vertebrae articulate with ribs by means of articular facets. Attached to all thoracic spinous processes are the trapezius muscle, the rhomboid muscle to the upper spinous processes, and the latissimus dorsi to the lower spinous processes. Deeper muscles of the back also attach to spinous and transverse processes (Fig. 14-2).

Thoracic Spine Injuries
Back Conditions in the Young Athlete

Young athletes who complain of thoracic spine pain may in fact have:
Spondylolysis
Spondylolisthesis
Scoliosis
Scheuermann's disease

Because young athletes are much less likely to sustain back strains and nerve root irritation, back pain could indicate a vertebral growth disturbance. Three such conditions that could have serious disabling consequences are spondylolisthesis (see Chapter 13), scoliosis, and Scheuermann's disease.

Scoliosis Any time a young athlete complains of back pain, scoliosis should be considered. Because a lateral-rotary condition of the spine can be progressively disabling if not promptly treated, referral to a physician must be made at once by the trainer (see Chapter 6).

Figure 14-1

Many sports place a great deal of stress on the upper and lower spine.

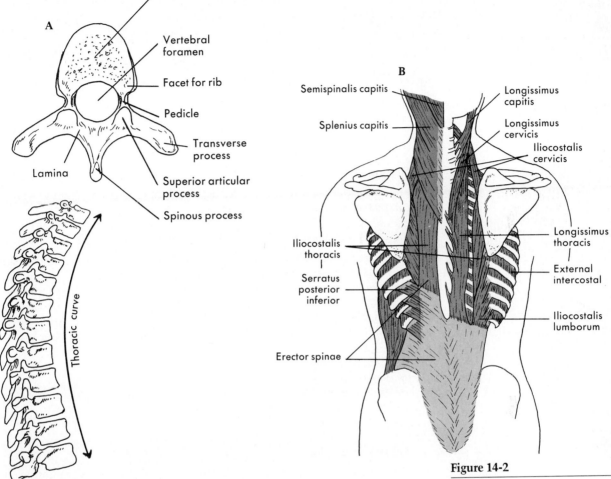

A

Body

Vertebral
foramen

Facet for rib

Pedicle

Transverse
process

Superior articular
process

Spinous process

Lamina

Thoracic curve

B

Semispinalis capitis

Splenius capitis

Iliocostalis
thoracis

Serratus
posterior
inferior

Erector spinae

Longissimus
capitis

Longissimus
cervicis

Iliocostalis
cervicis

Longissimus
thoracis

External
intercostal

Iliocostalis
lumborum

Figure 14-2

Anatomy of the thoracic
region. **A**, Thoracic spine. **B**,
Muscles of the back.

Scheuermann's disease   Adolescents who engage in sports such as gymnastics and swimming the butterfly stroke may be prone to Scheuermann's disease. This is a condition where there is a degeneration of the vertebrae growth regions. The athlete who complains of backache following physical activity should routinely be referred to a physician for examination.

CERVICAL SPINE

The cervical spine consists of seven vertebrae that function to support the head and allow rotation, lateral flexion, forward flexion, and backward extension (Figs. 14-3 and 14-4).

Cervical Spine Injuries

Because the neck is so mobile, it is extremely vulnerable to a wide range of sports injuries. Although relatively uncommon, severe sports injury to the neck can produce a catastrophic impairment of the spinal cord.

The very mobile neck carrying the relatively heavy head can incur a wide range of sports injuries.

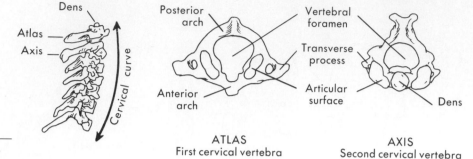

Figure 14-3

Cervical spine, atlas, and axis.

ATLAS
First cervical vertebra

AXIS
Second cervical vertebra

Figure 14-4

Relation of cord and spinal nerves to the vertebral column.

Long-necked football players or wrestlers are at risk and need to establish neck stability through strengthening exercises.

Evaluation of Neck Injuries

Evaluation of the neck injury can be divided into on-site emergency evaluation and off-site (sidelines or training room) evaluation.

On-site Emergency Evaluation

Unconscious athletes should be treated as if they have a cervical fracture (see Chapter 5). Every sports program should have an emergency system for caring for the severely injured athlete, especially when a neck injury is suspected.

An athlete who has sustained a neck injury, where fracture has been ruled out, should be carefully evaluated by the trainer or physician. Any one or more of the following signs should preclude the athlete from further sports participation:

1. Neck pain on passive, active, or resistive movement
2. Tingling or burning sensation in the neck, shoulder, or arm
3. Neck motion that causes an abnormal sensation, such as numbness or burning sensation
4. Muscle weakness in the upper or lower limbs

Off-site Evaluation

Even when an athlete comes into the training room from an evaluation of neck discomfort, fracture should always be considered as a possibility until it is ruled out. If there is doubt about a fracture, immediate referral to a physician for x-ray examination should be made.

Causes of Injury

A number of sports can place the cervical spine at risk. Among those activities in the highest risk category are diving, tackle football, and wrestling. Diving into shallow water causes many catastrophic neck injuries. The diver usually dives into water that is less than 5 feet deep, failing to keep the arms extended in front of the face; the head strikes the bottom producing a cervical fracture and/or subluxation. (Fig. 14-5).

Prevention of Neck Injuries

Prevention of neck injuries depends on the flexibility of the neck, its muscle strength, the state of readiness of the athlete, a knowledge of proper

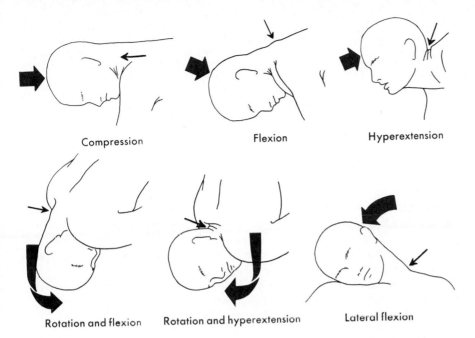

Compression   Flexion   Hyperextension

Rotation and flexion   Rotation and hyperextension   Lateral flexion

Figure 14-5

Mechanisms of neck injuries.

technique, and the use of proper protective equipment. Neck-strengthening flexibility exercises should be performed by the athlete daily.

During participation the athlete should constantly be in a "state of readiness" and, when making contact with an opponent, should "bull" the neck. This is accomplished by elevating both shoulders and isometrically contracting the muscles surrounding the neck.

Strength   Athletes with long, weak necks are especially at risk. Tackle football players and wrestlers must have highly stable necks. Specific strengthening exercises are essential for the development of this stability; a variety of different exercises can be employed that incorporate isotonic, isometric, or isokinetic contractions.

Manual resistance should *not* be performed just before an individual engages in a collision-type sport, such as football or ice hockey, to avoid the danger of participating in these activities with fatigued neck muscles.

Manual neck resistance   Manual resistance can provide an excellent means for helping to prevent neck injuries.

1. Extension, flexion, lateral flexion, and rotation are performed.
2. Each exercise is repeated 4 to 6 times in sets of 3.
3. The resisting partner accommodates to the varied strength of the mover, through a full range of motion.
4. Weaker spots in the range of motion can be strengthened with isometric resistance that is held for 6 seconds (Fig. 14-6).

Flexibility   In addition to strong muscles, the athlete's neck should have a full range of motion. Ideally the athlete should be able to place the chin on the chest and to extend the head back until the face is parallel with the ceiling. There should be at least 40 to 45 degrees of lateral flexion and enough rotation to allow the chin to reach a level even with the tip of the shoulder. Flexibility is increased by stretching exercises and strength exercises that are in

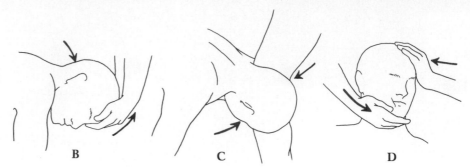

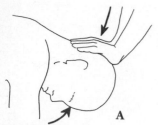

Figure 14-6

Manual resistance can provide an excellent means for helping to prevent neck injuries. **A,** Extension. **B,** Flexion. **C,** Lateral flexion. **D,** Rotation.

Figure 14-7

A collar for neck protection in football.

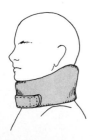

Figure 14-8

Wearing a soft cervical collar helps reduce pain and spasm in an injured neck.

full range of motion. Where flexibility is restricted, manual static stretching can be beneficial.

Protective neck devices   The protective neck roll and restrictive neck strap are used to reduce the severity of football neck injuries. The neck roll or collar can be custom-made with stockinette placed over sponge rubber, a towel, or other resilient material, or can be of the commercial inflatable type. It should encircle the entire neck (Fig. 14-7).

Restrictive neck straps are being used by some football teams on a trial basis. A 1 1/2-inch (3.75 cm) wide semielastic strap is fixed to the back of the helmet and shoulder pad to restrict excessive flexion.

Neck Injuries

Acute torticollis (wryneck)   Acute torticollis is a very common condition, more frequently called wryneck or "stiff neck." The athlete usually complains of pain on one side of the neck on awakening. This problem typically follows exposure to a cold draft of air or holding the head in an unusual position over a period of time.

On inspection, there is palpable point tenderness and muscle spasm. Head movement is restricted to the side opposite the irritation. X-ray examination will rule out a more serious injury. Management usually involves the wearing of a cervical collar for several days to relieve muscle stress and daily therapy with superficial heat (Fig. 14-8).

Acute strains of the neck and upper back   In a strain of the neck or upper back the athlete has usually turned the head suddenly or has forced flexion or extension. Muscles involved are typically the upper trapezius or sternocleidomastoid. Localized pain, point tenderness, and restricted motion are present. Care usually includes use of ICE-R immediately after the strain occurs and the wearing of a soft cervical collar. Follow-up care may include cryotherapy or superficial heat and analgesic medications as prescribed by the physician.

Cervical sprain (whiplash)   A cervical sprain can occur from the same mechanism as the strain but usually results from a more violent motion. More commonly the head snaps suddenly such as when the athlete is tackled or blocked while unprepared (Fig. 14-9).

The sprain displays all the signs of the strained neck but to a much greater degree. Besides injury to the musculature, the sprained neck also produces tears in the supporting ligaments. Along with the sprain, an intervertebral disk may be ruptured.

Pain usually is not experienced initially but appears the day after the trauma. Pain stems from tissue tear and a protective muscle spasm that restricts motion.

Care   As soon as possible the athlete should have an x-ray examination to rule out the possibility of fracture, dislocation, or disk injury. Neurological examination is performed by the physician to ascertain spinal cord or nerve root injury. A soft collar is applied to reduce muscle spasm. ICE-R is employed for 48 to 72 hours while the injury is in the acute stage of healing. In severe injury the physician may prescribe 2 or 3 days of bed rest, along with oral analgesics and anti-inflammation agents. Therapy might include cryotherapy or heat and massage. Mechanical traction may also be prescribed to relieve pain and muscle spasm.

Contusions to the throat and neck   Blows to the neck are not frequent in sports, but occasionally an athlete may receive a kick or blow to the throat. One type of trauma is known as "clotheslining," in which the athlete strikes or is struck in the throat region. Such a force could conceivably injure the carotid artery, causing a clot to form that occludes the blood flow to the brain. This same clot could become dislodged and migrate to the brain.[12] In either case serious brain damage may result. Immediately after throat trauma the athlete could experience severe pain and spasmodic coughing, speak with a hoarse voice, and complain of difficulty in swallowing.

Fracture of throat cartilages is rare, but it is possible and may be indicated by an inability to breathe and expectoration of frothy blood. Cyanosis may be present. Throat contusions are extremely uncomfortable and are often frightening to the athlete.

If the more severe signs appear, an emergency condition exists. In most situations cold may be applied intermittently to control superficial hemorrhage and swelling, and, after a 24-hour rest period, moist hot packs may be applied. For the most severe neck contusions, stabilization with a well-padded collar is beneficial.

Cervical fractures   The cervical vertebrae can be fractured in a number of ways. A compression fracture is created by a sudden forced flexion of the neck, such as striking the head when diving into shallow water. If the head is also rotated when making contact, a dislocation may occur along with the fracture. Fractures can also occur in a sudden forced hyperextension of the neck (Fig. 14-10).

The athlete may have one or more of the following signs of cervical fracture:
1. Cervical pain and pain in chest and extremities
2. Numbness in trunk and/or limbs
3. Weakness or paralysis in limbs and/or trunk
4. A loss of bladder and/or bowel control
5. Neck point tenderness and restricted movement
6. Cervical muscle spasm

Care   Extreme caution must be used in moving the athlete. The coach or athletic trainer must always be thinking of the possibility of the athlete's sustaining a catastrophic spinal injury from improper handling and transportation (see Chapter 5). **NOTE:** An unconscious athlete should be treated as if a serious neck injury is present until this is ruled out by the physician.

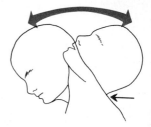

Figure 14-9

Whiplash.

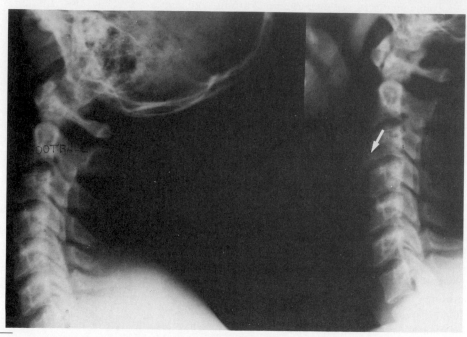

Figure 14-10

Fracture of the third cervical vertebra from playing football.

A unilateral cervical dislocation can cause the neck to be tilted toward the dislocated side, with tight muscles on the elongated side and relaxed muscles on the tilted side.

Cervical dislocations   Cervical dislocations are not common but occur much more frequently in sports than do fractures. They usually result from violent flexion and rotation of the head. Most injuries of this type happen in pool-diving accidents. The mechanism is analogous to the situation that occurs in football when blocks and tackles are poorly executed. The cervical vertebrae are more easily dislocated than are the vertebrae in other spinal regions because of their shape and relationship to one another.

For the most part, a cervical dislocation produces many of the same signs as a fracture. Both can result in considerable pain, numbness, and muscle weakness or paralysis. The most easily discernible difference is the position of the neck in a dislocation: a unilateral dislocation causes the neck to be tilted toward the dislocated side with extreme muscle tightness on the elongated side and a relaxed muscle state on the tilted side.

Cervical cord and peripheral nerve injuries   Neck and back injuries should always be treated with caution. The spinal cord is well protected by a connective tissue sheath, fat, and fluid cushioning, but even with protection, sudden abnormal forces can result in catastrophic paralysis and quadriplegia.

The spinal cord and nerve roots may be injured in five basic ways: laceration by bony fragments, hemorrhage, contusion, shock, and stretching. These may be combined into a single trauma or may act as separate conditions.

Laceration   Laceration of the cord is usually produced by the combined dislocation and fracture of a cervical vertebra. The jagged edges of the fragmented vertebral body cut and tear nerve roots or the spinal cord and can cause varying degrees of paralysis below the point of injury.

Hemorrhage   Hemorrhage develops from all vertebral fractures and from most dislocations, as well as from sprains and strains. It seldom causes harmful effects in the musculature, extradurally or even within the arachnoid space, where it dissipates faster than it can accumulate. However, hemorrhage within the cord itself causes irreparable damage.

Contusion   Contusion in the cord or nerve roots can arise from any force applied to the neck violently but without causing a cervical dislocation or fracture. Such an injury may result from a sudden displacement of a vertebra that compresses the cord and then returns to its normal position. This compression causes a swelling within the cord, resulting in various degrees of temporary or permanent damage.

Spinal cord shock   Occasionally a situation arises in which an athlete, after receiving a severe twist or snap of the neck, presents all the signs of a spinal cord injury. The athlete is unable to move certain parts of the body and complains of a numbness and a tingling sensation in his or her arms. After a short while all these signs leave; the athlete is then able to move his or her limbs quite freely and has no other symptoms other than a sore neck. This condition is considered a spinal cord shock and is caused by a mild compression on the spinal cord. In such cases athletes should be cared for in the same manner employed in any severe neck injury.

Cervical nerve stretch syndrome ("burner")   Stretching (cervical nerve stretch syndrome) or cervical nerve pinch is a condition that has received more recognition in recent years. Other terms for this condition are cervical radiculitis, "hot shots," "pinched nerve," or "burner." The mechanism of injury is one in which an athlete receives a violent lateral wrench of the neck from a head or shoulder block. The player complains of a burning sensation and pain extending from the neck down the arm to the base of the thumb with some numbness and loss of function of the arm and hand that lasts 10 to 20 seconds. It is speculated that an overriding of the articular facet has caused the electric shock–like sensation. However, it also may be an indication of a slipped cervical disk or a congenital vertebral defect. Repeated nerve stretch may result in neuritis, muscular atrophy, and a permanent loss of muscle function. This condition requires immediate medical evaluation. After cervical nerve stretch, medical clearance is required before the athlete can return to sports activity. In some cases functional damage is such that the athlete must not participate in certain sports. Conditions for returning to the sport include above-average neck strength and wearing of protective neckwear when using the head and neck in a sports activity. A similar condition can be produced by a nerve compression.

Neck Rehabilitation

The neck should be pain free before exercise rehabilitation begins. The first consideration should be restoration of the neck's normal range of motion. If the athlete had a prior restricted range of motion, increasing it to a more normal range is desirable. A second goal is to strengthen the neck as much as possible.

When the athlete has gained near-normal range of motion, a strength program should be instituted. All exercises should be conducted pain free.

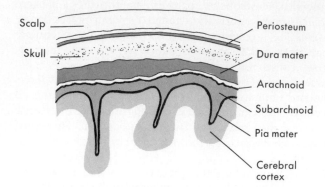

Figure 14-11

The meninges covering the brain.

Scalp — Periosteum

Skull — Dura mater

Arachnoid

Subarchnoid

Pia mater

Cerebral cortex

THE HEAD

The *brain* or encephalon is the part of the central nervous system that is contained within the bony cavity of the cranium and is divided into four sections: the cerebrum, the cerebellum, the pons, and the medulla oblongata. Investing the spinal cord and the brain are the *meninges*, which are three membranes that give protection to the brain and spinal cord (Fig. 14-11).

Cerebral Injuries

Despite its considerable protection, the brain is subject to traumatic injury, and a great many of the head injuries incurred in sports have serious consequences.[2] For this reason it is necessary to give special consideration to this part of the body. A constant supply of oxygen and blood to the brain is vital and critical to its survival. Although the incidence of serious head injuries from football has decreased in past years when compared to catastrophic neck injuries, their occurrence is of major concern. Every coach and athletic trainer must be able to recognize the signs of serious head injury and to act appropriately.

Most traumas of the head result from direct or indirect blows and may be classified as concussion injuries. Literally, "concussion" means an agitation or a shaking from being hit, and "cerebral concussion" refers to the agitation of the brain by either a direct or an indirect blow. Surgeons define concussion as a clinical syndrome characterized by immediate and transient impairment of neural function, such as alteration of consciousness, disturbance of vision, equilibrium, and so on, caused by mechanical forces.[3] The direct concussion most often comes either from a violent fall, in which sitting down transmits a jarring effect through the vertebral column to the brain, or from a blow to the chin. In most cases of cerebral concussion there is a short period of unconsciousness, having mild to severe results.

Most authorities agree that unconsciousness comes from a brain anoxia that is caused by constriction of the blood vessels. Depending on the force of the blow and the tolerance of the athlete to withstand such a blow, varying degrees of cerebral hemorrhage, edema, and tissue laceration may occur that in turn will cause tissue changes. Because of the fluid suspension of the brain, a blow to the head can effect an injury to the brain either at the point of contact or on the opposite side. After the head is struck, the brain continues to move in the fluid and may be contused against the opposite side. This causes a *contrecoup type of injury.* An athlete who is knocked unconscious by a blow to the head may be presumed to have received some degree of concussion. Most often the blow simply stuns the athlete, who recovers quite rapidly.

In determining the extent of head injury one must be aware of basic gross signs by which concussions may be evaluated. Concussions are described as being mild (first degree), moderate (second degree), or severe (third degree) and are graded from I through IV. Grades I and II come under the category of mild or first degree. Grade III is considered a moderate or second degree injury, and a grade IV concussion is considered a severe or third degree condition.

Grade I Concussion

Grade I concussions are minimal in intensity and represent the most common type in sports. In general the athlete becomes dazed and disoriented but does not become amnesic or have other signs associated with a more serious condition.

Grade II Concussion

A grade II cerebral concussion is also considered to be of mild intensity. There is no loss of consciousness, but there may be a slight temporary memory loss at the moment of impact or 5 to 10 minutes later, some minor mental confusion, unsteadiness, a ringing in the ears (tinnitus), and perhaps minor dizziness. A dull headache may also follow.[12] This is what is commonly called being "dinged" or having one's "bells rung." These athletes may also develop a postconcussion syndrome, characterized by difficulty in concentrating, recurring headaches, and irritability.

Grade III Concussion

Considered moderate in intensity, the grade III concussion can pose a serious medical problem. There is a loss of consciousness (up to 4 minutes); moderate tinnitus; retrograde amnesia, which constitutes a condition in which the athlete is unable to remember recent events; mental confusion; balance disturbance; and headache. Automatism, that is, automatic behavior before consciousness or full awareness has been achieved, may occur.[5]

The three major types of intracranial hemorrhage are:
Epidural
Subdural
Intracerebral

Grade IV Concussion

The grade IV cerebral concussion is obviously the most severe of the so-called knocked-out states. It implies many serious consequences: a prolonged period of unconsciousness (over 5 minutes); mental confusion for an extended period with retrograde amnesia (lasting over 5 minutes); and other symptoms such as tinnitus, dizziness, balance difficulties, automatic behavior, and convulsions.

Intracranial Hemorrhage

A blow to the head can cause intracranial bleeding. It may arise from rupture of a blood vessel aneurysm or tearing of the sinus separating the two brain hemispheres (Fig. 14-12). Venous bleeding may be slow and insidious, whereas arterial hemorrhage may be evident in a few hours. In the beginning the athlete may be quite lucid, with few or none of the symptoms of serious head

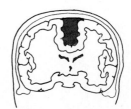

Figure 14-12

Intracranial hemorrhage.

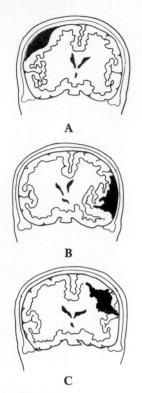

Figure 14-13

The three major types of intracranial hemorrhage. **A**, Epidural. **B**, Subdural. **C**, Intracerebral.

If neck injuries are suspected in the unconscious athlete, the jaw is brought forward, but the neck is not hyperextended to clear the airway.

injury, and then gradually display severe head pains, dizziness, nausea, inequality of pupil size, or sleepiness.[1] Later stages of cerebral hemorrhage are characterized by deteriorating consciousness, neck rigidity, depression of pulse and respiration, and convulsions. Of course, this becomes a life-and-death situation necessitating urgent neurosurgical care.

Skull fracture   Any time an athlete sustains a severe blow to the unprotected head, a skull fracture should be suspected. Skull fractures can be difficult to ascertain. Swelling of the scalp may mask a skull depression or deformity.[14] Until the more obvious signs caused by intracranial bleeding are present, the skull fracture, even on x-ray examination, can be missed.

Intracerebral bleeding   Intracerebral hemorrhage is bleeding within the brain itself. Most commonly it results from a compressive force to the brain[12] (Fig. 14-13). Deterioration of neurological function occurs rapidly, requiring immediate hospitalization.

Evaluation of Cerebral Injuries

Cases of serious head injury almost always represent a life-threatening situation that requires that the athlete be admitted to a hospital within a crucial 30-minute period.

On-site Evaluation

One must be adept at recognizing and interpreting the signs that an unconscious athlete presents. Priority first aid for any head injury must always deal with any life-threatening condition such as impaired airway or hemorrhage.[13] When an athlete is unconscious, a neck injury is also assumed. Without moving the athlete, evaluation includes:

1. Looking for the possibility of airway obstruction. If breathing is obstructed:
   a. Remove face mask by cutting away from the helmet, but leave helmet in place
   b. Stabilize head and neck
   c. Bring jaw forward to clear air passage (do not hyperextend neck)
   d. Take pulse: if absent, CPR is given; if present, oxygen may be given
   e. **NOTE**: Ammonia fumes should not be used for reviving an injured person. The athlete who is dazed or unconscious may jerk the head and exacerbate a spinal fracture after smelling the pungent ammonia fumes.
2. A quick observation of the following physical signs of concussion or skull fracture:
   a. Face color may be red or pale
   b. Skin may be cool or moist
   c. Pulse, if present, may be strong and slow or rapid and weak
   d. Breathing, if present, may be deep or shallow
   e. Pupils may be dilated or unequal
   f. Head may show swelling or deformity over area of injury
3. The athlete is removed carefully from the playing site on a spine board (see Chapter 5 instructions)

Further Evaluation of the Athlete with a Cerebral Injury

Athletes with grade III or IV concussions having distinct clinical signs should automatically be sent to the hospital for medical care. In grade I and II concussions it is often difficult for the coach or athletic trainer to determine exactly how serious the problem is. Also, grade I and II conditions can slowly—or even quickly—deteriorate to a higher grade. This makes certain evaluative procedures imperative even in so-called very minor cases (Table 14-1).

It must be noted that following a cerebral injury, an athlete must be completely free of symptoms before returning to competition.

Questioning the athlete   When the athlete regains consciousness, testing for mental orientation and memory should be done. Questions might include:
- What is your name?
- How old are you?
- Where are you?
- What game are you playing?
- What period is it?
- What is the score?
- What is your assignment on the 23 trap play?

Testing eye signs   Because of the direct connection between the eye and the brain, pupillary discrepancies provide important information. The athlete should be observed and tested for:

1. Dilated and/or irregular pupils. A check on pupil sizes may be particularly difficult at night and under artificial lights. To ensure accuracy, the athlete's pupil size should be compared with that of an official or another player present. It should be remembered, however, that some individuals normally have pupils that differ in size.

2. Blurred vision determined by a difficulty or inability to read a game program or the score board.

3. Inability for the pupils to rapidly accommodate to light variance. Eye accommodation should be tested by covering one eye with a hand. The covered eye normally will dilate, while the uncovered pupil will remain the same. When the hand is removed, the previously covered pupil normally will accommodate readily to the light. A slow accommodating pupil may be an indicator of cerebral injury.

4. Ability of eyes to track smoothly. The athlete is asked to hold the head in a neutral position, eyes looking straight ahead. The athlete is then asked to follow the top of a pen or pencil, first up as far as possible, then down as far as possible. The eyes are observed for smooth movement and any signs of pain. Next, the tip of the pen or pencil is slowly moved from left to right to determine whether the eyes follow the tip smoothly across the midline of the face or whether they make involuntary movements. A constant involuntary back and forth, up and down, or rotary movement of the eyeball is called *nystagmus*, indicating possible cerebral involvement.

Testing balance   If the athlete can stand, the degree of unsteadiness must be noted. A cerebral concussion of grade II or more can produce balance difficulties (positive Romberg's sign). To test Romberg's sign the athlete is told to stand tall with the feet together, arms at sides, eyes closed. A positive sign[15]

Checking eye signs can yield crucial information about possible brain injury.

TABLE 14-1

Cerebral concussion

	First Degree		Second Degree	Third Degree
	Grade I	Grade II	Grade III	Grade IV
Disorientation	+	+	+ +	+ + +
Dizziness		+	+ +	+ + +
Amnesia		+	+ +	+ + +
Headache			+/+ +	+ + +
Loss of conscious- ness			+/+ +	+ + +
Problems in concen- trating		+	+ +	+ + +
Tinnitus		+	+ +	+ + +
Balance problems		+	+ +	+ + +
Automatism			+/+ +	
Pupillary discrepencies			+/+ +	+ + +

+ Mild
+ + Moderate
+ + + Severe

Following a cerebral injury, an
athlete must be free of
symptoms and signs before
returning to competition.

is one in which the athlete begins to sway, cannot keep eyes closed, or obviously loses balance. Having the athlete attempt to stand on one foot is also a good indicator of balance.

Finger-to-nose test The athlete stands tall with eyes closed and arms out to the side. The athlete is then asked to touch the index finger of one hand to the nose and then to touch the index finger of the other hand to the nose. Inability to perform this task with one or both fingers is an indication of physical disorientation and precludes reentry to the game.

It must be noted that following a cerebral injury, an athlete must be completely free of symptoms before returning to competition.

THE FACE

The facial skin covers primarily subcutaneous bone with very little protective muscle, fascia, or fat. The supraorbital ridges house the frontal sinuses. In general the facial skeleton is composed of dense bony buttresses combined with thin sheets of bone.[16] The middle third of the face consists of the maxillary bone, which supports the nose and nasal passages.[16] The lower aspect of the face consists of the lower jaw or mandible. Besides supporting teeth, the mandible also supports the larynx, trachea, upper airway, and upper digestive tract[16] (Fig. 14-14).

Facial Injuries

Serious injuries to the face have been reduced significantly from the past by requiring proper protection in high-risk sports. The most prevalent cause of facial injury is a direct blow that injures soft and bony tissue. Very common are skin abrasions, lacerations, and contusions; less common are fractures.[10]

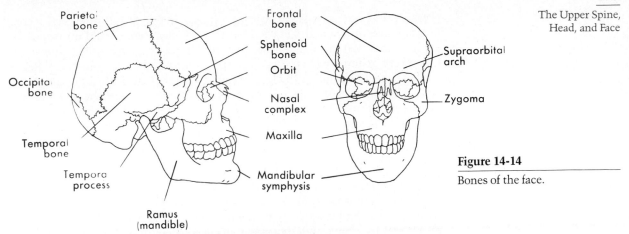

Figure 14-14

Bones of the face.

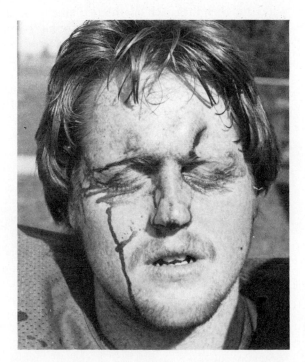

Figure 14-15

Skin wounds about the face
must be carefully managed to
avoid infection.

Facial Wounds

Special consideration must be given to skin wounds of the head and face because of their high vascularity and nearness to the brain (Fig. 14-15). The many irregular angles of the face make it susceptible to both abrasions and lacerations.

The face is generally perspiring and dirty during activity and should be cleansed thoroughly with soap and water before cleansing and debriding an abrasion. Debridement is carried out with antiseptic soap, water, and a soft brush. Once the wound has been completely cleansed, a mild antiseptic is applied, followed by a medicated ointment to keep the injury moist. A nonadhering sterile pad is placed over the wound and is taped in place. Regular daily checks should be made to ascertain whether any infection is present.

Lacerations especially common to the facial area are those occurring around the orbital socket, particularly at the brow line, and about the chin. As is done with other wounds, the facial laceration is cleansed completely and the hemorrhage is controlled by the use of a cold compress or an astringent. Most lacerations about the face can be adequately protected until the game is over and can then be sutured by a physician.

Mouth lacerations   Lacerations about the mouth usually occur from a blow to the mouth that forces soft tissue against the teeth. Lacerations of the mouth occur most frequently to the lips and tongue. Deep cuts will need to be sutured by a physician, but most lacerations are minor and will not keep the athlete out of activity.

For inspecting this type of injury, the athlete should rinse the mouth with water, and then the coach or athletic trainer should examine the teeth for possible fractures. After the extent of injury has been determined, a solution of hydrogen peroxide is used as an antiseptic and is followed by an astringent-antiseptic solution. Swelling and hemorrhaging can be controlled by having the athlete suck on ice.

Scalp lacerations   The care of scalp lacerations poses a special problem because of the general inaccessibility of these injuries. Bleeding is often extensive, which makes it difficult to pinpoint the site of the wound. Matted hair and dirt can also disguise the actual point of injury.

EMERGENCY CARE OF FACIAL LACERATIONS

The following procedure has been found beneficial in caring for lacerations during competition.

Materials needed: Antiseptic, tape adherent, flexible collodion or plastic spray, butterfly bandages, gauze, and 1-inch (2.5 cm) tape.

Position of the athlete: The athlete lies on the table, the wound upward.

Position of the operator: The operator faces toward the athlete's head, standing alongside the table on the same side as the injury.

Procedure

1. After the injury has been washed and dried, it may have to be shaved if it is in the vicinity of the eyebrow. After shaving it is again cleansed thoroughly and an antiseptic solution is applied.
2. Tape adherent is painted around the wound, and a coating of flexible collodion is placed directly over the wound.
3. A butterfly bandage stitch or a special light and stretchable plastic tape is applied across the wound, pulling it together. Two or more bandage stitches will be needed if the laceration is over 1/2-inch (1.25 cm) long. Each stitch is started below the tear and pulled upward, against gravity, to ensure maximum closure.
4. A gauze bandage is placed lengthwise over the butterfly bandage stitches to give added protection.

CARE OF SCALP LACERATIONS

Materials needed: Antiseptic soap, water, antiseptic, 4-inch (10 cm) gauze pads, sterile cotton, and hair clippers.
Position of the athlete: The athlete lies on the table with the wound upward.
Position of the operator: The operator stands at the side of the table, facing the injured side of the athlete's head.
Procedure
1. The entire area of bleeding is thoroughly cleansed with antiseptic soap and water. Washing the wound to remove dirt and debris is best done in lengthwise movements.
2. After the injury site is cleansed and dried, it is exposed and, if necessary, the hair clipped away. Enough scalp should be exposed so that a bandage and tape may be applied.
3. Firm pressure or an astringent can be used to reduce bleeding if necessary.
4. Wounds that are more than 1/2 inch (1/25 cm) in length and 1/8 inch (.03 cm) in depth should be referred to a physician for treatment. In less severe wounds the bleeding should be controlled and an antiseptic applied, followed by the application of a protective coating such as collodion and a sterile gauze pad. A tape adherent is then painted over the skin area to ensure that the tape sticks to the skin.

Injuries of the Mandible (Jaw)

Jaw fracture   Fractures of the lower jaw (Fig. 14-16) occur most often in collision sports. They are second in incidence of all facial fractures. Because it has relatively little padding and sharp contours, the lower jaw is prone to injury from a direct blow. The most frequently fractured area is near the jaw's frontal angle.

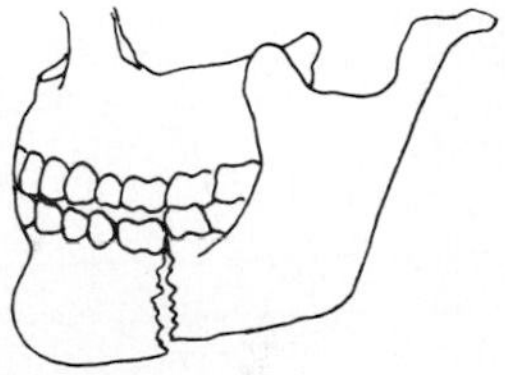

The main indications of a fractured mandible are deformity, loss of normal occlusion of the teeth, pain on biting down, bleeding around the teeth, and lower lip anesthesia.[9]

Figure 14-16

Mandibular fracture.

Care   Care usually includes cold packs to the side of the face, immobilization by a four-tailed bandage, and immediate referral to a physician.

Jaw dislocations   A dislocation of the jaw, or *mandibular luxation* involves the temporomandibular joint, which is formed by the condyle of the mandible and the mandibular fossa of the temporal bone. This area has all the features of a hinge and gliding articulation. Because of its wide range of movement and the inequity of size between the mandibular condyle and the temporal fossa, the jaw is somewhat prone to dislocation. The mechanism of injury in dislocations is usually initiated by a side blow to the open mouth of the athlete, thus forcing the mandibular condyle forward out of the temporal fossa. This injury may occur as either a luxation (complete dislocation) or a subluxation (partial dislocation).

The major signs of the dislocated jaw are a locked-open position, with jaw movement being almost impossible, and/or an overriding malocclusion of the teeth.

Care   In cases of first-time jaw dislocation the initial treatment includes immediately applying a cold compress to control hemorrhage, splinting the jaw by the use of a four-tailed bandage, and referring the athlete to a physician for reduction. Without a physician it is not advisable to attempt the reduction of a jaw dislocation unless it is of a chronically recurrent type.

Dental Injuries

The tooth is a composite of mineral salts of which calcium and phosphorus are most abundant. It is a complex of many structures composed of enamel, pulp, dentin, cementum, and root canal (Fig. 14-17).

With the use of face guards and properly fitting mouth guards most dental injuries can be prevented. Any blow to the upper or lower jaw can potentially injure the teeth. Injuries to the tooth below the gum line may repair themselves because of the abundant blood supply. However, fractures of the tooth below the gum line may not heal if there is an injury to the tooth pulp. Even though not obvious, a tooth could sustain a mild blow that disrupts its blood and nerve supply.[4]

The Fractured Tooth

Fracture of the crown of the tooth is an enamel fracture and can usually be repaired by smoothing, capping, or even removal of the entire tooth. In contrast, fractures that involve the dentin exposing the pulp may predispose the tooth to infection and tooth death.[16]

Teeth in which the enamel or dentin is chipped fail to rejuvenate because they lack a direct blood supply. They can be capped for the sake of appearance. A tooth that is fractured or loosened may be extremely painful because of the damaged or exposed nerve. In such cases a small amount of calcium hydroxide (Dycol) applied to the exposed nerve area will inhibit the pain until the athlete is seen by a dentist.

A fractured tooth is usually very sensitive to air and requires the athlete to keep the mouth closed. If there is no bleeding of the gums, the athlete can continue to play and see the dentist after the game.[4]

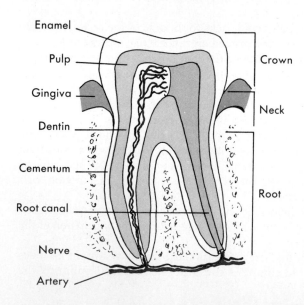

Figure 14-17

Normal tooth anatomy.

The Partially or Completely Dislocated Tooth

A tooth that has been knocked crooked should be manually realigned to a normal position as soon as possible. One that has been totally knocked out should be cleaned off with water and replaced in the tooth socket, if possible. If repositioning the dislocated tooth is difficult, the athlete should keep it under the tongue until the dentist can replace it.[4] If this is inconvenient, a dislodged tooth can also be kept in a glass of water. If a completely dislodged tooth is out of the mouth for more than 30 minutes the chances of saving it are very tenuous; therefore, the athlete should immediately be sent to a dentist for splinting.

A tooth that has been completely dislocated intact should be rinsed off with water and replaced in the socket.

Nasal Injuries

Nasal Fractures and Chondral Separation

A fracture of the nose is one of the most common fractures of the face. It appears frequently as a separation of the frontal processes of the maxilla, a separation of the lateral cartilages, or a combination (Fig. 14-18).

Figure 14-18

Nasal fracture.

The force of the blow to the nose may either come from the side or be a straight frontal force. A lateral force causes greater deformity than a "straight-on" blow. In nasal fractures hemorrhage is profuse because of laceration of the mucous lining. Swelling is immediate. Deformity is usually present if the nose has received a lateral blow. Gentle palpation may reveal abnormal mobility and emit a grating sound (crepitus).

Care One should control the bleeding and then refer the athlete to a physician for x-ray examination and reduction of the fracture. Simple and uncomplicated fractures of the nose will not hinder or be unsafe for the athlete, and he or she will be able to return to competition within a few days. Adequate protection can be provided by splinting.

Nosebleed (Epistaxis)

Nosebleeds in sports are usually the result of direct blows that cause varying degrees of contusion to the septum.

Hemorrhages arise most often from the highly vascular anterior aspect of the nasal septum. In some situations the nosebleed presents only a minor problem and stops spontaneously after a short period of time. However, there are persistent types that require medical attention and, probably, cauterization.

Care The following steps should be followed when caring for the acute nosebleed:

1. The athlete lies on the same side as the bleeding septum, his or her head comfortably elevated. (In this position the blood will be confined to one nostril.)
2. A cold compress is placed over the nose.
3. The athlete applies finger pressure to the affected nostril for 5 minutes.

If this method fails to stop the bleeding within 5 minutes, more extensive measures should be taken by a physician or athletic trainer. The application of a gauze or cotton pledget will provide corking action and encourage blood clotting. If a pledget is used, the ends should protrude from the nostrils at least 1/2 inch (1.25 cm) to facilitate removal. After bleeding has ceased the

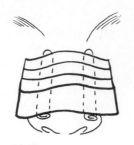

Figure 14-19

Splinting the fractured nose.

NOSE SPLINTING

The following procedure is used for nose splinting (Fig. 14-19).
Materials needed: Two pieces of gauze, each 2 inches (5 cm) long and rolled to the size of a pencil; 3 strips of 1 1/2-inch (3.75 cm) tape, cut about 4 inches (10 cm) long; and clear tape adherent.
Position of the athlete: The athlete lies supine on the training table.
Position of the operator: The operator stands facing the athlete's head.
Procedure
1. The rolled pieces of gauze are placed on either side of the athlete's nose.
2. Gently but firmly, 4-inch (10 cm) lengths of tape are laid over the gauze rolls.

---

athlete may resume activity, but he or she should be reminded not to blow the nose under any circumstances for at least 2 hours after the initial insult.

Foreign Body in the Nose

During participation the athlete may have insects or debris become lodged in one nostril; if the object is large enough, the mucous lining of the nose reacts by becoming inflamed and swollen. In most cases the foreign body will become dislodged if the nose is gently blown while the unaffected side is pinched shut. Probing and blowing the nose violently will only cause additional irritation. The removal of difficult objects may be aided by placing a few drops of olive or mineral oil into the nostril to soothe and prevent swelling of the mucosa. If oil is unavailable, the application of a nasal vasoconstrictor will help to shrink the mucous membranes.

Ear Problems

The ear (Fig. 14-20) is responsible for the sense of hearing and equilibrium. It is composed of three parts: the external ear; the middle ear (tympanic membrane) lying just inside the skull; and the internal ear (labyrinth), which is formed, in part, by the temporal bone of the skull. The middle ear and internal ear are structured to carry auditory impulses to the brain. Aiding the organs of hearing and equalizing pressures between the middle and the internal ear is the eustachian tube, a canal that joins the nose and the middle ear.

Sports injuries to the ear occur most often to the external portion. The external ear is separated into the auricle (pinna) and the external auditory canal (meatus). The auricle, which is shaped like a shell, collects and directs waves of sound into the auditory canal. It is made up of flexible yellow cartilage, muscles, and fat padding, and is covered by a closely adhering, thin layer of skin. Most of the blood vessels and nerves of the auricle turn around its borders, with just a few penetrating the cartilage proper.

Hematoma Auris (Cauliflower Ear)

Contusions, wrenching, or extreme friction of the ear can lead to hematoma auris, commonly known as a "cauliflower ear" (Fig. 14-21).

This condition usually occurs from repeated injury to the ear and is seen most frequently in boxers and wrestlers. However, recently it has been held to a minimum because of the protective measures that have been initiated.

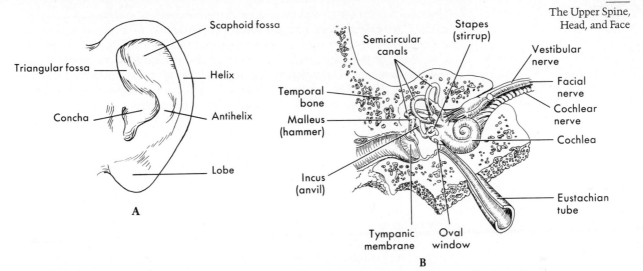

Figure 14-20

Ear anatomy. **A**, Normal
external ear. **B**, Inner ear.

Figure 14-21

The cauliflower ear.

Trauma may tear the overlying tissue away from the cartilaginous plate, resulting in hemorrhage and fluid accumulation. A hematoma usually forms before the limited circulation can absorb the fluid. If the hematoma goes unattended, a sequence of coagulation, organization, and fibrosis results in a keloid that appears elevated, rounded, white, nodular, and firm, resembling a cauliflower. Quite often it forms in the region of the helix fossa or concha; once developed, the keloid can be removed only by surgery. To prevent this disfiguring condition from arising, some friction-proofing agent such as petroleum jelly should be applied to the ears of athletes susceptible to this condition. They should also routinely wear ear guards in practice and in competition.

Care If an ear becomes "hot" because of excessive rubbing or twisting, the immediate application of a cold pack to the affected spot will alleviate hemorrhage. Once swelling is present in the ear, special care should be taken to prevent the fluid from solidifying; a cold pack should be placed immediately over the ear and held tightly by an elastic bandage for at least 20 minutes. If the swelling is still present at the end of this time, aspiration by a physician is needed, usually followed by a rigid compress such as the silicone cast.

Foreign Body in the Ear

The ears offer an opening as do the nose and eyes, in which objects can become caught. Usually these objects are pieces of debris or flying insects. They can be dislodged by having the athlete tilt the head to one side. If removal is difficult, syringing the ear with a solution of lukewarm water may remove the object. Care should be exercised to avoid striking the eardrum with the direct stream of water.

Swimmer's Ear

A common condition in athletes engaged in water sports is "swimmer's ear," a general term for ear infection caused by *Pseudomonas*, a type of bacillus.

Contrary to current thought among swimming coaches, swimmer's ear is not usually associated with a fungal infection. Water can become trapped in the ear canal as a result of various obstructions created by cysts, bone growths, ear wax plugs, or swelling caused by allergies. The athlete may complain of itching, discharge, or even a partial hearing loss. Under these circumstances the athlete should be sent immediately to a physician for treatment. Protection of the athlete with a mild ear infection can be successfully accomplished by plugging the ear with lamb's wool combined with lanolin. Prevention from ear infection can best be attained by drying the ears thoroughly with a soft towel, using ear drops containing a mild acid (3% boric acid) and alcohol solution before and after each swim, and avoiding situations that can cause ear infections, such as overexposure to cold wind or sticking foreign objects into the ear.

Eye Injuries

The eye has many anatomical protective devices. It is firmly retained within an oval socket formed by the bones of the head. A cushion of soft fatty tissue surrounds it, and a thin skin flap (the eyelid), which functions by reflex action, covers the eye for protection. Foreign particles are prevented from entering the eye by the lashes and eyebrows, which act as a filtering system. A soft mucous lining that covers the inner conjunctiva carries and spreads tears, which are secreted by many accessory lacrimal glands. A larger lubricating organ is located above the eye and secretes heavy quantities of fluid through the lacrimal duct to help wash away foreign particles. The eye proper is well protected by the sclera, a tough, white outer layer possessing a transparent center portion called the cornea (Fig. 14-22).

Eye Protection

The eye can be injured in a number of different ways. Shattered eyeglass or goggle lenses can lacerate; ski pole tips can penetrate; fingers, racquetballs, and larger projectiles can seriously compress and injure the eye. High-injury sports such as ice hockey, football, and lacrosse require full-face and helmet

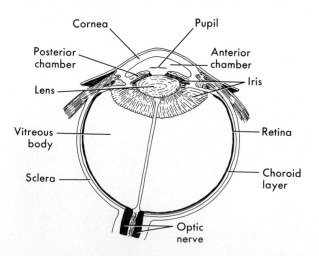

Figure 14-22

Eye anatomy.

protection while low-injury sports such as racquetball and tennis require eye guards that rest on the face.[6,16] Protective devices must provide protection from front and lateral blows.[7,8]

Immediate and follow-up care   Proper care of eye injuries is essential. The coach or athletic trainer must use extreme caution in handling eye injuries. If there appears to be a retinal detachment, perforation of the globe, foreign object embedded in the cornea, blood in the anterior chamber, decreased vision, loss of the visual field, poor pupillary adaptation, double vision, laceration, or impaired lid function, the athlete should be immediately referred to a hospital where there is an ophthalmologist.[13,15] Ideally, the athlete with a serious eye injury should be transported to the hospital by ambulance in a recumbent position. Both eyes must be covered during transport. At no time should pressure be applied to the eye. In cases of surrounding soft tissue injury, a cold compress can be applied for 30 to 60 minutes to control hemorrhage.[13]

Orbital Hematoma (Black Eye)

Although well protected, the eye may be bruised during sports activity. The severity of eye injuries varies from a mild bruise to an extremely serious condition affecting vision to the fracturing of the orbital cavity. Fortunately, most of the eye injuries sustained in sports are mild. A blow to the eye may initially injure the surrounding tissue and produce capillary bleeding into the tissue spaces. If the hemorrhage goes unchecked, the result may be a classic "black eye." The signs of a more serious contusion may be displayed in a subconjunctival hemorrhage or in faulty vision.

Care   Care of an eye contusion requires cold application for at least half an hour, plus a 24-hour rest period when the athlete has distorted vision. Under no circumstances should an athlete blow the nose following an acute eye injury, as hemorrhaging might be increased.

Foreign Body in the Eye

Foreign bodies in the eye are a frequent occurrence in sports and are potentially dangerous. A foreign object produces considerable pain and disability. No attempt should be made to rub the body out or to remove it with the fingers. Have the athlete close the eye until the initial pain has subsided and

---

REMOVING A FOREIGN BODY FROM THE EYE

Materials needed: One applicator stick, sterile cotton-tipped applicator, eyecup, and eyewash (solution of boric acid).

Position of the athlete: The athlete lies supine on a table.

Position of the operator: The operator should stand facing the athlete, on the side of the affected eye.

Procedure

1. Gently pull the eyelid down and lay an applicator stick crosswise at its base.
2. Have the athlete look down; then grasp the lashes and turn the lid back over the stick.
3. Holding the lid and the stick in place with one hand, use the sterile cotton swab to lift out the foreign body.

then attempt to determine if the object is in the vicinity of the upper or lower lid. Foreign bodies in the lower lid are relatively easy to remove by depressing the tissue and then wiping it with a sterile cotton applicator. Foreign bodies in the area of the upper lid are usually much more difficult to localize. Two methods may be used. In the first technique, which is quite simple, gently pull the upper eyelid over the lower lid, as the subject looks downward. This causes tears to be produced, which may flush the object down to the lower lid. If this method is unsuccessful, the second technique, described in the box above. should be used.

After the foreign particle is removed, the affected eye should be washed with a boric acid eye solution or with a commercial eyewash. Quite often after debridement there is a residual soreness, which may be alleviated by the application of petroleum jelly or some other mild ointment. If there is extreme difficulty in removing the foreign body or if it has become embedded in the eye itself, the eye should be closed and "patched" with a gauze pad, which is held in place by strips of tape. The athlete should be referred to a physician as soon as possible.

Corneal Abrasions

An athlete who gets a foreign object in the eye will usually try to rub it away. In doing so, the cornea can become abraded. The athlete will complain of severe pain and watering of the eye, photophobia, and a spasm of the orbicular muscle of the eyelid. The eye should be patched and the athlete sent to a physician. Corneal abrasion is diagnosed by application of a fluorescein strip to the abraded area, staining it a bright green.[15]

Hyphema

A blunt blow to the anterior aspect of the eye can produce a *hyphema*, which is a collection of blood within the anterior chamber. The blood settles inferiorly or may fill the entire chamber. Vision is partially or completely blocked. The coach or athletic trainer must be aware that a hyphema is a major eye injury that can lead to serious problems of the lens, choroid, or retina.[11,15]

Rupture of the Globe

A blow to the eye by an object smaller than the eye orbit produces extreme pressure that can rupture the globe. A golf ball or racquetball fits this category; however larger objects such as a tennis ball or a fist will often fracture the bony orbit before the eye is overly compressed.[13] Even if it does not cause rupture, such a force can cause internal injury that may ultimately lead to blindness.

Blowout Fracture

A blow to the face that strikes the eye and orbital ridge can cause what is commonly called a *blowout fracture* of the orbit. Because of the sudden increase in internal pressure of the eye, the very thin bone located in the inferior aspect of the orbit can fracture. Hemorrhage occurs around the inferior margins of the eye. The athlete commonly complains of double vision and pain on moving the eye. With such symptoms and signs, immediate referral to a physician is necessary.

Retinal Detachment

A blow to the athlete's eye can partially or completely separate the retina from its underlying retinal pigment epithelium. Retinal detachment is more common among athletes who have myopia (nearsightedness). Detachment is painless; however, early signs include seeing specks floating before the eye, flashes of light, or blurred vision. As the detachment progresses, the athlete complains of a "curtain" falling over the field of vision. Any symptoms of detachment must be immediately referred to an ophthalmologist.

SUMMARY

The postural defect scoliosis, which is a lateral-rotary deviation of the spine, can be progressively disabling. Spondylolisthesis and Sheuermann's disease can also cause severe pain in the thoracic spine.

Because of its mobility, the cervical spine is vulnerable to a wide range of sports injuries. The catastrophic neck injury is one that produces varying degrees of quadriplegia. The unconscious athlete should be treated as if he or she has a serious neck injury. A major means to preventing neck injury is to maximize its strength and flexibility.

The neck and upper back are subject to a number of acute noncatastrophic injuries. The most common of which are the wryneck or "stiff neck" muscle strains and neck sprains, sometimes called whiplash, and throat contusion. The most serious neck injuries are the cervical fracture and dislocation.

Brain injuries, which can be life-threatening, often result from blows that can be classified as concussion injuries. Depending on the severity of the concussion, the athlete may display signs of disorientation, dizziness, amnesia, headache, loss of consciousness, problems in concentrating, tinnitus, balance problems, automatism, and pupillary discrepancies.

Brain concussion is categorized in four grades. In grade I the athlete becomes dazed and disoriented. In grade II there is slight temporary memory loss, mental confusion, balance difficulties, tinnitus, dizziness, and headache. Grade III produces all of the symptoms present in grades I and II plus retrograde amnesia and automatism and loss of conscious for up to 4 minutes. In grade IV, the athlete has a loss of consciousness for 5 minutes or more; convulsions may accompany the other signs of concussion. The forces that are produced in a brain concussion can cause hemorrhage within the skull.

The face is subject to many different types of traumatic sports injuries. The most common are facial wounds, with lacerations ranking at the top. Less common, but usually more serious, are such injuries as jaw fractures and dislocations, dental injuries, and nasal injuries. A potentially disfiguring ear injury is the hematoma auris or cauliflower ear. The eye is also at risk; therefore, it is essential that the eye be protected against fast-moving projectiles.

REVIEW QUESTIONS AND CLASS ACTIVITIES

1. What major sports conditions occur in the immature thoracic spine?
2. Describe the on-site emergency evaluation of neck injuries.
3. Describe the causes of catastrophic neck injuries and how they may be prevented. Include in your answer practices, exercises, and protective devices.

4. Indicate the major causes and immediate care of the following acute neck injuries:
   a. wryneck
   b. whiplash
   c. throat contusion
5. Describe the signs of the cervical neck stretch, commonly called the "burner."
6. Pair off with another student, one being the coach/trainer and the other the injured athlete. The athletes simulates concussions of various grades. The coach/trainer gives an evaluation attempting to determine the grade of concussion.
7. List the on-site evaluation steps that should be taken when cerebral injuries occur.
8. Demonstrate the following procedures in evaluating a cerebral injury:
   a. questioning the athlete
   b. testing eye signs
   c. testing balance
   d. finger-to-nose test
9. List the emergency procedures for a serious neck injury.
10. Contrast a grade II to a grade III concussion.
11. What immediate care procedures should be taken for facial lacerations?
12. Discuss the immediate care procedures that should be taken when (a) a tooth is fractured and (b) when it is dislocated.
13. Describe the procedures that should be taken in a nose bleed.
14. How does one prevent a cauliflower ear?
15. The eye can sustain an extremely serious injury during some sports activities. What are the major indicators of a possible serious eye injury?

REFERENCES

1. Albright, L.: Head and neck injuries. In Smith, N.J. (editor): Sports medicine: health care for young athletes, Evanston, Ill., 1983, American Academy of Pediatrics.
2. Albright, J.P., et al.: Head and neck injuries in college football: an eight-year analysis, Am. J. Sports Med. 13:147, May/June 1985.
3. Arnheim, D.D.: Modern principles of athletic training, ed. 6, St. Louis, 1985, Times Mirror/Mosby College Publishing.
4. Castaldi, C.R.: Injuries to the teeth. In Vinger, P.F., and Hoerner, E.F. (editors): Sports injuries: the unthwarted epidemic, Boston, 1982, John Wright, PSG, Inc.
5. Cooper, D.L.: This sporting life, Emerg. Med. 11:287, 1979.
6. Diamond, G.R., et al.: Ophthalmologic injuries. In Betts, J.M., and Eichelberger, M. (editors): Symposium on pediatric and adolescent sports medicine, Clinics in sports medicine, vol. 1, no. 3, Philadelphia, Nov. 1982, W.B. Saunders Co.
7. Esterbrook, M.: Eye injuries in racket sports: a continuing problem, Phys. Sportsmed. 9:91, 1981.
8. Esterbrook, M.: Eye protection for squash and racquetball players, Phys. Sportsmed. 9:79, 1981.
9. Halling, A.H.: The importance of clinical signs and symptoms in the evaluation of facial fractures, Athl. Train. 17:102, 1982.
10. Minor facial injuries, Sports Med. Digest, 7:4, June 1985.
11. Palmer, D.J.: Traumatic hyphema, J.A.M.A. 12:254, July 1985.
12. Rockett, R.Y.: Injuries involving the head and neck: clinical anatomic aspects. In Vinger, P.F., and Hoerner, E.F. (editors): Sports injuries: the unthwarted epidemic, Boston, 1982, John Wright, PSG, Inc.
13. Sandusky, J.C.: Field evaluation of eye injuries, Ath. Train. 16:254, 1981.

14. Torg, J.S.: Life-threatening conditions. In Straus, R.H. (editor): Sports medicine and physiology, Philadelphia, 1979, W.B. Saunders Co.

15. Vinger, P.F.: Eye injuries. In Vinger, P.F., and Hoerner, E.F (editors): Sports injuries: the unthwarted epidemic, Boston, 1982, John Wright, PSG. Inc.

16. Wilson, K.S.: Injuries to the face, ear-nose-throat and airway. In Vinger, P.F., and Hoerner, E.F. (editors): Sports injuries: the unthwarted epidemic, Boston, 1982, John Wright, PSG, Inc.

ANNOTATED BIBLIOGRAPHY

Cailliet, R.: Neck and arm pain, ed. 2, Philadelphia, 1981, F.A. Davis Co.
A detailed monograph covering neck anatomy, pain diagnosis, and the more common diseases causing chronic pain.

Williams, J.G.P.: Color atlas of injury in sport, Chicago, 1980, Year Book Medical Publishers.
Excellent pictorial coverage of the more common injuries occurring to the head, face, and neck in Chapters 4 and 5.

| # THE SHOULDER COMPLEX

When you finish this chapter, you will be able to:

Identify major shoulder injuries

Provide immediate care for major shoulder injuries

Provide follow-up care for major shoulder injuries

The shoulder complex, as the name implies, is an extremely complicated region of the human body. Sports using the shoulder in repetitive activities, such as throwing, blocking, tackling, or rolling over as in tumbling, may produce a serious injury.[5]

The shoulder complex and shoulder joint are comprised of the clavicle, scapula, and humerus bones (Fig. 15-1). The major joints of this region are the sternoclavicular joint, acromioclavicular joint, coracoclavicular joint, and glenohumeral joint, more commonly called the shoulder joint (Fig. 15-2). A highly complex system of muscles, bursa, joint capsules, and ligaments is also a part of the shoulder complex[4] (Figs. 15-3 to 15-5). Movements of the shoulder include abduction, flexion, and extension[4,8] (Fig. 15-6).

PREVENTING SHOULDER INJURIES

Proper physical conditioning is of major importance in preventing many shoulder injuries. As with all preventive conditioning, a program should be directed to general body development and development of specific body areas for a given sports.[14] If a sport places extreme, sustained demands on the arms and shoulders, or if the shoulder is at risk for sudden traumatic injury, extensive conditioning must be employed. Maximal strength of both intrinsic and extrinsic muscles must be gained, along with a full range of motion in all directions.

Proper warm-up must be performed gradually before explosive arm movements are attempted. This includes gaining a general increase in body temperature followed by sport-specific stretching of selected muscles.[10]

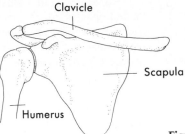

Clavicle

Scapula

Humerus

ANTERIOR

Figure 15-1

Bones of the shoulder complex.

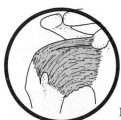

Sternoclavicular   Acromioclavicular   Coracoclavicular   Glenohumeral

Figure 15-2

Shoulder complex articulations.

Subacromial bursa

Subcoracoid bursa

Synovial capsule

Figure 15-3

Synovial capsule and bursae of the shoulder.

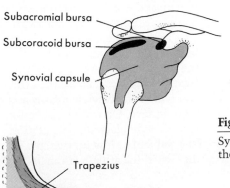

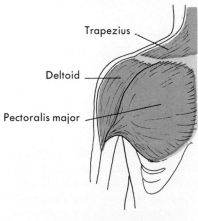

Trapezius

Deltoid

Pectoralis major

ANTERIOR VIEW

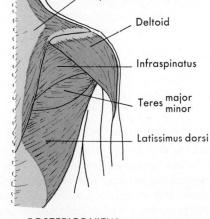

Trapezius

Deltoid

Infraspinatus

Teres major minor

Latissimus dorsi

POSTERIOR VIEW

Figure 15-4

Musculature of the shoulder.

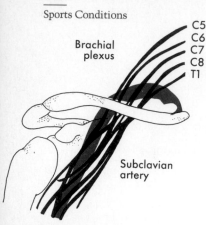

Figure 15-5

Brachial plexus and subclavian artery.

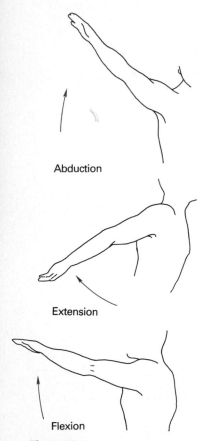

Figure 15-6

Movements of the shoulder.

All athletes in collision and contact sports should be instructed and drilled on how to fall properly. They must be taught to avoid trying to catch themselves with an outstretched arm. Performing a shoulder roll is a safer way to absorb the shock of the fall. Specialized protective equipment, such as shoulder pads, must be properly fitted to avoid some shoulder injuries in tackle football.

To avoid overuse shoulder injuries, it is essential that athletes be correctly taught in the appropriate techniques of throwing, spiking, overhead smashing, overhand serving, proper crawl and butterfly swimming strokes, and tackling and blocking.

SHOULDER COMPLEX INJURIES

Contusions and Strains

Injuries to the soft tissue in the area of the shoulder complex are common in sports.

Contusions

Blows about the shoulder that produce injury are most prevalent in collision and contact sports. The muscles with the highest incidence are those located in the upper arm and shoulder. Characteristically, bruises of this region result in pain and restricted arm movement. The subcutaneous areas of the shoulder complex are subject to bruising in contact sports.

The shoulder pointer   The most vulnerable part of the clavicle is the enlarged lateral end (acromial end), which forms a projection just before it joins the acromion process. Contusions of this type are often called *shoulder pointers*, and they may cause the athlete severe discomfort. Contusion to the lateral end of the clavicle causes a bone bruise and subsequent irritation to the bony surface. On initial inspection this injury may be mistaken for a first degree acromioclavicular separation. Management requires proper immediate first aid and follow-up therapy. In most cases these conditions are self-limiting; when the athlete is able to freely move the shoulder, he or she may return to sports activities.

Strains and Impingements

Strains about the shoulder complex are common in those sports that use the arms to overcome a resistance or propel an object. Strains to the musculature of the shoulder joint frequently affect the deltoid superficially and affect the tendons of the rotator cuff internally.

Injuries from the Throwing Motion

Strains and impingements in the shoulder region occur mainly in athletes who use repetitive throwing-type motions in activities such as baseball pitching, tennis serving and overhead smashing (Fig. 15-7), and swimming the crawl or butterfly. Quarterbacking and volleyball spiking also can cause microtraumas, which can lead to an overuse syndrome. In general, these sports actions have three phases in common: cocking, acceleration, and follow-through and deceleration phase.[16]

Figure 15-7

The tennis serve can be a major cause of overuse syndromes of the shoulder.

Cocking Phase

The cocking phase can cause anterior shoulder pain as a result of strain of the greater pectoral muscle insertion and origin of the anterior deltoid, long head of the biceps, or internal rotator muscles.

Acceleration Phase

Friction injuries causing an impingement syndrome or bursitis in the region of the scapula and fatigue injuries can result in the following:

1. Tendinitis of the greater pectoral major muscle insertion
2. Tendinitis of the coracobrachial muscle and short head of the biceps where it joints the coracoid process
3. Synovitis of the sternoclavicular or acromioclavicular joint
4. "Little League shoulder" or osteochondrosis of the upper growth region of the humerus
5. Spontaneous throwing fractures of the proximal humerus stemming from a stress fracture

Follow-through and Deceleration Phase

In this phase an injury to the posterior rotator cuff and shoulder joint capsule may occur.

Rotator cuff strains The principal rotator cuff tendon injured is that of the supraspinatus muscle (Fig. 15-8). The mechanism of shoulder strains occurs mainly as the result of a violent pull to the arm, an abnormal rotation, or a fall on the outstretched arm, tearing or even rupturing tendinous tissue. The throwing mechanism can produce a variety of abnormal stresses to the soft tissues of the shoulder, for example, impingement, overstretching, torsion, subluxation, and entrapment of nerves and blood vessels. Besides throwing,

The rotator cuff consists of the supraspinatus, infraspinatus, teres minor, and subscapular muscles.

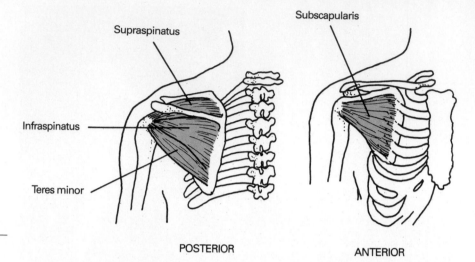

Figure 15-8

Rotator cuff muscles.

swimming in freestyle and butterfly events also place great stress on the shoulders' rotating mechanisms and can lead to an acute or chronic injury.

Rotator cuff impingement injury   The continual use of the arm or arms above the horizontal plane in an athletic endeavor has been known to lead to an impingement syndrome (Fig. 15-9). The major reason for impingement is the reduction of space through which the supraspinatus muscle can pass.[3,10]

The athlete with a rotator cuff injury may complain of the shoulder joint aching during activity or after activity. There also may be some restriction of shoulder motion (see Fig. 15-6).

Care   If the rotator cuff impingement injury is determined in its early stages, conservative care will usually be enough. This may include rest, coaching for proper arm usage, and superficial therapy such as cold or heat. Exercise rehabilitation should be concerned with full range of joint motion and strengthening of weak shoulder complex musculature.[10] If this condition is allowed to progress beyond its early stages, surgery may be necessary.

Proper coaching methods to prevent shoulder injuries must be undertaken for sports that involve throwing or throwinglike motions. Gradual warm-up should emphasize slow stretching and maximizing the extensibility of all major shoulder muscles. Strengthening shoulder muscles should be general at first and then emphasize the external and internal rotator muscles for good shoulder joint control.

Athletes displaying early symptoms of shoulder impingement must modify their arm movements. A swimmer may have to decrease his or her distance or change to a different stroke. Those athletes who throw or who perform throwinglike motions may have to decrease their force or develop a different technique.

Athletes experiencing shoulder pain and inflammation might benefit from cold application after workouts. This could be in the form of ice massage of an ice chip pack.

Heat of any form should be avoided after workouts. However, heat may be beneficial before workouts or at other times. Under the direction of a physi-

Figure 15-9

The butterfly stroke can be a major cause of the rotator cuff impingement syndrome.

cian, the trainer may use both ultrasound to relieve inflammation and transcutaneous electrical nerve stimulation (TENS) to relieve pain from the shoulder impingement. Besides this, the physician may prescribe an oral anti-inflammatory drug for a short period of time.

Sprains

Sternoclavicular Sprain

Sternoclavicular sprain (Fig. 15-10) is a relatively uncommon occurrence in sports, but occasionally one may result from one of the various traumas affecting the shoulder complex.

The mechanism of the injury can be initiated by an indirect force transmitted through the upper arm to the shoulder joint by a direct force, such as from a blow that strikes the poorly padded clavicle or by twisting or torsion of

Sprains can occur in the three major joints of the shoulder complex:
  Sternoclavicular joint
  Acromioclavicular joint
  Glenohumeral joint

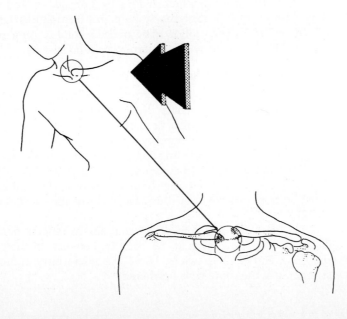

Figure 15-10

Sternoclavicular sprain and dislocation.

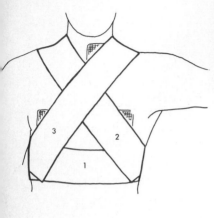

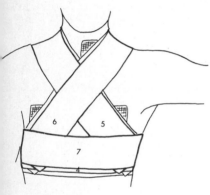

Figure 15-11

Sternoclavicular
immobilization.

STERNOCLAVICULAR IMMOBILIZATION

Materials needed: A felt pad of 1/4-inch (0.63 cm) thickness, cut to a circumference of 4 inches (10 cm), a 3-inch (7.5 cm) roll of elastic tape, two gauze pads, and tape adherent.

Position of the athlete: Reduction of the most common sternoclavicular dislocation is performed by traction with the athlete's arm abducted. Traction and abduction are maintained by an assistant while the immobilization taping is applied.

Position of the operator: The operator stands on the affected side of the athlete.

Procedure: Fig. 15-11 illustrates the proper procedure for sternoclavicular immobilization taping.

a backward elevated arm. Depending on the direction of force, the medial end of the clavicle can be displaced upward and forward, either posteriorly or anteriorly. Generally, the clavicle is displaced upward and forward.

Trauma resulting in a sprain to the sternoclavicular joint can be described in three degrees. The *first degree* is characterized by little pain and disability with some point tenderness but with no joint deformity. A *second degree* sprain displays subluxation of the sternoclavicular joint with visible deformity, pain, swelling, point tenderness, and an inability to abduct the shoulder in full range or to bring the arm across the chest, indicating disruption of stabilizing ligaments. The *third degree*, which is the most severe, presents a picture of complete dislocation with gross displacement of the clavicle at its sternal junction, swelling, and disability, indicating complete rupture of the supporting ligaments. If the clavicle is displaced backward, pressure may be placed on the blood vessels, esophagus, or trachea, causing a life or death situation.

Care Care of this condition is based on returning the displaced clavicle to its original position, which is done by a physician, and immobilizing it at that point so that healing may take place. Immobilization is usually maintained for 3 to 5 weeks, followed by graded reconditioning exercises. There is a high incidence of recurrence of sternoclavicular sprains.

Acromioclavicular Sprain

The acromioclavicular joint is extremely vulnerable to sprains among active sports participants, especially in collision sports. A program of prevention should entail proper fitting of protective equipment, conditioning to provide a balance of strength and flexibility to the entire shoulder complex, and teaching proper techniques of falling and the use of the arm in sports.

The mechanism of an acromioclavicular sprain is most often induced by a direct blow to the tip of the shoulder, pushing the acromion process downward, or by an upward force exerted against the long axis of the upper arm (Fig. 15-12).

The *first degree* acromioclavicular sprain reflects point tenderness and discomfort on movement at the junction between the acromion process and the other end of the clavicle. There is no deformity, indicating only a mild stretching of the supportive ligaments.

A *second degree* sprain indicates rupture of the ligaments supporting the clavicle to the acromion process. There is a definite displacement and prominence of the lateral end of the clavicle when compared to the unaffected side. In this moderate sprain there is point tenderness on palpation of the injury site, and the athlete is unable to fully abduct through a full range of motion or to bring the arm completely across the chest.[7,17] **NOTE:** The second degree sprain may require surgery to restore stability.[2]

Although occurring infrequently, the *third degree* injury is considered a dislocation, involving rupture of the supporting ligaments and major bony displacement.[15] The mechanics of the third degree subluxation/dislocation is a downward and outward force on the acromion process away from the clavicle. In such an injury there is gross deformity and prominence of the outer clavicular head, severe pain, loss of movement, and instability of the shoulder complex.[2,19]

Immediate and follow-up care Immediate care of the acromioclavicular sprain involves three basic procedures: (1) cold and pressure to control local hemorrhage, (2) stabilization of the joint by a sling and swathe bandage, and (3) referral to a physician for definitive diagnosis and treatment. Complete severance of the major supportive ligament may demand corrective surgery. Most second degree sprains require 4 to 6 weeks for fibrous healing to take place, and an extended period is needed for the restoration of general shoulder strength and mobility. A regimen of superficial moist heat will aid in resolving soreness. Movement in the pain-free range will be restored after the use of ice packs.[7]

Rehabilitative exercise is concerned with reconditioning the shoulder complex to the state it was before the injury. Full strength, flexibility, endurance, and function must be redeveloped. Protective taping may help support the first degree injury.

Glenohumeral Joint Sprain

Sprains of the shoulder joint involve injury to ligaments and the joint capsule. The pathological process of the sprain is comparable to that of an internal strain and, along with ligament and capsule injury, often affects the rotator cuff muscles.

The cause of this injury is the same as that which produces dislocation. Anterior capsular sprains occur when the arm is forced upward and sideward, such as making an arm tackle in football. Sprains also can occur from external rotation of the arm.

The athlete complains of pain on arm movement, especially when the sprain mechanism is reproduced. There also may be decreased range of motion and pain when the shoulder joint is palpated.

Immediate and follow-up care Care after acute trauma to the shoulder joint requires the use of a cold pack for 24 to 48 hours, elastic or adhesive compression, rest, and immobilization by means of a sling. After hemorrhage has subsided, a program of gentle mobilization following cold application is performed. Ultrasound and massage may also be applied by the trainer. Once the shoulder can execute a full range of movement without signs of pain, a resistance exercise program should be initiated. Any traumatic injury to the shoul-

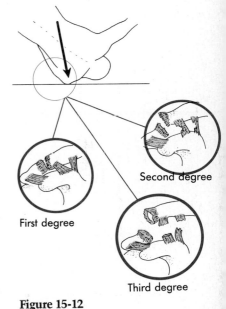

First degree

Second degree

Third degree

Figure 15-12

Mechanism of an acromioclavicular sprain.

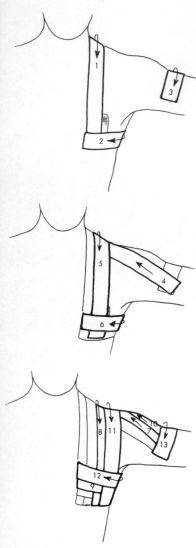

Figure 15-13

Protective acromioclavicular
taping.

PROTECTIVE ACROMIOCLAVICULAR TAPING

Protective acromioclavicular taping is designed to stabilize the acromioclavicular articulation in proper alignment and still allow normal movement of the shoulder complex.

Materials needed: One 1/4-inch (0.63 cm) thick felt pad, one roll of 2-inch (5 cm) adhesive tape, tape adherent, a 2-inch (5 cm) gauze pad, and a 3-inch (7.5 cm) elastic bandage.

Position of the athlete: The athlete sits in a chair with the affected arm resting in a position of abduction.

Position of the operator: The operator stands facing the athlete's abducted arm.

Procedure: Fig. 15-13 illustrates the proper procedure for applying the protective acromioclavicular taping.

der joint can lead to a chronic inflammation, which is encouraged when there is an absence of shoulder movement.

Subluxations and Dislocations

Dislocation of the humeral head is second only to finger dislocations in order of incidence in sports. When the shoulder joint is placed in an extreme range of motion, it is highly susceptible to dislocation. The most common kind of displacement is that occurring anteriorly (Fig. 15-14). Of those dislocations caused by direct trauma, 85% to 90% recur.[11]

Anterior Glenohumeral Dislocation

The anterior glenohumeral dislocation is caused when an arm is in a sideward or abducted position and is externally rotated. An arm tackle or an abnormal force to an arm that is executing a throw can cause a dislocation. Less often a fall or inward rotation and abduction of an arm may result in a dislocation.

The athlete with an anterior dislocation outwardly displays a flattened deltoid contour. Feeling the arm pit of the affected arm will reveal an obvious prominence of the humeral head.[12] The athlete carries the affected arm in slight abduction and external rotation and is unable to touch the opposite shoulder with the hand of the affected arm. There is often severe pain and disability.

In an anterior glenohumeral dislocation, the head of the humerus is forced out of the joint capsule in a forward direction and then forced upward to rest under the coracoid process. There also may be torn muscles and profuse bleeding. Additional complications may arise if the head of the humerus comes into contact with and injures the major complex, the brachial nerves and blood vessels (see Fig. 15-5).

Care Care of the shoulder dislocation requires immediate reduction by a physician, control of the hemorrhage by cold packs, immobilization, and the start of muscle reconditioning as soon as possible. The question often arises as to whether a first-time dislocation should be reduced or should receive medical attention. *Physicians generally agree that a dislocation may be associated with a fracture and nerve injury, and, therefore, it is beyond the scope of a coach's or athletic trainer's responsibilities.* Recurrent dislocations do not present the same complications or attendant dangers as the acute type; however, risk is always involved.[13]

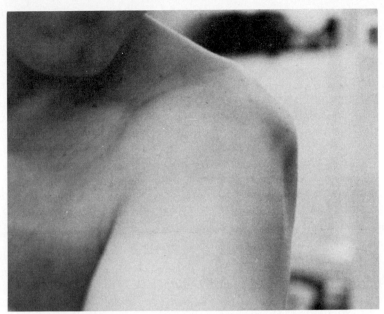

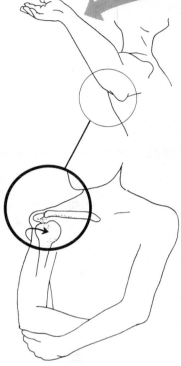

Figure 15-14

Anterior shoulder subluxation and dislocation.

After the dislocation has been reduced, immobilization and muscle rehabilitation are carried out. Immobilization takes place for about 3 weeks after reduction, with the arm maintained in a relaxed position of adduction and internal rotation.[13] While immobilized, the athlete is instructed to perform isometric exercises for strengthening the internal and external rotator muscles. After immobilization, the strengthening program progresses from isometrics to resisting rubber tubing and then to dumbbells and other resistance devices. A major criterion for the athlete's return to sports competition is that there must be internal and external rotation strength equal to 20% of the athlete's body weight.[13]

The Unstable Shoulder: Recurrent Subluxation and Dislocation

Recurrent subluxation   Subluxation of the shoulder usually begins with one traumatic event that places an abnormal stress on the joint or by repeated less forceful movements that stress the joint capsule.[20] Pitching, tennis serving, and crawl swimming may produce anterior capsular complaints, whereas swimming the backstroke or backhand stroking in tennis may cause problems with the posterior capsule. As the articular capsule becomes increasingly lax, more mobility of the glenohumeral head is allowed, eventually damaging the glenoid lip. With this damage and stretching of supportive ligamentous and tendinous structures, subluxation and dislocation can occur.[18]

When subluxation occurs, the athlete may complain that the shoulder felt like it came out of its socket, followed by sudden pain along the arm and numbness in the fingers.[17,18] The pain and numbness may last for several minutes, followed by extreme weakness of the entire arm.

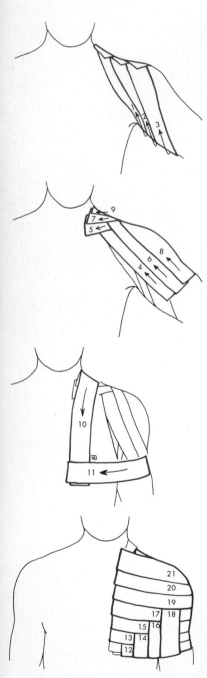

Figure 15-15

Taping for shoulder support
and restraint.

In conservative management, the shoulder is immobilized with a sling and swathe for 5 to 6 weeks. After immobilization and a decrease in inflammation, an exercise program is instituted emphasizing the rotator cuff, rhomboid, latissimus dorsi, and serratus anterior muscles.[18] A gradual program of strength and flexibility development is carried out over a 4- to 6-week period, followed by a slow return to sports activity over a period of 6 weeks.[18]

If a conservative approach is unsuccessful, surgery is usually performed. After surgery, a strength and development program is instituted.[9]

Recurrent shoulder subluxation and dislocation reduction With the permission of the team physician, the coach or athletic trainer can assist the athlete in reducing a recurrent shoulder subluxation or dislocation. The safest method is the *weight on the wrist technique*. In this method the athlete lies between two tables, with the head resting on one table and the body on the other. The affected arm extends between the two tables with a 5- to 10-pound weight tied to the wrist. As the muscles of the shoulder relax, a spontaneous reduction occurs.

Shoulder protection Every protection should be given to the athlete who may be prone to recurrent dislocations. Restraint by means of adhesive taping and a harness appliance should be used during any sports activity. Repeated dislocations continue to stretch the supporting structures and damage the articulating hyaline cartilage, which may eventually result in an arthritic condition.

Shoulder Bursitis

The shoulder joint is subject to subacute chronic inflammatory conditions resulting from trauma or from overuse in an abnormal fashion. An injury of this type may develop from a direct blow, a fall on the outstretched hand, or the stress incurred in throwing an object. Inflammation can occur in the shoulder, extensively affecting the soft tissues surrounding it or specifically affecting various bursae (Fig. 15-16). The bursa that is most often injured is the subacromial bursa, which lies underneath the deltoid muscle and the articular capsule and extends under the acromion process. The apparent pathological process in these conditions is fibrous buildup and fluid accumulation developing from a constant inflammatory state.

Recognition of these conditions follows the same course as in other shoulder afflictions. The athlete is unable to move the shoulder, especially in abduction; rotation and muscle atrophy also may ensue because of disuse.

TAPING FOR SHOULDER SUPPORT AND RESTRAINT

This taping is designed to support the soft tissues of the shoulder complex and to restrain the arm from abducting more than 90 degrees.

Materials needed: One roll of 2-inch (5 cm) tape, a 2-inch (5 cm) gauze pad, a cotton pad, tape adherent, and a 3-inch (7.5 cm) elastic bandage.

Position of the athlete: The athlete stands with the affected arm flexed at the elbow and the shoulder internally rotated.

Position of the operator: The operator stands facing the affected arm.

Procedure: Fig. 15-15 illustrates the proper taping procedure for shoulder support and restraint.

Care Care of low-grade inflammatory conditions must be initiated somewhat empirically. In some instances both the superficial heat from moist pads or infrared rays and the deep heat of diathermy or ultrasound are beneficial. In other instances heat may be aggravating, so cold applications by cold pack may be more useful. Whatever the mode of treatment, the athlete must maintain a consistent program of exercise, with the emphasis placed on regaining a full range of motion, so that muscle contractures and adhesions do not immobilize the joint.

Fractures of the Shoulder Complex

Fractures in the shoulder complex can be caused by a direct blow on the bone or indirectly by a fall on either an outstretched arm or the point of the shoulder.

Clavicular Fractures

Clavicular fractures (Fig. 15-17) are one of the most frequent fractures in sports. Over 80% occur in the middle third of the clavicle, which lacks ligamentous support.

Clavicular fractures are caused by either a direct blow or a transmitted force resulting from a fall on the outstretched arm. In junior and senior high school athletes these fractures are usually the greenstick type.

The athlete with a fractured clavicle usually supports the arm on the injured side and tilts his or her head toward that side, with the chin turned to the opposite side. On inspection the injured clavicle appears a little lower than the unaffected side. Palpation may also reveal swelling and mild deformity.

Care The clavicular fracture is cared for immediately by applying a sling and swathe bandage and by treating the athlete for shock, if necessary. The athlete is then referred to a physician, who in most instances will perform an x-ray examination of the area and then apply a shoulder figure-8 wrapping that will stabilize the shoulder in an upward and backward position.

UPPER ARM CONDITIONS

The upper arm can sustain varied stress and trauma, depending on the nature of the sport. Crushing blows may be directed to the area by collision and contact sports; severe strain can be imposed by the throwing sports and sports that afford muscle resistance, such as gymnastics.

Contusions

Contusions of the upper arm are frequent in contact sports. Although any muscle of the upper arm is subject to bruising, the area most often affected is the lateral aspect, primarily the brachial muscle and portions of the triceps and biceps muscles.

Bruises to the upper arm area can be particularly handicapping, especially if the radial nerve is contused through forceful contact with the humerus, producing transitory paralysis and consequently the inability to use the extensor muscles of the forearm.

Care Cold and pressure should be applied from 1 to 24 hours after injury, followed by cryotherapy or superficial heat therapy and massage. In most

Figure 15-16

Sports such as pole vaulting place extreme stress on the arm and shoulder complex; such overuse can lead to joint bursitis or inflammation of the synovium.

Figure 15-17

Clavicular fracture and associated brachial blood vessels and nerves.

Over 80% of all fractures to the clavicle occur in the middle third.

cases this condition responds rapidly to treatment, usually within a few days. If swelling and irritation last more than 2 or 3 weeks, *myositis ossificans* may have been stimulated, and massage must be stopped and protection afforded the athlete during sports participation.

Strains

Acute and chronic strains are common in the arm. The muscles most commonly affected are the biceps, triceps, and pectoral muscles. Two conditions that are unique to the arm area are bicipital tenosynovitis and biceps brachii rupture.

Bicipital Tenosynovitis

Tenosynovitis of the long head of the biceps muscle is common among athletes who execute a throwing movement as part of their event. It is more prevalent among pitchers, tennis players, and javelin throwers, for whom the repeated forced internal rotations of the upper arm may produce a chronic inflammatory condition in the vicinity of the synovial sheath of the long head of the biceps muscle. A complete rupture of the transverse ligament, which holds the biceps in its groove, may take place, or a constant inflammation may result in degenerative scarring or a subluxated tendon.

The athlete may complain of an ache in the front or the side of the shoulder; deep palpation reveals point tenderness in the region of the bicipital tendon.

Care Such conditions are best cared for by a period of complete rest for 1 to 2 weeks, with daily applications of cryotherapy or ultrasound. After the initial aching is gone, a gradual program of reconditioning can begin.

Biceps Brachii Ruptures

Ruptures of the biceps brachii (Fig. 15-18) occur mainly in gymnasts who are engaged in power moves. The rupture commonly takes place near the origin of the muscle. The athlete usually hears a resounding snap and feels a sudden, intense pain at the point of injury. A protruding bulge may appear near the middle of the biceps. When asked to flex the elbow joint of the injured arm, the gymnast displays a definite weakness. Care should include immediately applying a cold pack to control hemorrhage, placing the arm in a sling, and referring the athlete to the physician. Surgical repair is usually indicated.

Fractures

Fractures of the humeral shaft (Fig. 15-19) happen occasionally in sports, usually as the result of a direct blow or a fall on the arm.

The pathological process is characteristic of most uncomplicated fractures, except that there may be a tendency for the radial nerve, which encircles the humeral shaft, to be severed by jagged bone edges, resulting in radial nerve paralysis and causing wrist drop and inability to perform forearm supination.

Recognition of this injury requires immediate application of a splint, treatment for shock, and referral to a physician. The athlete will be out of competition for approximately 3 to 4 months.

Figure 15-18

Performing the iron cross on the rings can produce a biceps brachii rupture.

Fracture of the Upper Humerus

Fractures of the upper humerus (Fig. 15-20) pose considerable danger to nerves and vessels of that area. They result from a direct blow, a dislocation, or the impact received when falling onto the outstretched arm. Various parts of the end of the humerus may be involved. Such a fracture may be mistaken for a shoulder dislocation.

It may be difficult to recognize a fracture of the upper humerus by visual inspection alone; therefore, x-ray examination gives the only positive proof. Some of the more prevalent signs that may be present are pain, inability to move the arm, swelling, point tenderness, and discoloration of the superficial-tissue. Because of the proximity of the axillary blood vessels and the brachial plexus, a fracture to the upper end of the humerus may result in severe hemorrhaging or paralysis.

Care A suspected fracture of this type warrants immediate support with a sling and swathe bandage and referral to a physician. Incapacitation may range from 2 to 6 months.

Epiphyseal Fracture

Epiphyseal fracture of the head of the humerus (Fig. 15-21) is much more common in the young athlete than is a bone fracture. As epiphyseal injury in the shoulder region occurs most frequently in individuals 10 years of age and younger.[15] It is caused by a direct blow or by an indirect force traveling along the length of the axis of the humerus. This condition causes shortening of the arm, disability, swelling, point tenderness, and pain. There also may be a false joint. This type of injury should be suspected when such signs appear in young athletes. Initial treatment should include splinting and immediate referral to a physician. Healing is initiated rapidly; immobilization is necessary for only about 3 weeks. The main danger of such an injury is the possibility of damage to the epiphyseal growth centers of the humerus.

REHABILITATION OF THE SHOULDER COMPLEX

The shoulder complex and especially the glenohumeral joint have a tendency to become highly restricted in motion after injury or immobilization. In some cases a serious injury and immobilization lead to contractures and a tendency to develop fibrosis of the articular capsule. To prevent these problems, pain-free mobility is started as soon as possible without aggravating the injury.

Shoulder rehabilitation is highly complicated and depends on the nature of the injury and whether surgery has been performed. In general, rehabilitation progresses through early, intermediate, and advanced exercise stages.[1] Types of exercise can vary from isometrics, isotonics, isokinetics, stretching, and manual resistance.[6] The following exercises may be employed, depending upon the nature of injury.

Ball Squeeze

The athlete squeezes a tennis ball while performing pain-free shoulder movements in a sequence from abduction to flexion to external rotation and then moving to adduction, extension, and internal rotation (see Fig. 16-36). This exercise is performed twice daily, ten times in each direction.

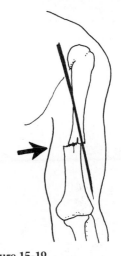

Figure 15-19

Humeral shaft fracture.

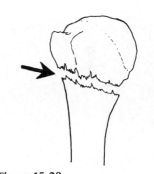

Figure 15-20

Fracture of the upper humerus.

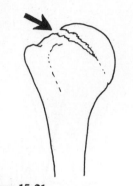

Figure 15-21

Epiphyseal fracture.

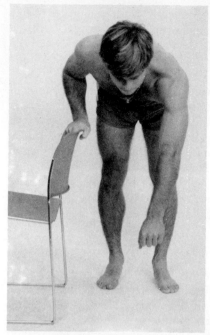

Figure 15-22

Codman's pendular exercise.

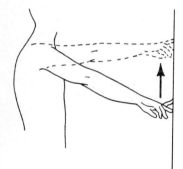

Figure 15-23

Finger wall climb.

Codman's Pendular Exercise

While bent over with the arm fully extended and the shoulder relaxed, the athlete moves the shoulder first in small circles in each direction and then in straight-line movements of flexion-extension and adduction-abduction. The distance of the swing is gradually increased. Exercises are performed twice daily with ten movements in each direction (Fig. 15-22).

Finger Wall Climb

Standing an arm's distance away from a wall, the athlete finger-walks up until there is pain. The first walking occurs facing the wall and then while the athlete stands sideways to the wall (Fig. 15-23). This is performed two or three times, twice daily.

Shoulder Wheel

The shoulder wheel provides an excellent means of gaining both shoulder flexibility and strength. The athlete stands sideways to the wheel and performs ten repetitions in each direction (Fig. 15-24). The exercises are repeated two or three times and performed three or four times a week.

Self-stretching

To stretch the posterior capsule, the athlete moves the arm to 90 degrees of flexion and with the opposite hand pulls the elbow into horizontal adduc-

Figure 15-24

Reconditioning with the shoulder wheel.

tion.[14] The exercise is performed twice daily, two or three times, holding each stretch for 20 to 30 seconds.

Next, the inferior capsule is stretched by placing the arm overhead as far as possible with the elbow flexed. The other hand grasps the opposite elbow to initiate the stretch[14] (Fig. 15-25).

Dumbbell Exercises

Strengthening the supraspinatus muscle entails having the athlete sit with the arms abducted 90 degrees, horizontally flexed 30 degrees, and internally rotated. The athlete then lifts and lowers a dumbbell in each hand. The exercise is performed ten times and repeated two or three times, three or four times a week.

To exercise the infraspinatus and teres minor muscles, the athlete lies on the side with the arm close to the body and the elbow bent 90 degrees. From a position of internal rotation, the athlete externally rotates the arm as far as possible (Fig. 15-26). This exercise is repeated ten times for two or three sets, three or four times a week.

To exercise the subscapularis muscle, the athlete lies supine, with the arm close to the side and the elbow flexed 90 degrees. From a position of full external rotation, the dumbbell is internally rotated as far as possible. The exercise is performed ten times for two or three sets, three or four times a week.

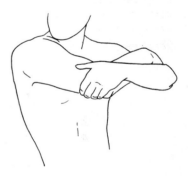

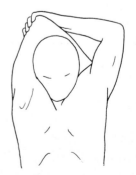

Bench Presses

The athlete progresses slowly from supporting a barbell or Universal weight in a "locked-out" bench press position (Fig. 15-27). Gradually, the athlete begins to bend the elbows until a press can be performed from a full range of motion. Ten presses are performed for two or three sets, three times a week.

Figure 15-25

Self-stretching.

Upright Rowing

A barbell is grasped in its center with both hands raised to a position underneath the athlete's chin (Fig. 15-28). The exercise is performed ten times for two or three sets, three times a week.

Light-resistance Shrugs

The athlete exercises the upper trapezius muscle by performing shrugs against a light dumbbell resistance. **NOTE**: The weight should not be allowed to hang loosely, which strains the acromioclavicular joint. Light-resistance shrugs are performed five to ten times, twice daily (Fig. 15-29). This exercise should take the shoulder from an anterior position to elevation (shrugs) and then to a posterior position.

Upright Rowing with Light Resistance

For strengthening the anterior deltoid muscle, the athlete performs upright rowing against a light resistance. Each exercise is performed for five to ten repetitions, twice daily.

Figure 15-26

Dumbbell exercises.

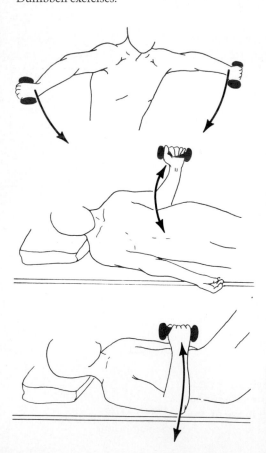

Figure 15-27

Bench presses.

Push-ups

Push-ups are an excellent way to strengthen the shoulder complex, especially the anterior aspect of the shoulder and chest. Push-ups are performed in two or three sets for ten repetitions, three or four times a week (Fig. 15-30).

Dips and Pull-ups

Parallel bar dips and horizontal bar pull-ups are also excellent intermediate exercises for shoulder rehabilitation. As with the other exercises, they should be performed in two or three sets of ten repetitions, three or four times a week.

SUMMARY

The shoulder complex is a highly complicated anatomical region that can sustain numerous sports injuries. Preventing shoulder complex injuries re-

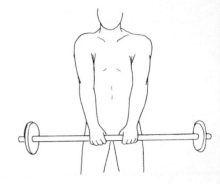

Figure 15-28

Upright rowing.

Figure 15-29

Dumbbell shoulder shrugs.

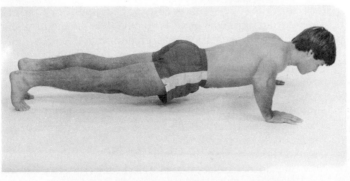

Figure 15-30

Push-ups.

quires general body conditioning as well as specific conditioning for the demands of an individual sport. Proper warm-up and learning how to fall can also help to prevent shoulder complex injuries.

Overuse injuries to the shoulder commonly stem from faulty form in pitching, tennis serving, overhead smashing, and swimming the crawl or butterfly stroke.

Contusions commonly occur to the soft tissue surrounding the shoulder complex as well as to the clavicle region. Strains and impingements are common in those sports that use the arms to overcome resistances or to propel objects. The rotator cuff muscles are common sites for strains and impingements. Sprains of the shoulder complex can occur at the sternoclavicular, acromioclavicular, and shoulder joints.

Shoulder joint dislocation is second only to finger dislocations in order of incidence in sports. The most common dislocation is the anterior glenohumeral dislocation. The athlete displays a flattened deltoid contour and carries the arm in slight abduction and external rotation.

The shoulder joint is also subject to the chronic problems of bursitis. Bursitis can stem from overuse or a sudden strain. The most often injured is the subacromial bursa that lies underneath the deltoid muscle and articular capsule and extends under the acromion process.

Fractures of the shoulder complex region can be caused directly by a blow to the bone or indirectly by a fall on either an outstretched arm or the point of a shoulder. The most prevalent fracture occurs to the clavicle. The scapula is fractured less often.

Injuries to the upper arm include contusions, strains, and fractures. A relatively common chronic strain site is the long head of the biceps and is called bicipital tenosynovitis. This tendon also can become ruptured. Fracture of the upper humeral shaft occurs only occasionally in sports, usually from a direct blow or a fall on the outstretched arm. A more common fracture site is the epiphysis of the humeral head in young athletes.

REVIEW QUESTIONS AND CLASS ACTIVITIES

1. How may shoulder injuries be prevented? Include in your answer conditioning and preventive equipment.
2. What are the usual causes of shoulder complex overuse injuries? How may some be related to improper throwing techniques?
3. Describe the shoulder point injury.
4. How may the superspinatus muscle be injured? List the stages of injury.
5. Differentiate the signs of a sternoclavicular and acromioclavicular sprain.
6. Describe the appearance of a glenohumeral sprain and differentiate it from a dislocation.
7. Why may a first-time shoulder joint dislocation be associated with a fracture?
8. Identify the reasons why glenohumeral subluxations and dislocations tend to recur. How are they commonly cared for?
9. Why does the subacromial bursa develop chronic inflammation? Can this condition be prevented?
10. Discuss the symptoms and signs of a fractured clavicle.
11. How may an athlete acquire bicipital tenosynovitis? How does this condition lead to a ruptured biceps tendon?

12. Develop an exercise rehabilitation program for:
    a. rotator cuff injury
    b. glenohumeral dislocation
    c. acromioclavicular sprain
13. Invite an athletic trainer or equipment manager to explain the difference between football shoulder pads and how they are fitted.

REFERENCES

1. Allman, F.L.: Exercise in sports medicine. In Basmagian, J.V. (editor): Therapeutic exercise, ed. 3, Baltimore, 1978, The Williams & Wilkins Co.
2. Bowers, K.D.: Treatment of acromioclavicular sprains in athletes, Phys. Sportsmed. 11:79, Jan. 1983.
3. Brunet, M.E., Haddad, R.J., and Porche, E.B.: Rotator cuff impingement syndromes in sports, Phys. Sportsmed. 10:86, Dec. 1982.
4. Carmichael, S.W., and Hart, D.L.: Anatomy of the shoulder joint, J. Ortho. Sports Phys. Ther. 6:255, Jan./Feb. 1985.
5. Duda, M.: Prevention and treatment of throwing-arm injuries, Phys. Sportsmed. 13:181, June 1985.
6. Einhorn, A.R.: Shoulder rehabilitation: equipment modifications, J. Ortho. Sports Phys. Ther. 6:247, Jan./Feb. 1985.
7. Gieck, J.: Injuries to the acromioclavicular joint—mechanisms, diagnosis, and treatment, Ath. Train. 14(1):22, 1979.
8. Hart, D.L., and Carmichael, S.T.: Biomechanics of the shoulder, J. Ortho. Sports Phys. Ther. 6(4):229, Jan./Feb. 1985.
9. Hastings, D.E., and Coughlin, L.P.: Recurrent subluxation of the glenohumeral joint, Am. J. Sports Med. 9:352, 1981.
10. Hawkins, R.J., and Hobeika, P.E.: Impingement syndrome in the athletic shoulder, Symposium on injuries to the shoulder in the athlete, Clinics in sports medicine, vol. 2, no. 2, Philadelphia, July 1983, W.B. Saunders Co.
11. Henry, J.H., and Genung, J.A.: Natural history of glenohumeral dislocation—revisited, Am. J. Sports Med. 10(3):135, 1982.
12. Henry, J.H.: How I manage dislocated shoulder, Phys. Sportsmed. 12:65, Sept. 1984.
13. Matsen, F.A., and Zuckerman, J.D.: Anterior glenohumeral instability, Symposium on injuries to the shoulder in the athlete, Clinics in sports medicine, vol. 2, no. 2, Philadelphia, July 1983, W.B. Saunders Co.
14. Moynes, D.R.: Prevention of injury to the shoulder through exercises and therapy, Symposium on injuries to the shoulder in the athlete, Clinics in sports medicine, vol. 2, no. 2, Philadelphia, July 1983, W.B. Saunders Co.
15. O'Donoghue, D.H.: Treatment of injuries to athletes, ed. 4, Philadelphia, 1984, W.B. Saunders, Co.
16. Richardson, A.B.: Overuse syndrome in baseball, tennis, gymnastics and swimming, Symposium on injuries to the shoulder in the athlete, Clinics in sports medicine, vol. 2, no. 2, Philadelphia, July 1983, W.B. Saunders Co.
17. Strauss, M.B., et al.: The shrugged-off shoulder: a comparison of patients with recurrent shoulder subluxations and dislocations, Phys. Sportsmed. 11:85, March 1983.
18. Warren, R.F.: Subluxation of the shoulder in athletes, Symposium on injuries to the shoulder in the athlete, Clinics in sports medicine, vol. 2, no. 2, Philadelphia, July 1983, W.B. Saunders Co.
19. Wickiewicz, T.L.: Acromioclavicular and sternoclavicular injuries, Symposium on injuries to the shoulder in the athlete, Clinics in sports medicine, vol. 2, no. 2, Philadelphia, July 1983, W.B. Saunders Co.
20. Zarins, B., and Rowe, C.R.: Current concepts in the diagnosis and treatment of shoulder instability in athletes, Med. Sci. Sports Exer. 16:444, Oct. 1984.

ANNOTATED BIBLIOGRAPHY

Cailliet, R.: Shoulder pain, ed. 2, Philadelphia, 1981, F.A. Davis Co.

Detailed coverage of the major causes of shoulder pain including functional anatomy, pain caused by trauma, referred pain, and rotator cuff tears.

Jobe, F.W. (editor): Symposium on injuries to the shoulder in the athlete, Clinics in sports medicine, vol. 2, no. 2, Philadelphia, July 1983, W.B. Saunders Co.

An 18-chapter monograph on shoulder injuries caused by sports participation. Chapters include causes of injury, basic anatomy and biomechanics related to selected sports, and a discussion of the most common injuries in sports.

Chapter 16

THE ELBOW, FOREARM, WRIST, AND HAND

When you finish this chapter, you will be able to:

Identify common elbow, forearm, wrist, and hand injuries

Provide immediate care of elbow, forearm, wrist, and hand injuries

The upper limb consisting of the elbow, forearm, wrist, and hand is second to the lower limb in the number of sports injuries incurred. Due to how it is used and its relative exposure, the upper limb is highly prone to numerous acute and overuse conditions.

THE ELBOW JOINT

Although not as complicated as the knee or shoulder, the elbow still ranks as one of the more complex joints in the human body. It is composed of three bones; the humerus, the radius, and the ulna (Figs. 16-1 to 16-4). The elbow joint allows for the movements of flexion and extension. The radioulnar joint, which allows for forearm pronation and supination, is formed by the annular ligament and the head of the radius resting close to the rounded end of the humerus (capitulum).

Injuries to the Elbow Region

The two most common mechanisms of elbow injury:
Throwing
Falling on the outstretched hand

The elbow is subject to injury in sports because of its broad range of motion, weak lateral bone arrangement, and relative exposure to soft tissue damage in the vicinity of the joint.

Contusions, Strains, and Sprains

Contusions   Because of its lack of padding and its general vulnerability, the elbow often becomes contused in collision and contact sports. Bone bruises arise from a deep penetration or a succession of blows to the sharp projections of the elbow. A contusion of the elbow may swell rapidly after an irritation of the olecranon bursa or the synovial membrane and should be treated immediately with cold and pressure for at least 24 hours. If the injury is se-

327

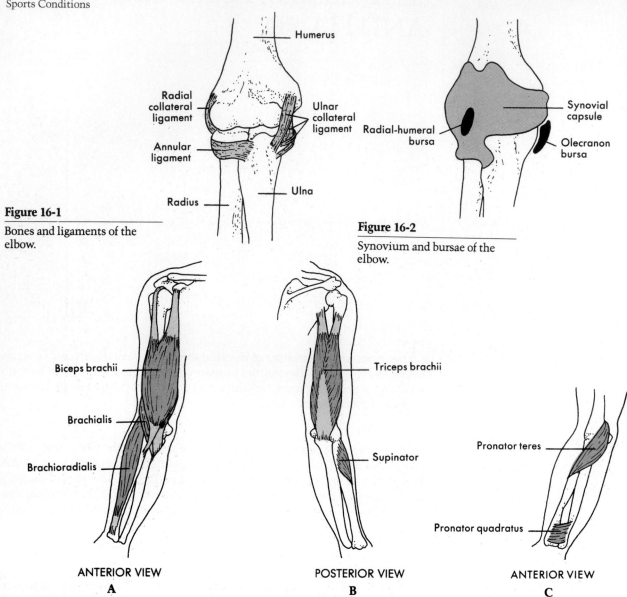

Figure 16-1

Bones and ligaments of the elbow.

Figure 16-2

Synovium and bursae of the elbow.

ANTERIOR VIEW
A

POSTERIOR VIEW
B

ANTERIOR VIEW
C

Figure 16-3

Muscles of the elbow joint. **A,** Anterior view. **B,** Posterior view. **C,** Forearm pronators.

vere, the athlete should be referred to a physician for x-ray examination to determine if a fracture exists.

Olecranon bursitis The olecranon bursa (Fig. 16-5), lying between the end of the olecranon process and the skin, is the most frequently injured bursa in the elbow. Its superficial location makes it prone to acute or chronic injury, particularly as the result of direct blows. The inflamed bursa produces pain, marked swelling, and point tenderness. Occasionally, swelling will appear almost spontaneously and without the usual pain and heat. If the condition is acute, a cold compress should be applied for at least 1 hour. Chronic olecranon bursitis requires a program of superficial therapy. In some cases aspiration by a physician will hasten healing. Although seldom serious, olecranon bursitis can be annoying and should be well protected by padding while the athlete is engaged in competition.

Strains The acute mechanisms of muscle strain associated with the elbow joint are usually excessive resistive motion, such as a fall on the outstretched hand with the elbow in extension that forces the joint into hyperextension. Repeated microtears causing chronic injury will be discussed under *epicondylitis*.

Immediate and follow-up care Immediate care includes ICE-R and sling support for the more severe cases. Follow-up care may include cryotherapy, ultrasound, and rehabilitative exercises. Conditions that cause moderate to severe loss of elbow function should routinely be referred for x-ray examination. It is important to rule out the possibility of an avulsion or epiphyseal fracture.

Sprains Sprains to the elbow are usually caused by hyperextension or a force that bends or twists the lower arm outward.

Immediate and follow-up care Immediate care for elbow sprains consists of cold and a pressure bandage for at least 24 hours with sling support fixed at 45 degrees of flexion. After hemorrhage has been controlled, superficial heat treatments in the form of the whirlpool may be started and combined with massage above and below the injury. Like fractures and dislocations, sprains also may result in abnormal bone proliferation if the area is massaged directly and too vigorously or exercised too soon. The main concern should be to gently aid the elbow in regaining a full range of motion and then, when the time is right, to commence active exercises until full mobility and strength have returned. Taping can help and should restrain the elbow from further injury, or it may be used while the athlete is participating in sports.

Epicondylitis Epicondylitis is a chronic condition that may affect athletes who execute repeated forearm twisting movements such as are performed in a variety of sports. The elbow is particularly predisposed to mechanical trauma in the activities of throwing and striking. Epicondylitis is variously identified as "pitcher's elbow," "tennis elbow," "javelin thrower's elbow," or "golfer's elbow" (Fig. 16-7).

Regardless of the sport or exact location of the injury, the symptoms and signs are similar. In addition to pain around the outside or inside of the elbow, there is usually point tenderness over an epicondyle and in some cases mild swelling. Passive twisting movement of the forearm seldom elicits pain, while active movement does.[4]

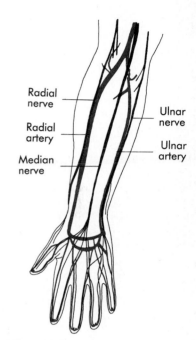

Radial nerve
Radial artery
Median nerve
Ulnar nerve
Ulnar artery

Figure 16-4

Arteries and nerves supplying the elbow joint, wrist, and hand.

ELBOW EXTENSION RESTRICTION TAPING

The procedure for taping the elbow to prevent hyperextension is as follows:

Materials needed: One roll of 1 1/2-inch (3.75 cm) tape, tape adherent, and a 2-inch (5 cm) elastic bandage.

Position of the athlete: The athlete stands with the affected elbow flexed at 90 degrees.

Position of the operator: The operator stands facing the side of the athlete's affected arm.

Procedure: Fig. 16-6 illustrates the proper procedure for applying the elbow extension restriction taping.

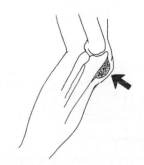

Figure 16-5

Olecranon bursitis.

Care Conservative care of moderate to severe epicondylitis usually includes a sling, rest, cold followed by gentle exercise, or heat. Analgesic or anti-inflammatory agents may be prescribed by a physician. A curvilinear brace applied just below the bend of the elbow is highly beneficial in reducing stress to the elbow. A conical brace provides counterforce, disseminating stress over a wide area and relieving the concentration of forces directly on the bony muscle attachments (Fig. 16-8). **NOTE**: In cases in which epicondylitis is related to tennis, there must be a concern for proper grip size and string tension.[9]

Elbow Osteochondritis Dissecans

Although osteochondritis dissecans is more common in knees, it also occurs in elbows. Its cause is unknown; however, impairment of the blood supply to the anterior surfaces leads to fragmentation and separation of a portion of the articular cartilage and bone, creating a loose body within the joint.[10]

The adolescent athlete usually complains of sudden pain and locking of the elbow joint. Range of motion returns slowly over a few days. Swelling, pain, and crepitation also may occur.

Care If there are repeated episodes of locking, surgical removal of the loose bodies may be warranted. If they are not removed, traumatic arthritis can eventually occur.

Dislocation of the Elbow

Dislocation of the elbow has a high incidence in sports activity and most often is caused either by a fall on the outstretched hand with the elbow in a

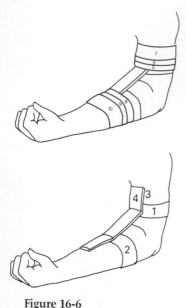

Figure 16-6

Elbow extension restriction taping.

Figure 16-7

Repeated throwing actions can produce the chronic elbow condition of epicondylitis.

position of hyperextension or by a severe twist while the elbow is in a flexed position. The bones of the forearm (ulna and radius) may be displaced backward, forward, or laterally. The appearance of the most common dislocation is a deformity of the olecranon process, whereby it extends backward, well beyond its normal alignment with the upper arm.

Elbow dislocations involve rupturing and tearing of most of the stabilizing ligamentous tissue, accompanied by profuse internal bleeding and subsequent swelling. There is severe pain and disability. The complications of such a trauma may include injury to the major nerves and blood vessels.

Immediate and follow-up care   The primary responsibility is to provide the athlete with a sling and immediately to refer the athlete to a physician for reduction. Reduction must be performed as soon as possible to prevent spasmodic constriction and prolonged derangement of soft tissue. In most cases the physician will administer an anesthetic before reduction to relax spasmed muscles. After reduction, the physician often will immobilize the elbow in a position of flexion and apply a sling suspension, which should be used for approximately 3 weeks. While the arm is maintained in flexion, the athlete should execute hand gripping and shoulder exercises. When initial healing has taken place, gentle, passive exercise and heat may be applied to help regain a full range of motion. Above-all, massage therapy and joint movements that are too strenuous should be avoided before complete healing has occurred because of the high probability of encouraging calcification of tendons and the joint capsule. Both range of movement and a strength program should be initiated by the athlete, but forced stretching must be avoided.

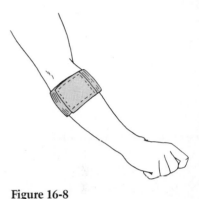

Figure 16-8

Curvelinear brace for tennis elbow.

Fractures of the Elbow

An elbow fracture can occur in almost any sports event and is usually caused by a fall on the outstretched hand or the flexed elbow or by a direct blow to the elbow. Children and young athletes have a much higher rate of this injury than do adults. A fracture can take place in any one or more of the bones that compose the elbow. A fall on the outstretched hand quite often fractures the humerus above the condyles. The bones of the forearm or wrist also may be the recipients of trauma that produces a fracture. An elbow fracture may or may not result in visible deformity. There usually will be hemorrhage, swelling, and muscle spasm in the injured area.

Common sports injuries that are forms of epicondylitis:
Pitcher's elbow
Tennis elbow
Javelin thrower's elbow
Golfer's elbow

Volkmann's Contracture

It is essential that athletes sustaining a serious elbow injury have their brachial or radial pulse monitored often. Swelling, muscle spasm, or pressure from a bone displacement can put pressure on the brachial artery and inhibit blood circulation to the forearm, wrist, and hand. Such inhibition of circulation can lead to muscle contracture and permanent paralysis.

The first indication of this problem is pain in the forearm that becomes progressively greater when the fingers of the affected arm are passively extended.

Volkmann's contracture is a major complication of a serious elbow injury.

Rehabilitation of the Elbow

While the elbow is immobilized after an acute injury, the athlete should perform general body exercises as well as exercises specific to the shoulder and wrist joint. In some cases isometric exercise is appropriate while the elbow is immobilized. Maintaining the strength of these articulations will speed the recovery of the elbow. After the elbow has healed and free movement is permitted by the physician, the first consideration should be restoration of the normal range of movement. Lengthening the contracted tendons and supporting tissue around the elbow requires daily gentle, active exercises. **NOTE:** Passive stretching may be detrimental to the athlete regaining full range of movement. *Forced stretching must be avoided at all times.* When the full range of motion has been regained, a graded, progressive resistance exercise program should be initiated, including elbow flexion and extension as well as forearm pronation and supination (Fig. 16-9). Protective taping must be continued until full strength and flexibility have been restored. Long-standing chronic conditions of the elbow usually cause gradual debilitation of the surrounding soft tissue. Elbows with conditions of this type should be restored to the maximal state of conditioning without encouraging postinjury aggravation.

THE FOREARM

The bones of the forearm are the ulna and the radius (Fig. 16-10). The ulna, which may be thought of as a direct extension of the humerus, is long, straight, and larger at its upper end than at its lower end. The radius, considered an extension of the hand, is thicker at its lower end than at its upper end. The forearm has three articulations: the superior, middle, and distal radioulnar joints.

The forearm muscles consist of flexors and pronators that are positioned anteriorly and of extensors and supinators that lie posteriorly. The flexors of the wrist and fingers are separated into superficial muscles and deep muscles (Fig. 16-11).

The major blood supply stems from the brachial artery, which divides into the radial and ulnar artery in the forearm.

Figure 16-9

A very gradual program of progressive resistance exercise is important to elbow rehabilitation.

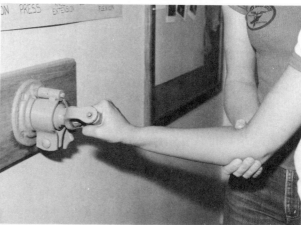

Except for the flexor carpi ulnaris and half of the flexor digitorum profundus, most of the flexor muscles of the forearm are supplied by the median nerve. The majority of the extensor muscles are controlled by the radial nerve.

Injuries to the Forearm

Lying between the elbow joint and the wrist and hand, the forearm is indirectly influenced by injuries to these areas; however, direct injuries can also occur.

Contusions

The forearm is constantly exposed to bruising in contact sports such as football. The ulnar side receives the majority of blows in arm blocks and, consequently, the greater amount of bruising. Bruises to this area may be classified as acute or chronic. The acute contusion can result in a fracture; but this happens only rarely. Most often a muscle or bone develops varying degrees of pain, swelling, and accumulation of blood (hematoma). The chronic contusion develops from repeated blows to the forearm with attendant multiple irritations. Extensive scar tissue may replace the hematoma and in some cases a bony callus replaces the scar tissue.

Immediate and follow-up care   Care of the contused forearm requires proper attention in the acute stages by application of ICE-R for 20 minutes every 1 1/2 waking hours, followed the next day by cold and exercise or superficial heat. Protection of the forearm is important for athletes who are prone to this condition. The best protection consists of a full-length sponge rubber pad for the forearm early in the season.

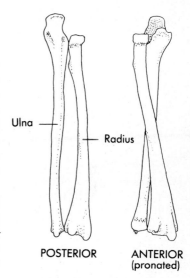

Figure 16-10

Bones of the forearm.

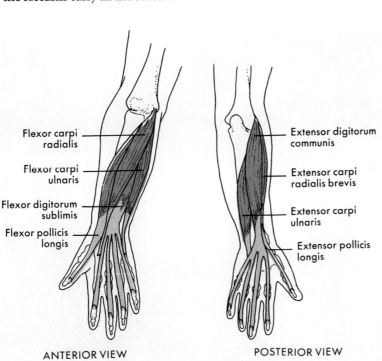

ANTERIOR VIEW
A

POSTERIOR VIEW
B

Figure 16-11

Muscles of the forearm. **A,** Anterior view. **B,** Posterior view.

Forearm splints, like
shinsplints, commonly occur
early and late in the sports
season.

Figure 16-12

A, A fracture of the radius and
ulna. **B**, A compound fracture
of the ulna.

A

Strains

Forearm strain can occur in a variety of sports; most such injuries come from repeated static contractions.

Forearm splints   Forearm splints, like shinsplints, are difficult to manage. They occur most often in gymnastics, particularly to those who perform on the side horse.

The main symptom is a dull ache of the extensor muscles, crossing the back of the forearm. Muscle weakness may also accompany the dull ache. Palpation reveals an irritation of the deep tissue between the muscles. The cause of this condition is uncertain; like shinsplints, forearm splints usually appear either early or late in the season, indicating poor conditioning or a factor of chronic fatigue. It is speculated that the reason for this problem is static muscle contractions of the forearm, as occurs when performing on the side horse. Constant static muscle contraction causes minute tears in the deep connective tissues of the forearm.

Care   Care of forearm splints is symptomatic. If the problem occurs in the early season, the athlete should concentrate on increasing the strength of the forearm through resistance exercises, but if it arises late in the season, emphasis should be placed on rest, cryotherapy, or heat and use of a supportive wrap during activity.

Fractures

Fractures of the forearm (Fig. 16-12) are particularly common among active children and youths and occur as the result of a blow or a fall on the out-

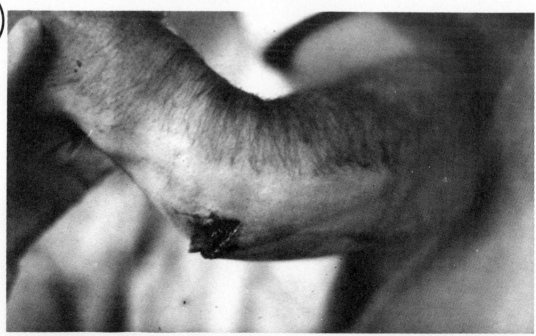

B

stretched hand. Fractures to the ulna or the radius singly are much rarer than simultaneous fractures to both. The break usually presents all the features of a long bone fracture: pain, swelling, deformity, and a false joint. The older the athlete, the greater the danger is of extensive damage to soft tissue and the greater the possibility of paralysis from Volkmann's contractures.

To prevent complications from arising, a cold pack must be applied immediately to the fracture site, the arm splinted and put in a sling, and the athlete referred to a physician. The athlete will usually be incapacitated for about 8 weeks.

Colles' Fracture Colles' fracture (Fig. 16-13) is among the most common type of forearm fractures and involves the lower end of the radius. The mechanism of injury is usually a fall on the outstretched hand, forcing the forearm backward and upward into hyperextension.

In most cases there is a visible deformity to the wrist. Sometimes no deformity is present, and the injury may be passed off as a bad sprain — to the detriment of the athlete. Bleeding is quite profuse in this area with the accumulated fluids causing extensive swelling in the wrist and, if unchecked, in the fingers and forearm. Ligamentous tissue is usually unharmed, but tendons may be torn away from their attachment, and there may possibly be median nerve damage.

Care The main responsibility is to apply a cold compress, splint the wrist, put the limb in a sling, and then refer the athlete to a physician for x-ray examination and immobilization. Severe sprains should always be treated as possible fractures. Lacking complications, the Colles' fracture will keep an athlete out of sports for 1 to 2 months. It should be noted that what appears to be a Colles' fracture in children and youths is often a lower epiphyseal separation. **NOTE:** Forearm exercise rehabilitation is discussed on page 343.

Figure 16-13

Common appearance of the forearm in Colles' fracture.

THE WRIST AND HAND

The wrist is formed by the union of the distal aspect of the radius and the articular disk of the ulna with three of the four proximal (of the eight diversely shaped) carpal bones (Fig. 16-14).

Injuries to the Wrist

Injuries to the wrist usually occur from a fall on the outstretched hand or repeated flexion, extension, or rotary movements[5] (Fig. 16-15).

Strains and Sprains

It is often very difficult to distinguish between injury to the muscle tendons crossing the wrist joint or the supporting structure of the carpal region. Therefore, emphasis will be placed on the condition of wrist sprains, whereas strains will be considered in the discussion of the hand.

A sprain is by far the most common wrist injury and in most cases is the most poorly managed injury in sports. It can arise from any abnormal, forced movement of the wrist. Falling on the hyperextended wrist is the most common cause, but violent flexion or torsion will also tear supporting tissue. Since the main support of the wrist is derived from posterior and anterior ligaments that carry the major nutrient vessels to the carpal bones, repeated sprains may disrupt the blood supply and, consequently, the nutrition to the carpal bones.

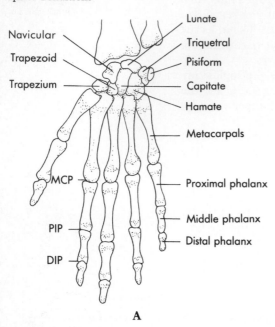

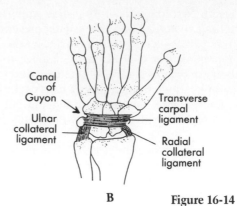

A

B

Figure 16-14

A, Bones of the wrist and hand.
B, Ligaments of the wrist.

Figure 16-15

Wrist injuries commonly occur from falls on the outstretched hand or from repeated flexion, extension, lateral, or rotary movements.

The sprained wrist may be differentiated from the carpal navicular fracture by recognition of the generalized swelling, tenderness, inability to flex the wrist, and absence of appreciable pain or irritation over the navicular bone. All athletes having severe sprains should be referred to a physician for x-ray examination to determine possible fractures.

Care Mild and moderate sprains should be given cold therapy and compression for at least 24 to 48 hours, after which cryotherapy is carried out or heat therapy is gradually increased. It is desirable to have the athlete start hand-strengthening exercises almost immediately after the injury has occurred.

Dislocations

Dislocations of the wrist are relatively infrequent in sports activity. Most occur from a forceful hyperextension of the hand. Of those dislocations that do occur, the bones that could be involved are the distal ends of the radius and ulna as well as a carpal bone, the lunate being the most commonly affected. This appears as a major deformity in the wrist region.

Fractures

Fractures of the wrist commonly occur to the distal ends of the radius and ulna and to the carpal bones; the carpal navicular bone is most commonly affected; the hamate bone is affected less often.

Navicular fracture The navicular bone is the most frequently fractured of the carpal bones. The injury is usually caused by a force on the outstretched hand, which compresses the navicular bone between the radius and the second row of carpal bones (Fig. 16-16). This condition is often mistaken for a severe sprain, and as a result the required complete immobilization is not carried out. Without proper splinting, the navicular fracture often fails to heal because of an inadequate supply of blood, thus degeneration and **necrosis** (bone death) occur. This condition is often called "atrophic necrosis" of the navicular bone. It is necessary to try, in every way possible, to distinguish between a wrist sprain and a fracture of the navicular bone because a fracture necessitates immediate referral to a physician.

The signs of a recent navicular fracture include swelling in the area of the carpal bones, severe point tenderness of the navicular bone in the anatomical snuffbox (Fig. 16-17), and navicular pain that is elicited by upward pressure exerted on the long axis of the thumb and by radial flexion.

Care With these signs present, cold should be applied, the area splinted, and the athlete referred to a physician for x-ray study and casting. In most cases cast immobilization lasts for about 8 weeks and is followed by strengthening exercises coupled with protective taping.

Hamate fracture A fracture of the hamate bone can occur from a fall, but more commonly occurs from being struck by an implement such as the handle of a tennis racquet, a baseball bat, or a golf club.[8] Wrist pain and weakness are experienced. Pull of the muscular attachments can cause nonunion; therefore, casting is usually the treatment of choice. Taping support should be maintained until the athlete has regained full strength and mobility.

Figure 16-16

Carpal navicular fracture.

necrosis
Death of tissue

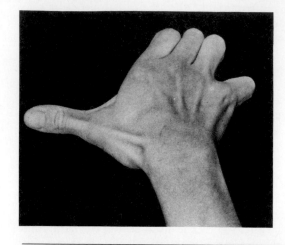

Figure 16-17

Anatomical "snuffbox" formed by extensor tendons of the thumb.

Figure 16-18

Wrist taping technique no. 1.

WRIST TAPING TECHNIQUES NO. 1

This wrist taping technique is designed for mild wrist strains or sprains.

Materials needed: One roll of 1-inch (2.5 cm) tape and tape adherent.

Position of the athlete: The athlete stands with the affected hand flexed toward the injured side and the fingers moderately spread to increase the breadth of the wrist for the protection of nerves and blood vessels.

Position of the operator: The operator stands facing the athlete's affected wrist.

Procedure: Fig. 16-18 illustrates the proper procedure for applying wrist taping technique no. 1.

WRIST TAPING TECHNIQUE NO. 2

This wrist taping technique is designed to stabilize and protect a badly injured wrist. The materials and positioning are the same as in technique no. 1.

Procedure: Fig. 16-19 illustrates the proper procedure for applying wrist taping technique no. 2.

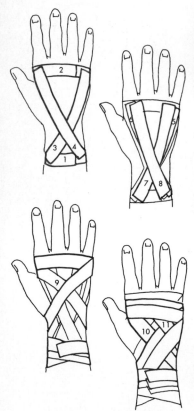

Figure 16-19

Wrist taping technique no. 2.

Wrist Ganglion of the Tendon Sheath

The wrist ganglion (Fig. 16-20) is often seen in sports. It is considered by many to be a herniation of the joint capsule or of the synovial sheath of a tendon; other authorities believe it to be a cystic structure. It usually appears slowly, after a wrist strain, and contains a clear, mucous fluid. The ganglion most often appears on the back of the wrist but can appear at any tendinous point in the wrist or hand. As it increases in size, it may be accompanied by a mild pressure discomfort. An old method of treatment was to first break down the swelling by means of finger pressure and then apply a felt pressure pad for a period of time to encourage healing. A newer approach is the combination of drawing the fluid off using a hypodermic needle and chemical cauterization, with subsequent application of a pressure pad. Neither of these methods prevents the ganglion from recurring. Surgical removal is the best method available.

Injuries to the Hand

Injuries to the hand occur frequently in sports, yet the injured hand is probably the most poorly managed of all body areas.

Contusions and Pressure Injuries of the Hand and Phalanges

The hand and phalanges, having irregular bony structure combined with little protective fat and muscle padding, are prone to bruising in sports. This condition is easily identified from the history of trauma and the pain and swelling of soft tissues. Cold, compression, and elevation should be applied immediately for 48 hours to avoid swelling. This should be followed by gradual warming of the part in whirlpool or immersion baths. Although soreness is still present, protection should be given by a sponge rubber pad.

A particularly common contusion of the finger is bruising of the distal phalanx, which results in a *subungual hematoma* (contusion of the fingernail). This is an extremely painful condition because of the accumulation of blood underneath the fingernail. The athlete should place the finger in ice water until the hemorrhage ceases, and the pressure of blood should then be released.

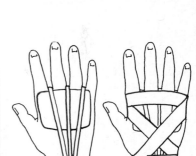

Figure 16-20

Wrist ganglion.

BRUISED HAND TAPING

The following method is used to tape a bruised hand.

Materials needed: One roll of 1-inch (2.5 cm) adhesive tape, one roll of 1/2-inch (1.25 cm) tape, a 1/4-inch (0.63 cm) thick sponge rubber pad, and tape adherent.

Position of the athlete: The fingers are spread moderately.

Position of the operator: The operator faces the athlete's hand.

Procedure: Fig. 16-21 illustrates the proper procedure for applying the bruised hand taping.

Figure 16-21

Bruised hand taping.

RELEASING BLOOD FROM BENEATH THE FINGERNAIL

The following are two common methods for releasing the pressure of the subungual hematoma.

Materials needed: Scalpel, small-gauge drill or paper clip, and antiseptic.

Position of the athlete: The athlete sits with the injured hand, palm downward, on the table.

Position of the operator: The operator sits facing the athlete's affected finger and stabilizes it with one hand.

Technique 1

1. The injured finger should be coated with an antiseptic solution.
2. A sharp scalpel point or small-gauge drill is used to penetrate the injured nail by a rotary action. If the hematoma extends out as far as the end of the nail, it may be best to release the blood by slipping the scalpel tip under the end of the nail (Fig. 16-22).

Technique 2

1. A paper clip is heated to a red-hot temperature.
2. The red-hot paper clip is laid on the surface of the nail with moderate pressure. This results in melting a hole through the nail to the site of the bleeding.

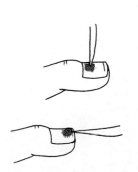

Figure 16-22

Releasing blood from beneath the fingernail, technique no. 1.

Figure 16-23

Mallet finger.

Figure 16-24

Splinting of the mallet finger.

Figure 16-25

Boutonnière deformity.

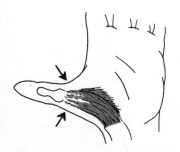

Figure 16-26

Sprained thumb.

Tendon Conditions

Tenosynovitis The tendons of the wrist and hand can sustain irritation from repeated movement that result in tenosynovitis. An inflammation of the tendon sheath results in swelling, crepitation, and painful movement. The extensor tendons of the wrist are most commonly affected.

deQuervain's disease The first tunnel of the wrist becomes contracted and narrowed due to an irritation. Two tendons move through the first tunnel, which is formed by a long groove.

Athletes who use a great deal of wrist motion in their sports are prone to deQuervain's disease. The symptoms are aching, which may radiate to the hand or forearm.[3] Movements of the wrist tend to increase the pain.

Care Care of deQuervain's disease involves wrist immobilization, rest, superficial cold or heat, and anti-inflammatory medication. Ultrasound and ice massage also have been found to be beneficial.

Mallet finger

The mallet finger is common in sports, particularly in baseball and basketball. It is caused by a blow from a thrown ball that strikes the tip of the finger completely tearing the extensor tendon from its insertion along with a piece of bone.

The athlete is unable to extend the finger, carrying it at about a 30-degree angle. There is also point tenderness at the site of the injury, and the pulled away bone chip often can be felt (Fig. 16-23).

Care Pain, swelling, and discoloration from internal hemorrhage are present. The distal phalanx should be splinted in a position of extension immediately, cold should be applied to the area, and the athlete should be referred to a physician. Most physicians will splint the mallet finger into extension and the proximal phalanx into flexion for 4 to 6 weeks (Fig. 16-24).

Boutonnière deformity The boutonnière, or buttonhole, deformity is caused by a rupture of the extensor tendon of the middle phalanx. Trauma forces the upper joint of the middle phalanx into excessive flexion.

The athlete complains of severe pain and inability to extend the finger. There is swelling, point tenderness, and an obvious deformity (Fig. 16-25).

Care Care of the boutonniere deformity includes cold application followed by splinting of the joint in extension. **NOTE**: If this condition is inadequately splinted, the classic boutonnière deformity will develop. Splinting is continued for 5 to 8 weeks. While splinted, the athlete is encouraged to flex the distal phalanx.[3]

Sprains, Dislocations, and Fractures

The phalanges, particularly the thumb (Fig. 16-26), are prone to sprains caused by a blow delivered to the tip or by violent twisting. The mechanism of injury is similar to that of fractures and dislocations. The sprain, however, mainly affects the capsular, ligamentous, and tendinous tissues. Recognition is accomplished primarily through the history and the sprain symptoms: pain, marked swelling, and bleeding.

Gamekeeper's thumb A sprain of the ulnar collateral ligament of the thumb is common among athletes, especially skiers and tackle football players. The cause of injury is usually a forceful abduction of the thumb's uppermost phalanx, which is occasionally combined with hyperextension.[6]

Care Since the stability of pinching can be severely deterred, proper immediate and follow-up care must be carried out. If there is instability in the joints, the athlete should be immediately referred to an orthopedist. If the joint is stable, x-ray examination should routinely be performed to rule out fracture. Splinting of the thumb should be applied for protection over a 3-week period or until it is pain free. The splint is applied with the thumb in a neutral position extending from the end of the thumb to above the wrist.[7] After splinting, a thumb spica taping should be worn during sports participation.

Collateral ligament sprain A collateral ligament sprain of a finger is very common in sports such as basketball, volleyball, and football. A common mechanism is an axial force producing the "jammed finger."[2]

There is severe point tenderness at the joint site, especially in the region of the collateral ligaments. There may be a lateral or medial instability when the joint is in 150 degrees of flexion.

Care Care includes ice packs for the acute stage, x-ray examinations, and splinting. Splinting of the joint is usually at 30 to 40 degrees of flexion for 10 days. If the sprain is to the first phalanx joint, splinting a few days in full extension assists in the healing process. If the sprains are minor, taping the injured finger to a noninjured one will provide protective support. Later, a protective checkrein can be applied for either thumb or finger protection.

It is important to elevate the hand for the first 48 hours after injury to prevent swelling into the fingers.

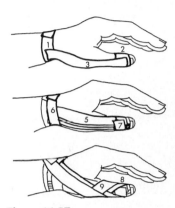

Figure 16-27

Sprained thumb taping.

SPRAINED THUMB TAPING

Sprained thumb taping is designed to give both protection of the muscle and joint and support to the thumb.
Materials needed: One roll of 1-inch (2.5 cm) tape and tape adherent.
Position of the athlete: The athlete should hold the injured thumb in a relaxed, neutral position.
Position of the operator: The operator stands in front of the athlete's injured thumb.
Procedure: Fig. 16-27 illustrates the proper procedure for applying the sprained thumb taping. The thumb spica with tape provides an excellent means of protection during recovery from an injury (Fig. 16-28).

Figure 16-28

Thumb spica.

FINGER AND THUMB CHECKREINS

The finger or thumb that has been sprained may require the additional protection afforded by a restraining checkrein.
Materials needed: One roll of 1-inch (2.5 cm) tape.
Postition of the athlete: The athlete spreads the injured fingers widely but within a range free of pain.
Position of the operator: The operator faces the athlete's injured finger.
Procedure: Fig. 16-29 illustrates the proper procedure for applying the finger and thumb checkreins.

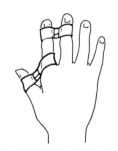

Figure 16-29

Finger and thumb checkreins.

Figure 16-30

Being hit on the tip of the finger can produce enough force to dislocate it.

Figure 16-31

Volleyball produces a high percentage of finger injuries.

Dislocations of the phalanges Dislocations of the phalanges (Fig. 16-30) have a high rate of occurrence in sports and are caused mainly by being hit on the tip of the finger by a ball (Fig. 16-31). The force of injury is usually directed upward from the palmar side, displacing either the first or second joint dorsally. The resultant problem is primarily a tearing of the supporting capsular tissue, accompanied by hemorrhaging. However, there may be a rupture of the flexor or extensor tendon and chip fractures in and around the dislocated joint. It is advisable to splint the dislocation as it is and refer to the team physician for reduction.

To ensure the most complete healing of the dislocated finger joints, splinting should be maintained for about 3 weeks in 30 degrees of flexion because an inadequate immobilization could cause an unstable joint and/or excessive scar tissue and, possibly, a permanent deformity.

Special consideration must be given to dislocations of the thumb and any second or third joints of the fingers. A properly functioning thumb is necessary for hand dexterity; consequently, any traumatic injury to the thumb should be considered serious. Thumb dislocations occur frequently at the second joint, resulting from a sharp blow to its tip, with the trauma forcing the thumb into hyperextension and dislocating the second joint downward. Any dislocation of the third joint of the finger can lead to complications and require the immediate care of an orthopedist. It should be noted that all hand dislocations must be x-rayed to rule out fracture.

Fractures of the hand The same mechanism that produces strains, sprains, and dislocations can cause fractures of the metacarpal bones and phalanges. Other mechanisms include crushing injuries.

Fractures of the metacarpal bones Fractures of the metacarpal bones (Fig. 16-32) are common in contact sports. They arise from striking an object with the fist or from having the hand stepped on. There is often pain, deformity, swelling, and abnormal mobility. In some cases no deformity occurs, and by palpation one is unable to distinguish between a severe contusion and a fracture. In this situation digital pressure should be placed on the knuckles and the long axes of the metacarpal bones. Pressure often will reveal pain at the fracture site. After the fracture is located, the hand should be splinted over a gauze roll splint, cold and pressure applied, and the athlete referred to a physician.

Fractures of the phalanges Fractures of the phalanges are among the most common fractures in sports and can occur as the result of a variety of mechanisms: the fingers being stepped on, hit by a ball, or twisted. The finger suspected of being fractured should be splinted in flexion around a gauze roll or a curved splint to avoid full extension. Flexion splinting reduces the deformity by relaxing the flexor tendons. Fracture of the end phalanx is less complicated than fracture of the middle or third phalanx.[1] The major concerns are to control bleeding, apply a splint properly, and then refer the athlete to a physician.

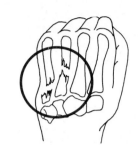

Figure 16-32

Fractures of the metacarpals.

Rehabilitation of the Forearm, Wrist, and Hand

Reconditioning of the hand, wrist, and forearm must commence as early as possible. Immobilization of the forearm or wrist requires that the muscles be exercised almost immediately after an injury occurs if atrophy and contractures are to be prevented. The athlete is not ready for competition until full strength and mobility of the injured joint have been regained. Grip strength is an excellent way to determine the state of reconditioning of the hand, wrist, and forearm. The hand dynamometer may be used to ascertain strength increments during the process of rehabilitation. Full range of movement and strength must be considered for all the major articulations and muscles.

Once ligament or tendon injuries have healed to the point that movement will not disrupt, active mobilization is carried out.[11, 12] Exercise is graduated to increase grip and pinch strength. Some of the following exercises can be employed with success. **NOTE**: All exercises should be performed in a pain-free range of motion. Such exercises should be performed in sets of ten, working toward an ultimate program of three sets of ten, two or three times daily.

Suggested Forearm and Wrist Exercises

Proper forearm reconditioning is extremely important for injuries to the wrist and hand, as well as the forearm. An excellent beginning exercise is the towel twist, in which the athlete twists the towel in each direction as if wringing out water (Fig. 16-33). A wrist roll exercise (Fig. 16-34) against a resistance is also an excellent forearm, wrist, and hand strength developer. More specific strength development can be employed by the use of a resistance device such as a dumbbell. By stabilizing the bent elbow, the athlete can perform wrist flexion and extension and also forearm pronation and supination.

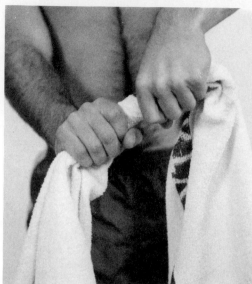

Figure 16-33

The towel twist exercise.

Figure 16-34

Wrist roll.

Figure 16-35

Wrist circles and finger spread and grip.

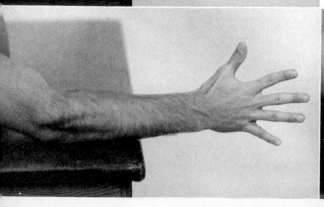

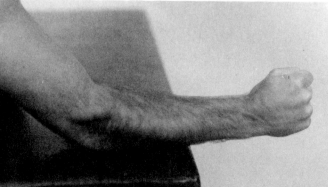

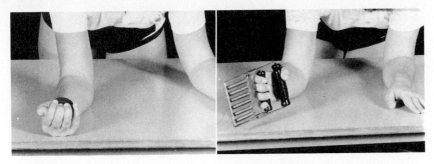

Figure 16-36

Restoring grip strength.

Wrist strength depends on forearm strength and freedom of movement in the wrist joint. Circumduction exercise helps to maintain joint integrity. Circling must be performed in each direction (Fig. 16-35).

Suggested Hand and Wrist Exercises

Two exercises that are highly beneficial are gripping and spreading the hand and squeezing a ball. Resistance exercises also can be used successfully for restoring grip strength (Fig. 16-36).

SUMMARY

The upper limb including the elbow, forearm, wrist, and hand is second to the lower limb in incidence of sports injuries.

The elbow is anatomically one of the more complex joints in the human body. The elbow joint allows for the movements of flexion and extension, and the radioulnar joint allows for forearm pronation and supination. The major sports injuries of the elbow are contusions, strains, sprains, and dislocations. The chronic strain, which produces the pitcher's, tennis, javelin, and golfer's elbow, is more formally known as epicondylitis.

The forearm is composed of the ulna and radius bones as well as associated soft tissue. Sports injuries to the region commonly consist of contusions, chronic forearm splints, acute strains, and fractures.

Injuries to the wrist usually occur from a fall or repeated movement of flexion, extension, and rotation. Common injuries are sprains, lunate carpal dislocation, navicular carpal fracture, and hamate fracture.

Injuries to the hand occur frequently in sports activities. Common injuries include those caused by contusions and chronic pressure; tendons receiving sustained irritation, which lead to tenosynovitis; and tendon avulsions. Sprains, dislocations, and fractures of the fingers are also common.

REVIEW QUESTIONS AND CLASS ACTIVITIES

1. Describe how and why the elbow becomes chronically strained from throwing mechanisms.
2. Describe a dislocated elbow: its causation, appearance, and care.
3. How does the elbow sustain epicondylitis?
4. Compare elbow and knee osteochondritis dissecans. How does each occur?
5. What causes a Volkmann's contracture? How may it be detected early?

6. Discuss the many aspects of elbow exercise rehabilitation.
7. Compare forearm splints and shinsplints. How does each occur?
8. Describe the Colles' fracture of the forearm: its cause, appearance, and care.
9. What healing problems occur with navicular carpal fractures? Why?
10. How do you relieve a subungual hematoma?
11. What causes stenosing tenosynovitis in the hand?
12. A mallet finger and the boutonnière deformity are produced by what situation in baseball? How should each be cared for?
13. A sprained thumb is common in sports activities. How does it occur and what care should be given?
14. Should a dislocated finger be reduced by a coach? Explain your answer.
15. Have a hand surgeon discuss the need for proper immediate care, early referral to a physician, and proper rehabilitation of hand injuries.

REFERENCES

1. Birnbaum, J.S.: The musculoskeletal manual, New York, 1982, Academic Press, Inc.
2. Brunet, M.E., et al.: How I manage sprained fingers in athletics, Phys. Sportsmed. 12:99, Aug. 1984.
3. Cailliet, R.: Hand pain and impairment, ed. 3, Philadelphia, 1982, F.A. Davis Co.
4. Cyriax, J.: Textbook of orthopaedic medicine, vol. 1, Diagnosis of soft tissue lesions, ed. 8, Eastbourne, England, 1982, Baillière Tindall.
5. Dobyns, J.H., et al.: Sports stress syndrome of the hand and wrist, Am. J. Sports Med. 6(5):236, 1978.
6. Gerber, C., et al.: Skier's thumb: surgical treatment of recent injuries to the ulnar collateral ligament of the thumb's metacarpophalangeal joint, Am. J. Sports Med. 9:171, May/June 1981.
7. Maroon, B.R.: Orthopedic aspects of sports medicine. In Appenzeller, O., and Atkinson, R. (editors): Sports medicine, Baltimore, 1981, Urban & Schwarzenberg, Inc.
8. McCue, F.C., III, et al.: Hand and wrist injuries in the athlete, Am. J. Sports Med. 7(5):275, 1979.
9. Physical therapy program for tennis elbow syndrome, Sports Med. Digest, 7:4, April 1985.
10. Singer, K.M., and Roy, S.P.: Osteochondrosis of the humeral capitellum, Am. J. Sports Med. 12:351, Sept./Oct. 1984.
11. Wilson, R.L., and Carter, M.S.: Joint injuries in the hand: preservation of proximal interphalangeal joint function. In Hunter, J.M., et al. (editors): Rehabilitation of the hand, ed. 2, St. Louis, 1984, The C.V. Mosby Co.
12. Wilson, R.L., and Carter, M.S.: Management of hand fractures. In Hunter, J.M., et al. (editors): Rehabilitation of the hand, ed. 2, St. Louis, 1984, The C.V. Mosby Co.

ANNOTATED BIBLIOGRAPHY

Cailliet, R.: Hand pain and impairment, ed. 3, Philadelphia, 1982, F.A. Davis Co.
An excellent monograph on hand conditions. It offers a good review of key anatomy and causes of injury and pain.
Hunter, J.M., et al. (editors): Rehabilitation of the hand, St. Louis, 1978, The C.V. Mosby Co.
Although written for the physician and therapist, it has parts that should be of value to the coach or athletic trainer. The chapter on splinting is especially interesting.

Chapter 17

OTHER HEALTH CONDITIONS AND THE ATHLETE

When you finish this chapter, you will be able to:

Explain reasons for the cause of the most common skin infections related to the physically active person

Identify the symptoms and signs of sexually transmitted diseases, respiratory infections, communicable viral diseases, and gastrointestinal complaints

Explain physical activity as it relates to respiratory conditions

Describe common gastrointestinal complaints as they relate to physical activity

Explain the reasons for diabetes mellitus as well as recognize the signs of diabetic coma and insulin shock and provide the proper immediate care in each case

Explain the reasons for epilepsy and provide proper immediate care for an epileptic seizure

Explain menstrual irregularities as they are related to the physically very active female

In addition to musculoskeletal injuries, the athlete is often exposed to many other common illnesses. Those that will be considered in this chapter include skin conditions, respiratory disorders, common communicable diseases, gastrointestinal conditions, diabetes, convulsive disorders, menstrual irregularities, and sexually transmitted diseases.

SKIN INFECTIONS

The skin is the largest organ of the human body. It is composed of three layers—epidermis, dermis, and subcutis (Fig. 17-1). The most common skin infections seen in sports are caused by viruses, bacteria, and fungi.

Viral Infections

Common viruses that attack the skin of athletes:
Herpes
Verruca
Molluscum contagiosum

Viruses are ultramicroscopic organisms that are parasitic to living cells. Common virus infections are the herpes simplex—labalis (cold sore) and gladiatorum (side of the face, neck, or shoulders); the verruca virus (plantar and flat warts); and water warts (molluscum contagiosum).[13]

Bacterial Infections

Bacteria are single-celled, plantlike microorganisms that lack chlorophyll. There are three primary forms of bacteria: ovoid shaped, rod shaped, and spiral forms.

The two types of ovid forms associated with skin infections are staphylococci aureus strain and streptococci (Fig. 17-2) causing the common conditions of impetigo contagiosa, boils, infected hair follicles, and infected sweat glands.

347

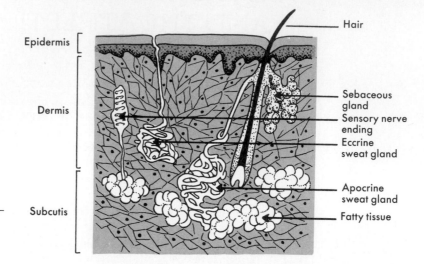

Figure 17-1

The skin is the largest organ of the human body, weighing 6 to 7 1/2 pounds in the adult.

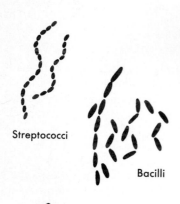

Figure 17-2

Common disease organisms.

The bacillus bacterium causes a number of serious diseases of which tetanus is of major concern in athletics. Tetanus (lockjaw) is an acute disease causing fever and convulsions. Tonic spasm of skeletal muscles is always a possibility for any nonimmunized athlete. The tetanus bacillus enters an open wound as a spore and, depending on individual susceptibility, acts on the motor end plate of the central nervous system. After initial childhood immunization by tetanus toxoid, boosters should be given every 10 years. An athlete not immunized should receive an injection of tetanus immune globulin (Hyper-Tet) immediately after injury.

The spiral bacterial form (spirilla and spirochete) is represented by the spirochete of syphilis, a very serious venereal disease (see page 349).

Fungal Infections

Fungi are plantlike organisms having no chlorophyll. Fungus can invade the skin's keratin, the most common general condition of which is ringworm. Ringworm (or tinea) is named for the area of the infected skin such as tinea capitis (head), tinea corporis (body), tinea unguium (toenails and fingernails), tinea cruris (jock rash), and tinea pedis (athlete's foot).

Sexually Transmitted Diseases

Sexually transmitted diseases are discussed in this section because of their relationship to the skin and mucous membrane. It is important that athletes who appear to have a disease related to sexual activity be immediately referred for proper medical care. The classic venereal diseases, such as gonorrhea and syphilis, are much less prevalent than in the past because effective antibiotic treatments have been developed. Diseases such as nonspecific urethritis, trichomoniasis, genital candidiasis, herpes genitalis, genital warts, molluscum contagiosum, and parasitic infections of pediculosis pubis and scabies are more commonly seen today.

Gonorrhea

Gonorrhea, commonly called "clap," is an acute venereal disease that can infect the urethra, cervix, and rectum. The organism of infection is the gonococcal bacteria *Neisseria gonorrhoeae*, which is usually spread by sexual intercourse.

In men the incubation period is from 2 to 10 days. The onset of the disease is marked by a tingling sensation in the urethra, followed in 2 or 3 hours by greenish-yellow discharge of pus and painful urination. Sixty percent of infected women are asymptomatic. For those who have symptoms, onset is between 7 and 21 days. In these cases symptoms are very mild with some vaginal discharge. Gonorrheal infection of the throat and rectum are also possible.

Care   Penicillin in high doses is usually the drug of choice. Other antibiotics may be used if the strain of bacteria is resistant to treatment.

Complications   Because of embarrassment some individuals fail to secure proper medical help and, although the initial symptoms will disappear, such an individual is not cured and can still spread the infection. Untreated gonorrhea becomes latent and will manifest itself in later years, usually causing sterility and/or arthritis. Treatment consists of large amounts of penicillin or other antibiotics. Recent experimental evidence suggests an increasing resistance of the gonococci to penicillin. Evidence of any of the symptoms should result in immediately remanding the individual to a physician for testing and treatment. *All sexual contact must be avoided* until it has been medically established that the disease is cured. Because of the latent residual effects that are the end result of several diseases in this group, including sterility and arthritis, immediate medical treatment is mandatory. Although outward signs may disappear, the disease is still insidiously present in the body. Additionally, such treatment will alleviate the discomfort that accompanies the initial stages of the disease.

Acquired Syphilis

Acquired syphilis is known as the "great imitator," since its lesions resemble those of other diseases, masking it and making detection difficult.

Syphilis is a contagious systemic disease caused by the motile spirochete *Treponema pallidum*. It enters the body through a mucous membrane or skin abrasion. In just a few hours the spirochete disseminates throughout the body.

Acquired syphilis is separated into three phases: primary, secondary, and tertiary. The incubation period varies from 1 to 13 weeks but most commonly 3 to 4 weeks. During the primary phase the site of inoculation develops a red papule that erodes into a single painless ulcer (chancre). Around the ulcer is a red areola. The lymph glands in the area become painlessly enlarged. After about 6 to 12 weeks the *secondary phase* appears. During this time there may be a mild illness including headache, loss of appetite, nausea, fever, general aching of joints, and a rash. The skin rash can imitate a variety of conditions. The rash is pinkish or pale red in light-skinned individuals and pigmented in dark-skinned individuals. The rash is found frequently on the hands and soles of the feet. The rash occurs in crops of papules, macules, or pustules. This phase, if not treated, may last a short period of time or may persist for months. Eventually the outward signs disappear and the *tertiary* or *late phase* may begin. In one third of the untreated cases late or tertiary syphilis occurs. In this phase the heart, spinal cord, brain, and other body organs can incur permanent damage.

Genital Herpes

Type 2 herpes simplex virus is associated with herpes genital infection, which is now the most prevalent cause of general ulcerations. Signs of the disease appear about 4 to 7 days after sexual contact.

The first signs in men are itching and soreness, but women may be asymptomatic in the vagina and cervix. It is estimated that 50% to 60% of individuals who have had one attack of herpes genitalis will have no further episodes, or if they do, the lesions are few and insignificant.[12] Like herpes labialis and gladiatorum, lesions develop that eventually become ulcerated with a red areola. Ulcerations crust and heal in about 10 days, leaving a scar.

Care There is no cure for genital herpes. Recently systemic medications, specifically antiviral medications such as acycloguanosine (Zovirax, Acyclovir) and viderabine (Vira-A) are being used to lessen the early symptoms of the disease.[2]

Complications Of major importance to a pregnant woman with a history of genital herpes is whether there is an active infection when she is nearing delivery. Herpes simplex can be fatal to a newborn child. There is also some relationship (although this is unclear) between a higher incidence of cervical cancer and the incidence of herpes genitalis.[12]

Condyloma Acuminata (Venereal Warts)

Another form of the verruca virus that should be recognized and referred to a physician is condyloma acuminata or venereal warts. These warts are transmitted by sexual activity and commonly occur from poor hygiene. It appears on the glans penis, vulva, or anus.

This form of verruca virus produces nodules that have a cauliflowerlike lesion or can be singular. In their early state they are soft, moist, pink or red swellings that rapidly develop a stem with a flowerlike head.[1] They may be mistaken for secondary syphilis or carcinoma.

Moist condylomas often are carefully treated by the physician with a solution containing 20% to 25% podophyllin. Dry warts may be treated with a freezing process such as liquid nitrogen.

RESPIRATORY TRACT CONDITIONS

The respiratory tract is an organ system through which various communicable diseases can be transmitted. It is commonly the port of entry for acute infectious diseases that are spread from person to person or by direct contact. Some of the more prevalent conditions affecting athletes are the common cold, sore throat, asthma, hay fever, and air pollution.

A   B

Figure 17-3

Proper applications of nose
drops. **A**, Head tilted back. **B**,
Head down.

The Common Cold (Coryza)

Upper respiratory tract infections, especially colds and associated conditions,
are common in the sports program and can play havoc with entire teams. The
common cold is attributed to a filterable virus, which produces an infection
of the upper respiratory tract within a susceptible individual.

The susceptible person is believed to be one who has, singly or in combination, any of the following characteristics:

1. Physical debilitation from overwork or lack of sleep
2. Chronic inflammation from a local infection
3. Inflammation of the nasal mucosa from an allergy
4. Inflammation of the nasal mucosa from breathing foreign substances
   such as dust
5. Sensitivity to stress

The onset of coryza is usually rapid, with symptoms varying in each individual. The typical effects are a general feeling of malaise with an accompanying headache, sneezing, and nasal discharge. Some individuals may register a
fever of 100° to 102° F (38° to 39° C) and have chills. Various aches and pains
may also accompany the symptoms. The nasal discharge starts as a watery
secretion, gradually becoming thick and discolored from the inflammation.

Care   Care of the cold is usually symptomatic, with emphasis placed on
isolation, bed rest, and light eating. Palliative medications include aspirin for
relieving general discomfort, rhinitis tablets for drying the secreting mucosa,
and nasal drops or an inhaler containing ephedrine to relieve nasal congestion
(Fig. 17-3). If a cough is present, various syrups may be given to afford relief.

Sore Throat (Pharyngitis)

The sore throat, or pharyngitis, is usually of viral origin or due to streptococcal, pneumococcal, or staphylococcal organisms. A sore throat usually is associated with a common cold or sinusitis, as the result of postnasal drip. It
may also be an indication of a more serious condition. Frequently it starts as a
dryness in the throat, progressing to soreness, with pain and swelling. It is
sometimes accompanied by a headache, a fever of 101° to 102° F (38° to 39° C),
chills, coughing, and a general feeling of fatigue. On examination, the throat
may appear dark red and swollen, and mucous membranes may be coated.

Figure 17-4

Studies show that long, continuous running compared to intermittent running causes the most severe exercise-induced asthma.

Care In most cases bed rest is considered the best treatment, combined with the use of symptomatic medications such as aspirin and a hot saltwater gargle. Antibiotics and a silver nitrate throat swab may be used by a physician if other measures are inadequate.

Asthma

As one of the most common respiratory diseases, bronchial asthma can be produced from a number of stressors, such as a viral respiratory tract infection, emotional upset, changes in barometric pressure or temperature, exercise, inhalation of a noxious odor, or exposure to a specific allergen.[3]

Bronchial asthma is characterized by a spasm of the bronchial smooth muscles, edema, and inflammation of the mucous lining. In addition to narrowing the airway, copious amounts of mucus are produced. Difficulty in breathing may cause the athlete to hyperventilate, resulting in dizziness. The attack may begin with coughing, wheezing, shortness of breath, and a sense of fatigue.

The Asthmatic Athlete

An asthmatic attack has been known to be stimulated by exercise in some individuals and may be provoked in others only on rare occasions during moderate exercise.[10] The exact cause of exercise-induced asthma (EIA) is not clear. Metabolic acidosis, postexertional hypocapnia, stimulation of tracheal irritant receptors, adrenergic abnormalities such as defective catecholamine

The athlete undergoing a sudden asthmatic attack should:

Be relaxed and reassured
Use a previously specified medication
Drink water
Perform controlled breathing
Be removed from what might be triggering the attack

metabolism, and psychological factors have been suggested as possible causes.[9,10]

A number of studies have been carried out to determine the most desirable exercise and training methods for EIA. Continuous running for long periods of time, compared to intermittent running, causes the most severe bronchospasm[11] (Fig. 17-4). Swimming is found to be the least bronchospasm producing, which may be due to the moist, warm air environment.[4] It is generally agreed that a regular exercise program can benefit asthmatics and nonasthmatics as well. Fewer symptoms occur with short intense work followed by rest compared to sustained exercise.[10] There should be gradual warm-up and cool-down. The duration of exercise should build up slowly to 30 to 40 minutes, four or five times a week.[5] Exercise intensity and loading also should be graduated slowly. An example would be 10 to 30 seconds of work, followed by 30 to 90 seconds of rest. Aerosol asthmatic agents are taken before exercise. Asthmatic athletes who receive medication for their condition should make sure that what they take is legal for competition.[10]

Hay Fever (Pollinosis)

Hay fever is an acute seasonal allergic condition that occurs from airborne pollens. In the early stages, the athlete's eyes, throat, mouth, and nose begin to itch. This is followed by watering of the eyes, sneezing, and a clear, watery,

---

MANAGEMENT OF THE ACUTE ASTHMATIC ATTACK

Athletes who have a history of asthma usually know how to care for themselves when an attack occurs. However, the coach or athletic trainer must be aware of what to look for and what to do if called on.

Early Symptoms and Signs
Anxious appearance
Sweating and paleness
Flared nostrils
Breathing with pursed lips
Fast breathing
Vomiting
Hunched over body posture
Physical fatigue unrelated to activity
Indentation in the notch below the Adam's apple
Rib spaces sink in as the athlete inhales
Coughing for no apparent reason
Excess throat clearing
Irregular, labored breathing or wheezing

Actions to Take
Attempt to relax and reassure the athlete.
If medication has been cleared by the team physician, have the athlete use it.
Encourage the athlete to drink water.
Have the athlete perform controlled breathing along with relaxation exercises.
If an environmental factor triggering the attack is known, remove it or the athlete from the area.
If these procedures do not help, immediate medical attention may be necessary.

TABLE 17-1

Some infectious diseases*

Sites Involved	Mode of Transmission	Incubation Period	Chief Symptoms	Duration	Period of Contagion	Treatment	Prophylaxis
Measles (rubeola)							
Skin, respiratory tract, and conjunctivae	Contact or droplet	7-14 days	Appearance—like common cold with fever, coryza, cough, conjunctivitis, photophobia, and spots in throat followed by skin rash	4-7 days after symptoms appear	Just before coldlike symptoms through about 1 week after rash appears	Bed rest and use of smoked glasses; symptomatic	Vaccine available
German measles (rubella)							
Skin, respiratory tract, and conjunctivae	Contact or droplet	14-21 days	Cold symptoms, skin rash, and swollen lymph nodes behind ear	1-2 days	2-4 days before rash through 5 days afterward	Symptomatic	Vaccine available; gamma globulin given in postexposure situations
Chickenpox (varicella)							
Trunk; then face, neck, and limbs	Contact or droplet	14-21 days	Mild cold symptoms followed by appearance of vesicles	1-2 weeks	1 day before onset through 6 days afterward	Symptomatic	None; avoid exposure

nasal discharge. The athlete may complain of a sinus-type headache, emotional irritability, difficulty in sleeping, red and swollen eyes and nasal mucous membranes, and a wheezing cough. Relief is usually fast after the oral ingestion of an antihistamine.

COMMON COMMUNICABLE VIRAL DISEASES

It is not within the purview of this text to describe in detail all the various infectious diseases to which athletes may be prone. However, on occasion an athlete may exhibit recognizable symptoms of such a disease; one should know the symptoms and be able to identify them (Table 17-1). A player or other athlete indicating such symptoms should be referred to a physician without delay.

COMMON GASTROINTESTINAL COMPLAINTS

Like any other individual, the athlete may develop various complaints of the digestive system. The athlete may display various disorders of the gastrointestinal tract as a result of poor eating habits or the stress engendered from competition.

*Except as indicated, the common cause of each disease included in this table is a virus.
†Common cause, undetermined; probably a virus.

TABLE 17-1 *Continued.*

Some infectious diseases

Sites Involved	Mode of Transmission	Incubation Period	Chief Symptoms	Duration	Period of Contagion	Treatment	Prophylaxis
Mumps (epidemic parotidits)							
Salivary glands	Prolonged contact or droplet	18-21 days	Headache, drowsiness, fever abdominal pain, pain on chewing and swallowing, swelling of neck under jaw	10 days	1 week	Symptomatic	Temporary immunization by virus vaccine
Influenza (grippe)							
Respiratory tract	Droplet	1-2 days	Aching of low back, generalized aching, chills, headache, fever, and bronchitis	2-3 days		Symptomatic	Moderate temporary protection by polyvalent influenza virus
Cold (coryza)							
Respiratory tract	Droplet	12 hours to 4 days	Mild fever, headache, chills, and nasal discharge	1-2 weeks		Symptomatic	Possible help from vitamins and/or cold vaccine; avoid exposure
Infectious mononucleosis†							
Trunk	Contact	7-14 days	Sore throat, fever, skin rash, general aching, and swelling of lymph glands	3-4 weeks		Symptomatic	None; avoid extreme fatigue

Indigestion

Some athletes have certain food idiosyncrasies that cause them considerable distress after eating. Others develop reactions when eating before competition. The term given to digestive upset is indigestion (**dyspepsia**).

Indigestion can be caused by any number of conditions. The most common in sports are emotional stress, esophageal and stomach spasms, and/or inflammation of the mucous lining of the esophagus and stomach. These conditions cause an increased secretion of hydrochloric acid (sour stomach), nausea, and flatulence (gas).

Care Care of acute dyspepsia involves the elimination of irritating foods from the diet, development of regular eating habits, and avoidance of anxieties that may lead to gastric distress.

Constant irritation of the stomach may lead to chronic and more serious disorders such as gastritis, an inflammation of the stomach wall, or ulcerations of the gastrointestinal mucosa. Athletes who appear nervous and highstrung and suffer from dyspepsia should be examined by the sports physician.

dyspepsia
Imperfect digestion

Diarrhea

Diarrhea is the abnormal looseness or passage of a fluid, unformed stool and is categorized as acute and chronic, according to the type present. It is characterized by abdominal cramps, nausea, and possibly vomiting, coupled with frequent elimination of stools, ranging from 3 to 20 a day. The infected person often has a loss of appetite and a light brown or gray, foul-smelling stool. Extreme weakness caused by the fluid dehydration is usually present.

Care   The cause of diarrhea is often difficult to establish. It is conceivable that any irritant may cause the loose stool. This can include an infestation of parasitic organisms or an emotional upset. Management of diarrhea requires a knowledge of its cause. Less severe cases can be cared for by (1) omitting foods that cause irritation, (2) drinking boiled milk, (3) eating bland food until symptoms have ceased, and (4) using pectins two or three times daily for the absorption of excess fluid.

Constipation

Some athletes are subject to constipation, the failure of the bowels to evacuate feces. There are numerous causes of constipation, the most common of which are (1) lack of abdominal muscle tone, (2) insufficient moisture of the feces, causing it to be hard and dry, (3) lack of a sufficient proportion of roughage and bulk in the diet to stimulate peristalsis, (4) poor bowel habits, (5) nervousness and anxiety, and (6) overuse of laxatives and enemas.

Care   The best means of overcoming constipation is to regulate eating patterns to include foods that will encourage normal defecation. Cereals, fruits, vegetables, and fats stimulate bowel movement, whereas sugars and carbohydrates tend to inhibit it. Some persons become constipated as the result of psychological factors. In such cases it may be helpful to try to determine the causes of stress and, if need be, to refer the athlete to a physician or school psychologist for counseling. Above all, laxatives or enemas should be avoided unless their use has been prescribed by a physician.

DIABETES MELLITUS

Diabetes mellitus is a complex hereditary or developmental disease of carbohydrate metabolism. Decreased effectiveness of insulin or an insufficient amount is responsible for most cases. Until recently diabetics were usually discouraged or forbidden competitive sports participation. Today an ever-increasing number of diabetics are active sports participants, functioning effectively in almost all sports. Since the key to the control of diabetes is the control of blood sugar, the insulin-dependent athlete must constantly juggle food intake, insulin, and exercise to maintain the blood sugar in its proper range if he or she is to perform to maximum. Diet, exercise, and insulin are the major factors in the everyday life-style of the diabetic athlete, who out of necessity must develop an ordered and specific living pattern to cope with the demands of daily existence and strenuous physical activity.

Diabetic athletes engaging in vigorous physical activity should eat before exercising, and, if the exercise is protracted, should have hourly glucose supplementation. As a rule, the insulin dosage is not changed, but food intake is increased. The response of diabetics varies among individuals and depends on many variables. Although there are some hazards, with proper medical evaluation and planning by a consultant in metabolic diseases, diabetics can feel free to engage in most physical activities.

Management of the Diabetic Coma and Insulin Shock

It is important that those who work with athletes who have diabetes mellitus are aware of the major symptoms of diabetic coma and insulin shock and the proper actions to take when either one occurs.

Diabetic Coma

If not treated adequately through proper diet and intake of insulin, the diabetic athlete can develop acidosis. A loss of sodium, potassium, and ketone bodies through excessive urination, produces a problem of ketoacidosis that can lead to coma. The signs of a diabetic coma include:
- Labored breathing or gasping for air
- Fruity smelling breath caused by acetone
- Nausea and vomiting
- Thirst
- Dry mucous lining of the mouth and flushed skin
- Mental confusion or unconsciousness followed by coma

Care Because of the life-threatening nature of the diabetic coma, early detection of ketoacidosis is essential. The injection of insulin into the athlete will normally prevent coma.

Insulin Shock

Unlike diabetic coma, insulin shock occurs when too much insulin is taken into the body, resulting in hypoglycemia and shock. It is characterized by the following:
- Physical weakness
- Moist and pale skin
- Drooping eye lids
- Normal or shallow respirations

Care The diabetic athlete who engages in intense exercise and metabolizes large amounts of glycogen could inadvertently take too much insulin and thus have a severe reaction. To avoid this problem the athlete must adhere to a carefully planned diet that includes a snack before exercise. The snack should contain a combination of a complex carbohydrate and protein, such as cheese and crackers. Activities that last for more than 30 to 40 minutes should be accompanied by snacks and simple carbohydrates. Some diabetics carry with them a lump of sugar or have candy or orange juice readily available in the event an insulin reaction seems imminent.

CONVULSIVE DISORDERS (EPILEPSY)

Epilepsy is not a disease but a symptom that can be manifested by a large number of underlying disorders. **Epilepsy** is defined as "a recurrent paroxysmal disorder of cerebral function characterized by sudden, brief attacks of altered consciousness, motor activity, sensory phenomena, or inappropriate behavior."[3] For some types of epilepsy there is a genetic predisposition and a low threshold to having seizures. In others, altered brain metabolism or a history of injury may be the cause. A seizure can range from extremely brief episodes

epilepsy
Recurrent paroxysmal disorder characterized by sudden attacks of altered consciousness, motor activity, sensory phenomena, or inappropriate behavior

For individuals who have major daily or weekly seizures, collision-type sports may be prohibited.

Figure 17-5

Each person with epilepsy must be considered individually as to whether he or she should be considered for competitive sports participation.

menarche
Onset of menses

Girls who have moderate to severe dysmenorrhea require examination by a physician.

(petit mal seizures) to major episodes (grand mal seizures), unconsciousness, and tonic-clonic muscle contractions.

Each person with epilepsy must be considered individually as to whether he or she should engage in competitive sports (Fig. 17-5). It is generally agreed that if an individual has daily or even weekly major seizures, collision sports should be prohibited.[14] This prohibition is not because hitting the head will trigger a seizure but because unconsciousness during participation could result in a serious injury. If the seizures are properly controlled by medication or only occur during sleep, little, if any, sports restriction should be imposed, except for scuba diving, swimming alone, or participation at a great height.

Management of the Epileptic Seizure

Often the epileptic athlete will experience an aura, which is a sign of an impending seizure. In such instances the athlete can take measures to provide protection, such as sitting or lying down. When a seizure occurs without warning, the following steps should be taken:

- Be emotionally composed.
- If possible, cushion the athlete's fall.
- Keep the athlete from injury-producing objects.
- Loosen restrictive clothing.
- Prevent the athlete from biting the mouth by placing a soft cloth between the teeth.
- Allow the athlete to awaken normally after the seizure.

MENSTRUAL IRREGULARITIES

Women in the United States are increasingly participating in sports activities and have been training harder than ever before. What impact does this have on menstruation?

Menarche may be delayed in highly physically active women. Absence of menses and diminished flow have been common in professional female ballet dancers, gymnasts, and long-distance runners.[6,7] Runners who suddenly decrease training, such as when an injury is incurred , often report a return of regular menses.[8] Weight gain, together with less intense exercise, also are reported to reverse these conditions.[6] Although these irregularities may be a normal aspect of thinness and hard physical training, it is advisable that a physician be consulted. To date, there is no indication that these conditions will adversely affect the health of the athlete.[14] Almost any type of menstrual irregularity can be caused by overly stressful and demanding sports activity.

Dysmenorrhea (painful menstruation) appears to be less prevalent among more active women; however, it is inconclusive whether specific sports participation can alleviate or produce **dysmenorrhea**. For girls with moderate to severe dysmenorrhea, gynecological consultation is warranted to rule out a serious pathological condition.[14]

Painful menstruation is caused by a lack of normal blood flow to the pelvic organs or by a possible hormonal imbalance. This syndrome, which is identified by cramps, nausea, lower abdominal pain, headache, and on occasion emotional lability, is the most common disorder. Mild to vigorous exercises that help alleviate painful menstruation are usually prescribed by physicians. Physicians generally advise a continuance of the usual sports participation during the menstrual period, provided the performance level of the individual does not drop below her customary level of ability. Among athletes, swimmers have the highest incidence of painful menses, quite probably as the result of strenuous sports participation during the menses. Generally, a decrease in flow appears more common in those sports that require strenuous exertion over a long period of time, for example, long-distance running, rowing, cross-country skiing, basketball, tennis, or field hockey. Since great variation exists among female athletes in respect to the menstrual pattern, its effect on physical performance, and the effect of physical activity on the menstrual pattern, each individual must learn to make adjustments to her cycle that will permit her to function effectively and efficiently with a minimum of discomfort or restriction. The use of pills, devices, and other methods, to alter or stop the menstrual cycle is inadvisable. Evidence to date indicates that top performances are possible in all phases of the cycle.[15]

SUMMARY

The most common skin infections in athletes are caused by viruses, bacteria, and fungi. Viral infections include herpes simplex (e.g., the cold sore), verruca (warts), and the molluscum contagiosum (water warts). Tetanus, which can cause lock jaw, is another major concern in athletics. Bacterial infections are represented by impetigo contagiosa, boils, and infected hair follicles and sweat glands. Ringworm or tinea is the fungus infection commonly attacking all areas of the body; tinea pedis (athlete's foot) is the most common. Sexually transmitted diseases can be caused by virus (herpes simplex 2), and bacteria can cause gonorrhea and syphilis.

The common cold, sore throat, hay fever, and asthma are respiratory tract conditions that can adversely affect the athlete. Asthma can be chronic (e.g., bronchial) or induced by physical activity. Care of the acute asthmatic attack requires understanding the early symptoms and signs and responding accordingly.

Because communicable viral diseases such as German measles, mumps, or infectious mononucleosis can infect many athletes on a team, early recognition is necessary. When suspected the athlete should be isolated from other athletes and immediately referred to a physician for diagnosis.

Gastrointestinal complaints such as indigestion, diarrhea, and constipation are as common among athletes as nonathletes. Minor problems should be distinguished from major complaints such as factors that may indicate an appendicitis condition.

Diabetes mellitus is a complex hereditary or developmental disease of carbohydrate metabolism. Decreased effectiveness of insulin or an insufficient amount is responsible for most cases. The diabetic athlete must carefully monitor his or her energy output to ensure there is a balance of food intake and the burning of sugars via insulin. If this does not occur, diabetic coma or insulin shock may result.

Epilepsy is defined as "a recurrent paroxysmal disorder of cerebral function characterized by sudden, brief attacks of altered consciousness, motor activity, sensory phenomena, or inappropriate behavior."[3] A coach or athletic trainer must recognize an athlete going into seizure and be able to provide proper immediate care.

Women athletes engaging in hard physical training may be prone to menstrual irregularities. Types of irregularities are absence of menses, diminished flow, excessive flow, frequent abnormal flow, and painful menstruation. A decrease in the intensity and amount of exercise often ameliorates this condition.

REVIEW QUESTIONS AND CLASS ACTIVITIES

1. Describe the organisms underlying the most common skin infections seen in athletes. Name a representative disease under each causation.
2. Discuss the appearance of genital herpes, syphilis, and gonorrhea. Why are these serious diseases?
3. Why are some individuals susceptible to the common cold and others are not? List the typical cold symptoms. How should the cold be managed?
4. Differentiate between bronchial asthma and exercise-induced asthma. Indicate the management of an acute asthmatic attack.
5. Describe the most common gastrointestinal complaints. How are they acquired and cared for?
6. What is diabetes mellitus? What value might exercise have for the person with diabetes mellitus? Describe diabetic coma and insulin shock and how they are managed.
7. What causes grand mal seizures? How should they be managed?
8. Discuss menstrual irregularities related to the highly active athlete. Why do they occur? How should they be managed?

REFERENCES

1. Anderson, W.A.D., and Scotti, T.M.: Synopsis of pathology, ed. 10, St. Louis, 1980, The C.V. Mosby Co.
2. Bergfeld, W.F.: The skin. In Strauss, R.H. (editor): Sports medicine, Philadelphia, 1984, W.B. Saunders Co.
3. Berkow, R. (editor): The Merck manual, ed. 10, Rahway, N.J., 1982, Merck & Co., Inc.
4. Bundgaord, A., et al.: Exercise induced asthma after swimming and bicycle exercise, Eur. J. Respir. Dis. 63:245, May 1982.
5. Bundgaord, A.: Exercise and the asthmatic, Sports Med. 2:254, 1985.
6. Caldwell, F.: Menstrual irregularity in athletes: the unanswered question, Phys. Sportsmed. 10:142, May 1982.
7. Cohen, J.L., et al.: Exercise, body weight, and amenorrhea in professional ballet dance, Phys. Sportsmed. 10:79, April 1982.
8. Dale, E., et al.: Menstrual dysfunction in distance runners, Obstet. Gynecol. 54:47, 1979.
9. Kolski, G.B.: The athlete with asthma and allergies, Symposium on pediatric and adolescent sports medicine, Clinics in sports medicine, vol. 1, no. 1, Philadelphia, Nov. 1982, W.B. Saunders Co.
10. Morton, A.R.: Physical activity and the asthmatic, Phys. Sportsmed. 9:51, March 1981.
11. Morton, A.R., et al.: Continuous and intermittent running in the provocation of asthma, Ann. Allergy 48:123, Feb. 1982.
12. Murphy, K., and Corey, L.: Misinformation persists about genital herpes, Skin and Allergy News 12(1):16, 1981.
13. Rees, R.B.: Warts: a clinician's view, Cutis, 28:177, 1981.
14. Smith, N.J. (editor): Sports participation for children and adolescents with chronic health problems. In Sports medicine: health care for young athletes, Evanston, Ill., 1983, American Academy of Pediatrics.
15. Stager, J.M.: Reversibility of amenorrhea in athletes, Sports Med. 1:337, Oct. 1984.

ANNOTATED BIBLIOGRAPHY

Athletic training and sports medicine, Chicago, 1984, American Academy of Orthopaedic Surgeons.

Part II, "Special Medical Considerations," contains many well-written chapters. Of special interest to the reader will be: Chapter 42, Women Athletes; Chapter 43, The Diabetic Athlete; Chapter 44, The Asthmatic Athlete; Chapter 46, Communicable Diseases; and Chapter 47, Common Dermatological Problems.

Strauss, R.H. (editor): Sports medicine, Philadelphia, 1984, W.B. Saunders Co.
Numerous chapters detail health conditions among athletes. Of particular interest are: Chapter 6, The Skin; Chapter 7, The Respiratory System; Chapter 10, The Gastrointestinal System; Chapter 13, Metabolic Responses to Exercise in Normal and Diabetic Individuals; and Chapter 17, Factors Important to Women Engaged in Vigorous Physical Activity.

Walsh, M.M. (editor): Symposium on the athletic woman, vol. 3, no. 4, Clinics in sports medicine, Philadelphia, Oct. 1984, W.B. Saunders Co.
A symposium covering the athletic woman who engages in hard physical training. It discusses health conditions unique to the gender.

UNITS OF MEASURE

TEMPERATURE

To convert a Fahrenheit temperature to Celsius (centigrade):

$$°C = (°F - 32) \div 1.8$$

To convert a Celsius temperature to Fahrenheit:

$$°F = (1.8 \times °C) + 32$$

On the Fahrenheit scale, the freezing point of water is 32° F and the boiling point is 212° F. On the Celsius scale, the freezing point of water is °0 C and the boiling point is 100° C.

DISTANCE

Equivalent Metric Unit	Equivalent English Unit
1 centimeter (cm)	0.3937 inch
2.54 centimeters	1 inch
1 meter (m)	3.28 feet; 1.09 yards
0.304 meters	1 foot
1 kilometer (km)	0.62 mile
1.61 kilometers	1 mile

POWER AND ENERGY

Power = Work divided by time; measured in horsepower (HP), watts, etc.

1 HP = 746 watts

Energy = Application of a force through a distance

1 kilocalorie (kcal) = Amount of energy required to heat 1 kilogram (kg) of water 1 ° Celsius

INDEX

GLOSSARY

abduction A movement of a body part away from the mid line of the body, 201

accident Occurring by chance or without intention, 10

acute injury An injury with sudden onset and short duration, 10

ad libitum The amount desired, 115

adduction A movement of a body part toward the mid line of the body, 201

afferent nerve fibers Carry messages toward the brain, 161

agonist muscles Muscles directly engaged in contraction as related to muscles that relax at the same time, 21

ambulation Move or walk from place to place, 187

ameboid action A leukocyte moving through a capillary wall through the process of diapedisis, 157

analgesia Pain inhibition, 163

anesthesia Partial or complete loss of sensation, 162

anomaly Deviation from the normal, 270

anoxia A lack of oxygen, 262

antagonist muscles Muscles that counteract the action of the agonist muscles, 21

anterior Before or in front of, 82

anteroposterior Refers to the position of front to back, 128

apophysis A bone outgrowth to which muscles attach, 151

arrhythmical movement Irregular movement, 170

arthroscopic examination Viewing the inside of a joint via the arthroscope, which utilizes a small camera lens, 231

asymmetries (body) A lack of symmetry of sides of the body, 135

automatism Automatic behavior before consciousness or full awareness has been achieved

following a brain concussion, 289

avascular necrosis Death of tissue due to a lack of blood supply, 253

avulsion A tearing away, 73

axilla Arm pit, 84

bandage A strip of cloth or other material used to cover a wound, 70

biomechanics Branch of study that applies the laws of mechanics to living organisms and biological tissues, 3

bipedal Having two feet or moving on two feet, 126

bradykinin Peptide chemical that causes pain in an injured area, 161

calisthenic Exercise involving free movement without the aid of equipment, 22

catastrophic injury Relates to a permanent injury to the spinal cord leaving the athlete quadriplegic or paraplegic, 14

cerebrovascular accident Stroke, 94

chondromalacia A degeneration of a joint's articular surface, leading to softening, 132

chronic injury An injury with long onset and long duration, 10

clavis durum Hard corn, 183

clavis molle Soft corn, 183

clonic muscle contraction Alternating involuntary muscle contraction and relaxation in quick succession, 144

collagenous tissue The white fibrous substance composing connective tissue, 31

collision sport A sport in which athletes use their bodies to deter or punish opponents, 11

communicable disease A disease that may be transmitted directly or indirectly from one individual to another, 347

concentric muscle contraction Refers to muscle shortening, 24

conduction Heating by direct contact with a hot medium, 164

conjunctivae Mucous membrane that lines the eyes, 268

contact sport A sport in which athletes do make physical contact but not with the intent to produce bodily injury, 11

contracoup brain injury After head is struck brain continues to move within the skull and becomes injured on the opposite side of the force, 289

convection Heating indirectly through another medium such as air or liquid, 164

conversion Heating by other forms of energy (e.g., electricity), 164

corticosteroid A steroid produced by the adrenal cortex, 194

counterirritant An agent that produces a mild inflammation and in turn acts as an analgesic when applied locally to the skin (e.g., liniment), 21

crepitation A crackling sound heard on the movement of ends of a broken bone, 149

cryokinetics Cold application combined with exercise, 162

cryotherapy Cold therapy, 162

cyanosis Slightly bluish, grayish, slatelike, or dark purple discoloration of the skin due to a reduced amount of blood hemaglobin, 268

debride Removal of dirt and dead tissue from a wound, 71

deconditioning A state whereby the athlete's body loses its competitive fitness, 19

degeneration Deterioration of tissue, 205

dermatome A segmental skin area innervated by various spinal cord segments, 160

diapedisis Passage of blood cells by ameboid action through the intact capillary wall, 157

diaphragm A musculomembraneous wall separating the abdomen from the thoracic cavity, 262

diarthrodial joint Ball and socket joint, 128

diastolic blood pressure The residual pressure caused when the heart is between beats, 95

distal Farthest from a center, mid line, or from the trunk, 171

dorsiflexion Bending toward the dorsum or rear, opposite of plantar flexion, 134

dorsum The back of a body part, 189

dressing Medicine applied to a material such as gauze and then applied to a wound, 70

dyspepsia Impaired digestive function, 264

dyspnea Difficulty in breathing, 268

eccentric muscle contraction Refers to muscle lengthening, 24

ecchymosis Black and blue skin discoloration due to hemorrhage, 144

ectopic calcification Calcification occurring in an abnormal place, 152

electrotherapy Treating disease by electrical devices, 10

encephalon The brain, 288

endurance Refers to the body's ability to engage in prolonged physical activity, 38

epidemiological approach The study of sports injuries involving the relationship of as many factors as possible, 12

epilepsy Recurrent paroxysmal disorder characterized by sudden attacks of altered consciousness, motor activity, sensory phenomena, or inappropriate behavior, 357

epiphysis The cartilagenous growth region of a bone, 145

epistaxis Nose bleed, 297

etiology Pertaining to the cause of a condition, 151

eversion of the foot To turn the foot outward, 62

exostoses Benign bony outgrowths that protrude from the surface of a bone and are usually capped by cartilage, 193

extraoral mouth guard A protective device that fits outside the mouth, 54

exudates Accumulation of a fluid in an area, 164

fascia Fibrous membrane that covers, supports, and separates muscles, 31

fasciitis Fascia inflammation, 189

fibrinogen A protein present in blood plasma that is converted into a fibrin clot, 157

fibrocartilage A type of cartilage in which the matrix contains thick bundles of collagenous fibers (e.g., intervertebral disks), 221

foot pronation Combined foot movements of eversion and abduction, 188

genitourinary Pertaining to the reproductive and urinary organs, 263

genu valgum Knock knees, 136

genu varum Bow legs, 136

hemarthrosis Blood in a joint, 228

hematoma Blood tumor, 104

hematuria Blood in the urine, 263

hemoglobin Coloring substance of the red blood cells, 21

hemoglobinuria Hemoglobin in the urine, 163

hemophilia A hereditary blood disease in which coagulation is greatly prolonged, 245

hemothorax Bloody fluid in the pleural cavity, 266

hyperemia An unusual amount of blood in a body part, 166

hyperextension Extreme stretching out of a body part, 84

hyperflexibility Flexibility beyond a joint's normal range, 31

hypermobility Mobility of a joint that is extreme, 192

hyperventilation Abnormally deep breathing that is prolonged causing a depletion of carbon dioxide, a fall in blood pressure, and fainting, 263

hypoallergenic Low allergy producing, 74

hypoxia Lack of an adequate amount of oxygen, 103

idiopathic Cause of a condition is unknown, 262

inflammatory phase , 156

injury An act that damages or hurts, 10

innervation Nerve stimulation of a muscle, 24

interosseous membrane Connective tissue membrane between bones, 133

intervertebral Between two vertebrae, 128

intramuscular bleeding Bleeding within a muscle, 112

intraoral mouth guard A protective device that fits within the mouth and covers the teeth, 54

intravenous Substances administered to a patient via a vein, 120

inversion of the foot To turn the foot inward. Inner border of the foot lifts, 62

ischemia Local anemia, 217

isokinetic muscle resistance Accommodating and variable resistance, 24

isometric muscle contraction Muscle contracts statically without a change in its length, 23

isotonic muscle contraction Muscle shortens and lengthens through a complete range of joint motion, 23

keratolytic Loosening of the horny skin layer, 183

kyphosis Exaggeration of the normal thoracic spine, 136

labile Unsteady; not fixed and easily changed, 358

liability The legal responsibility to perform an act in a reasonable and prudent manner, 90

lordosis Abnormal lumbar vertebral convexity, 136

luxation Complete joint dislocation, 145

lysis To break down, 158

macerated skin Skin that has been softened through wetting, 183

menarche Onset of the menstrual function, 358

metabolites Products left after metabolism has taken place, 24

metatarsalgia Pain in the metatarsal arch, 191

metatarsophalangeal joint Joint where the phalanges meet with the metatarsal bones, 61

microtrauma Small musculoskeletal traumas that are accumulative, 128

mononucleosis (infectious) A disease, usually of young adults, causing fever, sore throat, and lymph gland swelling, 263

musculoskeletal Pertaining to muscles and the skeleton, 5

myoglobin A respiratory pigment in muscle tissue that is an oxygen carrier, 21

myotatic reflex Stretch reflex, 24

necrosis Death of tissue, 119

negative resistance Slow eccentric muscle contraction against a resistance, 24

nerve entrapment A nerve that is compressed between bone or soft tissue, 153

neuritis Inflammation of a nerve, 153

noncontact sport Not involved in any physical contact, 11

nystagmus A constant involuntary back and forth, up and down, or rotary movement of the eyeball, 291

orthosis Used in sports as an appliance or apparatus used to support, align, prevent, or correct deformities, or to improve function of a movable body part, 64

osteoarthritis A chronic disease involving joints in which there is destruction of articular cartilage and bone overgrowth, 253

osteochondral Refers to relationship of bone and cartilage, 228

osteochondritis dissecans Fragment of cartilage and underlying bone is detached from the articular surface, 234

osteochondrosis A disease state of a bone and its articular cartilage, 153

palpation Feeling an injury with the fingers, 103

papule Pimple, 349

paresthesia Abnormal sensation such as numbness, prickling, and tingling, 217

pathology Study of the nature and cause of disease, 145

pediatrician A specialist in the treatment of children's diseases, 5

periosteum The fibrous covering of a bone, 175

peristalis A progressive wavelike movement that occurs in the alimentary canal, 356

pes planus Flat feet, 213

phagocytosis Process of ingesting microorganisms, other cells, or foreign particles, commonly by monocytes or white cells, 157

phalanges Bones of the fingers and toes, 183

phalanx Any one of the bones of the fingers and toes, 187

photochromic lenses Glass lens spectacles that become color-tinted when exposed to sunlight, 55

photophobia Unusual intolerance of light, 302

plyometric exercise Produces an isometric-type muscle overload, using the stretch reflex, 24

pneumothorax A collapse of a lung due to air in the pleural cavity, 266

posterior Toward the rear or back, 82

prophylaxis Guarding against injury or disease, 78

proprioceptors Organs within the body that provide the athlete with an awareness of where the body is in space (kinesthesis), 40

prostoglandin Acidic lipids widely distributed in the body; in musculoskeletal conditions it is concerned with vasodilation, histaminelike effect; it is inhibited by aspirin, 161

prothrombin Interacts with calcium to produce thrombin, 157

proximal Nearest to the point of attachment, 171

quadriplegia Paralysis affecting all four limbs, 14

resorption Act of removal by absorption, 149

revascularize Restoration of circulation to an injured area, 254

scleral White outer coating of the eye, 56

scoliosis A lateral deviation curve of the spine, 136

sign Objective evidence of an abnormal situation within the body, 102

sling psychrometer Instrument for establishing the wet-bulb, globe temperature index, 115

spondylolisthesis Forward slipping of a vertebral body, usually a lumbar vertebrae, 270

staphylococcus A genus of micrococci, some of which are pathogenic causing pus and tissue destruction, 160

streptococcus Oval bacteria that appear in a chain, 160

stroke volume Capacity of heart to pump blood during exercise, 39

subcutaneous Beneath the skin, 20

subluxation A partially dislocated joint, 31

subthreshold Below the point at which a physiological effect begins to be produced, 149

symptom Subjective evidence of an abnormal situation within the body, 102

syndrome Group of typical symptoms or conditions that characterize a deficiency or disease, 217

synergy To work in cooperation with, 170

synovia A colorless, viscid, lubricating fluid of joints, bursae, and tendon sheaths, 153

synovitis Inflammation of a synovial membrane, 253

synthesis To build up, 158

systolic blood pressure The pressure caused by the heart pumping, 95

tendinitis Inflammation of a tendon, 152

tenosynovitis Inflammation of a tendon synovial sheath, 152

tetnus toxoid Tetnus toxin modified to produce active immunity against *Clostridium Tetani*, 348

thromboplastin Substance within the tissues that accelerates blood clotting, 157

tinea Ringworm; skin fungus disease, 348

tonic muscle spasm Rigid muscle contraction that lasts over a period of time, 144

tonus (muscle) Residual state of muscle contraction, 38

torsional A rotation or twisting of a part, 214

transitory paralysis Temporary paralysis, 262

traumatic Pertaining to the course of an injury or wound, 128

valgus Position of a body part that is bent outward, 228

varus Position of a body part that is bent inward, 231

vasoconstriction A decrease in the diameter of a blood vessel, 156

vasodilation An increase in the diameter of a blood vessel, 120

vasospasm Blood vessel spasm, 163

venule Tiny vein continuous with a capillary, 157

verruca Virus causing a wart, 347

viscera Internal organs, 259

viscus (organs) Any internal organ enclosed within a cavity, 265

CREDITS

Unit Openers Unit Three opener, Cramer Products, Inc., Gardner, Kans.

Chapter 1 PP. 3 and 5, Cramer Products, Inc., Gardner, Kans.; pp. 7 and 8, D. Bailey — California State University, Long Beach; pp. 12 and 15, G. Robert Bishop.

Chapter 2 PP. 23, 27, 28, and 29, Robert Freligh — California State University, Long Beach; p. 43, modified from Payne, W., and Hahn, D.: *Understanding your health*, St. Louis, 1986, Times Mirror/Mosby College Publishing.

Chapter 3 PP. 51, 54, 61, and 64, Robert Freligh — California State University, Long Beach; p. 58, G. Robert Bishop; p. 62, Donzis Protective Equipment, Houston, Tex.; p. 59, Douglas Child — Creative Support Systems of California, Irvine, Calif.; p. 62, Cramer Products, Inc., Gardner, Kans.; p. 63, Don Joy Orthopedic, Carlsbad, Calif.

Chapter 4 P. 71, From Booher, J., and Thibideau, G.: *Athletic injury assessment*, St. Louis, 1985, Times Mirror/Mosby College Publishing; p. 71, Dr. James Garrick — Center for Sports Medicine, St. Francis Memorial Hospital, San Francisco.

Chapter 5 PP. 91 and 116, Cramer Products, Inc., Gardner, Kans.; p. 116, modified from Berkow, R.: *The Merck manual of diagnosis and therapy*, ed. 14, Rahway, N. J., 1982, Merck and Co., Inc.

Chapter 6 PP.130, 132, and 134, Cramer Products Inc., Gardner, Kans.

Chapter 8 P. 157, Cramer Products, Inc., Gardner, Kans.; pp. 166 and 168, Robert Freligh — California State University, Long Beach.

Chapter 10 P. 210, Cramer Products, Inc., Gardner, Kans.

Chapter 11 P. 225, Pro-Fit Orthotics, Linnfield, Mass.; p. 229, From Booher, J., and Thibodeau, G.: *Athletic injury assessment*, St. Louis, 1985, Times Mirror/Mosby College Publishing; p. 229, Bill Oakes, Northern Iowan.

Chapter 13 P. 266, G. Robert Bishop.

Chapter 15 P. 311, Cramer Products, Inc., Gardner, Kans.; p. 315, From Booher, J. and Thibodeau, G.: *Athletic injury assessment*, St. Louis, 1985, Times Mirror/Mosby College Publishing; p. 315, Steve Yoneda — California Polytechnic State University, San Luis Obispo, Calif.

Chapter 16 P. 334, From Booher, J., and Thibodeau, G.: *Athletic injury assessment*, St. Louis, 1985, Times Mirror/Mosby College Publishing.